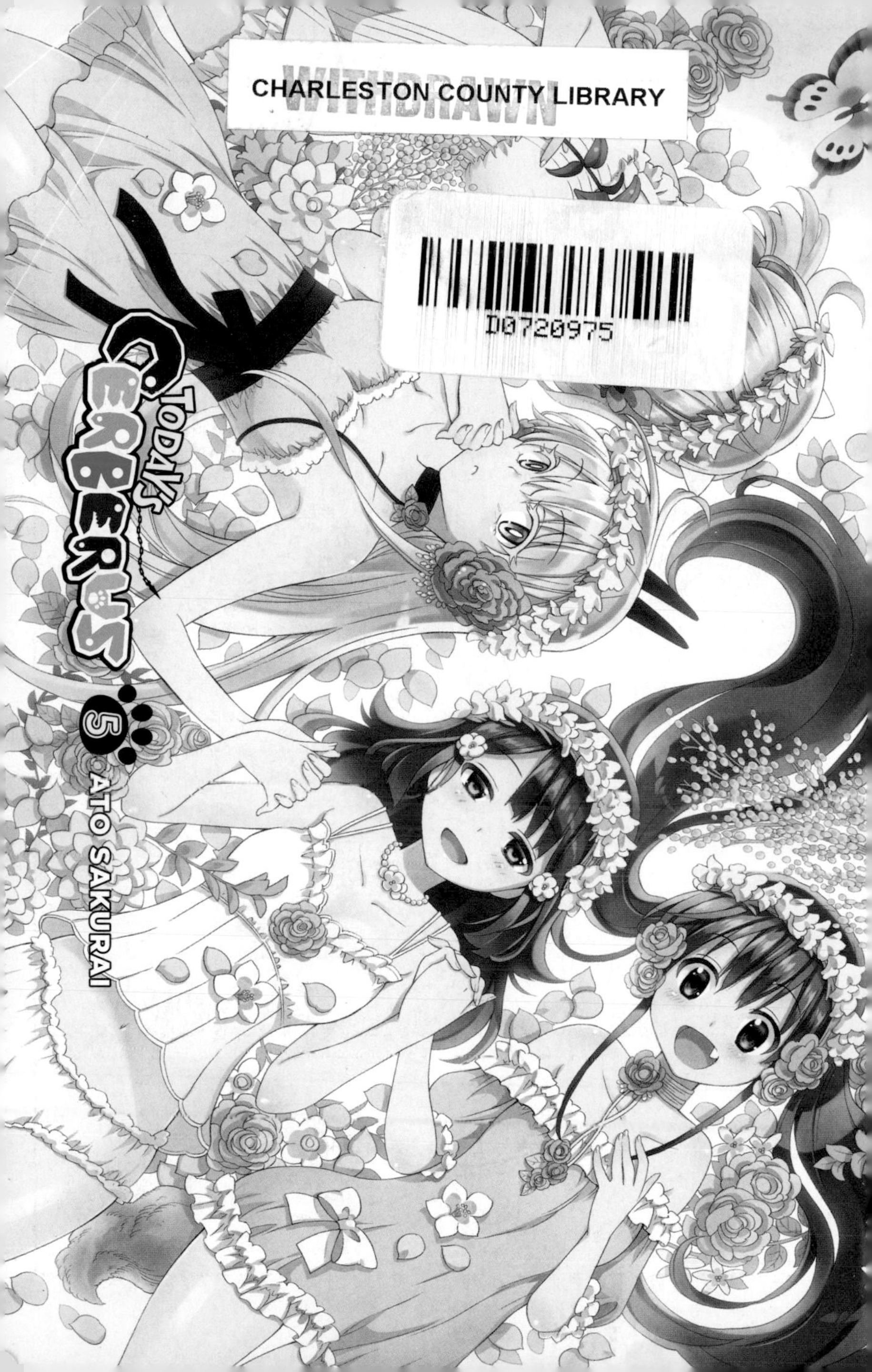
TODAY'S CERBERUS
5
ATO SAKURAI

CONTENTS

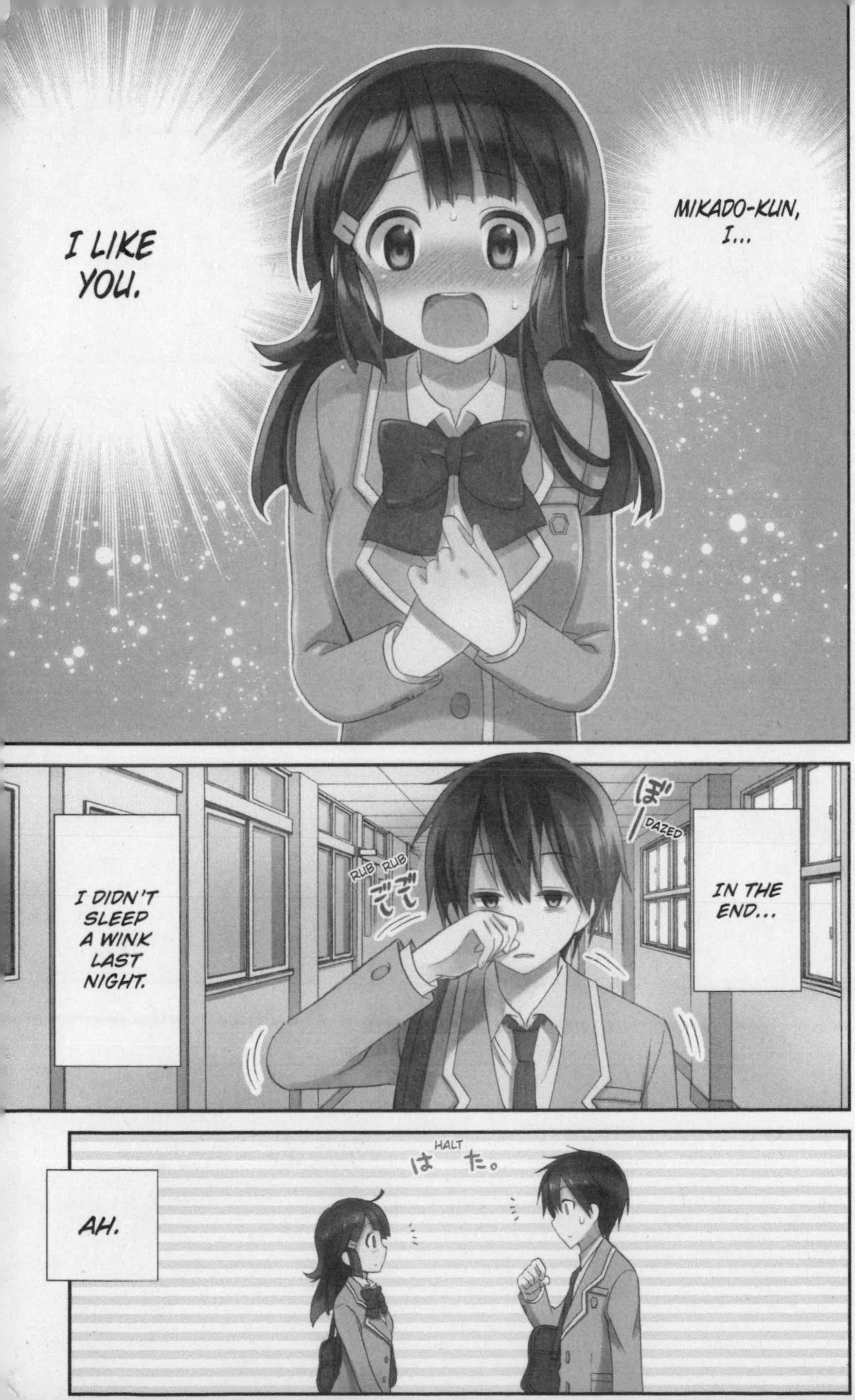
MIKADO-KUN, I...
I LIKE YOU.
IN THE END...
ぼー
DAZED
RUB RUB
ごご
I DIDN'T SLEEP A WINK LAST NIGHT.
HALT
はた。
AH.

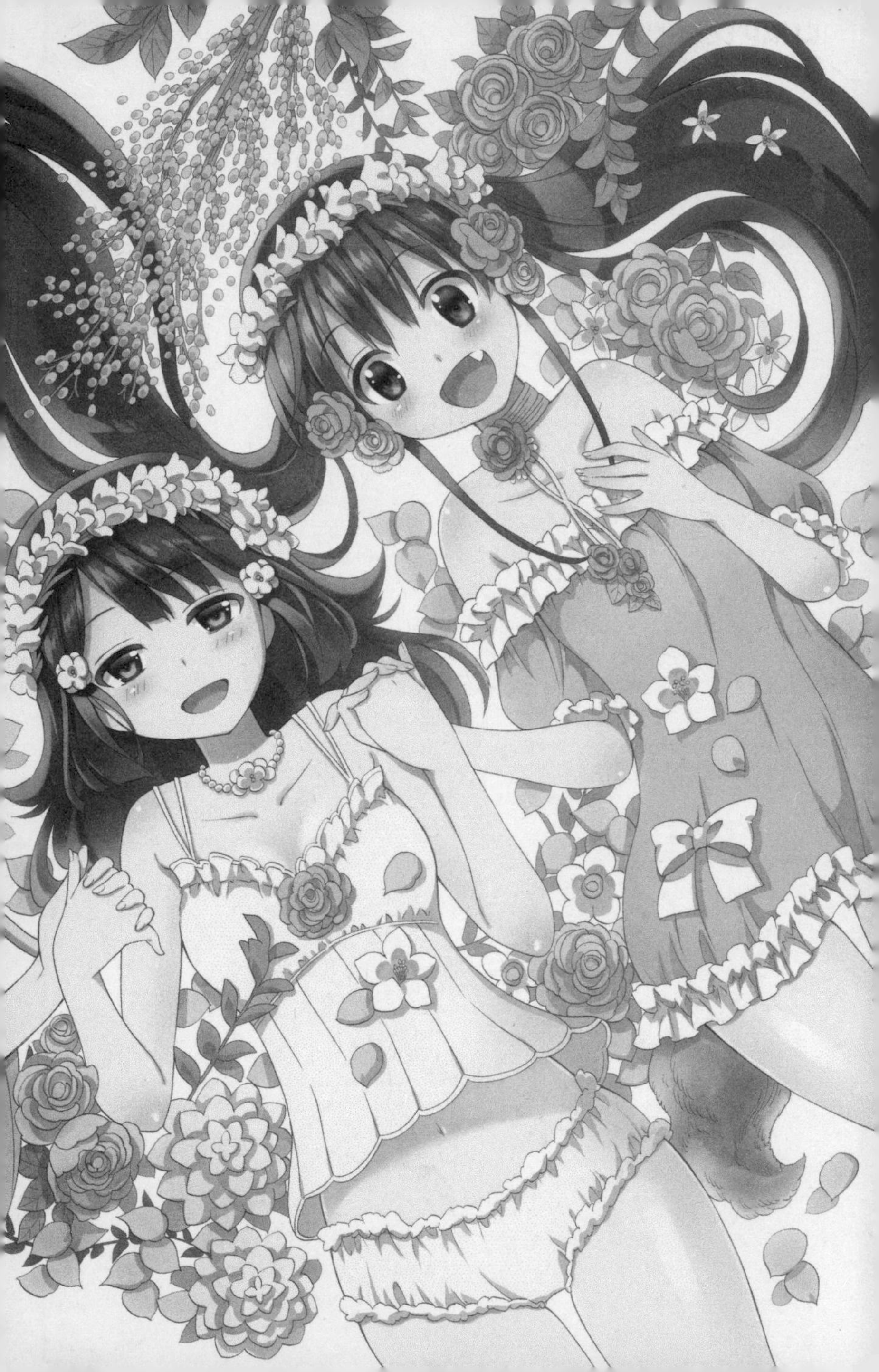

CHAPTER 20
UNSEEN HEART

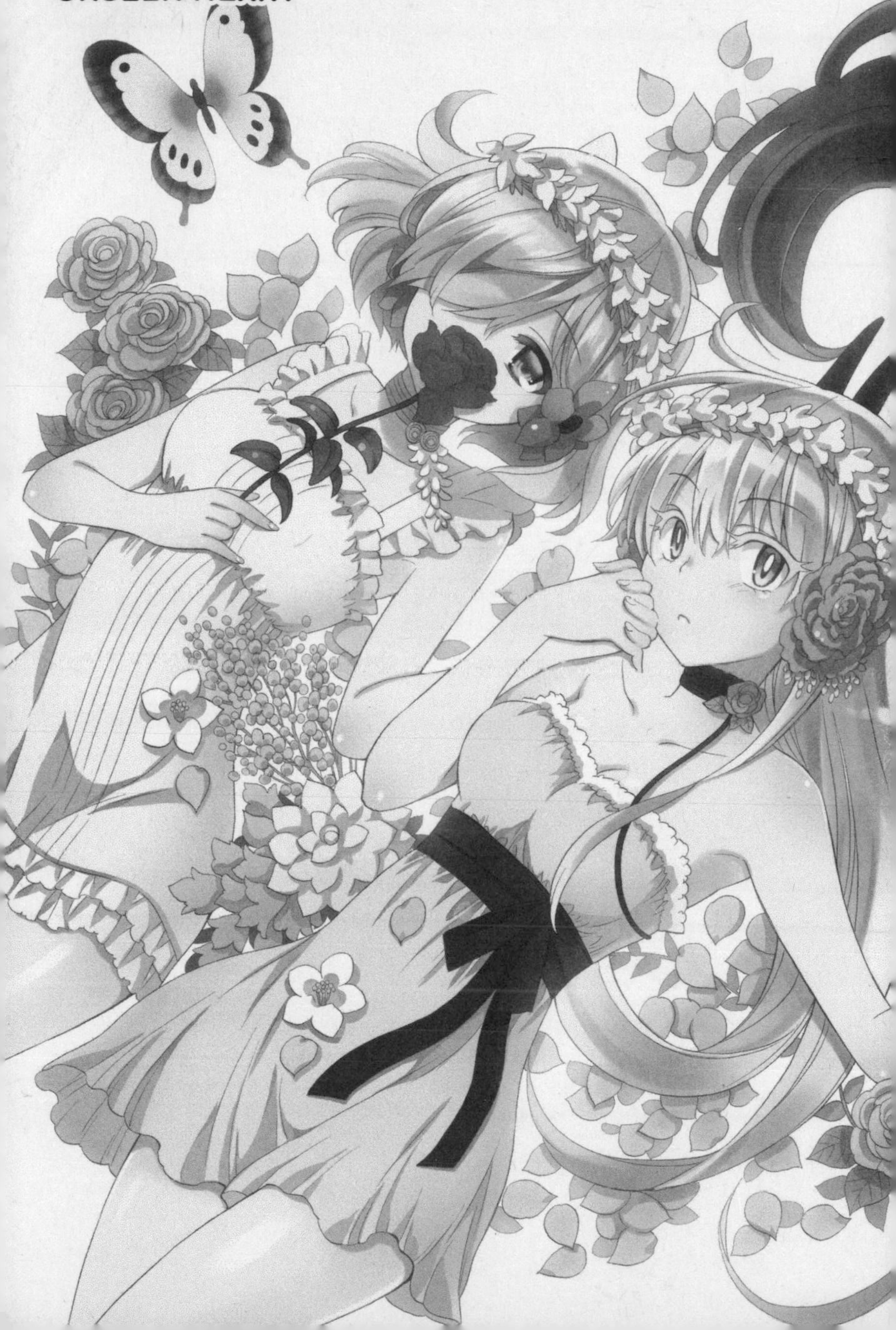

TODAY'S CERBERUS 🐾

I TOTALLY
FORGOT TO
PUT COATS ON
EVERYONE...

SORRY.

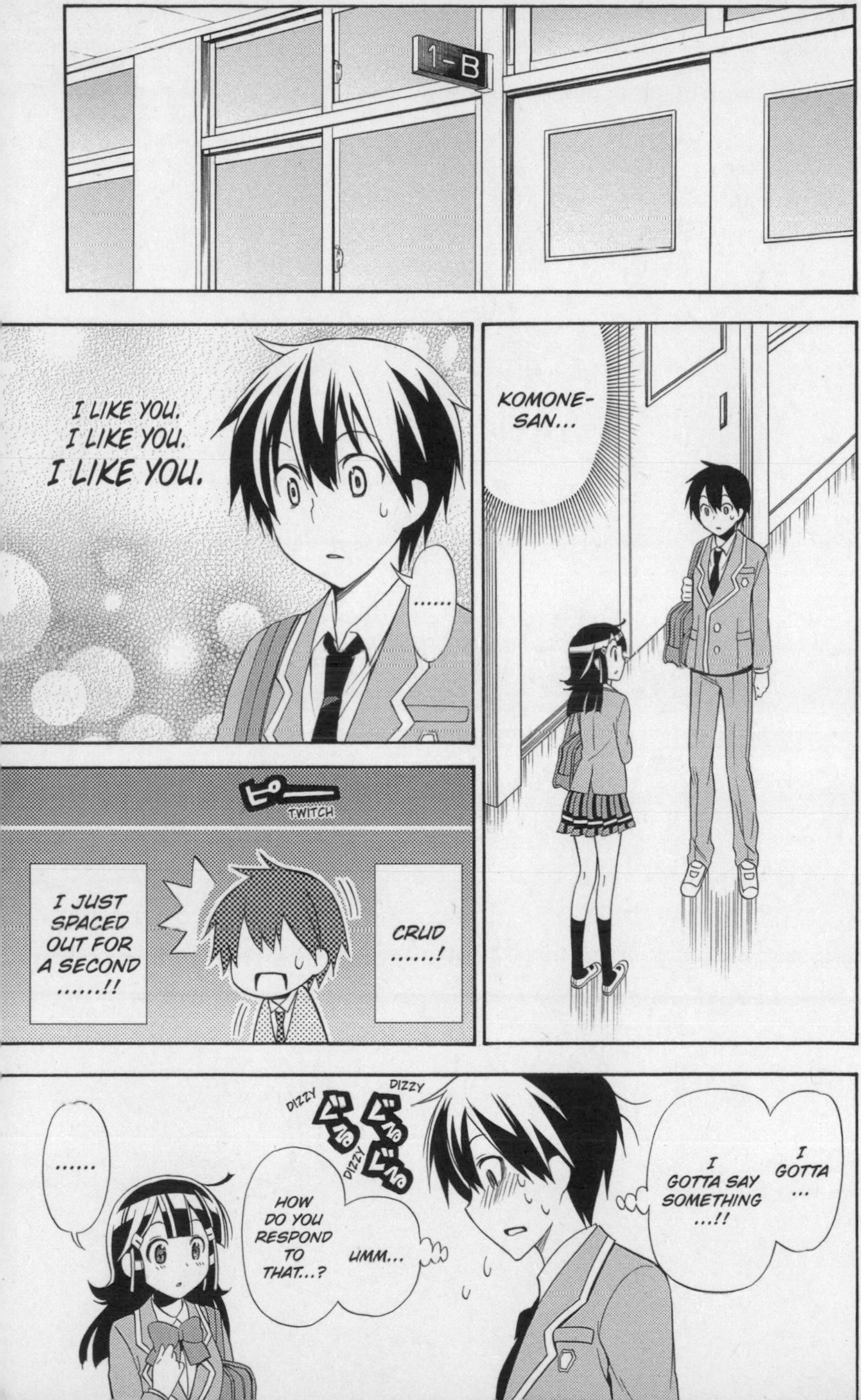
KOMONE-SAN...
I LIKE YOU.
I LIKE YOU.
I LIKE YOU.
......
ピー
TWITCH
CRUD ......!
I JUST SPACED OUT FOR A SECOND ......!!
I GOTTA ...
I GOTTA SAY SOMETHING ...!!
DIZZY
DIZZY
DIZZY
UMM...
HOW DO YOU RESPOND TO THAT...?
......

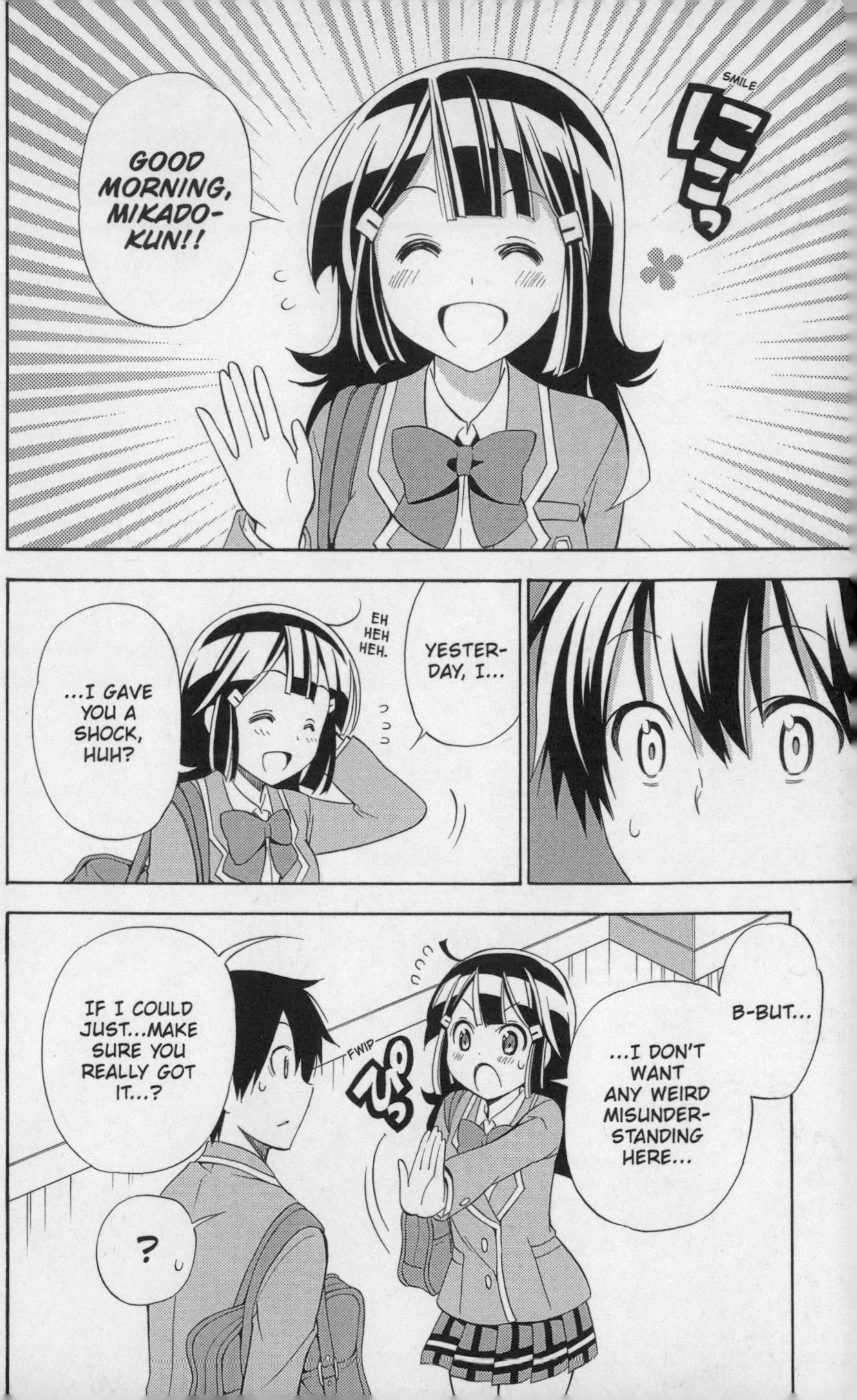
SMILE
GOOD MORNING, MIKADO-KUN!!
YESTER-DAY, I...
EH HEH HEH.
...I GAVE YOU A SHOCK, HUH?
B-BUT...
...I DON'T WANT ANY WEIRD MISUNDER-STANDING HERE...
FWIP
IF I COULD JUST...MAKE SURE YOU REALLY GOT IT...?
?

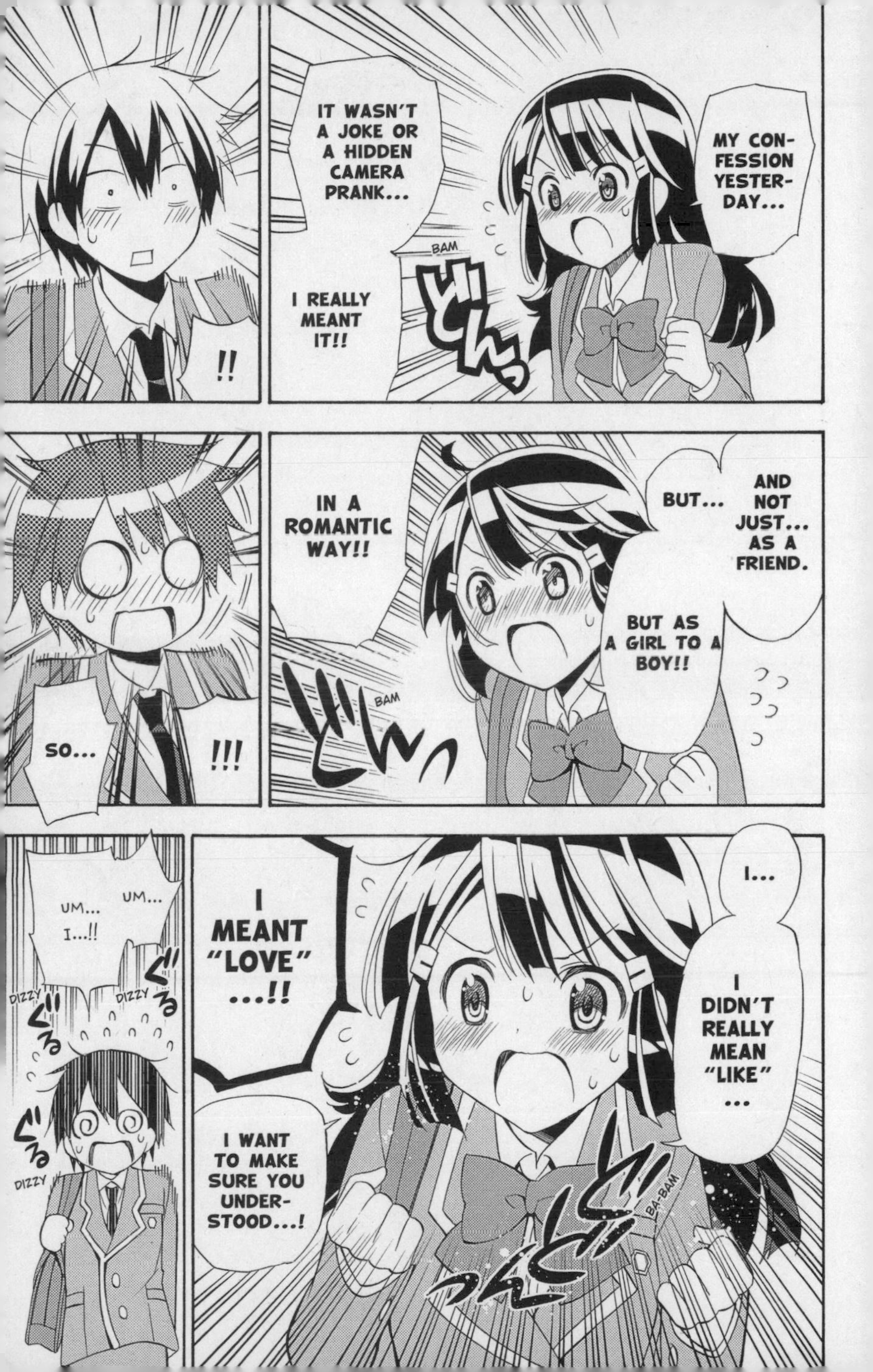
MY CON-FESSION YESTER-DAY...
IT WASN'T A JOKE OR A HIDDEN CAMERA PRANK...
BAM
I REALLY MEANT IT!!
!!
AND NOT JUST... AS A FRIEND.
BUT...
BUT AS A GIRL TO A BOY!!
IN A ROMANTIC WAY!!
BAM
!!!
SO...
I...
I DIDN'T REALLY MEAN "LIKE"...
I MEANT "LOVE"...!!
I WANT TO MAKE SURE YOU UNDER-STOOD...!
BA-BAM
UM...
UM... I...!!
DIZZY
DIZZY
DIZZY

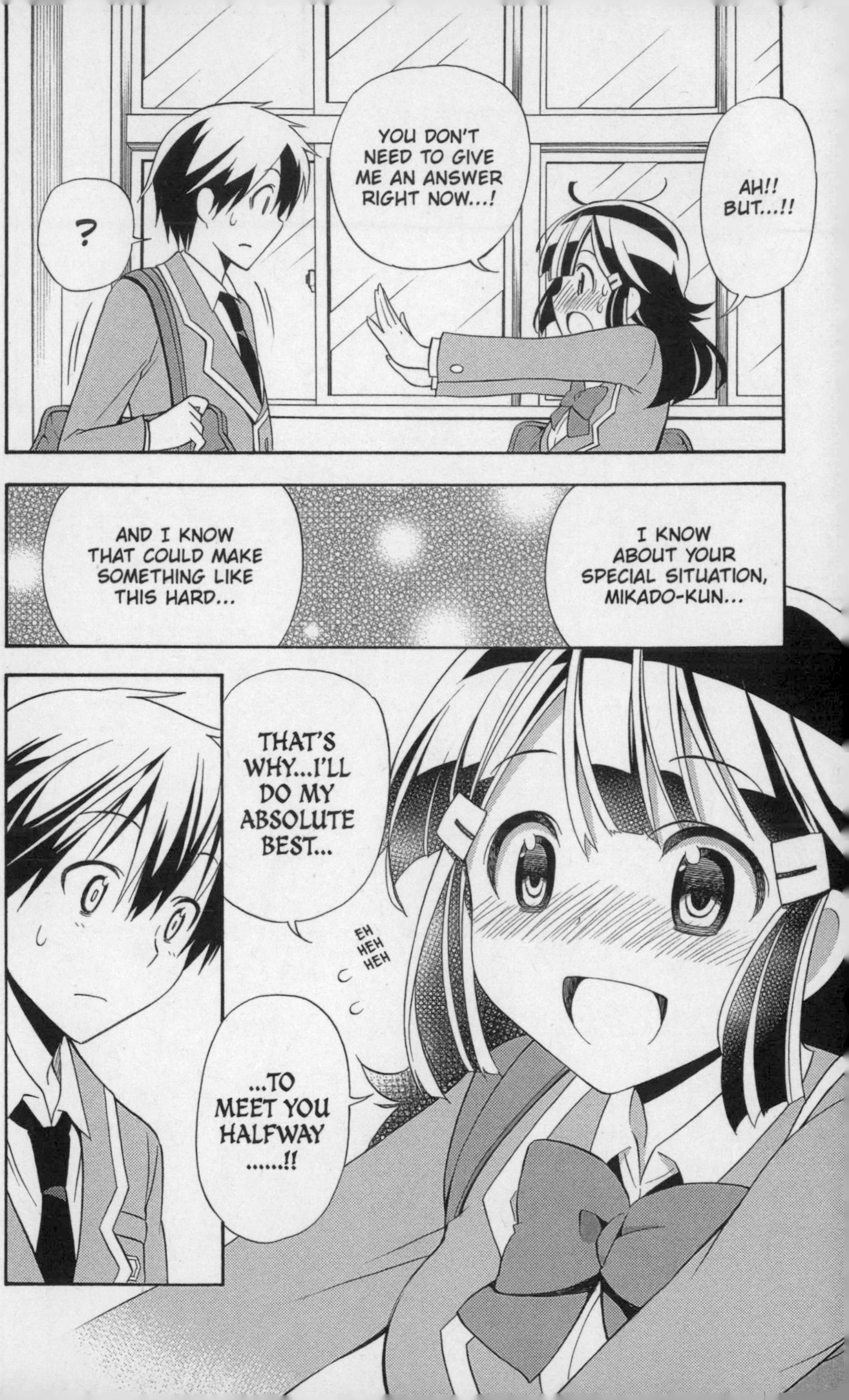
AH!! BUT...!!
YOU DON'T NEED TO GIVE ME AN ANSWER RIGHT NOW...!
?
I KNOW ABOUT YOUR SPECIAL SITUATION, MIKADO-KUN...
AND I KNOW THAT COULD MAKE SOMETHING LIKE THIS HARD...
THAT'S WHY...I'LL DO MY ABSOLUTE BEST...
EH HEH HEH
...TO MEET YOU HALFWAY ......!!

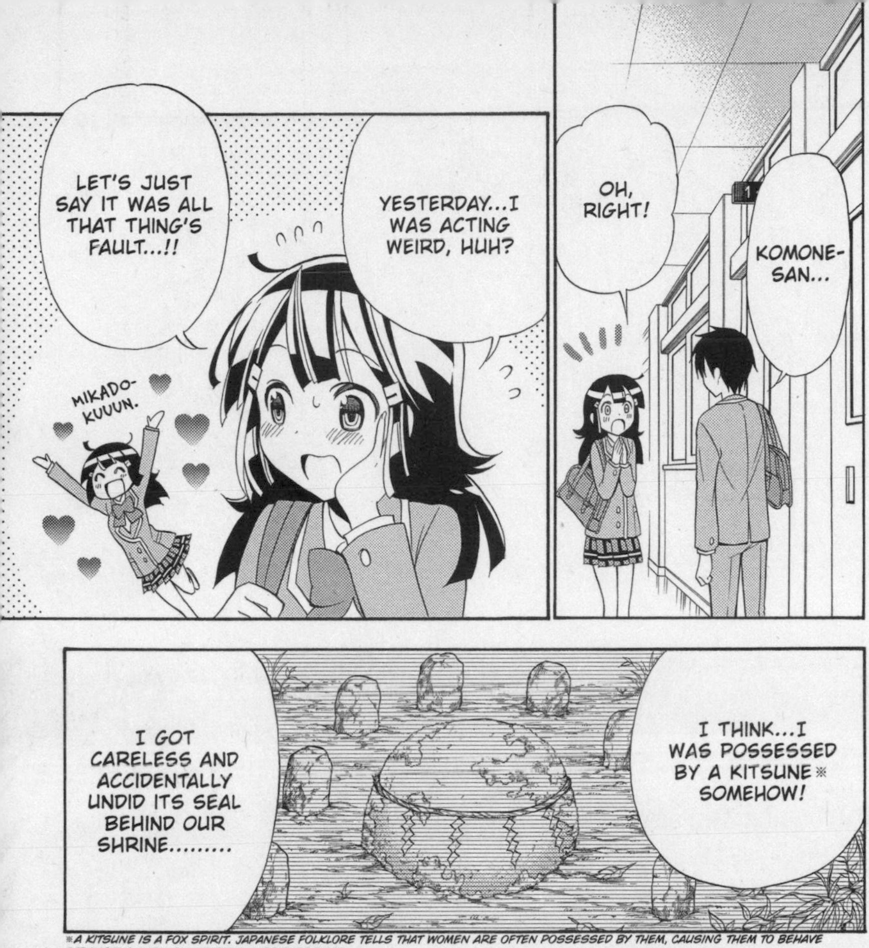
KOMONE-SAN...
OH, RIGHT!
YESTERDAY...I WAS ACTING WEIRD, HUH?
LET'S JUST SAY IT WAS ALL THAT THING'S FAULT...!!
MIKADO-KUUUN.
I THINK...I WAS POSSESSED BY A KITSUNE※ SOMEHOW!
I GOT CARELESS AND ACCIDENTALLY UNDID ITS SEAL BEHIND OUR SHRINE.........

※A KITSUNE IS A FOX SPIRIT. JAPANESE FOLKLORE TELLS THAT WOMEN ARE OFTEN POSSESSED BY THEM, CAUSING THEM TO BEHAVE STRANGELY UNTIL THE SPIRIT CAN BE EXORCISED.

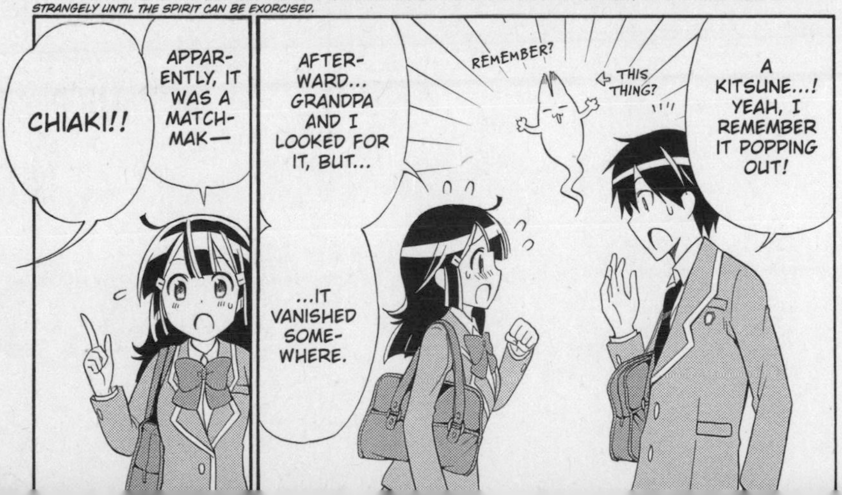
A KITSUNE...! YEAH, I REMEMBER IT POPPING OUT!
THIS THING?
REMEMBER?
AFTERWARD... GRANDPA AND I LOOKED FOR IT, BUT...
...IT VANISHED SOMEWHERE.
APPARENTLY, IT WAS A MATCHMAK—
CHIAKI!!

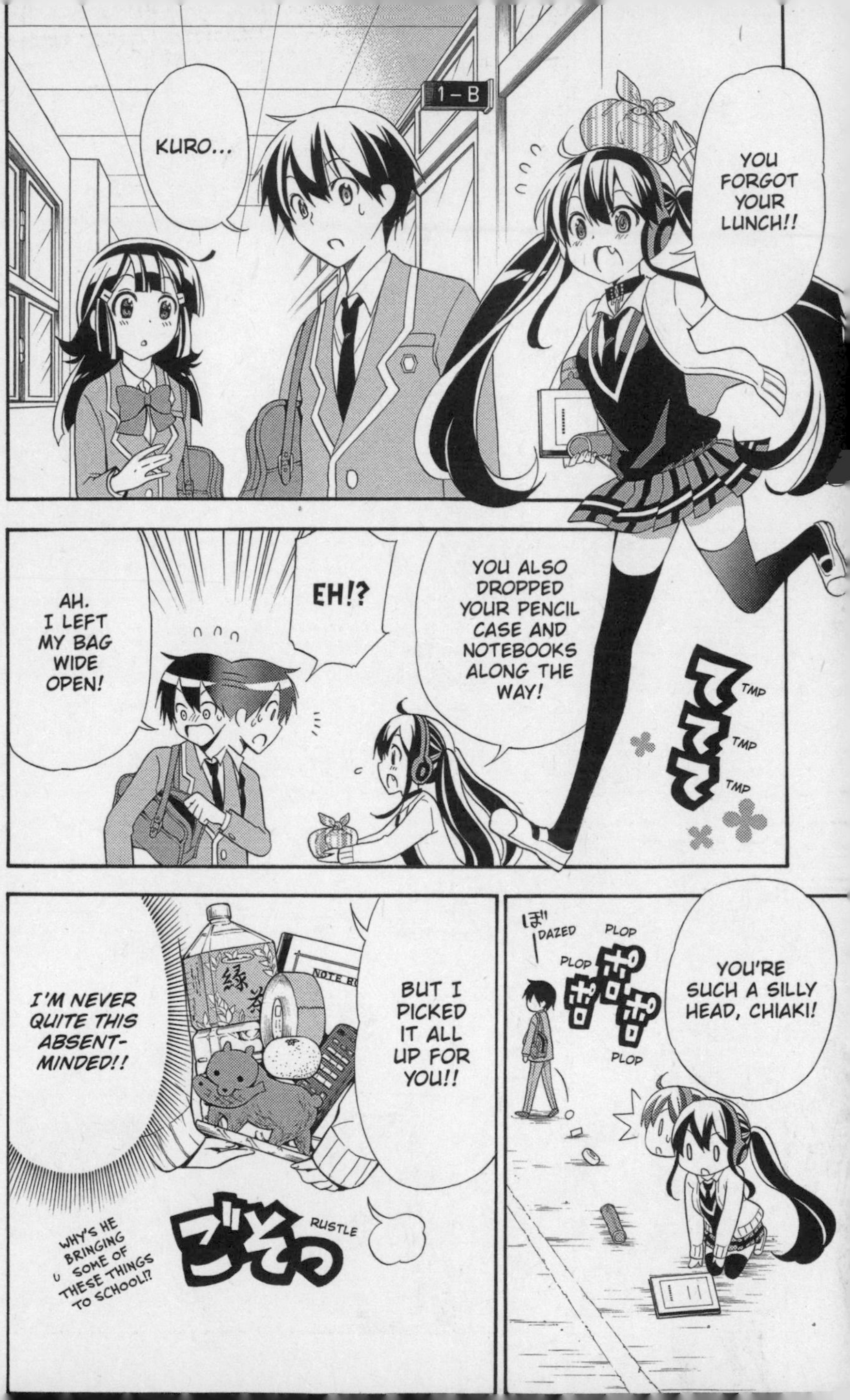

YOU FORGOT YOUR LUNCH!!
KURO...
1-B
YOU ALSO DROPPED YOUR PENCIL CASE AND NOTEBOOKS ALONG THE WAY!
ててて
TMP
TMP
TMP
EH!?
AH. I LEFT MY BAG WIDE OPEN!
YOU'RE SUCH A SILLY HEAD, CHIAKI!
ポロポロ
PLOP
PLOP
PLOP
ぼ
DAZED
BUT I PICKED IT ALL UP FOR YOU!!
I'M NEVER QUITE THIS ABSENT-MINDED!!
緑茶
ごそっ
RUSTLE
WHY'S HE BRINGING SOME OF THESE THINGS TO SCHOOL!?

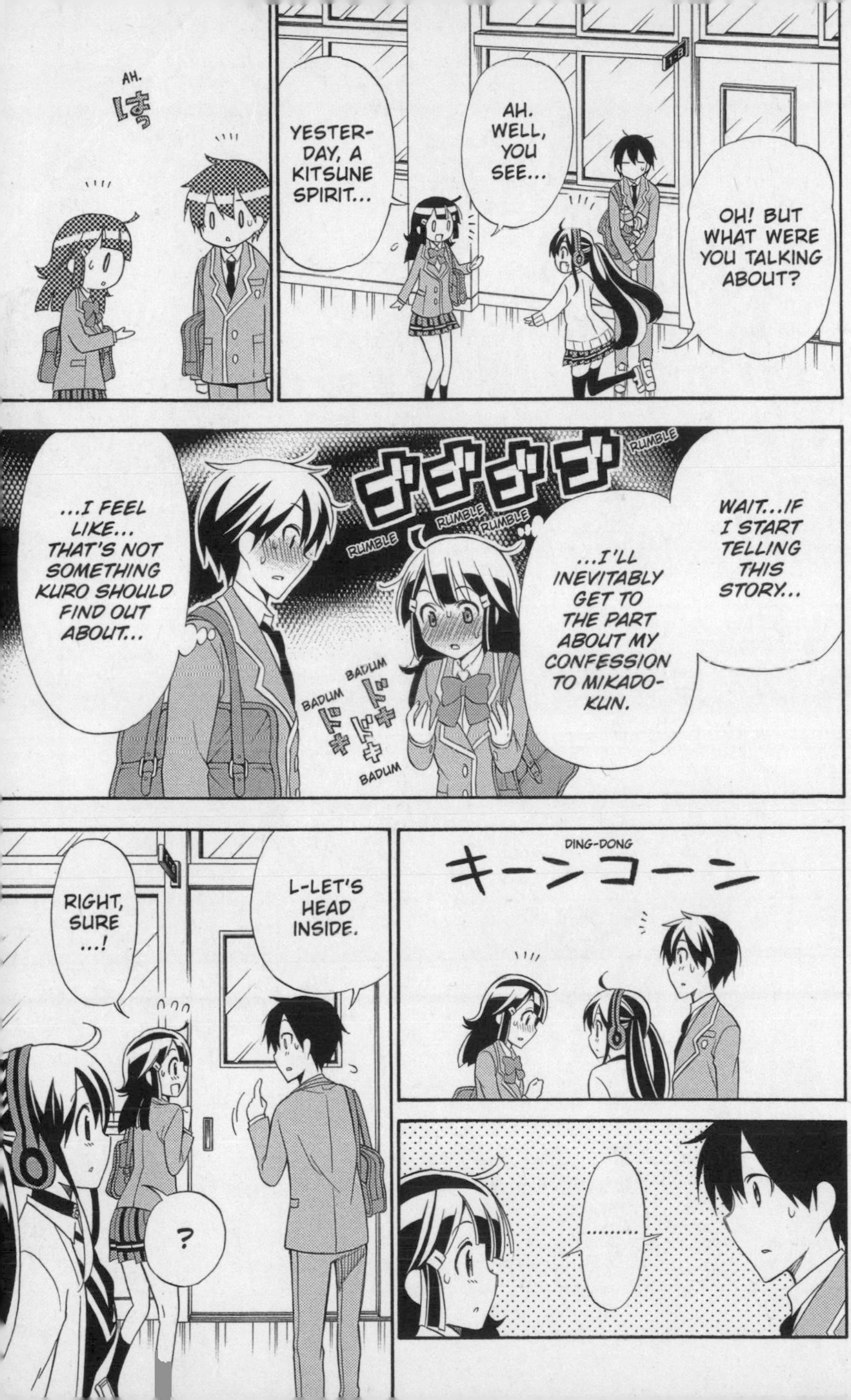
OH! BUT WHAT WERE YOU TALKING ABOUT?
AH. WELL, YOU SEE...
YESTER-DAY, A KITSUNE SPIRIT...
AH.
はっ
WAIT...IF I START TELLING THIS STORY...
...I'LL INEVITABLY GET TO THE PART ABOUT MY CONFESSION TO MIKADO-KUN.
ゴゴゴゴ
RUMBLE
RUMBLE
RUMBLE
RUMBLE
ドキドキドキ
BADUM
BADUM
BADUM
...I FEEL LIKE... THAT'S NOT SOMETHING KURO SHOULD FIND OUT ABOUT...
DING-DONG
キーンコーン
....
L-LET'S HEAD INSIDE.
RIGHT, SURE ...!
?

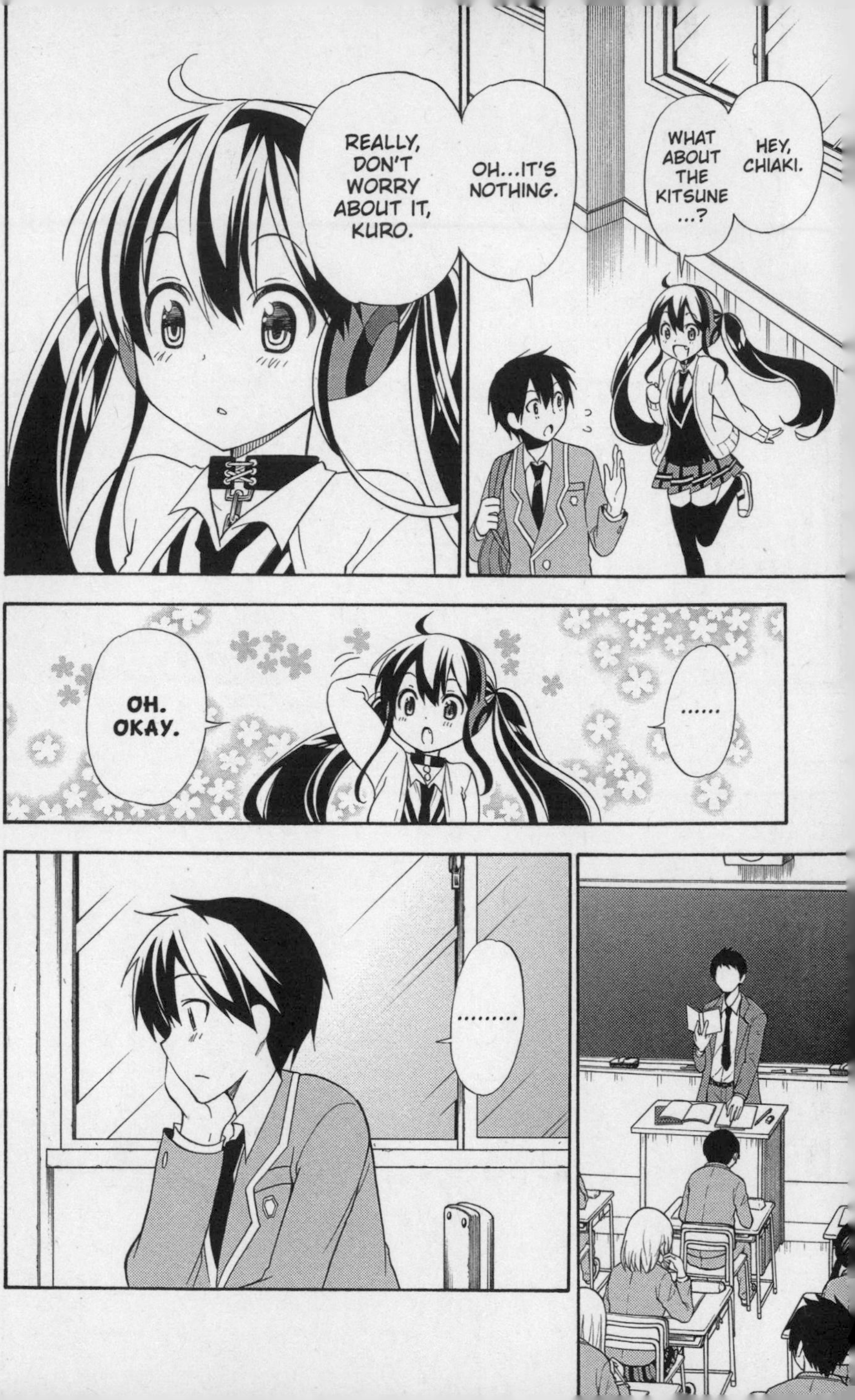
HEY, CHIAKI.
WHAT ABOUT THE KITSUNE ...?
OH...IT'S NOTHING.
REALLY, DON'T WORRY ABOUT IT, KURO.
......
OH. OKAY.
....

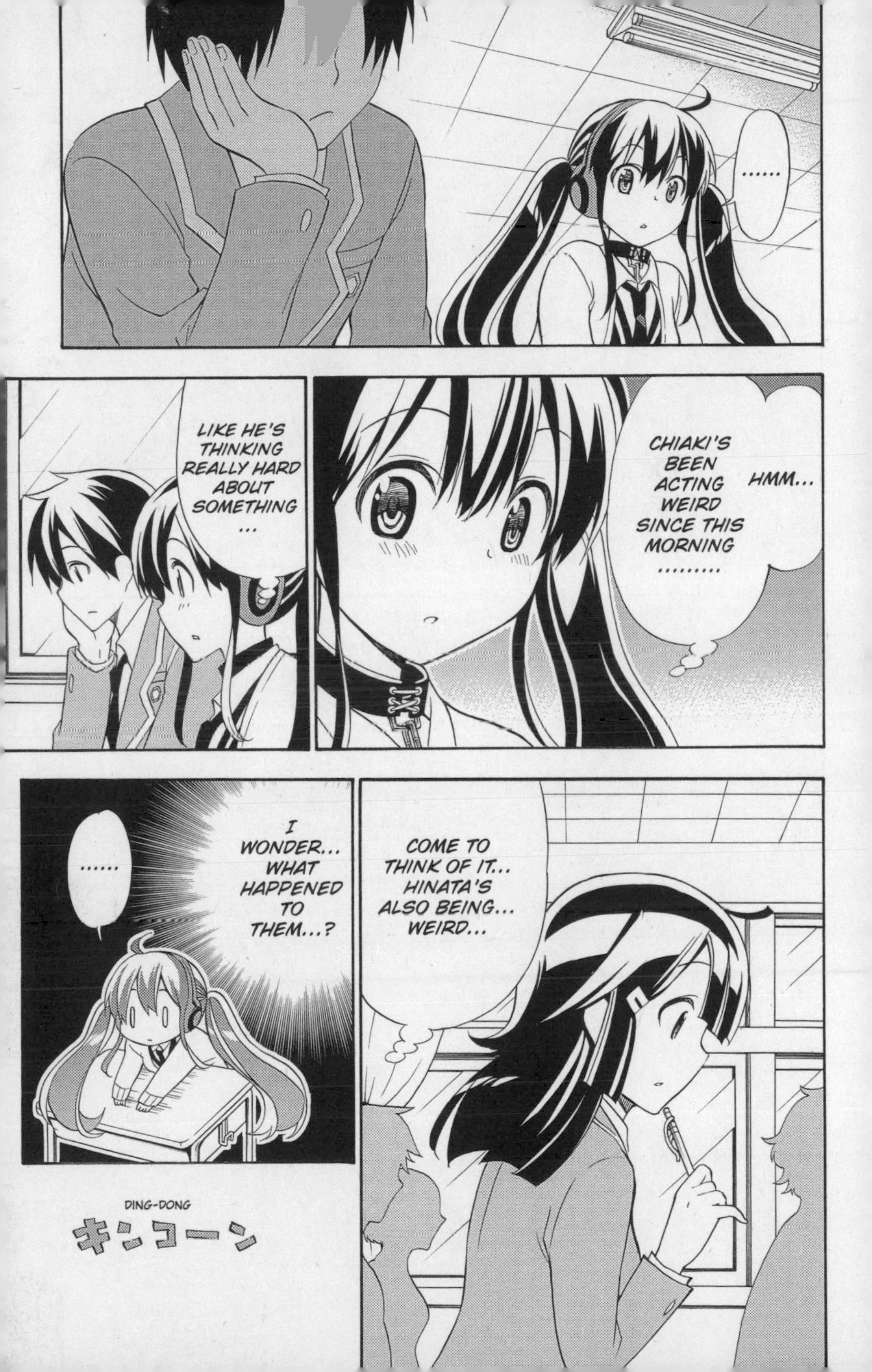
......
HMM...
CHIAKI'S BEEN ACTING WEIRD SINCE THIS MORNING ....
LIKE HE'S THINKING REALLY HARD ABOUT SOMETHING ...
COME TO THINK OF IT... HINATA'S ALSO BEING... WEIRD...
I WONDER... WHAT HAPPENED TO THEM...?
......
DING-DONG
キンコーン

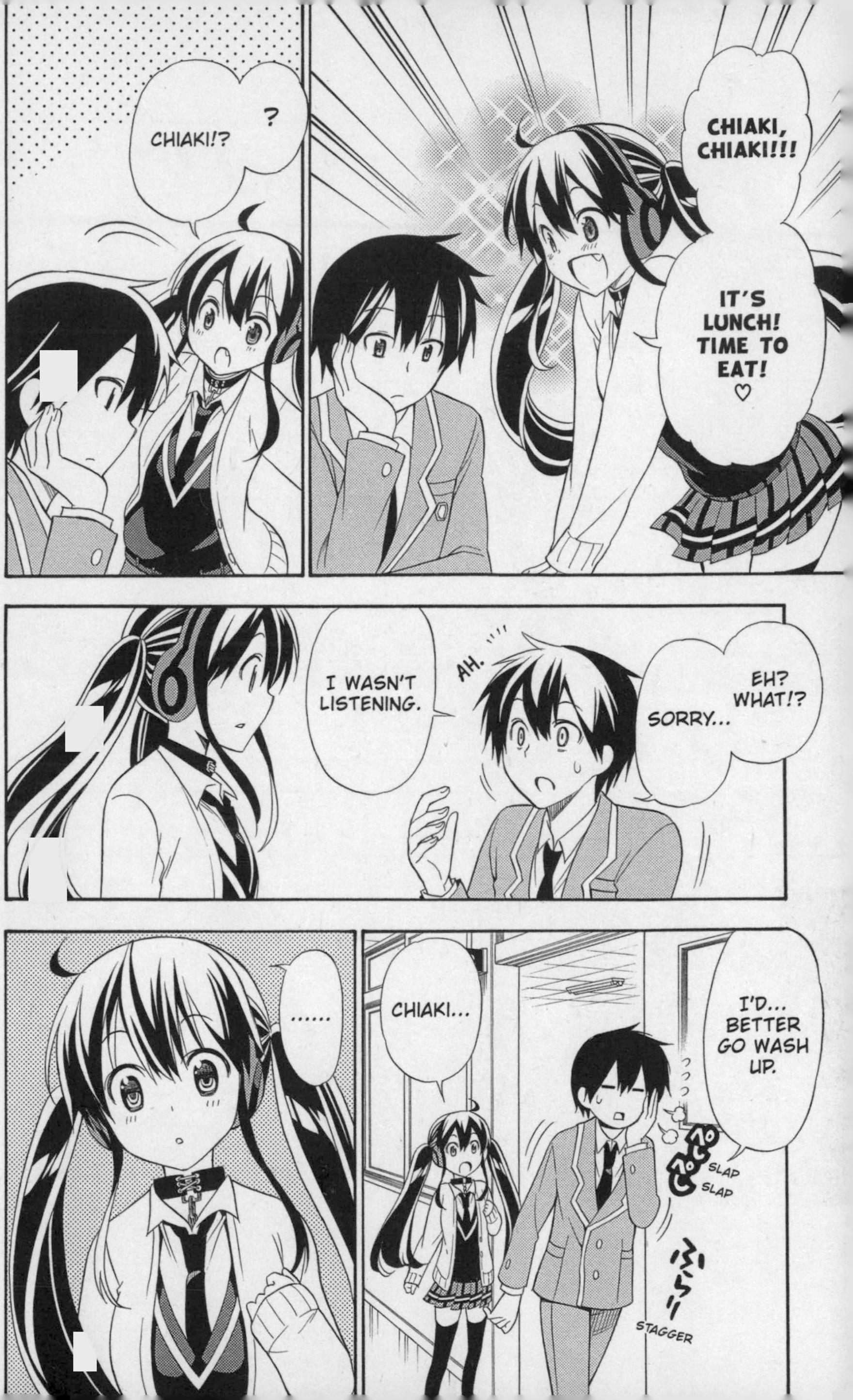
CHIAKI, CHIAKI!!!
IT'S LUNCH! TIME TO EAT! ♡
?
CHIAKI!?
EH? WHAT!?
SORRY...
AH.
I WASN'T LISTENING.
I'D... BETTER GO WASH UP.
SLAP SLAP
STAGGER
CHIAKI...
......

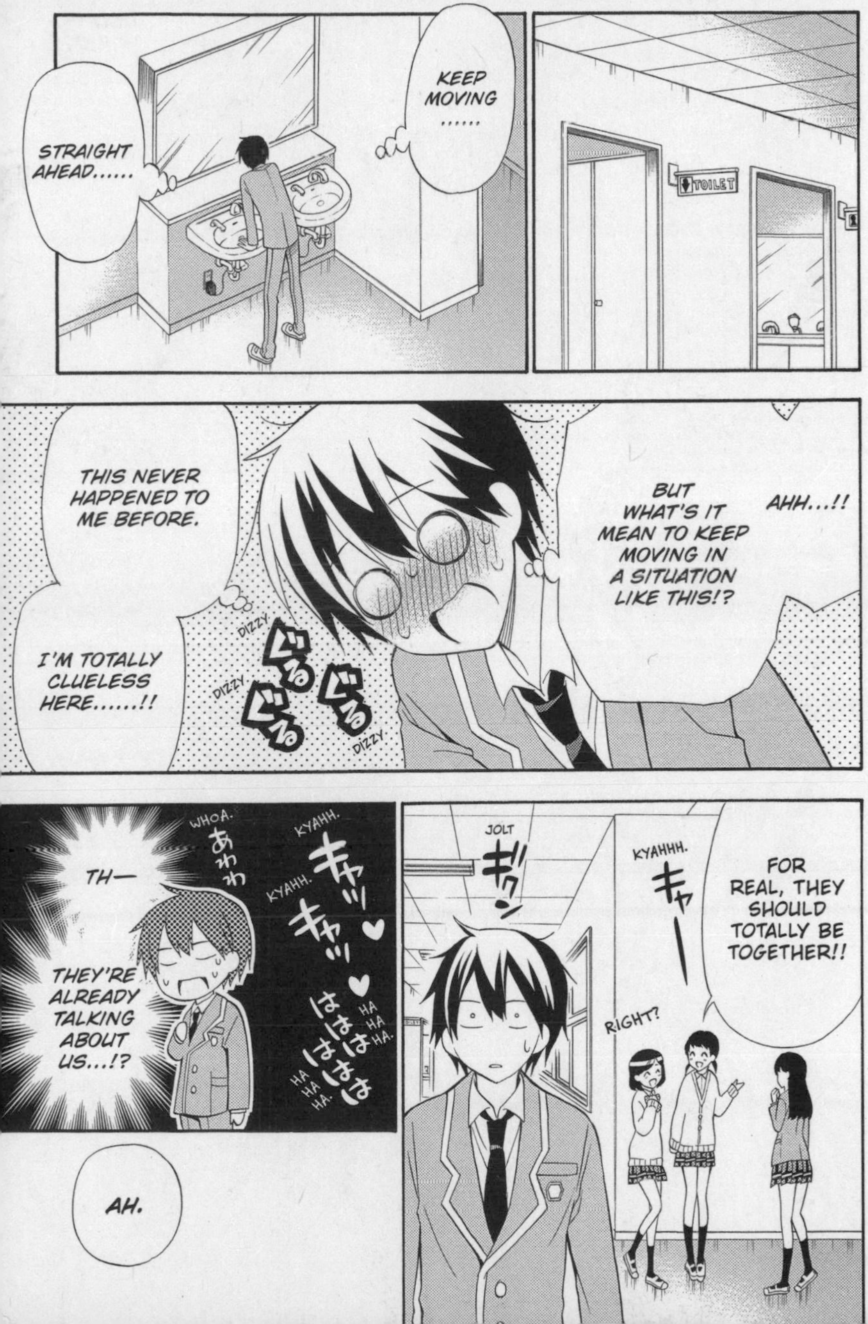
TOILET
KEEP MOVING ......
STRAIGHT AHEAD......
AHH...!!
BUT WHAT'S IT MEAN TO KEEP MOVING IN A SITUATION LIKE THIS!?
DIZZY. ぐる DIZZY. ぐる DIZZY. ぐる
THIS NEVER HAPPENED TO ME BEFORE.
I'M TOTALLY CLUELESS HERE......!!
FOR REAL, THEY SHOULD TOTALLY BE TOGETHER!!
KYAHHH. キャー
JOLT ギクン
RIGHT?
KYAHH. キャッ
KYAHH. キャッ
HA HA HA. ははは
HA HA HA. ははは
WHOA. あわわ
TH—
THEY'RE ALREADY TALKING ABOUT US...!?
AH.

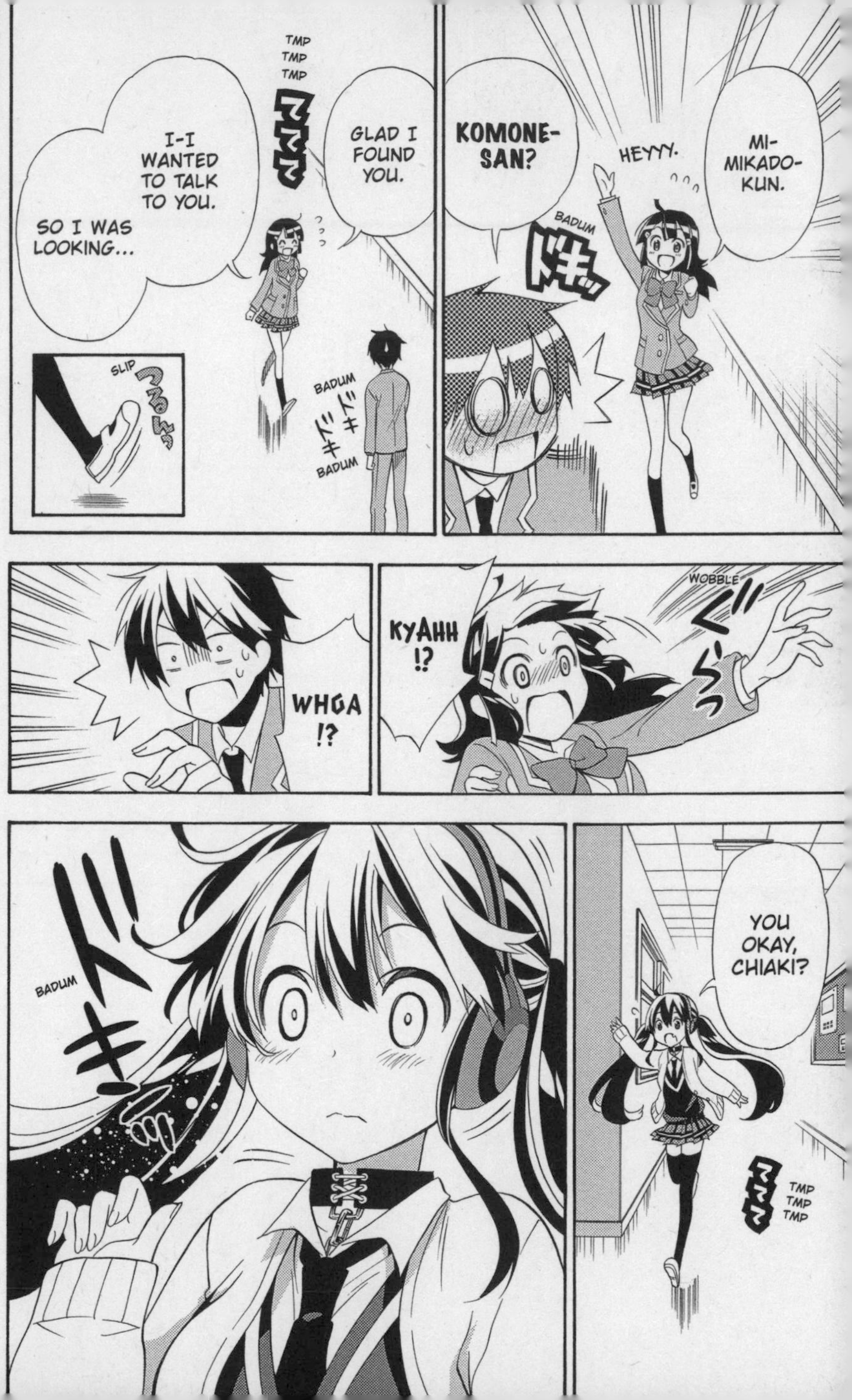
MI-MIKADO-KUN.
HEYYY.
KOMONE-SAN?
BADUM
ドキッ
GLAD I FOUND YOU.
TMP TMP TMP
I-I WANTED TO TALK TO YOU.
SO I WAS LOOKING...
BADUM ドキドキ BADUM
SLIP
つるんっ
WOBBLE
ぐらっ
KYAHH !?
WHGA !?
YOU OKAY, CHIAKI?
TMP TMP TMP
BADUM
ドキッ

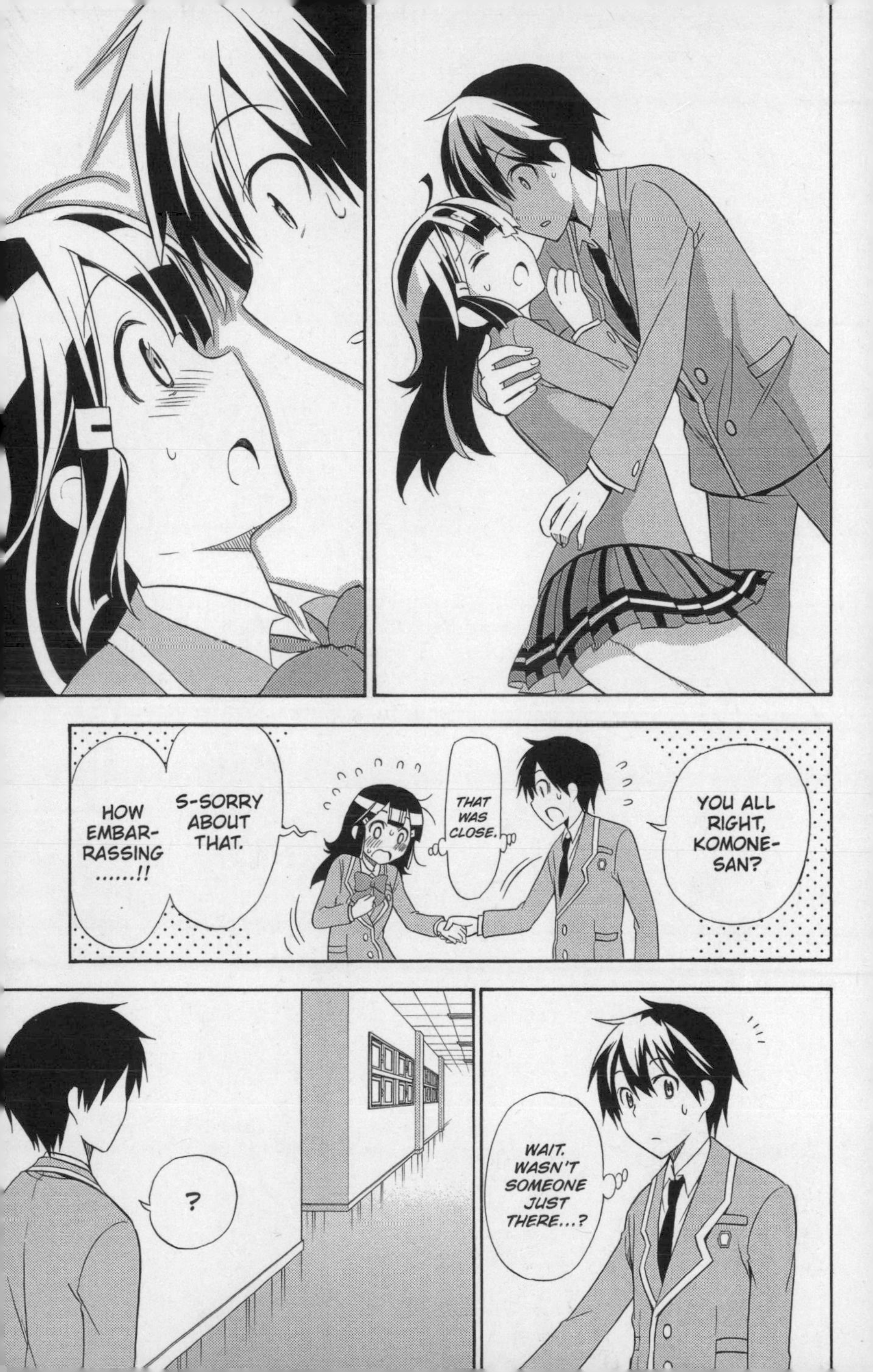
YOU ALL RIGHT, KOMONE-SAN?
THAT WAS CLOSE.
S-SORRY ABOUT THAT.
HOW EMBAR-RASSING ......!!
WAIT. WASN'T SOMEONE JUST THERE...?
?

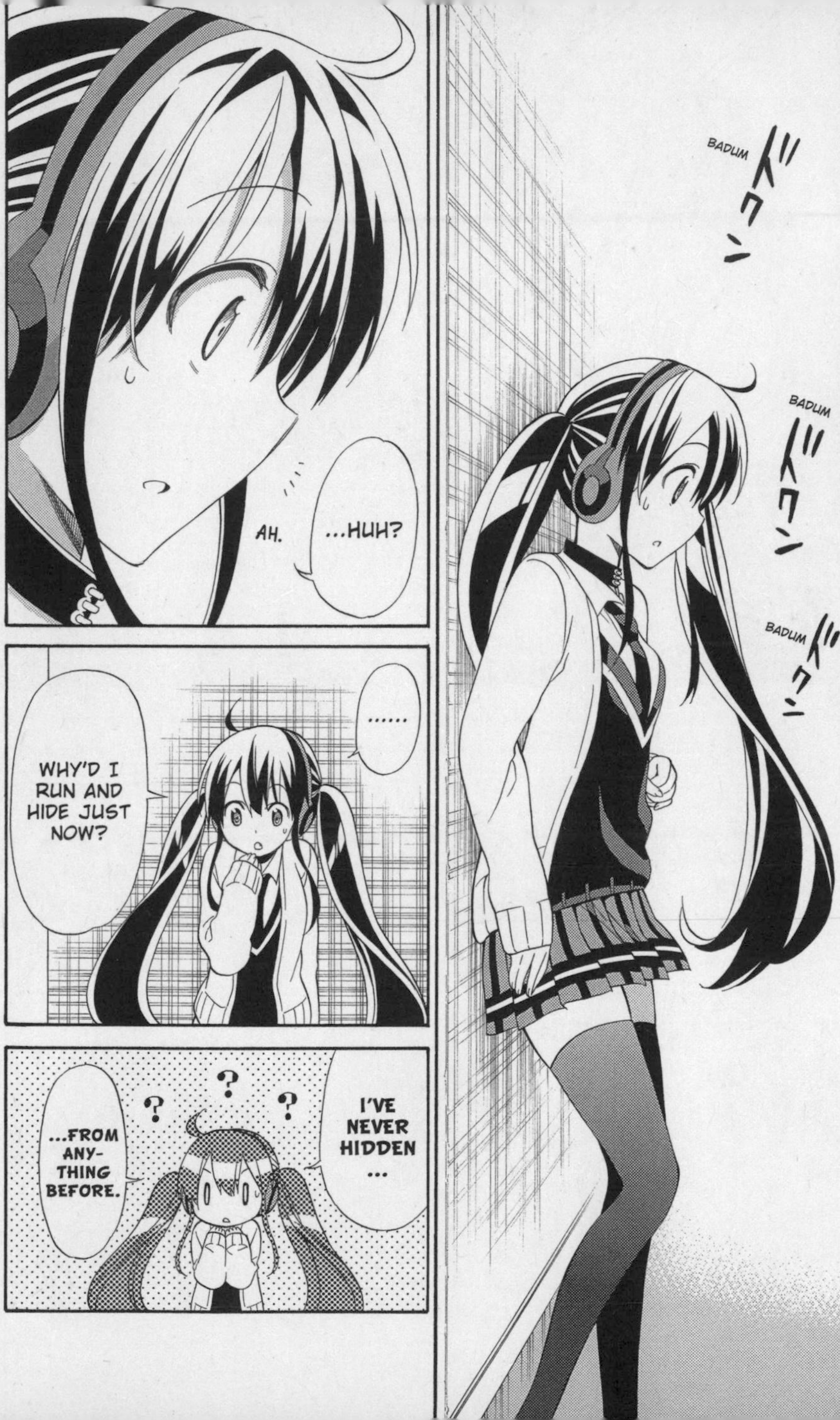
BADUM
ドクン
BADUM
ドクン
BADUM
ドクン
...HUH?
AH.
......
WHY'D I RUN AND HIDE JUST NOW?
?
?
?
I'VE NEVER HIDDEN ...
...FROM ANY-THING BEFORE.

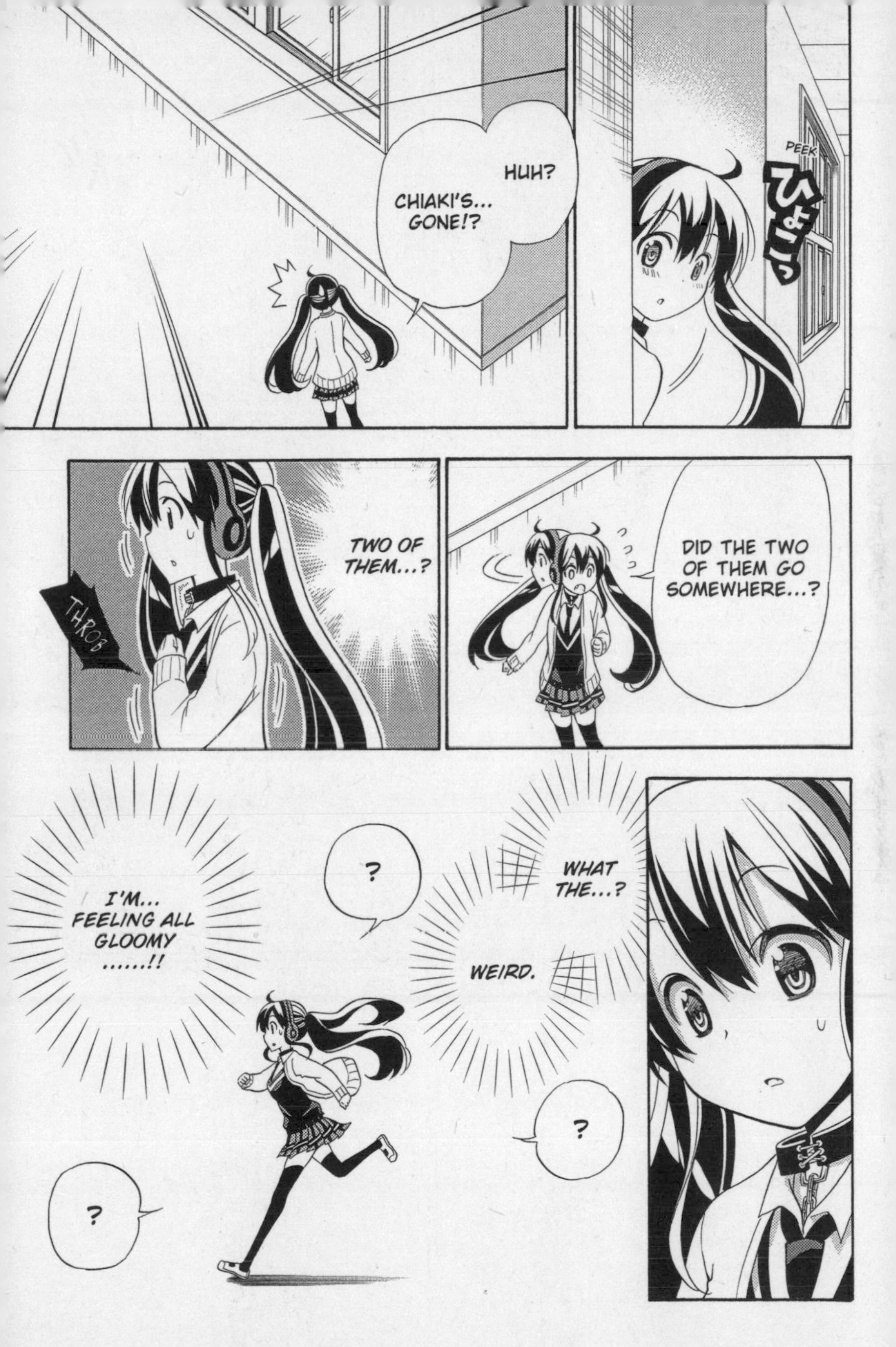
PEEK
ひょこっ
HUH?
CHIAKI'S... GONE!?
DID THE TWO OF THEM GO SOMEWHERE...?
TWO OF THEM...?
THROB
WHAT THE...?
?
WEIRD.
I'M... FEELING ALL GLOOMY ......!!
?
?

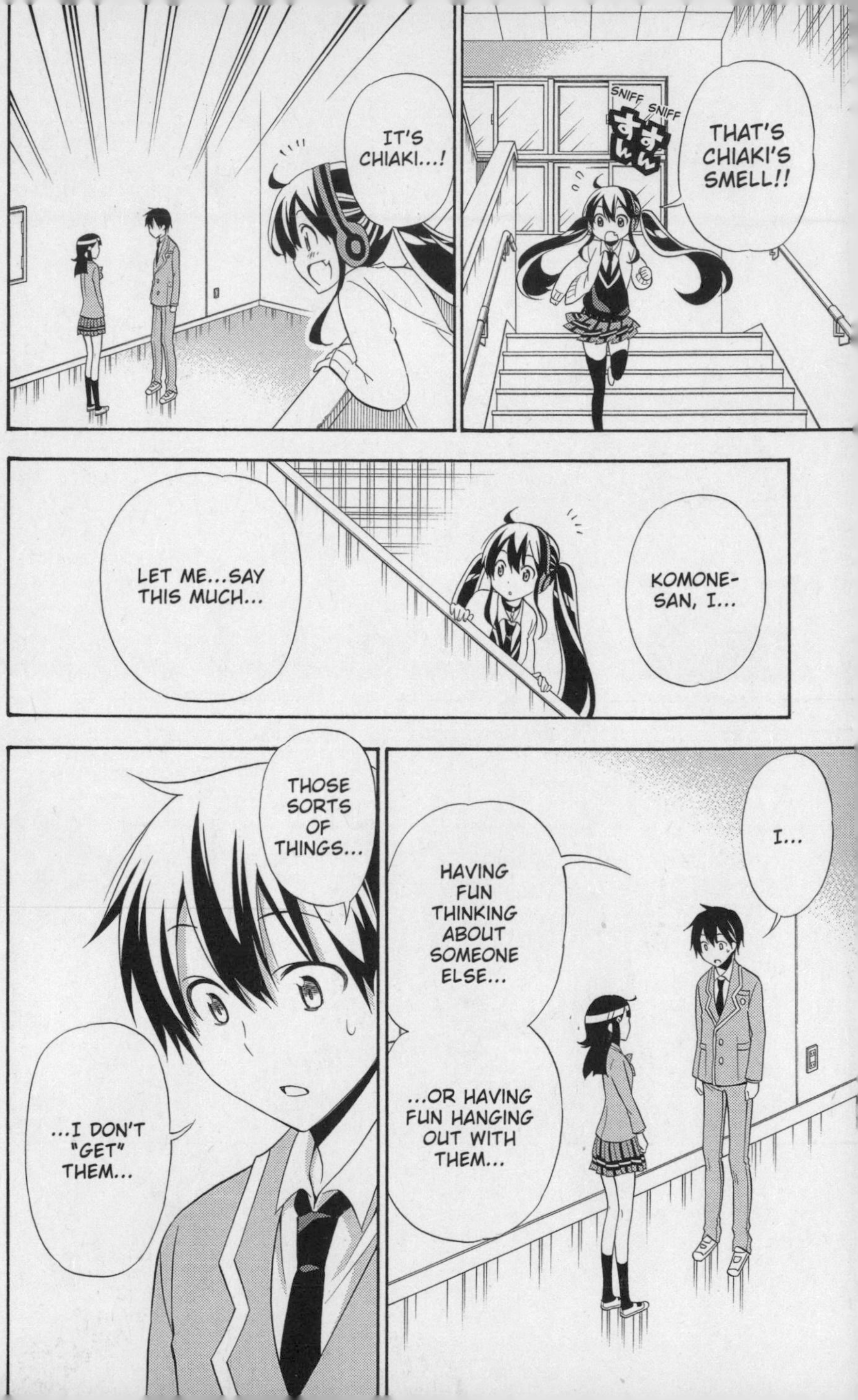
SNIFF SNIFF
すんすん
THAT'S CHIAKI'S SMELL!!
IT'S CHIAKI...!
KOMONE-SAN, I...
LET ME...SAY THIS MUCH...
I...
HAVING FUN THINKING ABOUT SOMEONE ELSE...
...OR HAVING FUN HANGING OUT WITH THEM...
THOSE SORTS OF THINGS...
...I DON'T "GET" THEM...

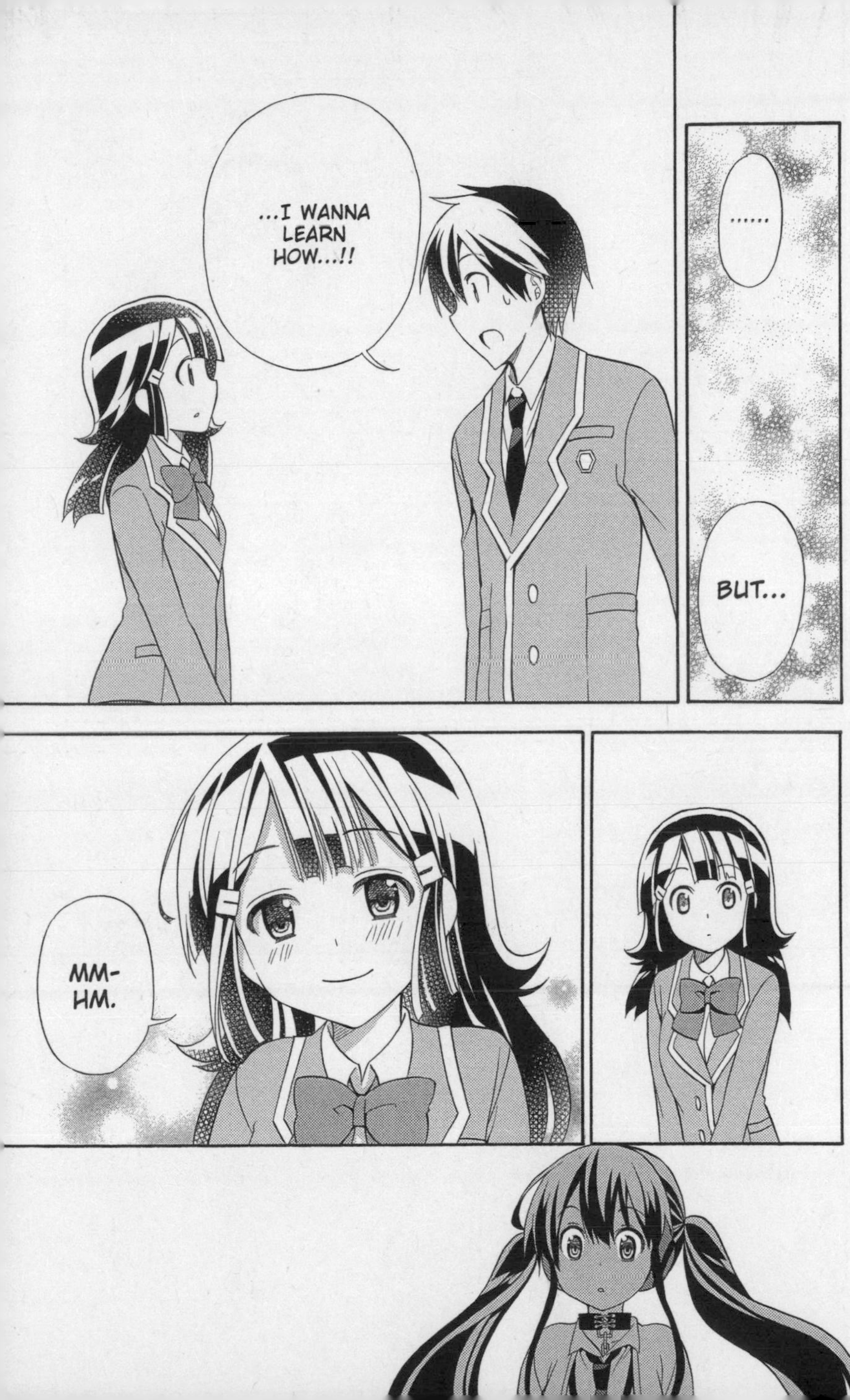
......
BUT...
...I WANNA LEARN HOW...!!
MM-HM.

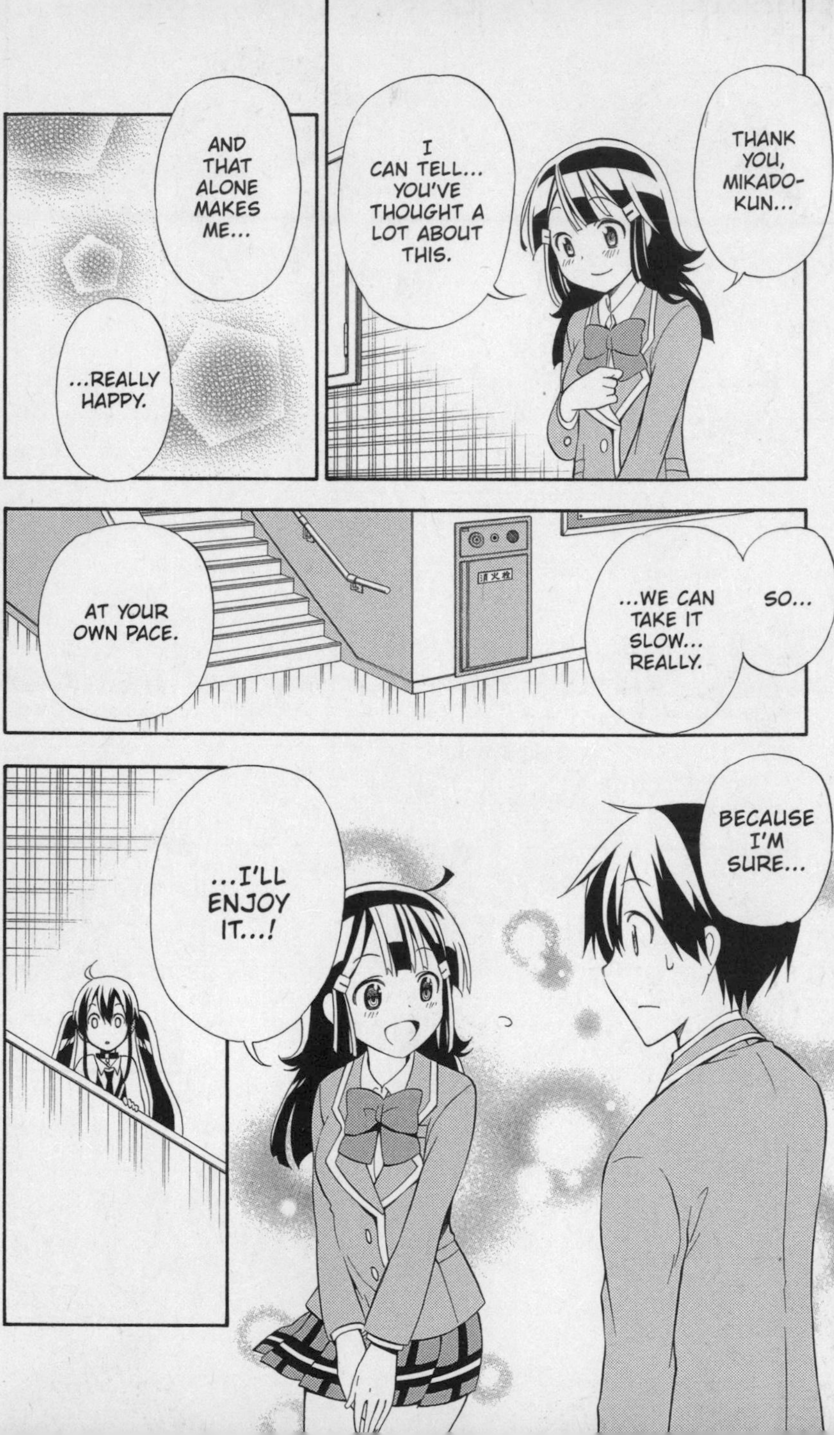
THANK YOU, MIKADO-KUN...
I CAN TELL... YOU'VE THOUGHT A LOT ABOUT THIS.
AND THAT ALONE MAKES ME...
...REALLY HAPPY.
SO...
...WE CAN TAKE IT SLOW... REALLY.
AT YOUR OWN PACE.
BECAUSE I'M SURE...
...I'LL ENJOY IT...!

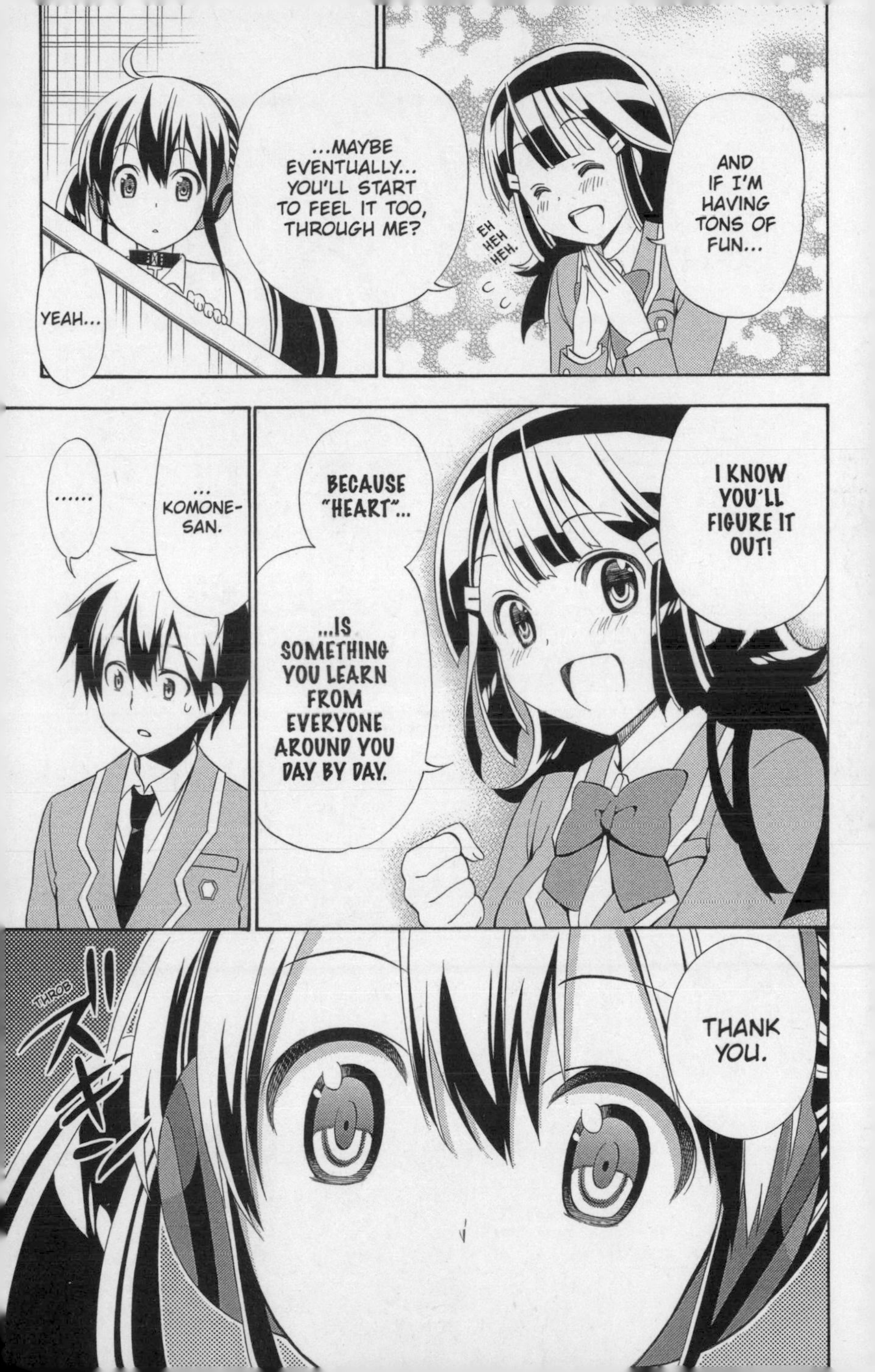
AND IF I'M HAVING TONS OF FUN...
EH HEH HEH.
...MAYBE EVENTUALLY... YOU'LL START TO FEEL IT TOO, THROUGH ME?
YEAH...
I KNOW YOU'LL FIGURE IT OUT!
BECAUSE "HEART"...
...IS SOMETHING YOU LEARN FROM EVERYONE AROUND YOU DAY BY DAY.
... KOMONE-SAN.
......
THANK YOU.
THROB

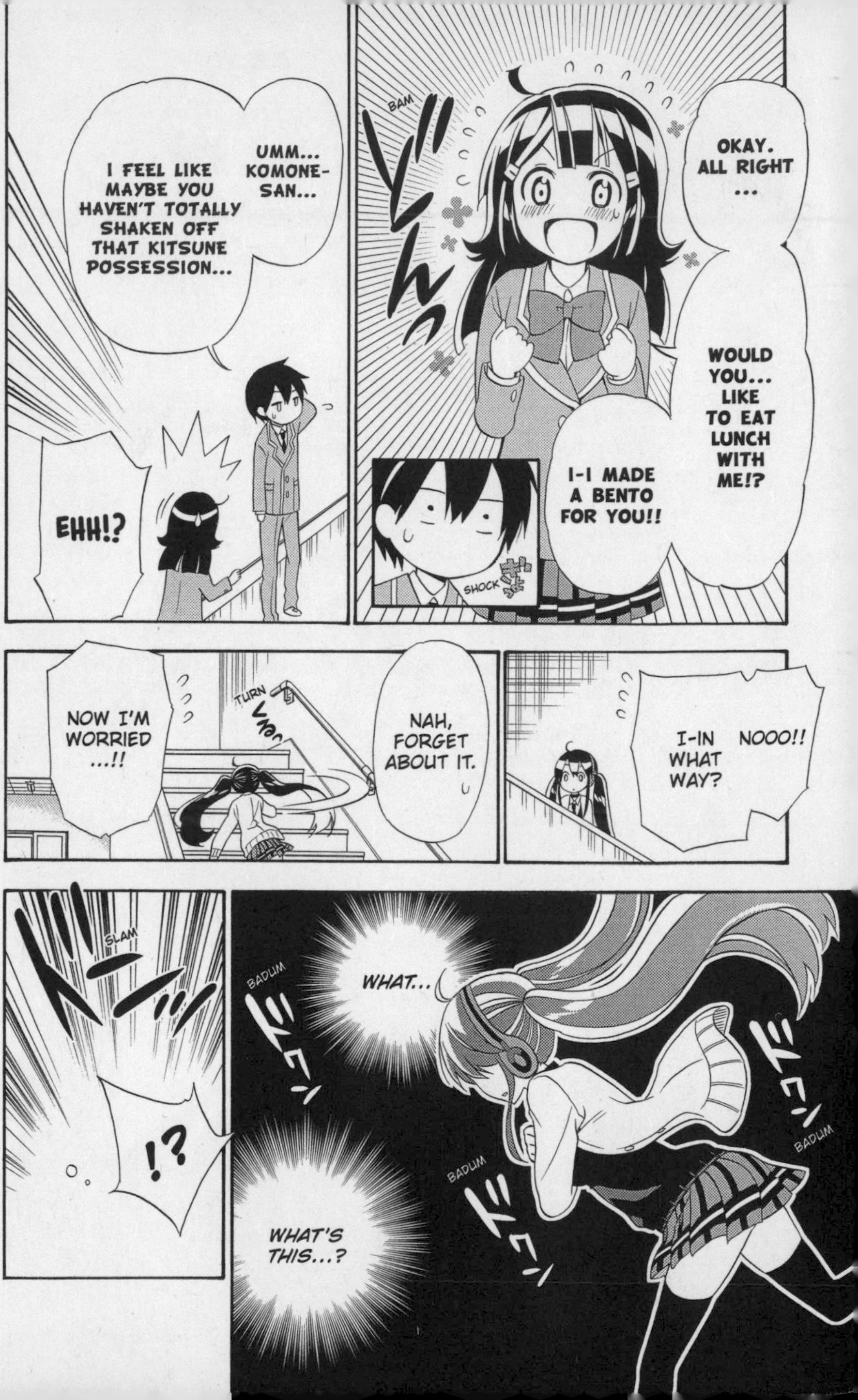
OKAY. ALL RIGHT ...
BAM
WOULD YOU... LIKE TO EAT LUNCH WITH ME!?
I-I MADE A BENTO FOR YOU!!
SHOCK
UMM... KOMONE-SAN...
I FEEL LIKE MAYBE YOU HAVEN'T TOTALLY SHAKEN OFF THAT KITSUNE POSSESSION...
EHH!?
NOOO!!
I-IN WHAT WAY?
NAH, FORGET ABOUT IT.
TURN
NOW I'M WORRIED ...!!
WHAT...
BADUM
WHAT'S THIS...?
BADUM
BADUM
SLAM
!?

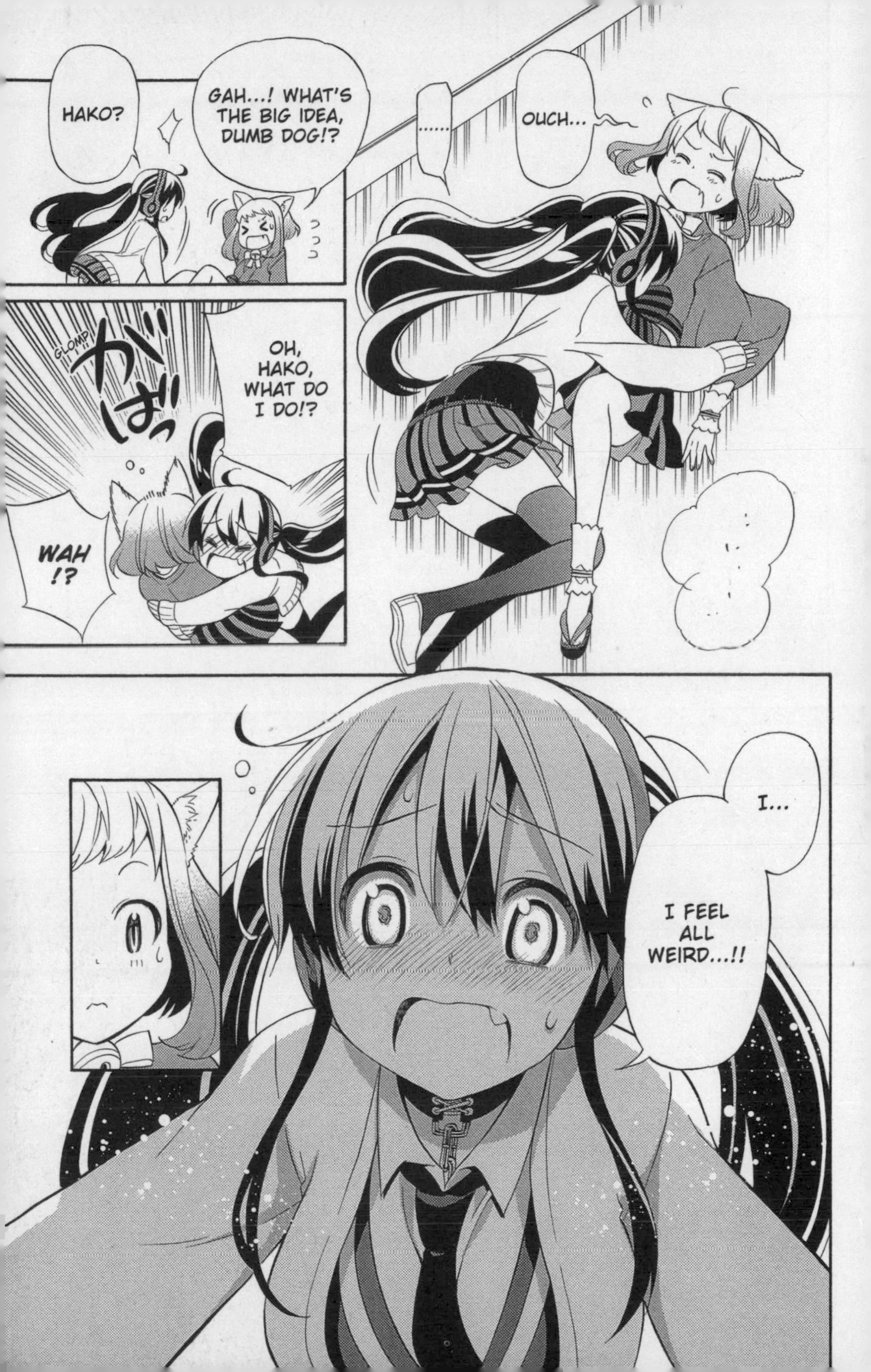
OUCH...
......
GAH...! WHAT'S THE BIG IDEA, DUMB DOG!?
HAKO?
OH, HAKO, WHAT DO I DO!?
GLOMP
WAH!?
I...
I FEEL ALL WEIRD...!!

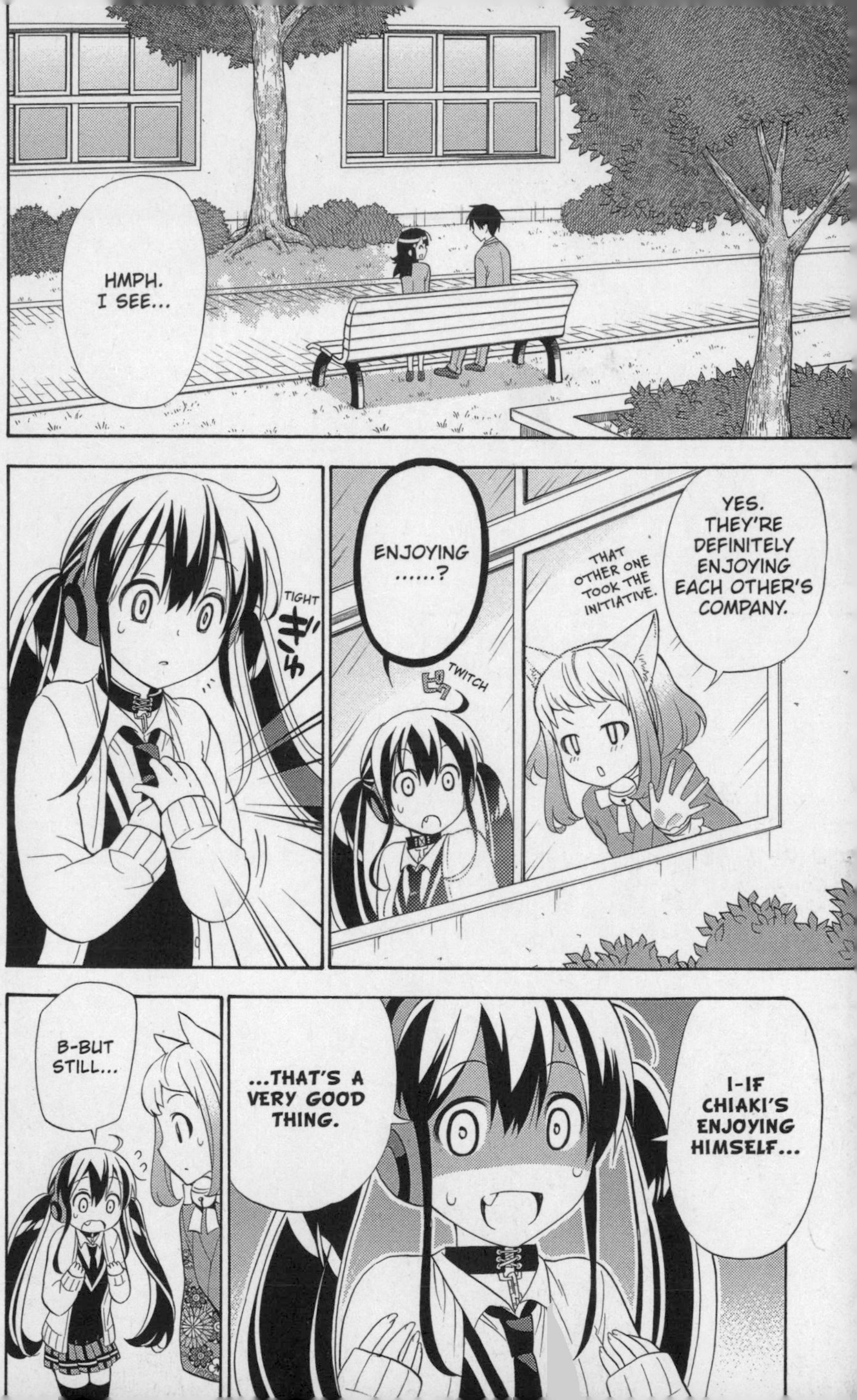
HMPH. I SEE...
YES. THEY'RE DEFINITELY ENJOYING EACH OTHER'S COMPANY.
THAT OTHER ONE TOOK THE INITIATIVE.
ENJOYING ......?
TWITCH
TIGHT
I-IF CHIAKI'S ENJOYING HIMSELF...
...THAT'S A VERY GOOD THING.
B-BUT STILL...

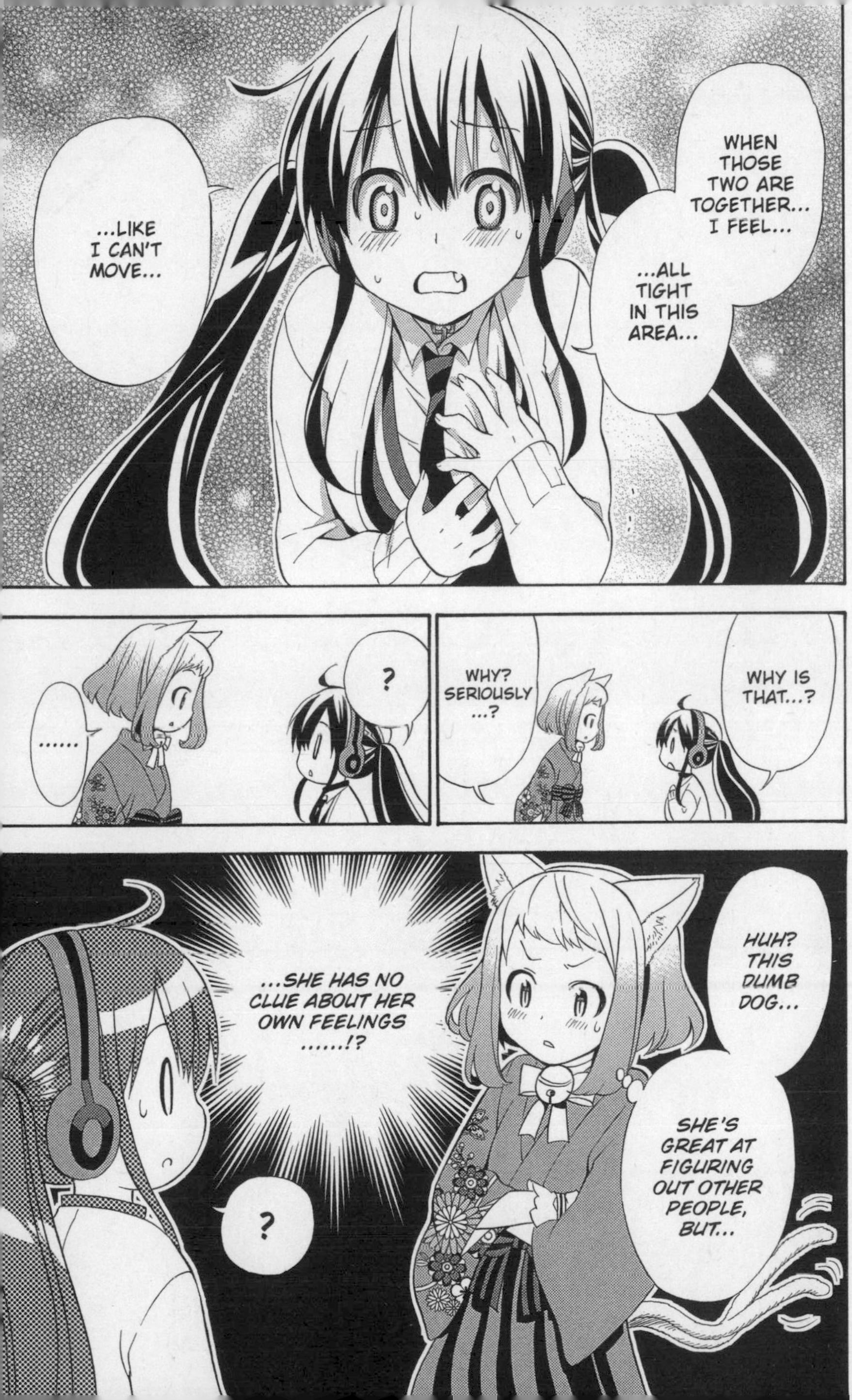
WHEN THOSE TWO ARE TOGETHER... I FEEL...
...ALL TIGHT IN THIS AREA...
...LIKE I CAN'T MOVE...
WHY IS THAT...?
WHY? SERIOUSLY ...?
?
......
HUH? THIS DUMB DOG...
SHE'S GREAT AT FIGURING OUT OTHER PEOPLE, BUT...
...SHE HAS NO CLUE ABOUT HER OWN FEELINGS ......!?
?

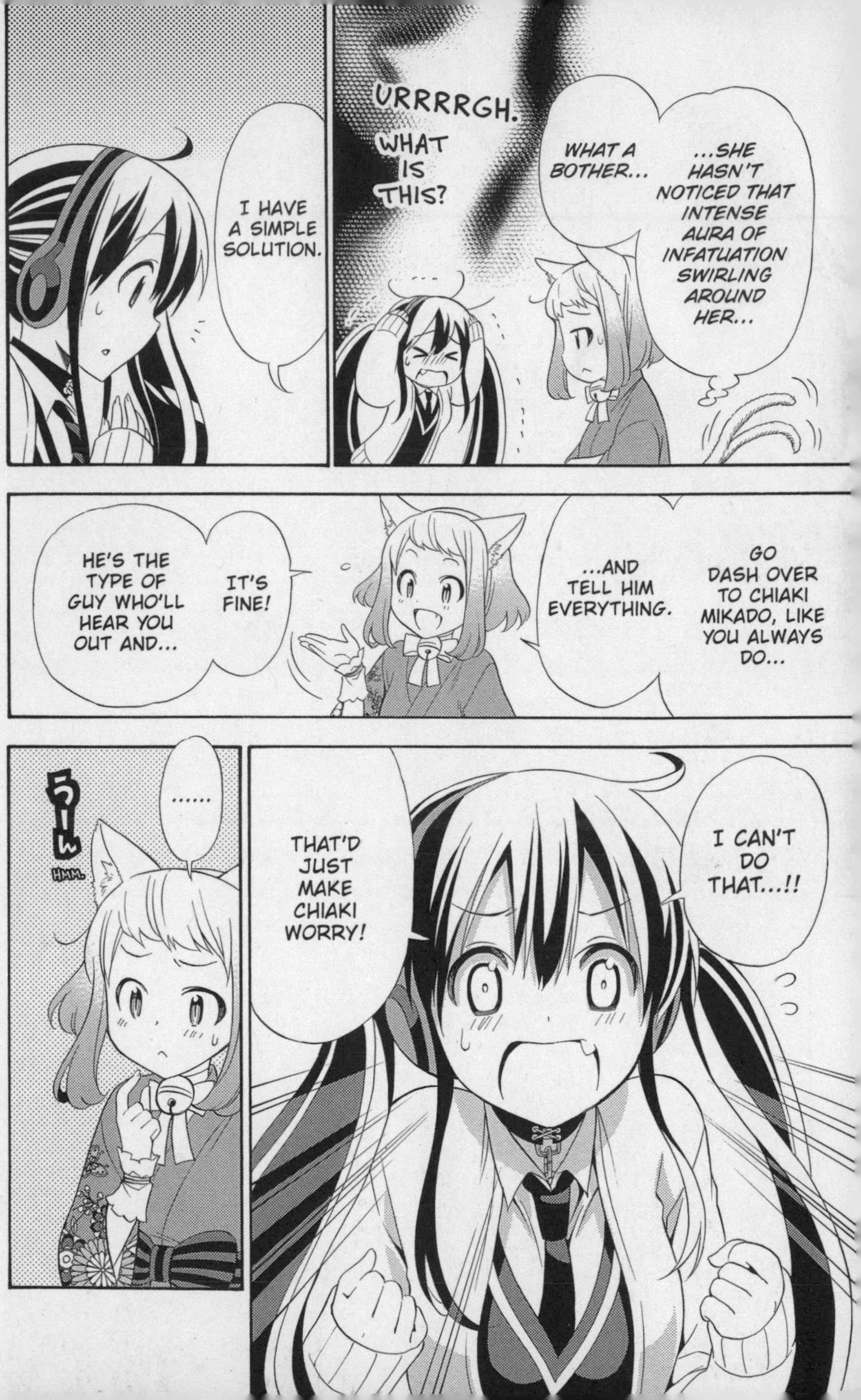
URRRRGH.
WHAT IS THIS?
...SHE HASN'T NOTICED THAT INTENSE AURA OF INFATUATION SWIRLING AROUND HER...
WHAT A BOTHER...
I HAVE A SIMPLE SOLUTION.
GO DASH OVER TO CHIAKI MIKADO, LIKE YOU ALWAYS DO...
...AND TELL HIM EVERYTHING.
IT'S FINE!
HE'S THE TYPE OF GUY WHO'LL HEAR YOU OUT AND...
I CAN'T DO THAT...!!
THAT'D JUST MAKE CHIAKI WORRY!
......
うーん
HMM.

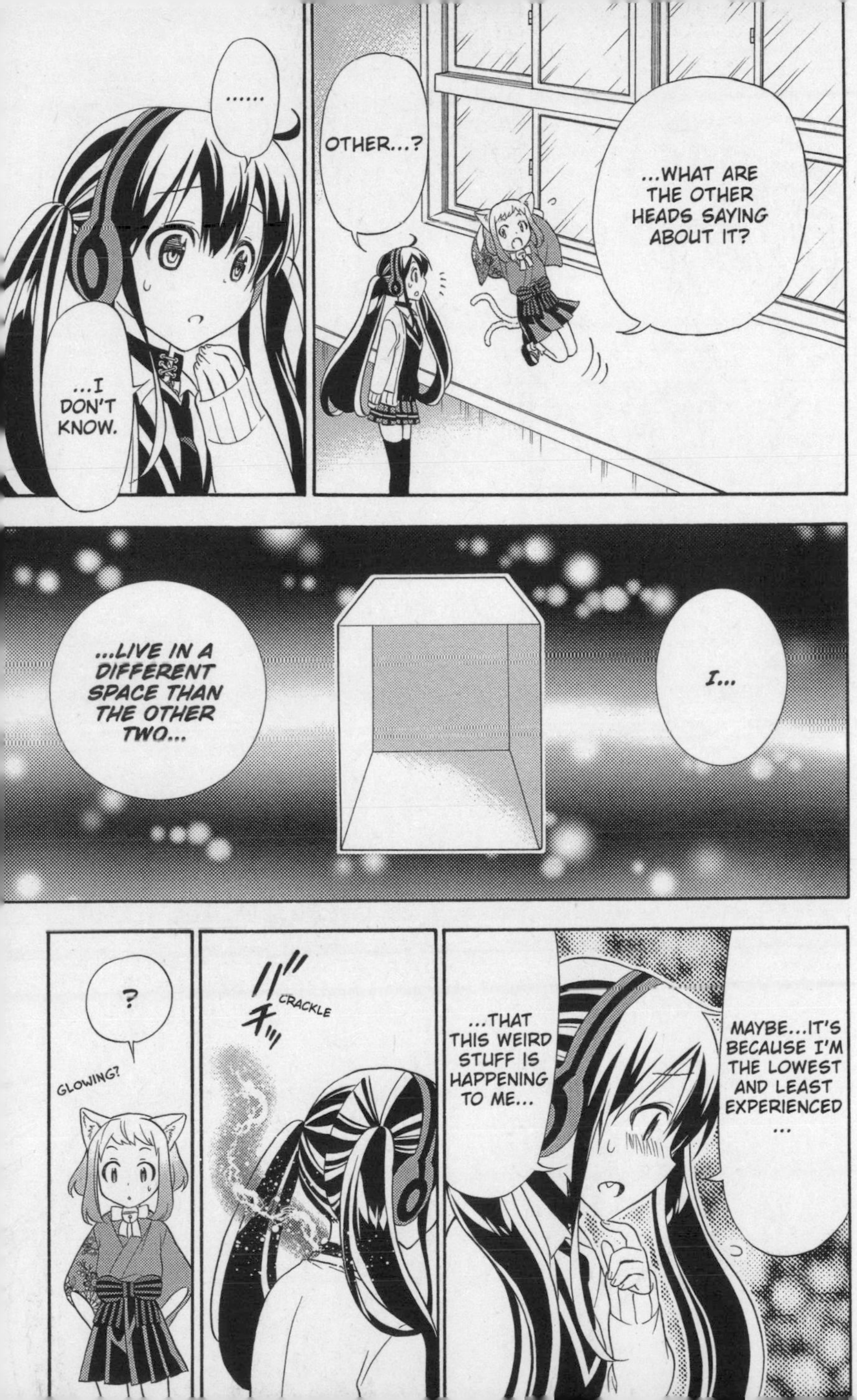
...WHAT ARE THE OTHER HEADS SAYING ABOUT IT?
OTHER...?
......
...I DON'T KNOW.
I...
...LIVE IN A DIFFERENT SPACE THAN THE OTHER TWO...
MAYBE...IT'S BECAUSE I'M THE LOWEST AND LEAST EXPERIENCED...
...THAT THIS WEIRD STUFF IS HAPPENING TO ME...
CRACKLE
?
GLOWING?

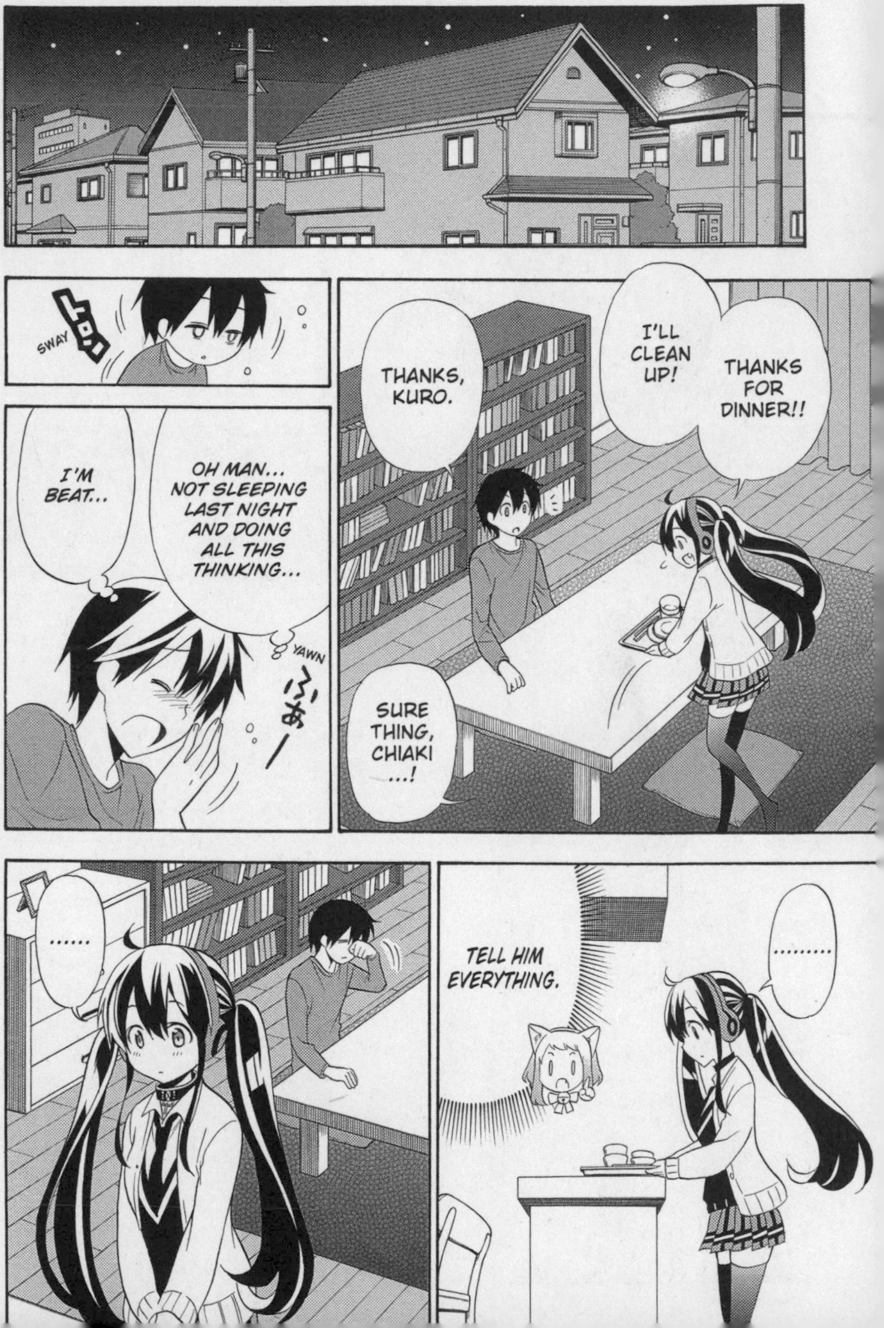
THANKS FOR DINNER!!
I'LL CLEAN UP!
THANKS, KURO.
SURE THING, CHIAKI ...!
SWAY
OH MAN... NOT SLEEPING LAST NIGHT AND DOING ALL THIS THINKING...
I'M BEAT...
YAWN
ふぁー
....
TELL HIM EVERYTHING.
......

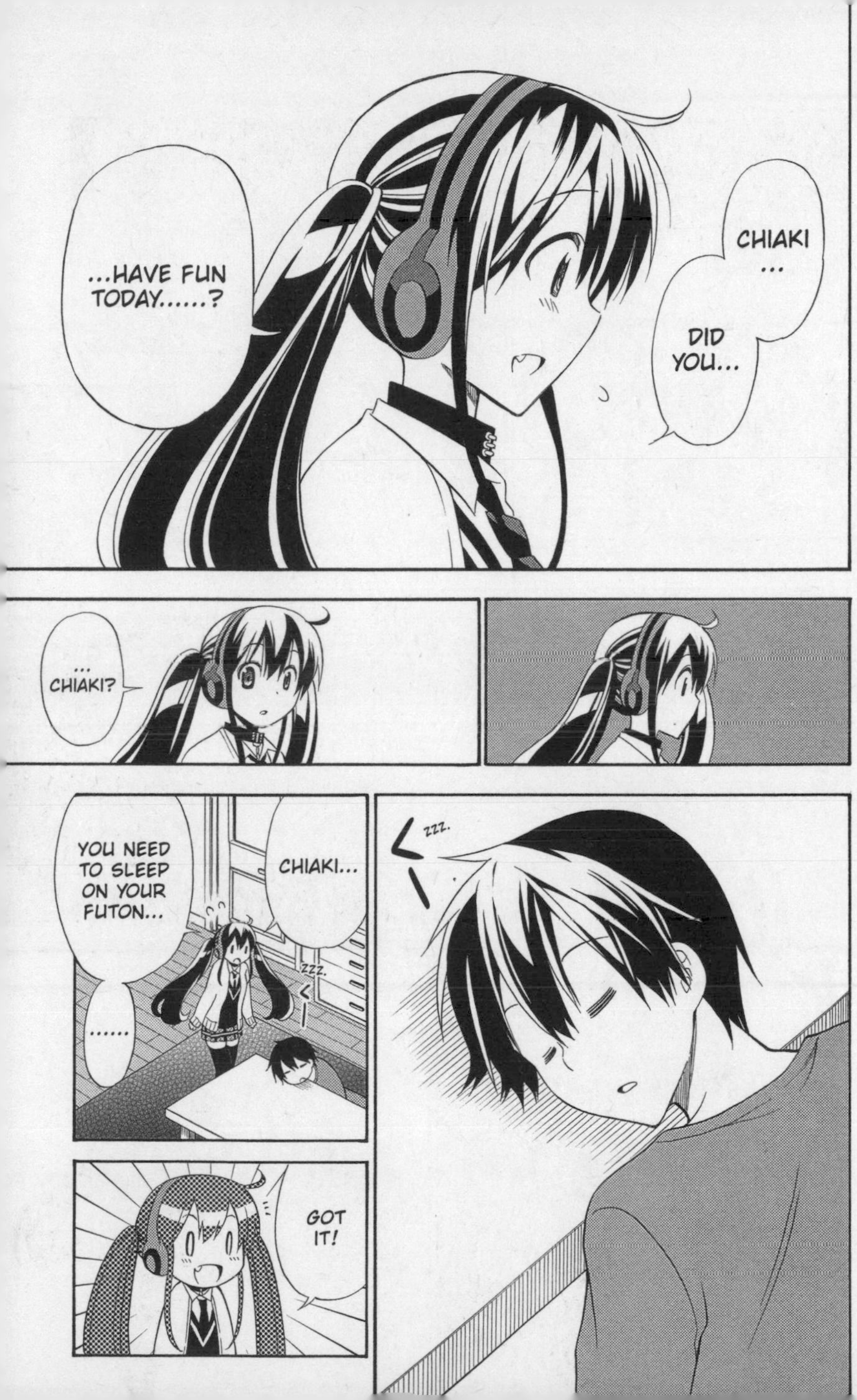
CHIAKI ...
DID YOU...
...HAVE FUN TODAY......?
... CHIAKI?
zzz.
CHIAKI...
YOU NEED TO SLEEP ON YOUR FUTON...
......
zzz.
GOT IT!

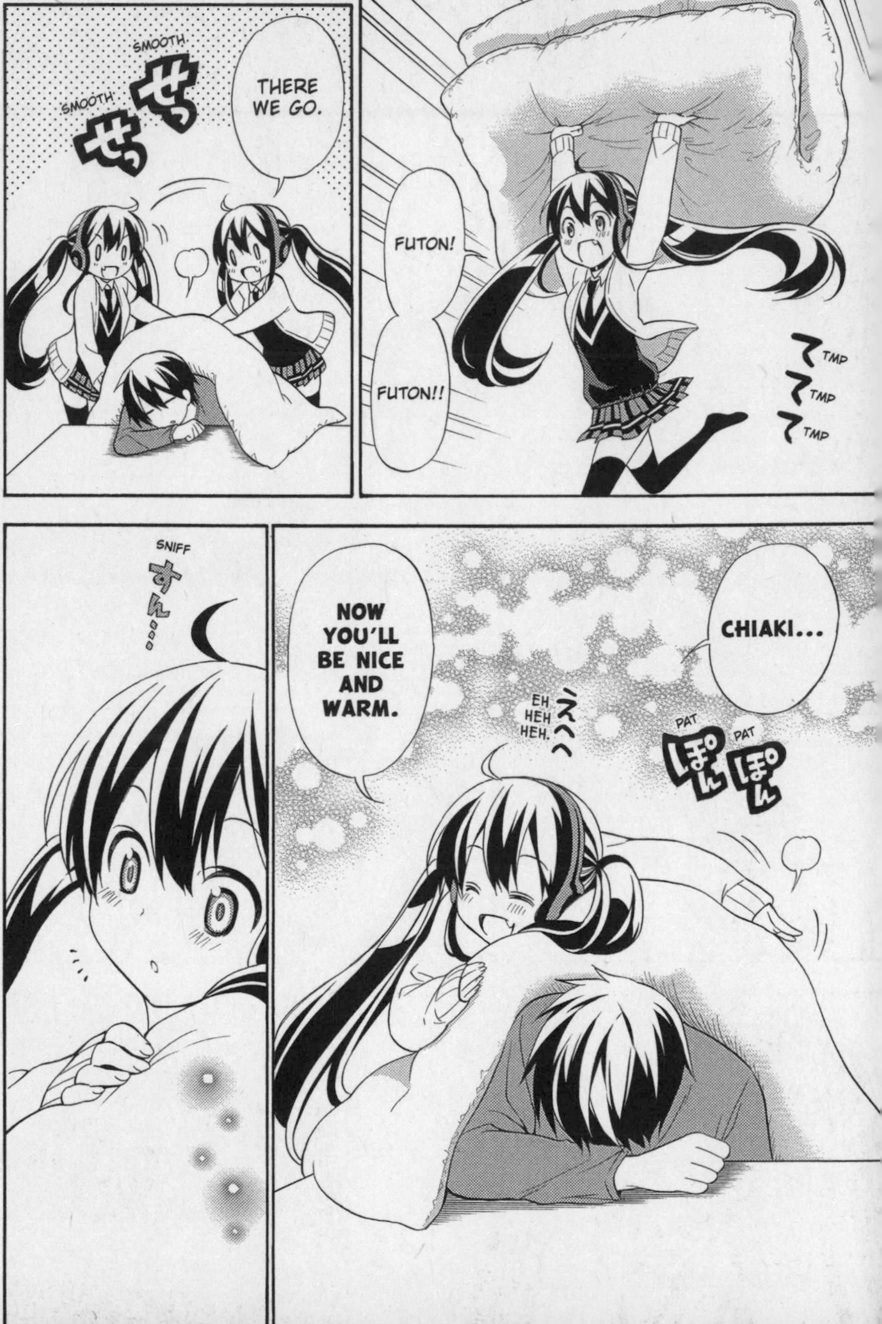
FUTON!
FUTON!!
てててTMP TMP TMP
THERE WE GO.
せっせっ SMOOTH SMOOTH
CHIAKI...
NOW YOU'LL BE NICE AND WARM.
えへへ EH HEH HEH.
ぽんぽん PAT PAT
すん... SNIFF

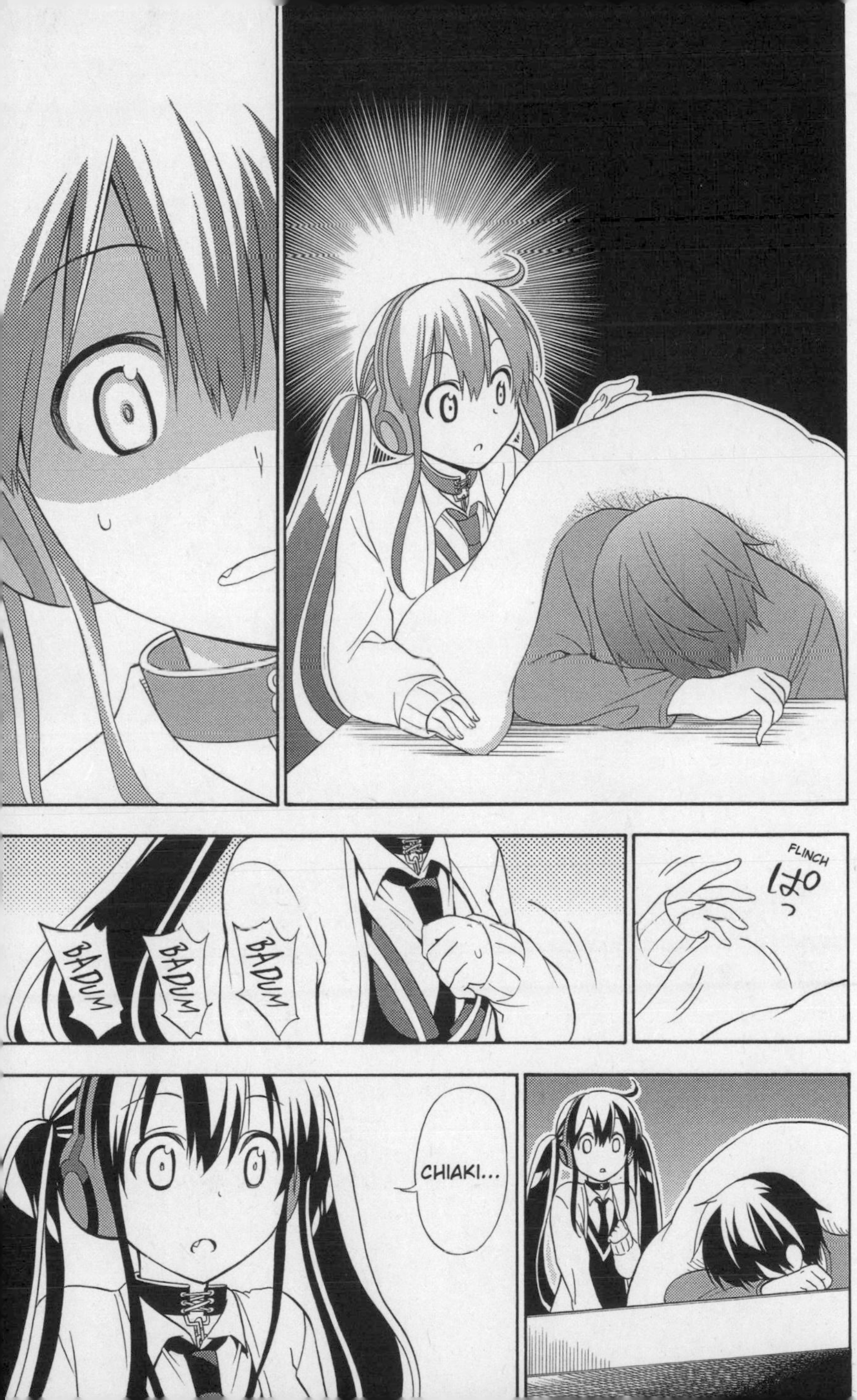
FLINCH
はっ
BADUM
BADUM
BADUM
CHIAKI...

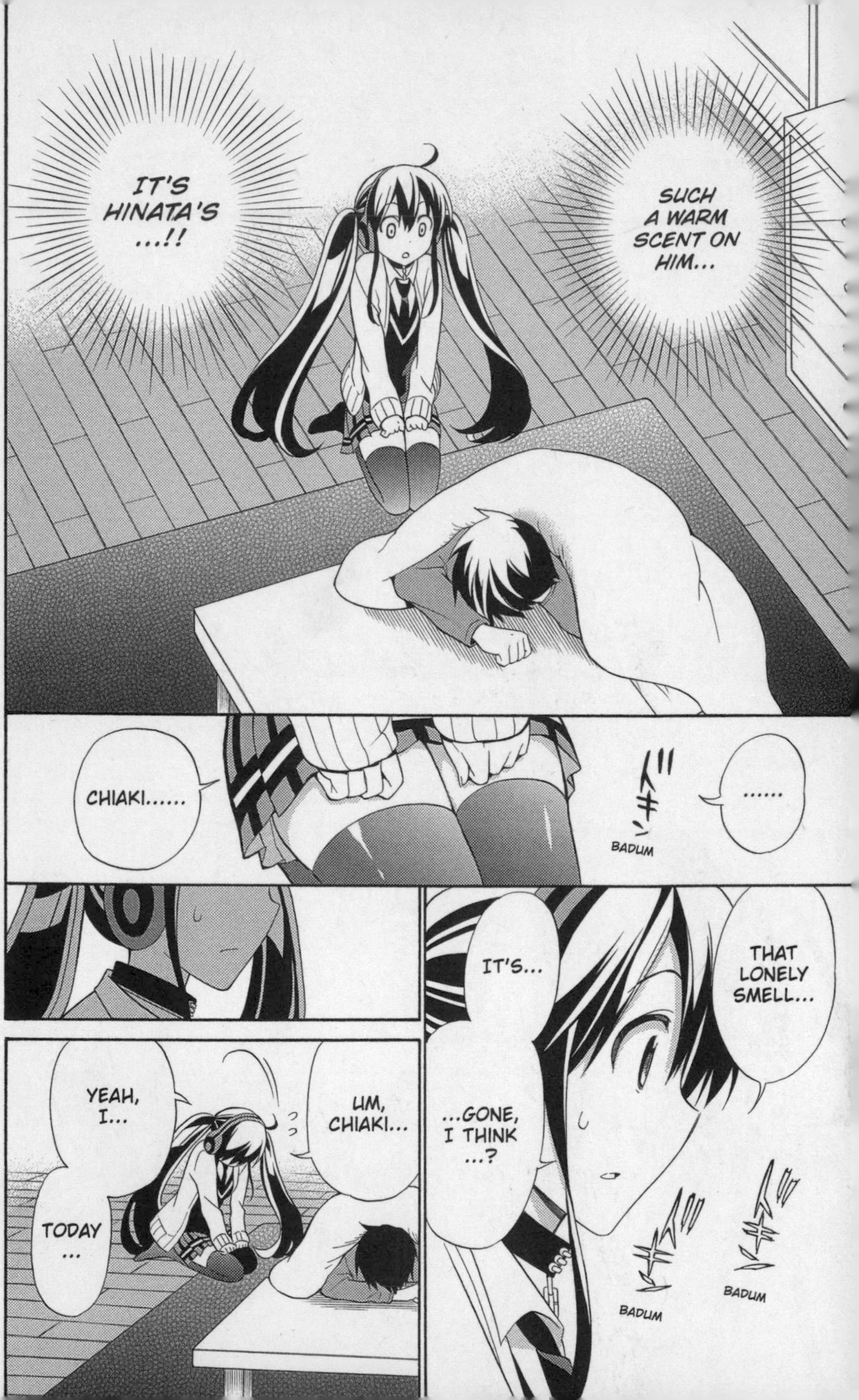
SUCH A WARM SCENT ON HIM...
IT'S HINATA'S ...!!
......
BADUM
CHIAKI......
THAT LONELY SMELL...
IT'S...
...GONE, I THINK ...?
BADUM
BADUM
UM, CHIAKI...
YEAH, I...
TODAY ...

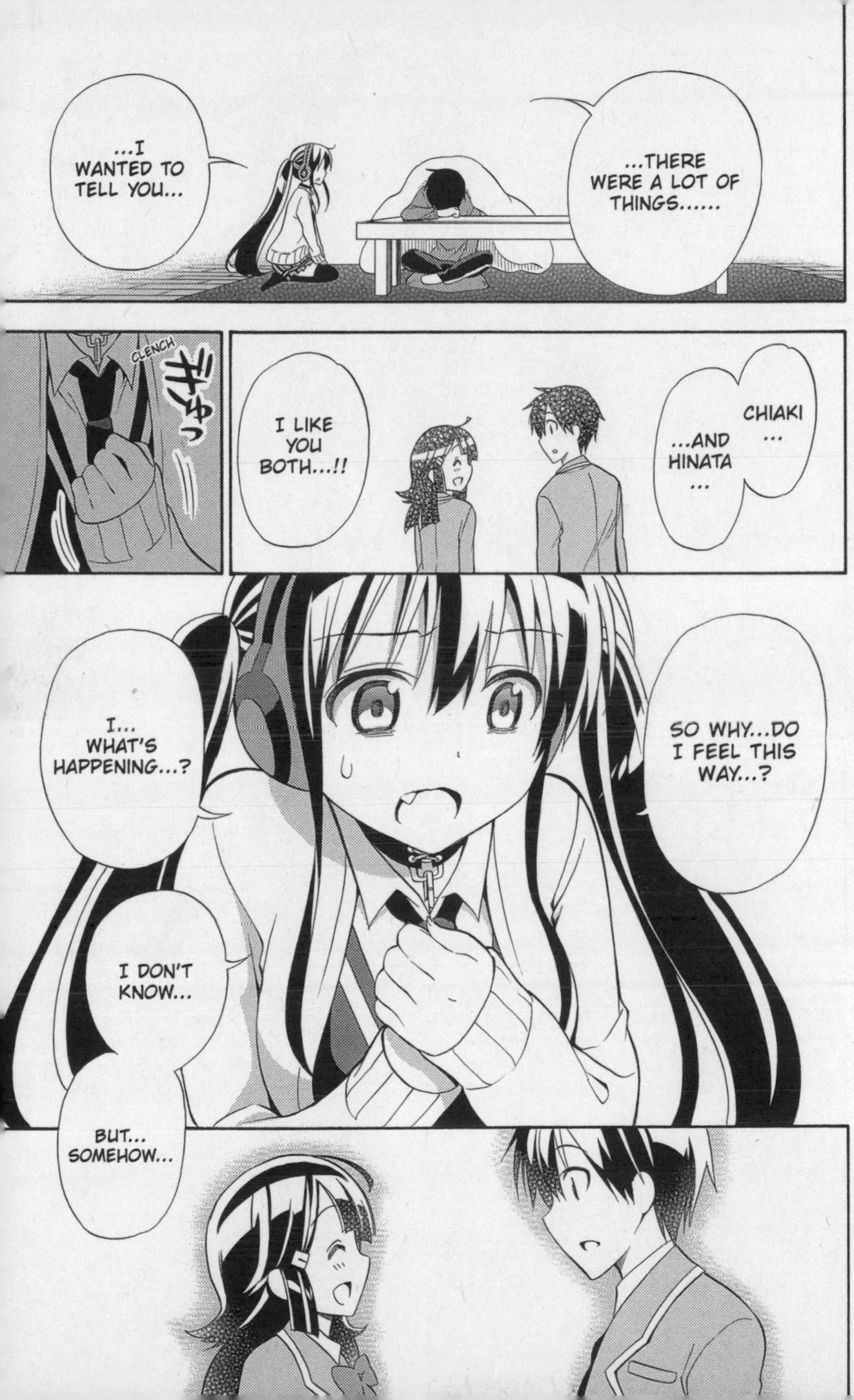
...THERE WERE A LOT OF THINGS......
...I WANTED TO TELL YOU...
CHIAKI ...
...AND HINATA ...
I LIKE YOU BOTH...!!
ぎゅっ
CLENCH
SO WHY...DO I FEEL THIS WAY...?
I... WHAT'S HAPPENING...?
I DON'T KNOW...
BUT... SOMEHOW...

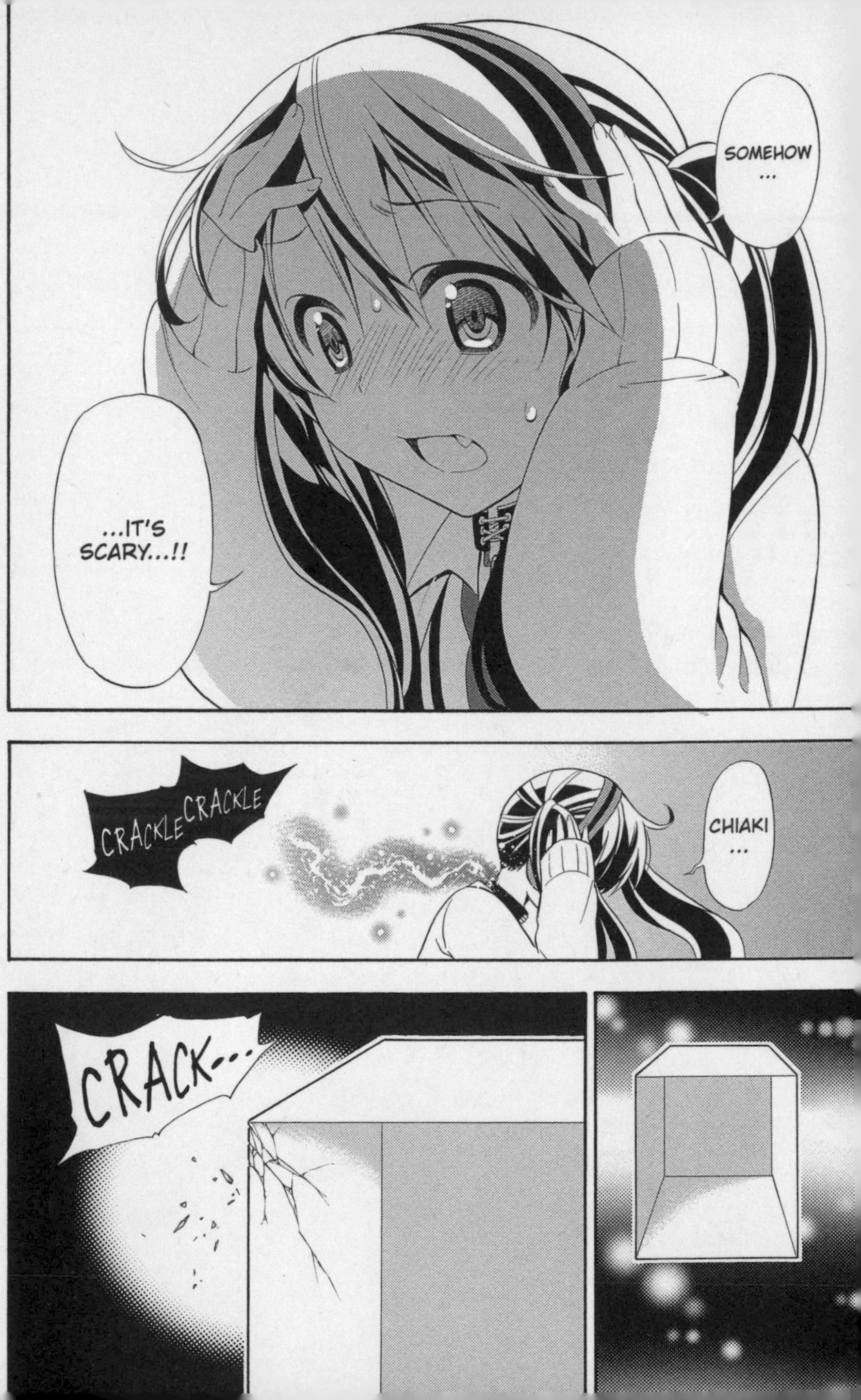
SOMEHOW ...
...IT'S SCARY...!!
CHIAKI ...
CRACKLE CRACKLE
CRACK...

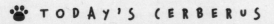
🐾 TODAY'S CERBERUS

?

HMM.

I WONDER IF
THAT DUMB
DOG IS
ALL RIGHT...?

TODAY'S CERBERUS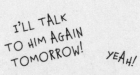

I'LL TALK TO HIM AGAIN TOMORROW!

YEAH!

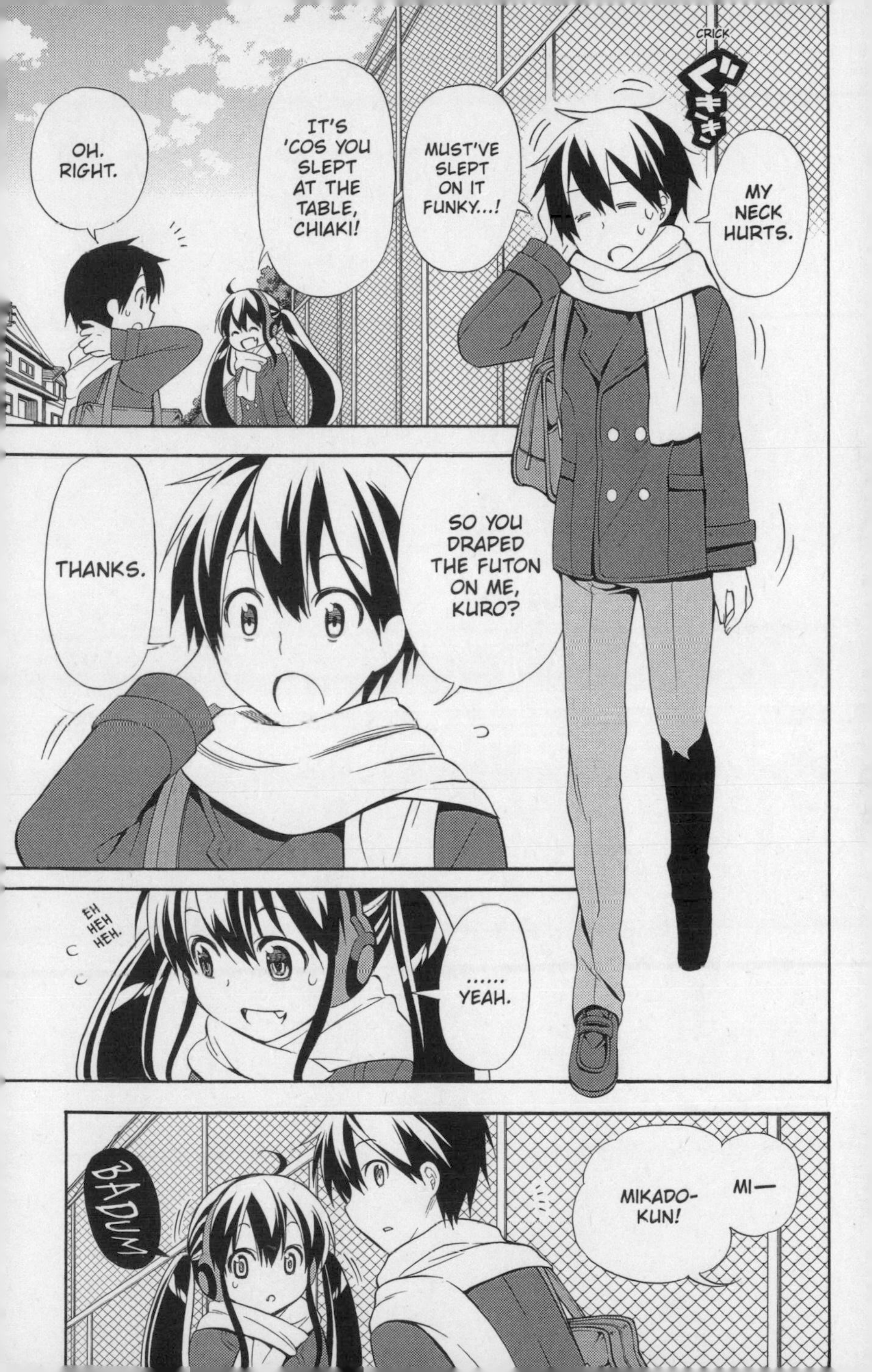
CRICK
MY NECK HURTS.
MUST'VE SLEPT ON IT FUNKY...!
IT'S 'COS YOU SLEPT AT THE TABLE, CHIAKI!
OH. RIGHT.
SO YOU DRAPED THE FUTON ON ME, KURO?
THANKS.
EH HEH HEH.
...... YEAH.
MI—
MIKADO-KUN!
BADUM

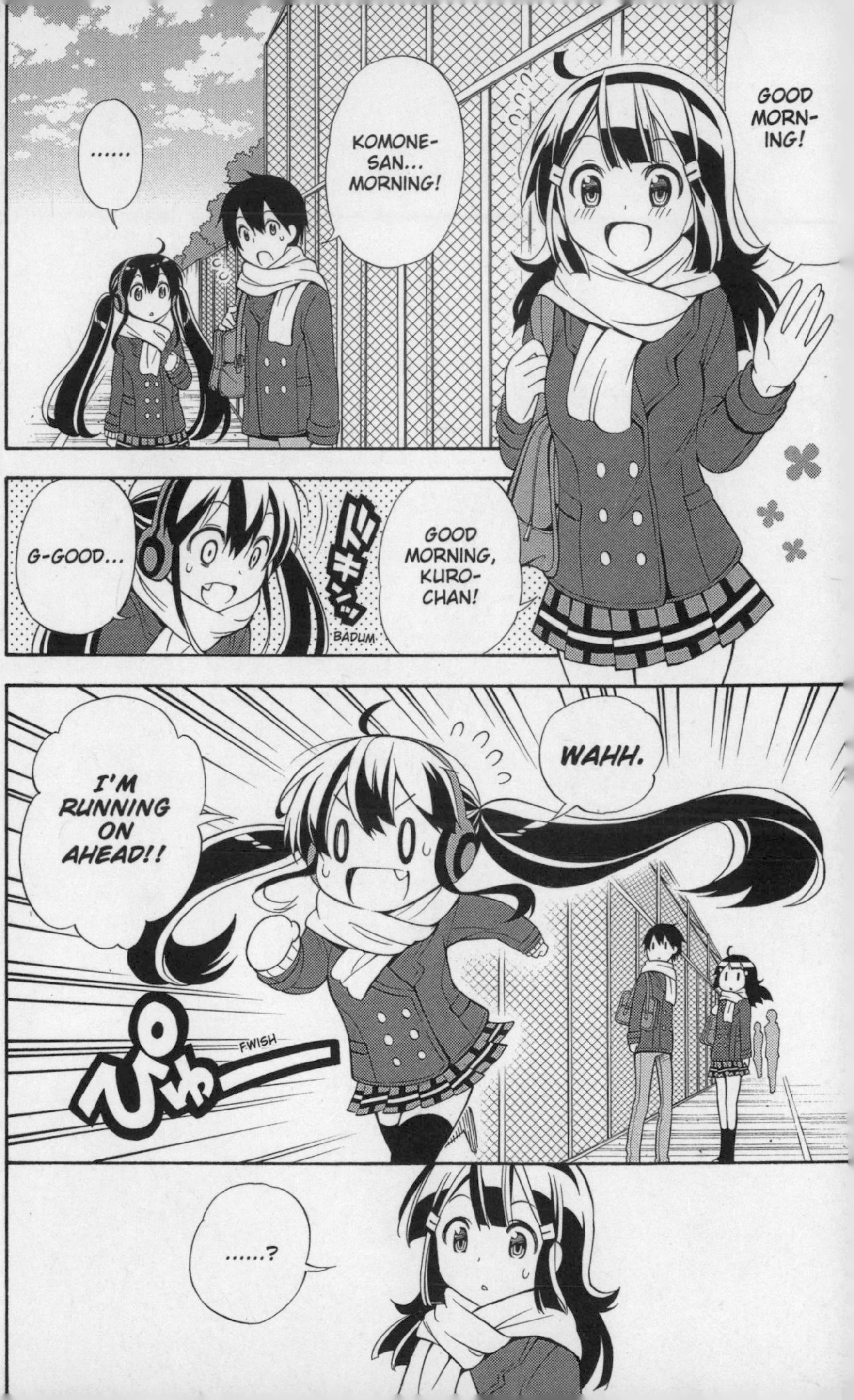
GOOD MORN-ING!
KOMONE-SAN... MORNING!
......
GOOD MORNING, KURO-CHAN!
BADUM
G-GOOD...
WAHH.
I'M RUNNING ON AHEAD!!
FWISH
......?

CHAPTER 21
EXPLOSION

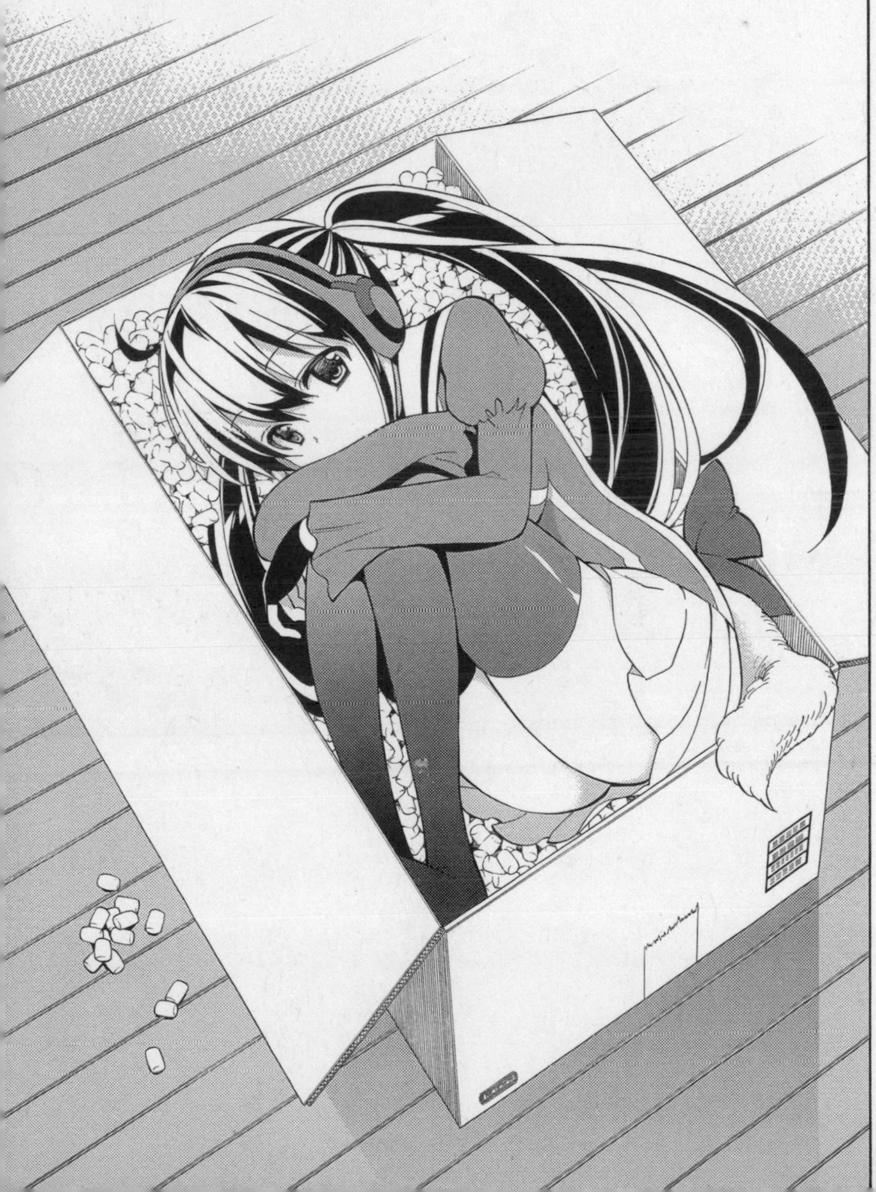

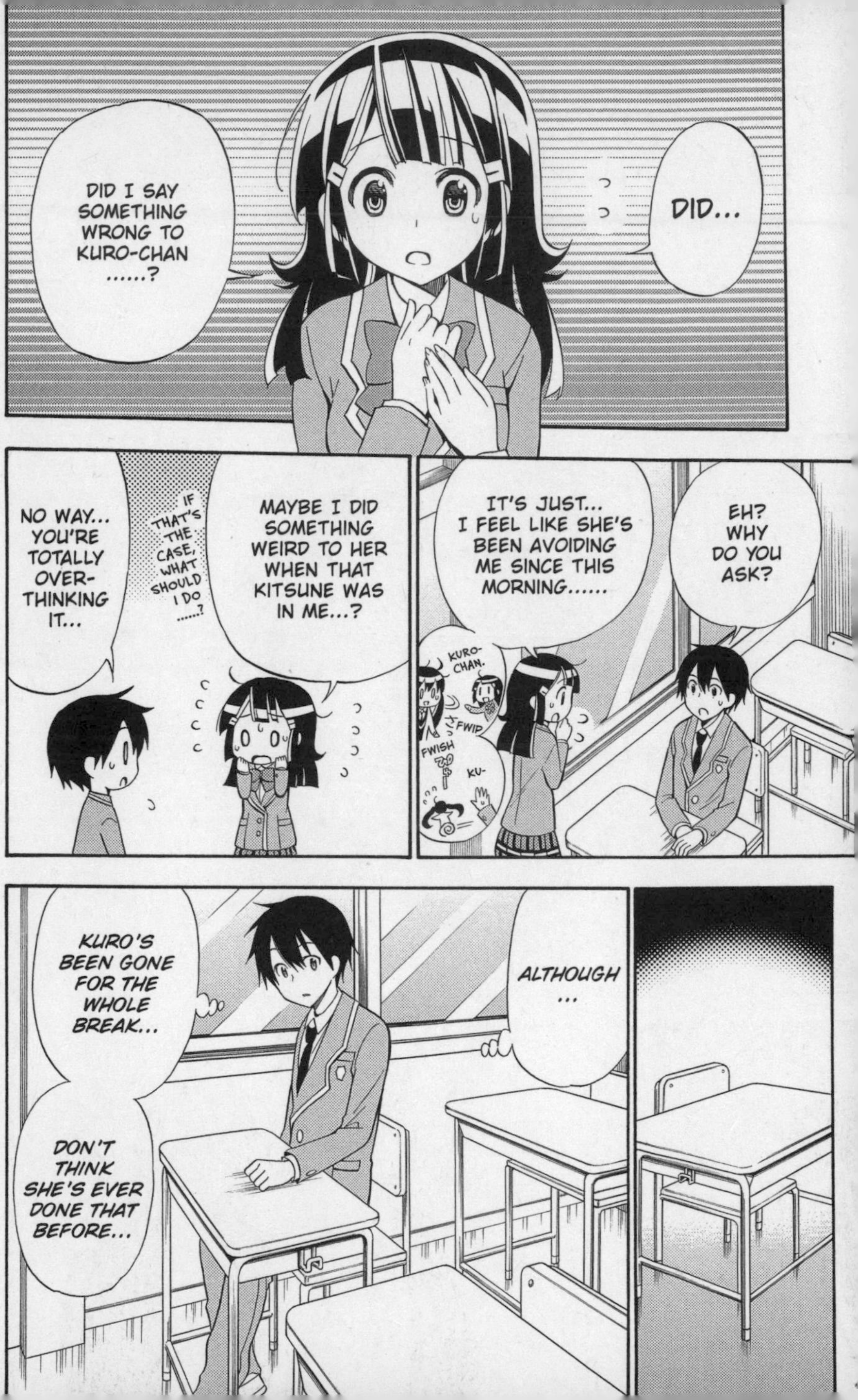
DID...
DID I SAY SOMETHING WRONG TO KURO-CHAN ......?
EH? WHY DO YOU ASK?
IT'S JUST... I FEEL LIKE SHE'S BEEN AVOIDING ME SINCE THIS MORNING......
KURO-CHAN.
FWIP
FWISH
KU-
MAYBE I DID SOMETHING WEIRD TO HER WHEN THAT KITSUNE WAS IN ME...?
IF THAT'S THE CASE, WHAT SHOULD I DO ......?
NO WAY... YOU'RE TOTALLY OVER-THINKING IT...
ALTHOUGH ...
KURO'S BEEN GONE FOR THE WHOLE BREAK...
DON'T THINK SHE'S EVER DONE THAT BEFORE...

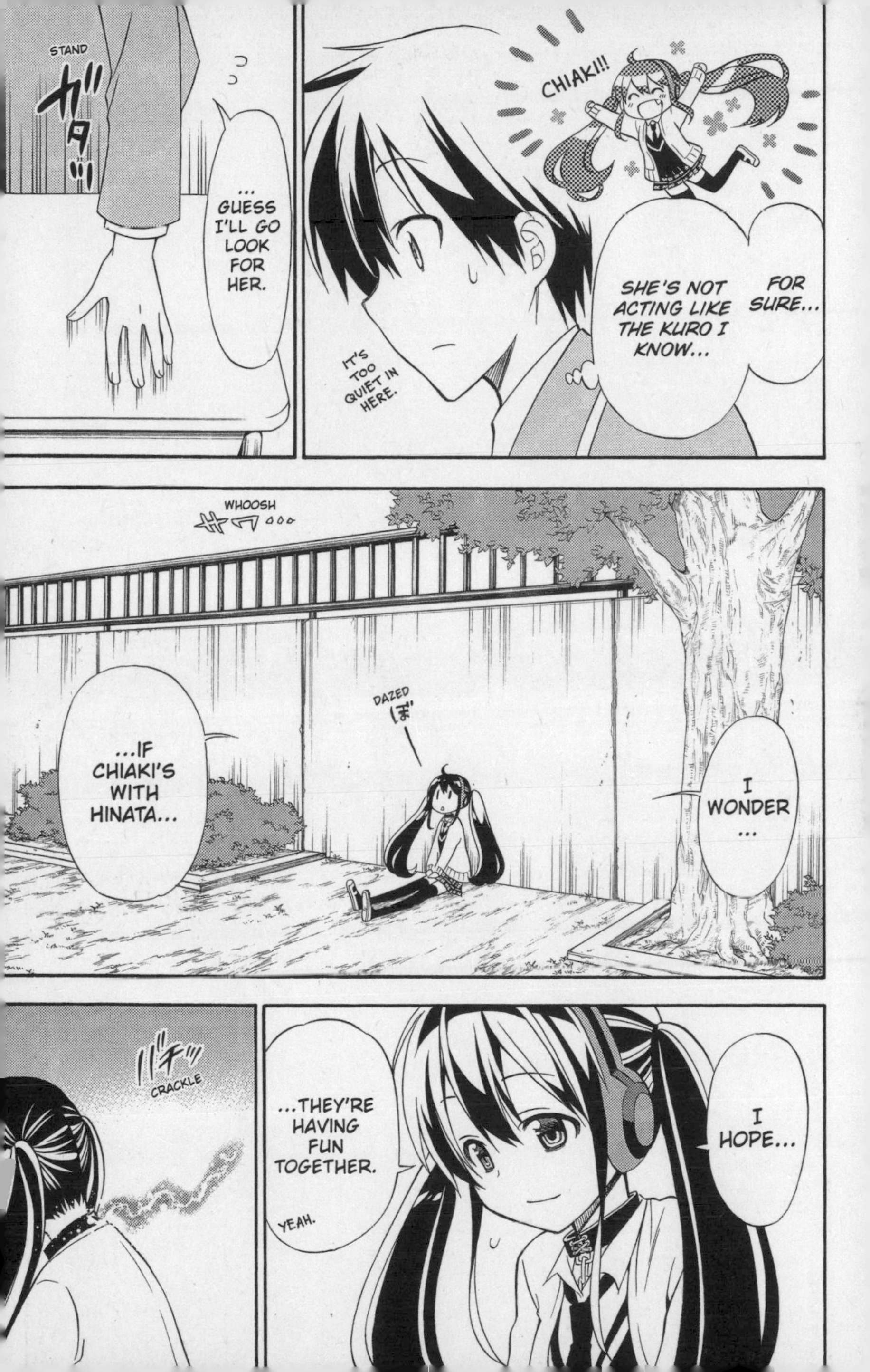
CHIAKI!!
FOR SURE...
SHE'S NOT ACTING LIKE THE KURO I KNOW...
IT'S TOO QUIET IN HERE.
STAND
... GUESS I'LL GO LOOK FOR HER.
WHOOSH
I WONDER ...
DAZED
...IF CHIAKI'S WITH HINATA...
I HOPE...
...THEY'RE HAVING FUN TOGETHER.
YEAH.
CRACKLE

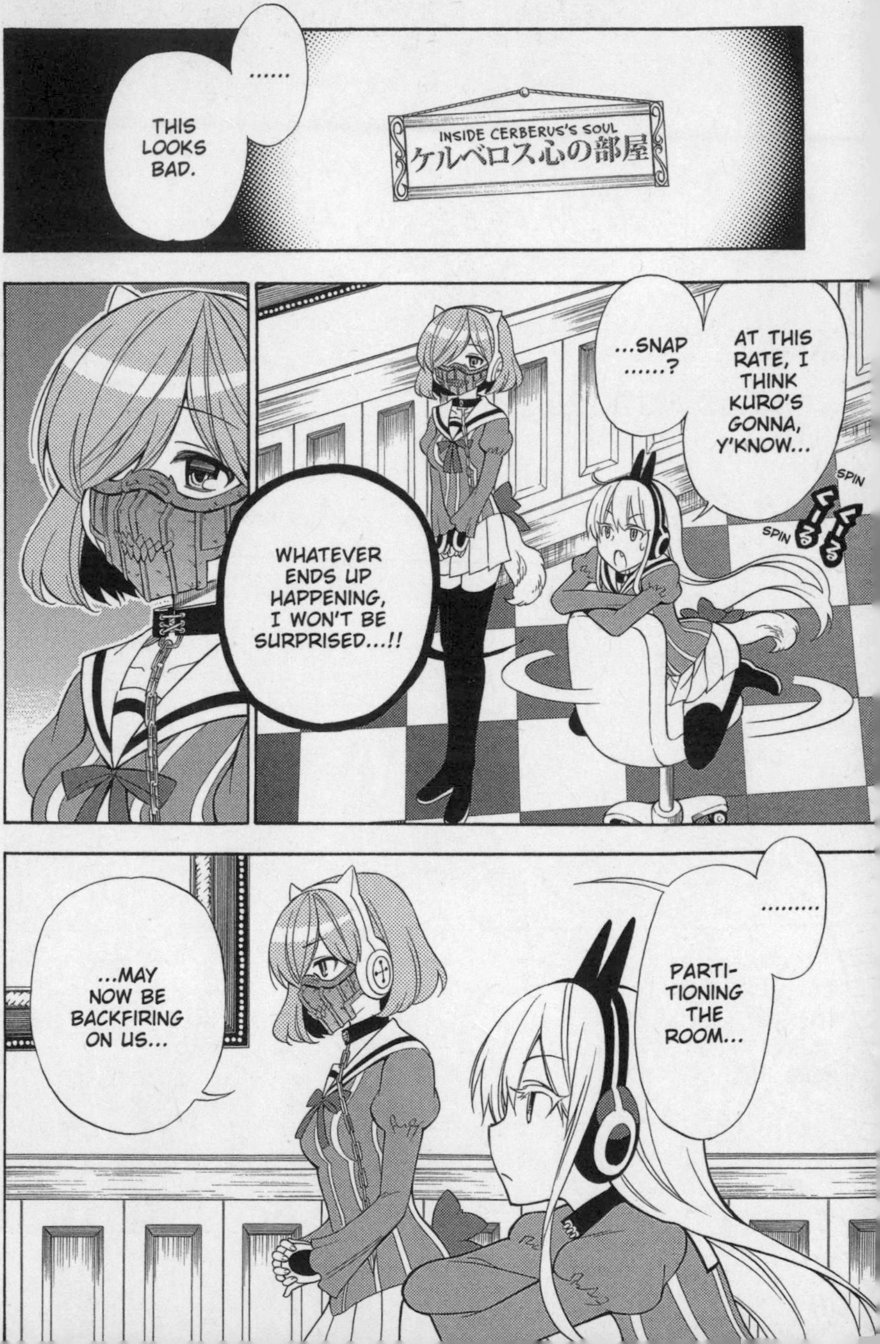
INSIDE CERBERUS'S SOUL
ケルベロス心の部屋
......
THIS LOOKS BAD.
AT THIS RATE, I THINK KURO'S GONNA, Y'KNOW...
...SNAP ......?
SPIN
SPIN
WHATEVER ENDS UP HAPPENING, I WON'T BE SURPRISED...!!
....
PARTI-TIONING THE ROOM...
...MAY NOW BE BACKFIRING ON US...

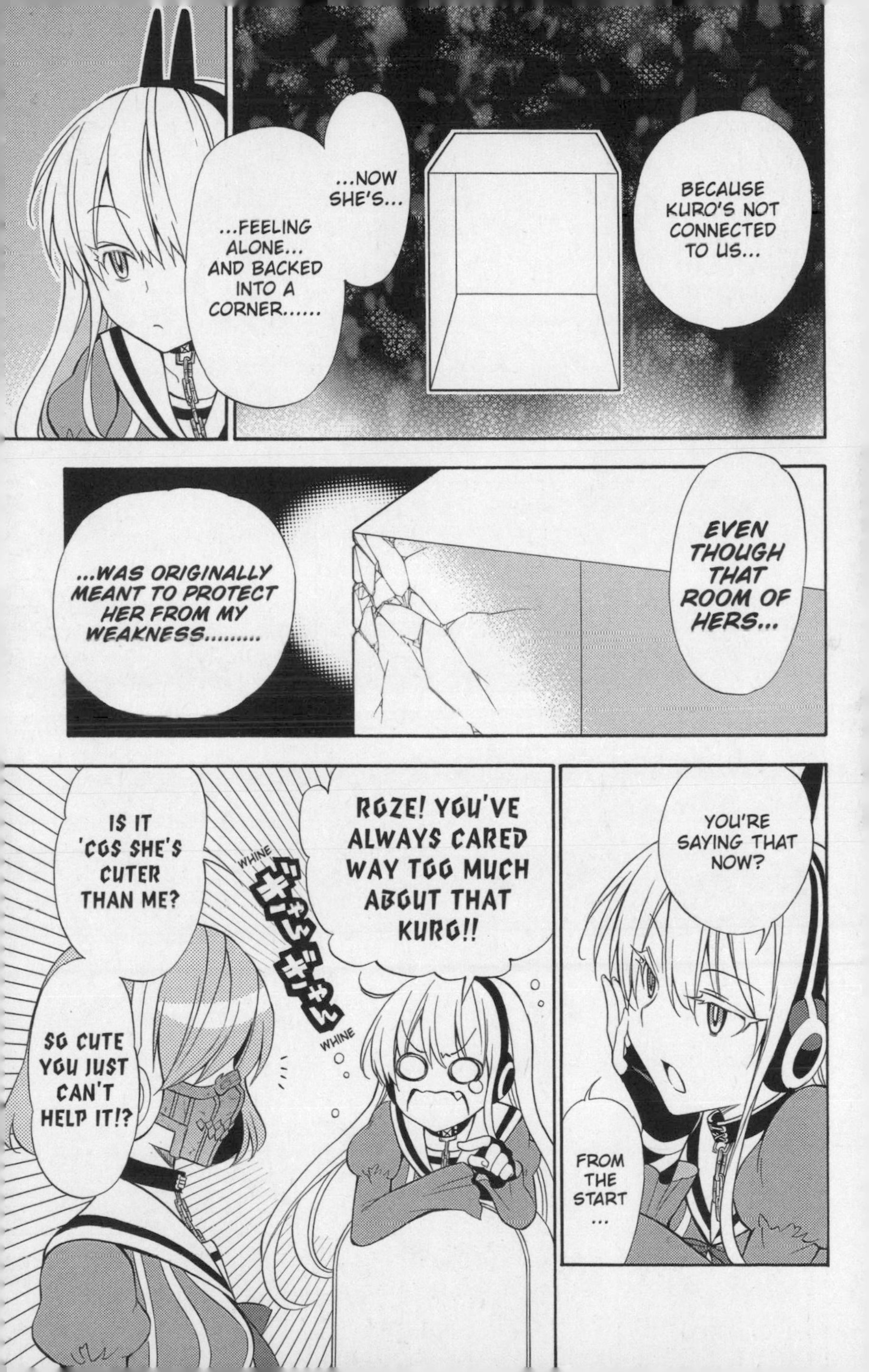
BECAUSE KURO'S NOT CONNECTED TO US...
...NOW SHE'S...
...FEELING ALONE... AND BACKED INTO A CORNER......
EVEN THOUGH THAT ROOM OF HERS...
...WAS ORIGINALLY MEANT TO PROTECT HER FROM MY WEAKNESS.........
YOU'RE SAYING THAT NOW?
FROM THE START ...
ROZE! YOU'VE ALWAYS CARED WAY TOO MUCH ABOUT THAT KURO!!
WHINE
WHINE
IS IT 'COS SHE'S CUTER THAN ME?
SO CUTE YOU JUST CAN'T HELP IT!?

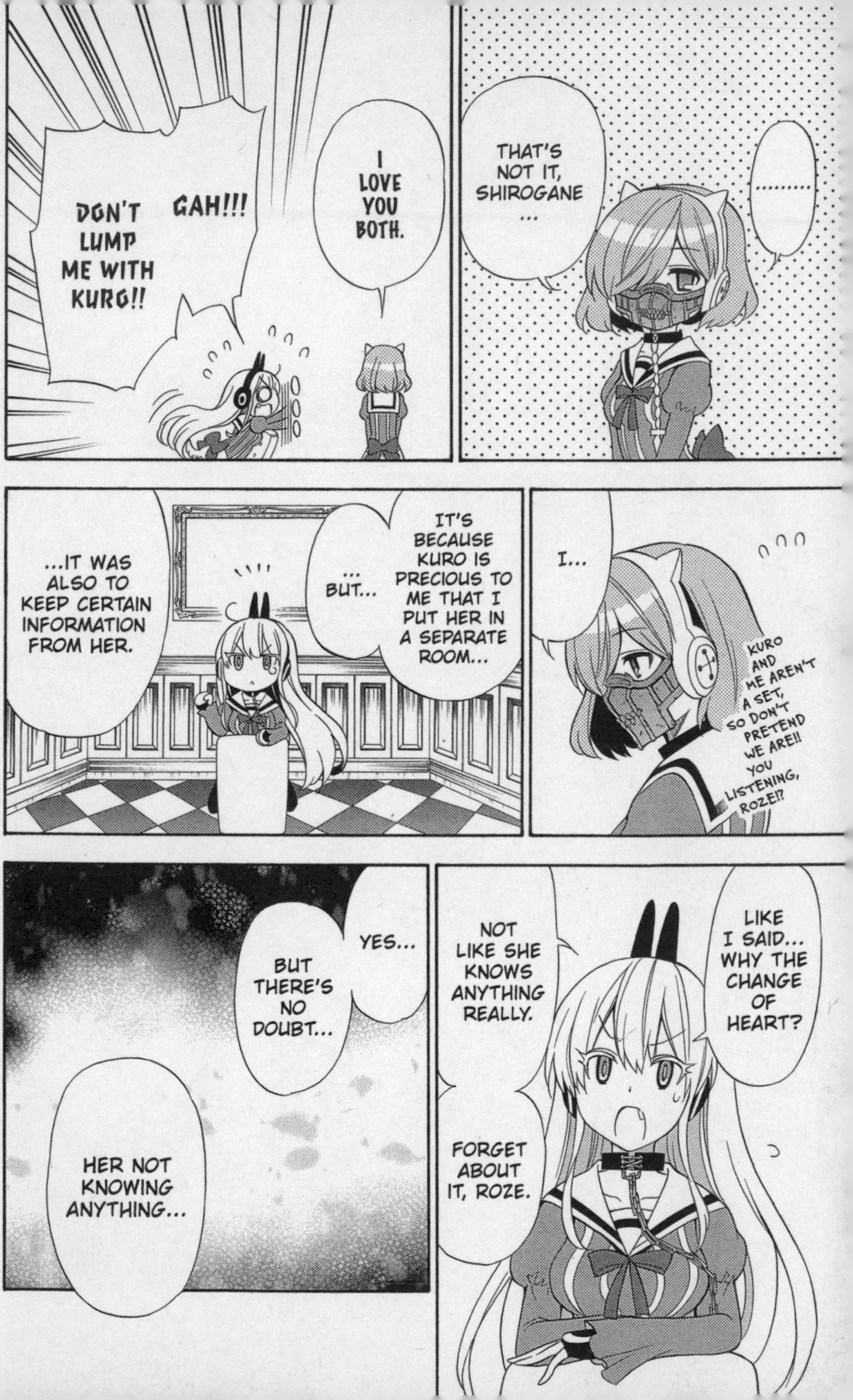
....
THAT'S NOT IT, SHIROGANE ...
I LOVE YOU BOTH.
GAH!!!
DON'T LUMP ME WITH KURO!!
I...
KURO AND ME AREN'T A SET, SO DON'T PRETEND WE ARE!! YOU LISTENING, ROZE!?
IT'S BECAUSE KURO IS PRECIOUS TO ME THAT I PUT HER IN A SEPARATE ROOM...
... BUT...
...IT WAS ALSO TO KEEP CERTAIN INFORMATION FROM HER.
LIKE I SAID... WHY THE CHANGE OF HEART?
NOT LIKE SHE KNOWS ANYTHING REALLY.
FORGET ABOUT IT, ROZE.
YES...
BUT THERE'S NO DOUBT...
HER NOT KNOWING ANYTHING...

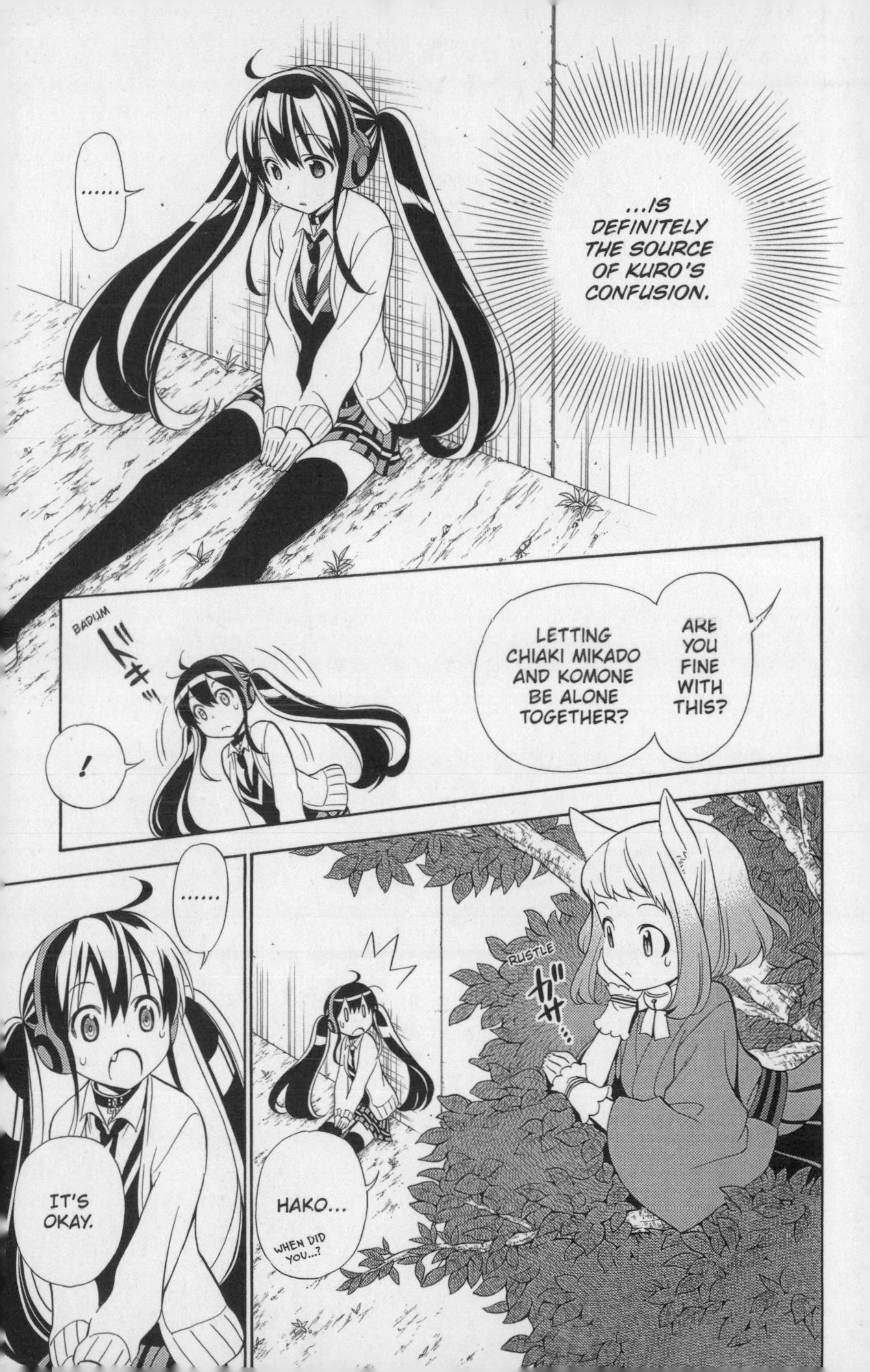

...IS DEFINITELY THE SOURCE OF KURO'S CONFUSION.
......
ARE YOU FINE WITH THIS?
LETTING CHIAKI MIKADO AND KOMONE BE ALONE TOGETHER?
BADUM
!
RUSTLE
HAKO...
WHEN DID YOU...?
......
IT'S OKAY.

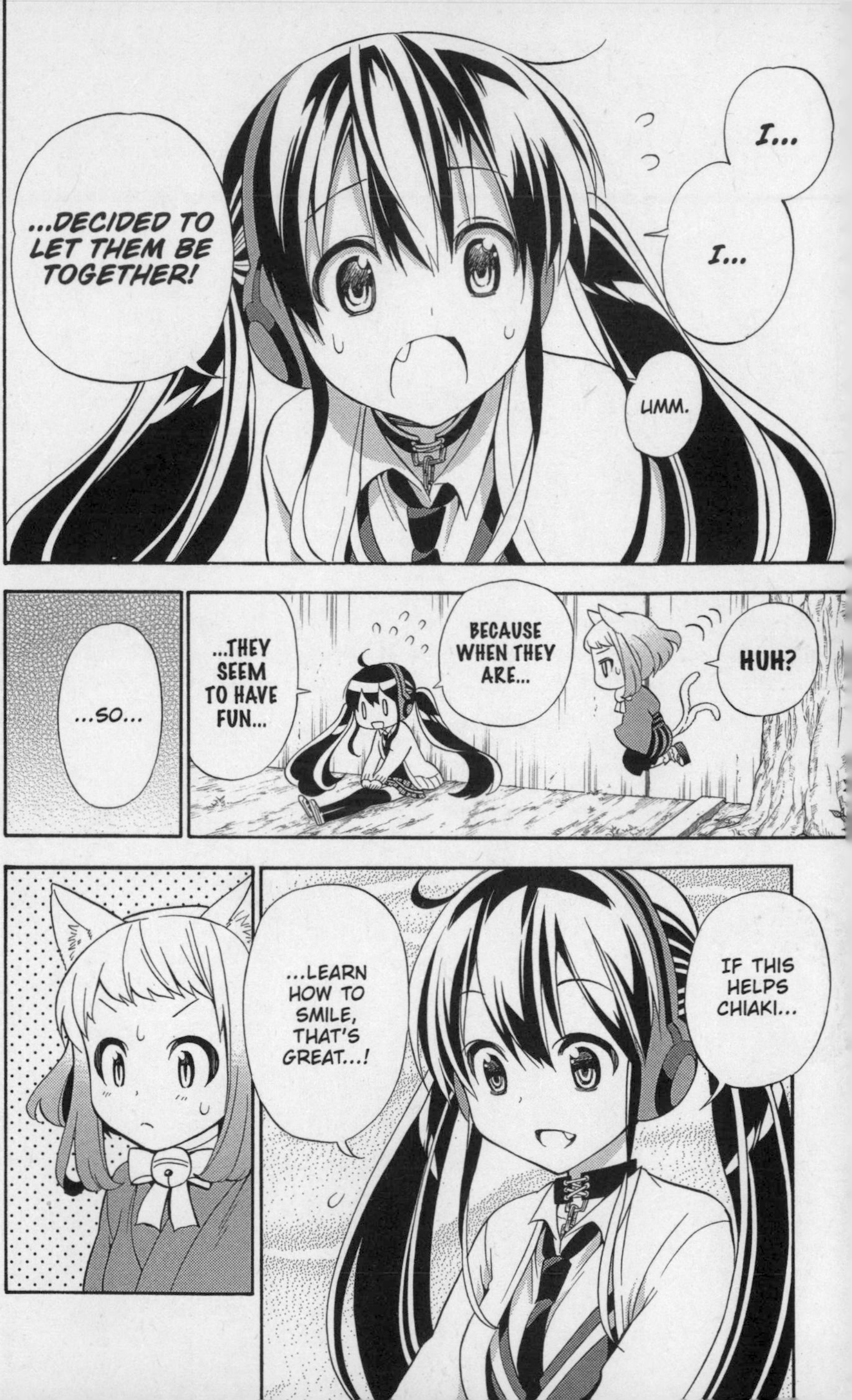
I...
I...
UMM.
...DECIDED TO LET THEM BE TOGETHER!
HUH?
BECAUSE WHEN THEY ARE...
...THEY SEEM TO HAVE FUN...
...SO...
IF THIS HELPS CHIAKI...
...LEARN HOW TO SMILE, THAT'S GREAT...!

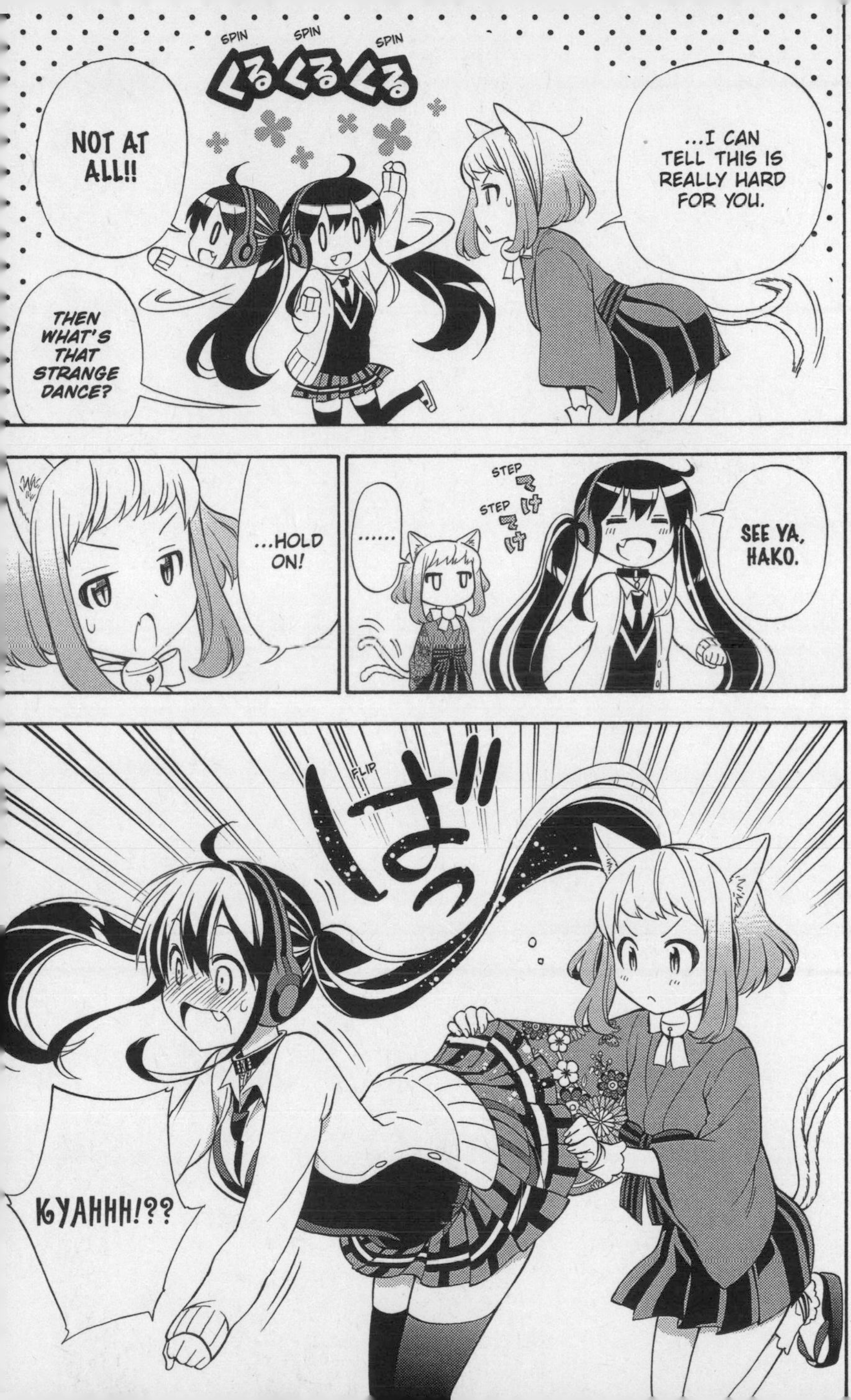
...I CAN TELL THIS IS REALLY HARD FOR YOU.
SPIN SPIN SPIN
くるくるくる
NOT AT ALL!!
THEN WHAT'S THAT STRANGE DANCE?
SEE YA, HAKO.
STEP
STEP
......
...HOLD ON!
FLIP
KYAHHH!??

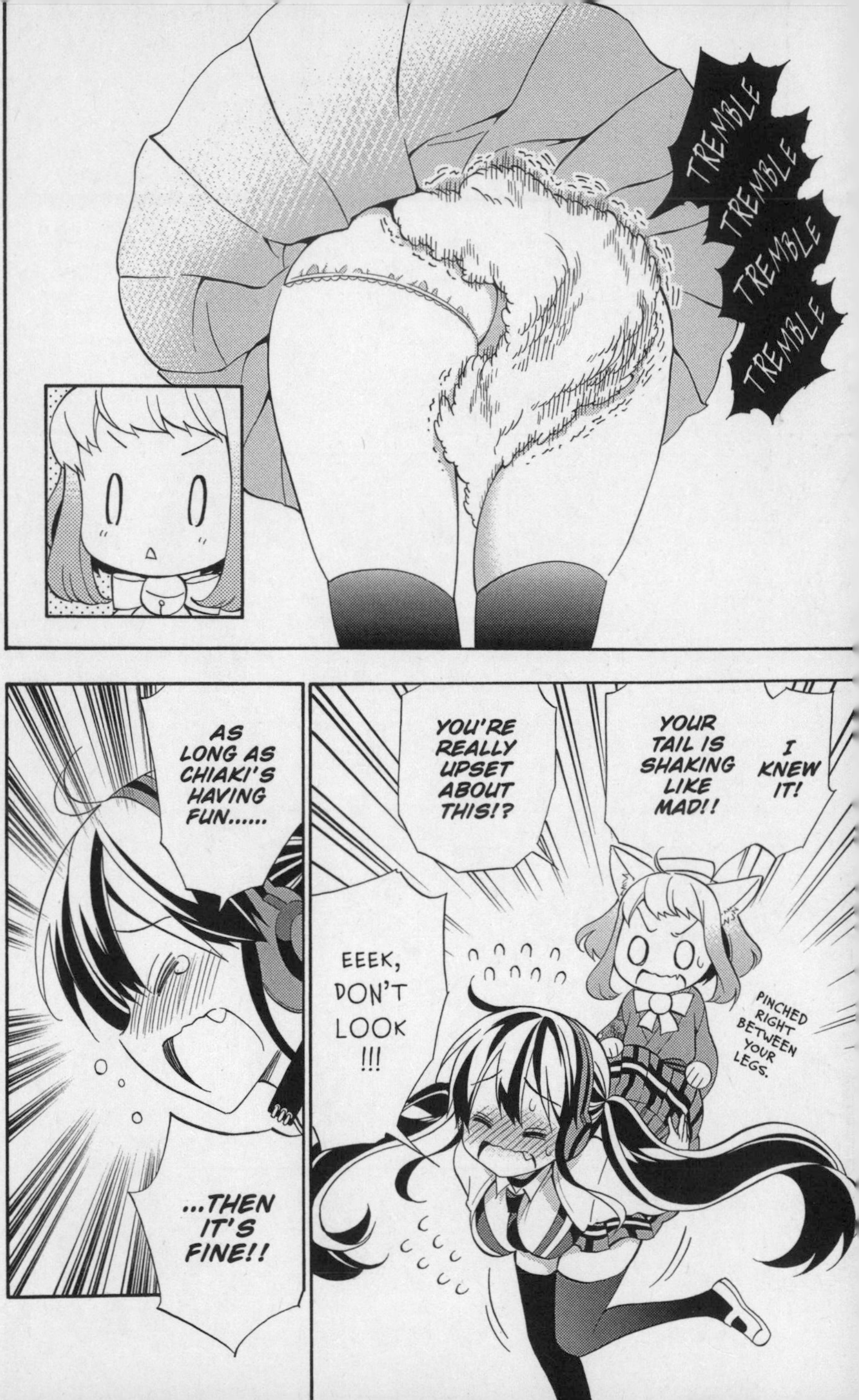
TREMBLE TREMBLE TREMBLE TREMBLE
I KNEW IT!
YOUR TAIL IS SHAKING LIKE MAD!!
YOU'RE REALLY UPSET ABOUT THIS!?
PINCHED RIGHT BETWEEN YOUR LEGS.
EEEK, DON'T LOOK!!!
AS LONG AS CHIAKI'S HAVING FUN......
...THEN IT'S FINE!!

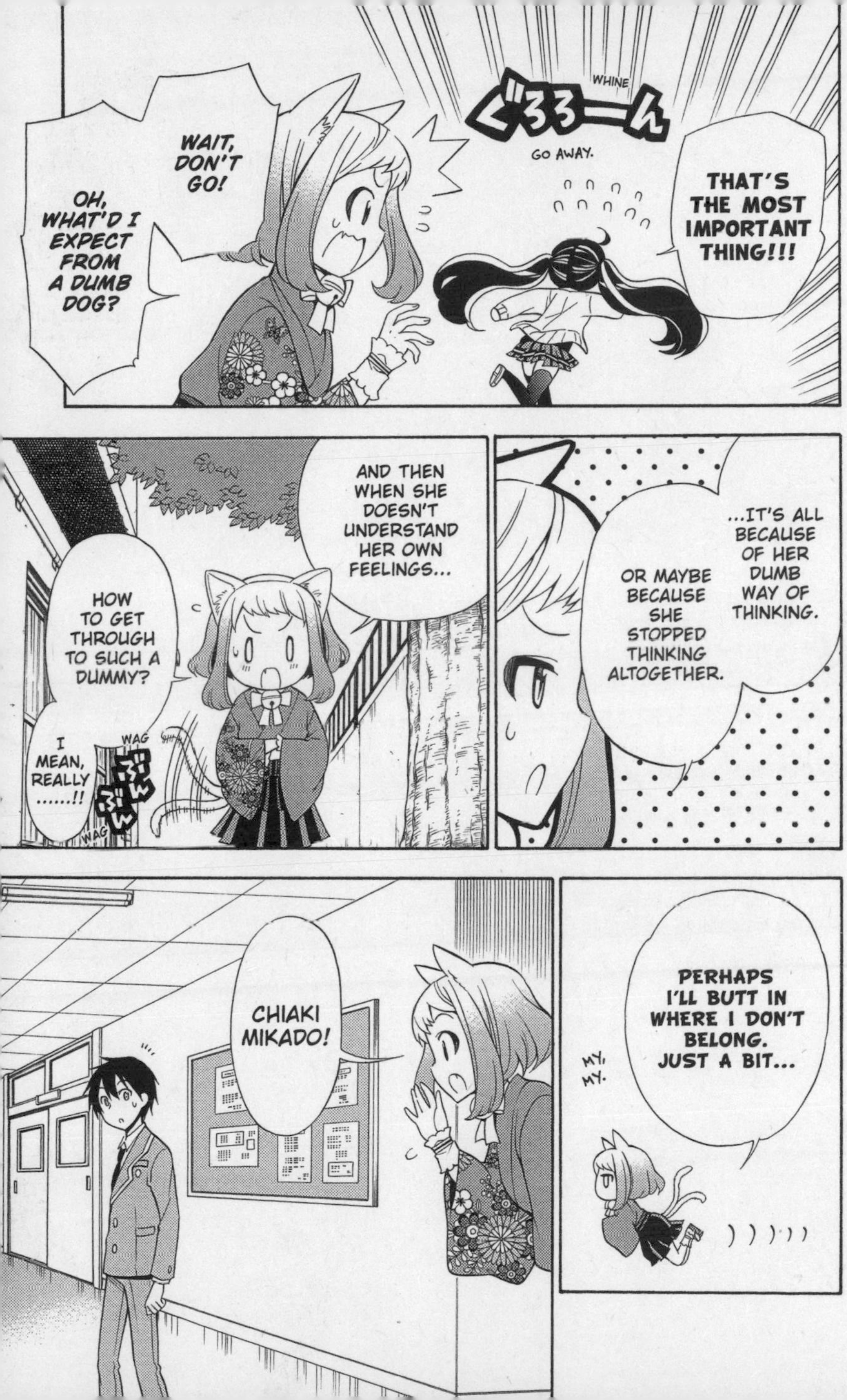
THAT'S THE MOST IMPORTANT THING!!!
ぐるるーん
WHINE
GO AWAY.
WAIT, DON'T GO!
OH, WHAT'D I EXPECT FROM A DUMB DOG?
...IT'S ALL BECAUSE OF HER DUMB WAY OF THINKING.
OR MAYBE BECAUSE SHE STOPPED THINKING ALTOGETHER.
AND THEN WHEN SHE DOESN'T UNDERSTAND HER OWN FEELINGS...
HOW TO GET THROUGH TO SUCH A DUMMY?
I MEAN, REALLY ......!!
WAG
WAG
PERHAPS I'LL BUTT IN WHERE I DON'T BELONG. JUST A BIT...
MY, MY.
CHIAKI MIKADO!

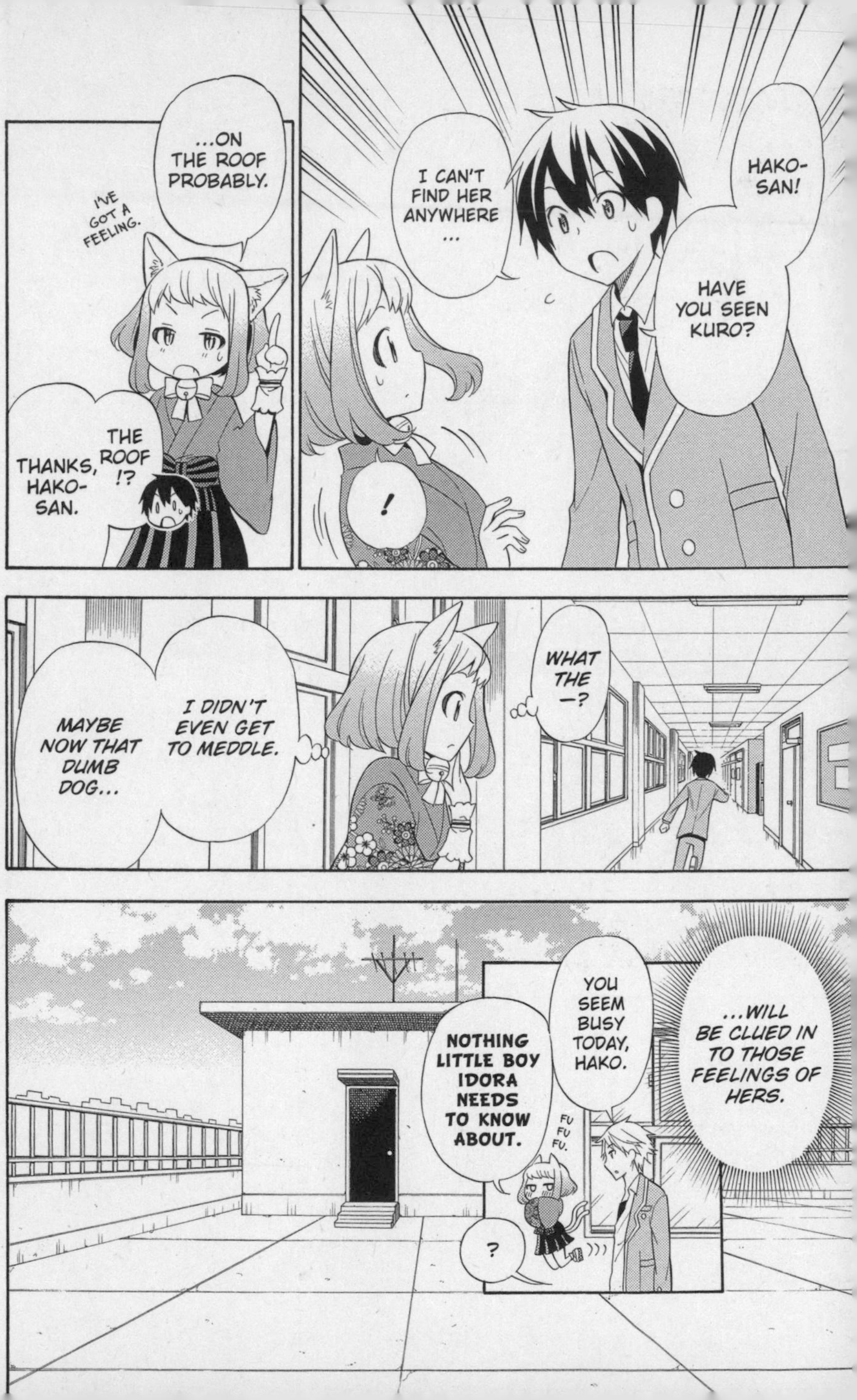
HAKO-SAN!
HAVE YOU SEEN KURO?
I CAN'T FIND HER ANYWHERE ...
!
...ON THE ROOF PROBABLY.
I'VE GOT A FEELING.
THE ROOF !?
THANKS, HAKO-SAN.
WHAT THE —?
I DIDN'T EVEN GET TO MEDDLE.
MAYBE NOW THAT DUMB DOG...
...WILL BE CLUED IN TO THOSE FEELINGS OF HERS.
YOU SEEM BUSY TODAY, HAKO.
NOTHING LITTLE BOY IDORA NEEDS TO KNOW ABOUT.
FU FU FU.
?

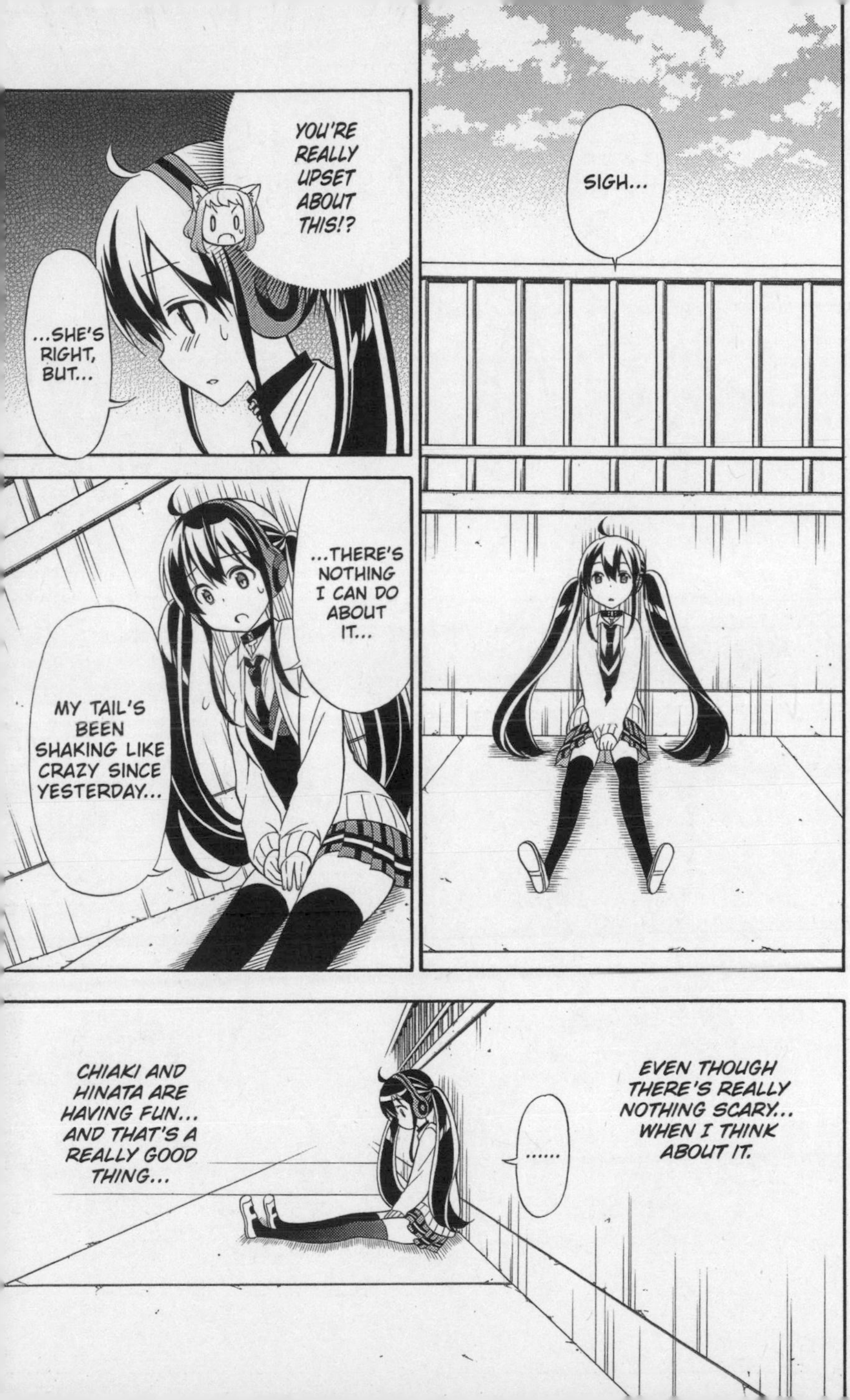
SIGH...
YOU'RE REALLY UPSET ABOUT THIS!?
...SHE'S RIGHT, BUT...
...THERE'S NOTHING I CAN DO ABOUT IT...
MY TAIL'S BEEN SHAKING LIKE CRAZY SINCE YESTERDAY...
EVEN THOUGH THERE'S REALLY NOTHING SCARY... WHEN I THINK ABOUT IT.
......
CHIAKI AND HINATA ARE HAVING FUN... AND THAT'S A REALLY GOOD THING...

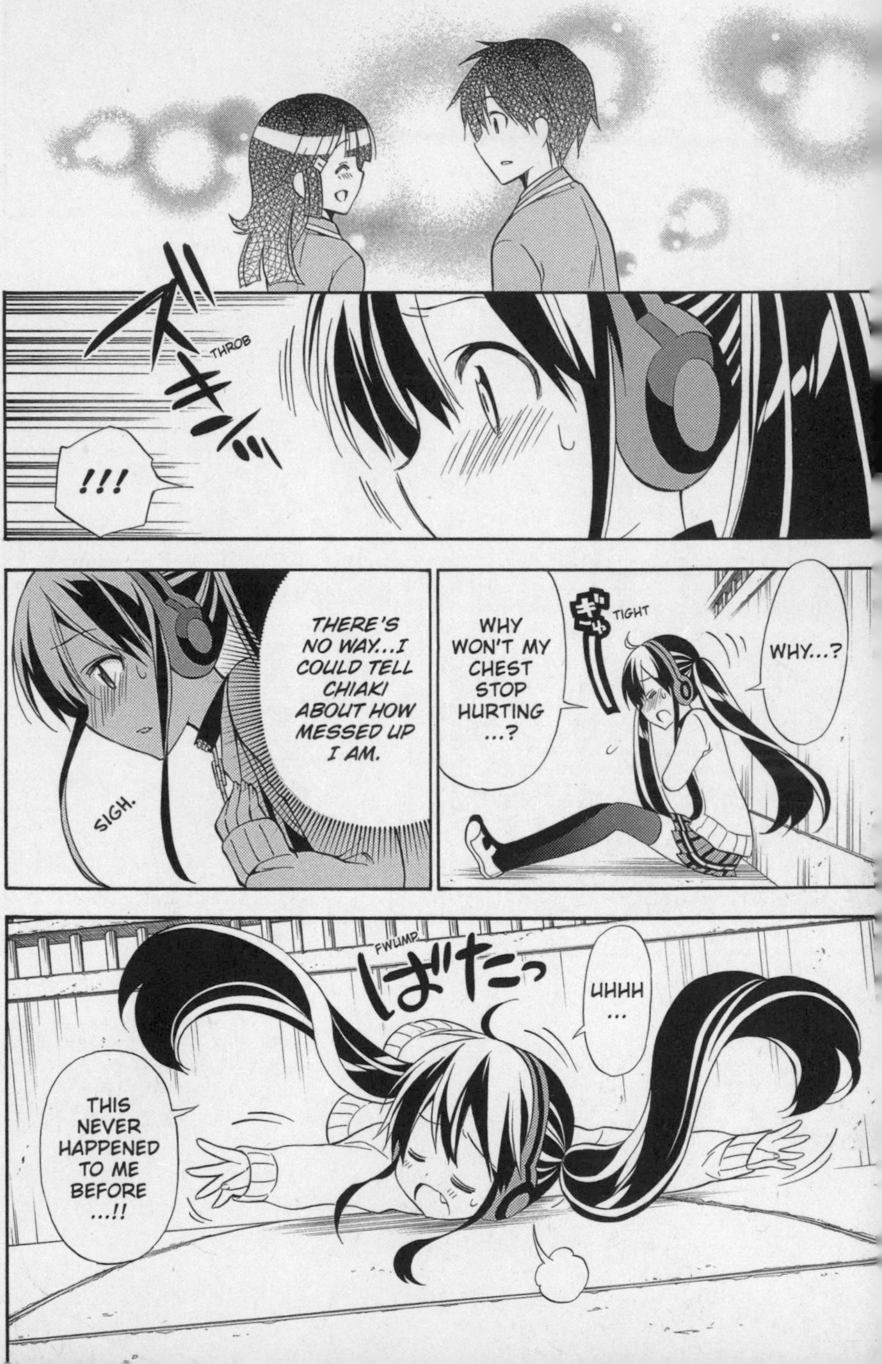
THROB
!!!
WHY...?
ぎゅ
TIGHT
WHY WON'T MY CHEST STOP HURTING ...?
THERE'S NO WAY...I COULD TELL CHIAKI ABOUT HOW MESSED UP I AM.
SIGH.
ばたっ
FWUMP
UHHH ...
THIS NEVER HAPPENED TO ME BEFORE ...!!

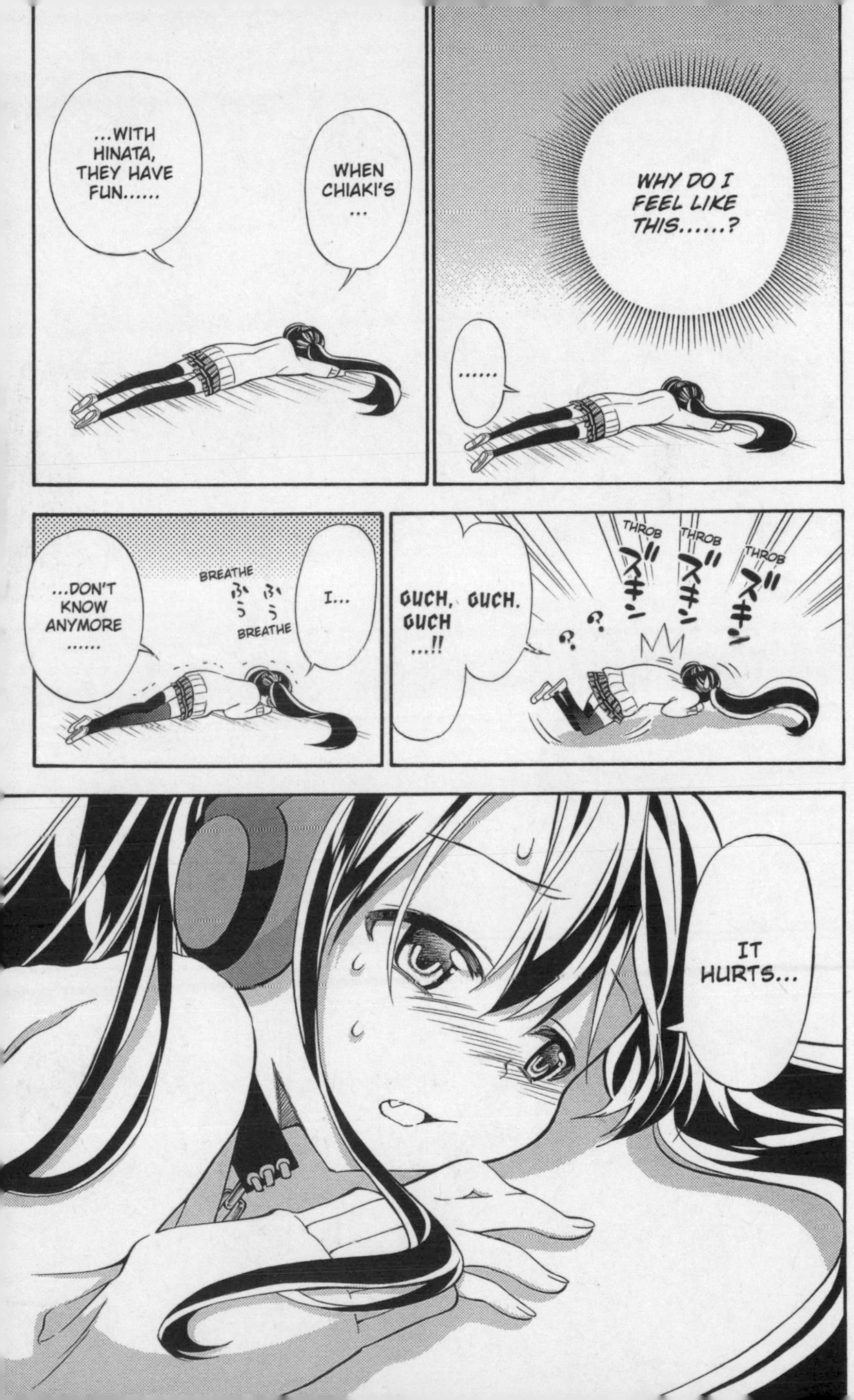
WHY DO I FEEL LIKE THIS......?
......
WHEN CHIAKI'S ...
...WITH HINATA, THEY HAVE FUN......
THROB ズキン
THROB ズキン
THROB ズキン
OUCH, OUCH. OUCH ...!!
I...
BREATHE ふぅ ふぅ BREATHE
...DON'T KNOW ANYMORE ......
IT HURTS...

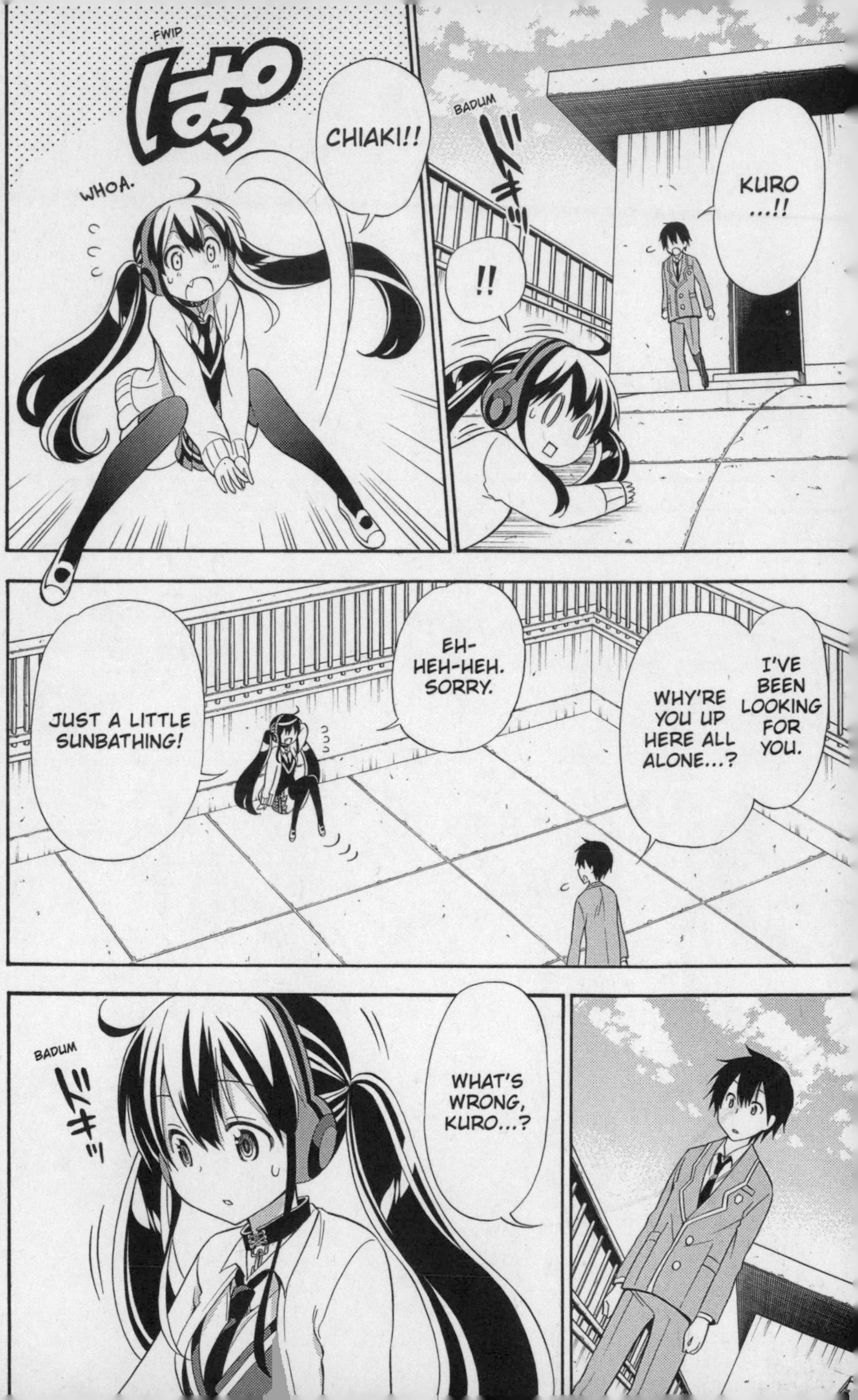
KURO ...!!
BADUM
ドキッ
!!
FWIP
ぱっ
CHIAKI!!
WHOA.
I'VE BEEN LOOKING FOR YOU.
WHY'RE YOU UP HERE ALL ALONE...?
EH-HEH-HEH. SORRY.
JUST A LITTLE SUNBATHING!
WHAT'S WRONG, KURO...?
BADUM
ドキッ

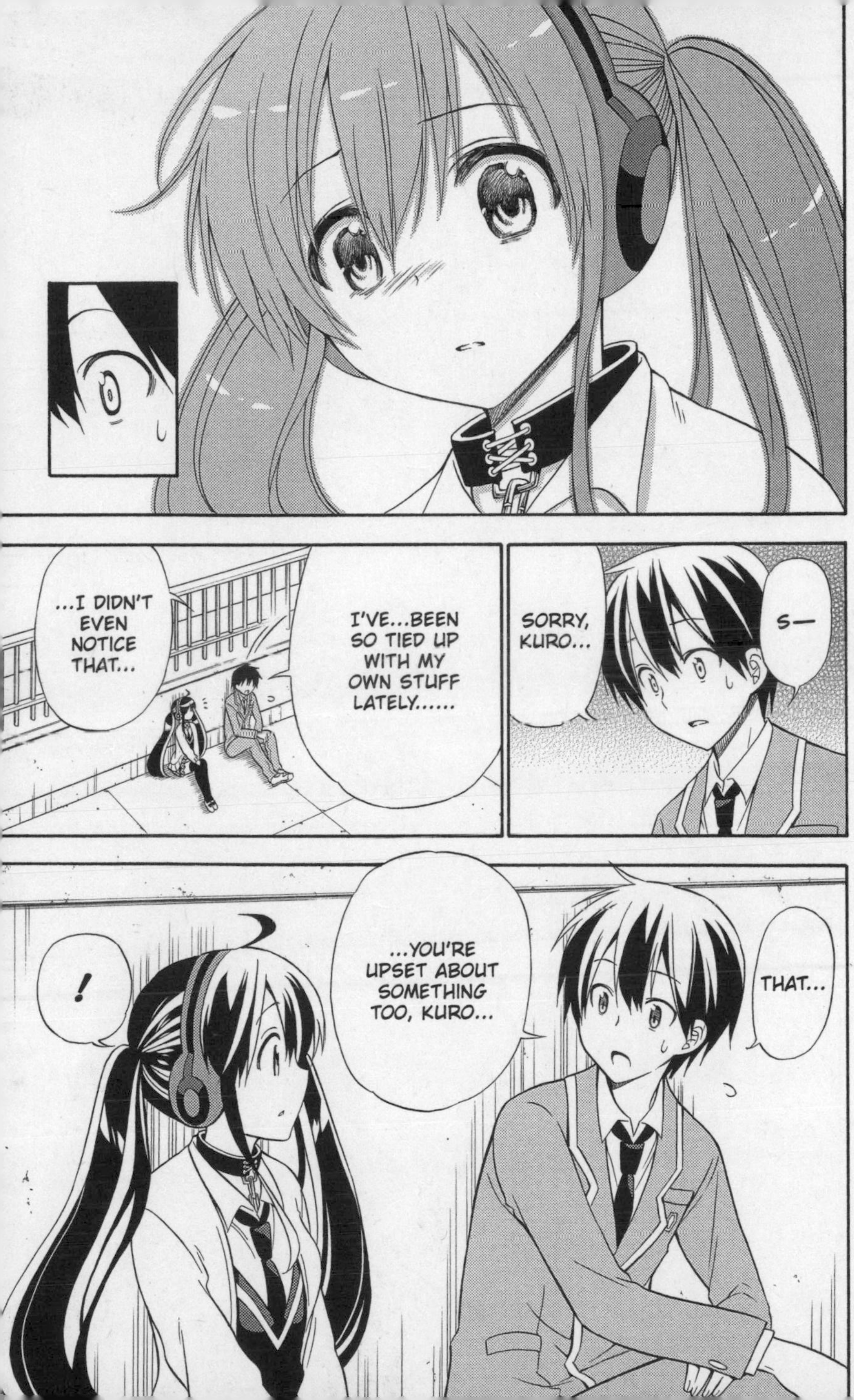
S—
SORRY, KURO...
I'VE...BEEN SO TIED UP WITH MY OWN STUFF LATELY......
...I DIDN'T EVEN NOTICE THAT...
THAT...
...YOU'RE UPSET ABOUT SOMETHING TOO, KURO...
!

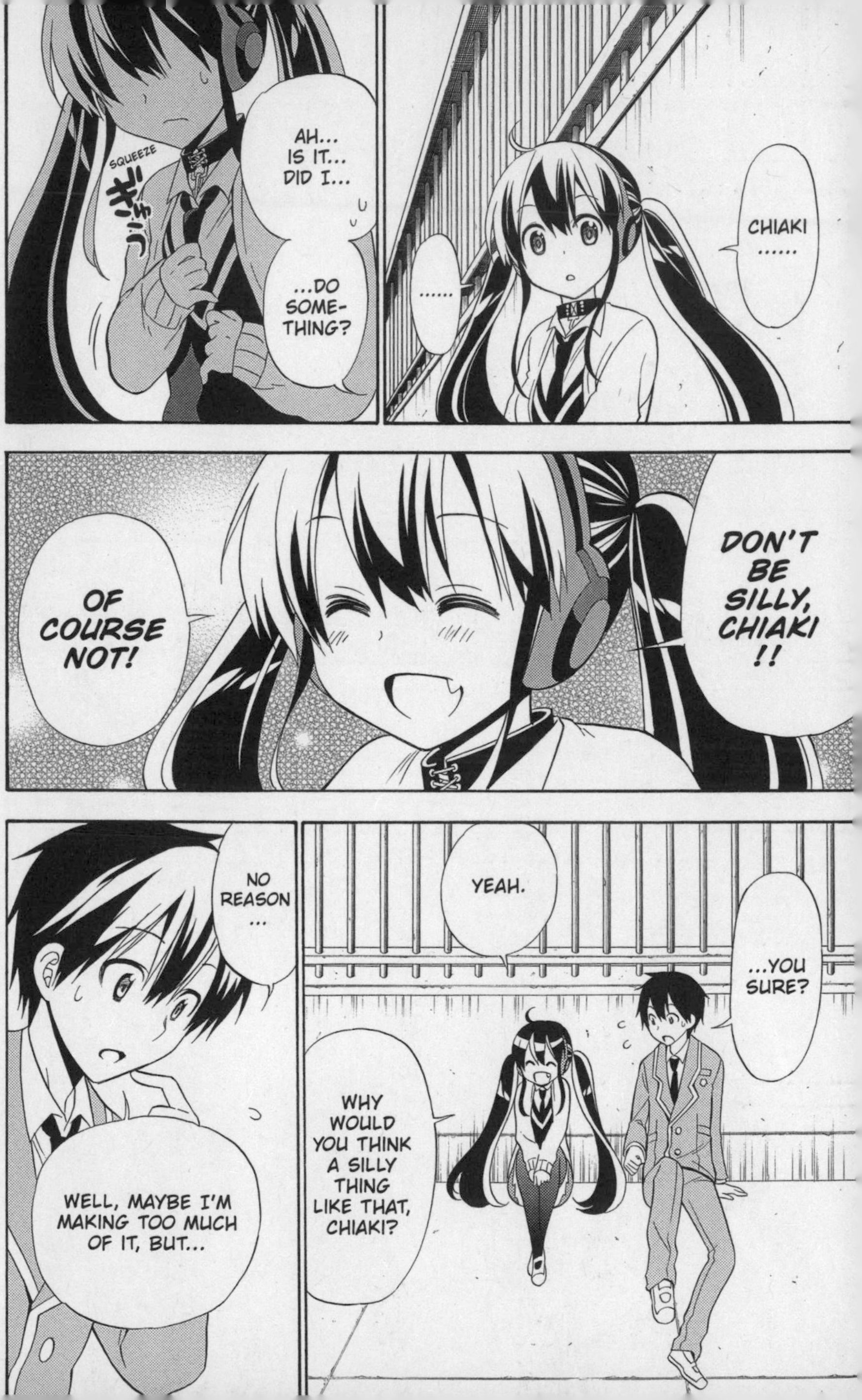
CHIAKI ......
......
AH... IS IT... DID I...
...DO SOME-THING?
SQUEEZE
ぎゅぅ
DON'T BE SILLY, CHIAKI!!
OF COURSE NOT!
...YOU SURE?
YEAH.
WHY WOULD YOU THINK A SILLY THING LIKE THAT, CHIAKI?
NO REASON...
WELL, MAYBE I'M MAKING TOO MUCH OF IT, BUT...

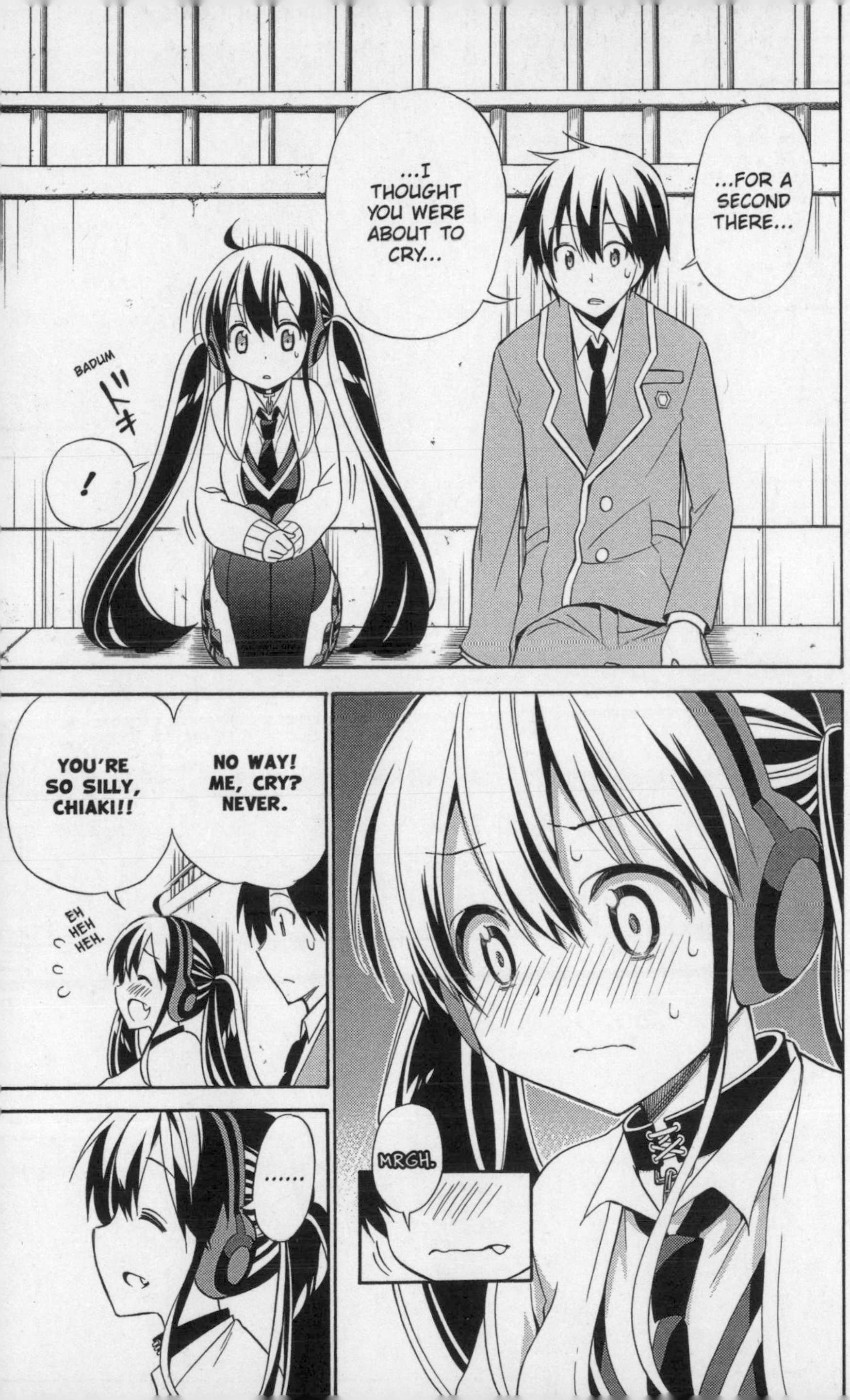
...FOR A SECOND THERE...
...I THOUGHT YOU WERE ABOUT TO CRY...
BADUM
ドキ
!
MRGH.
NO WAY! ME, CRY? NEVER.
YOU'RE SO SILLY, CHIAKI!!
EH HEH HEH.
......

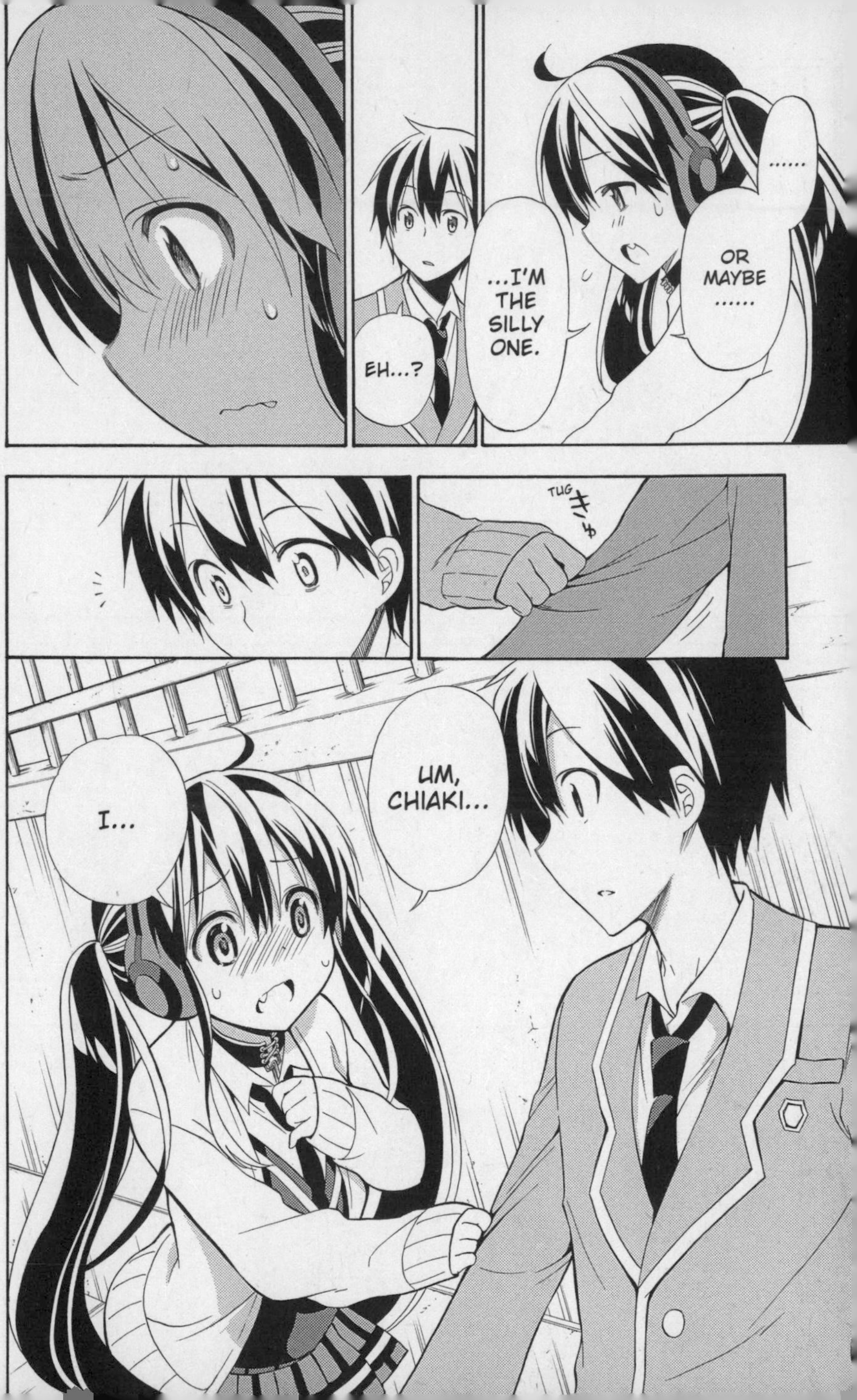
......
OR MAYBE ......
...I'M THE SILLY ONE.
EH...?
TUG
UM, CHIAKI...
I...

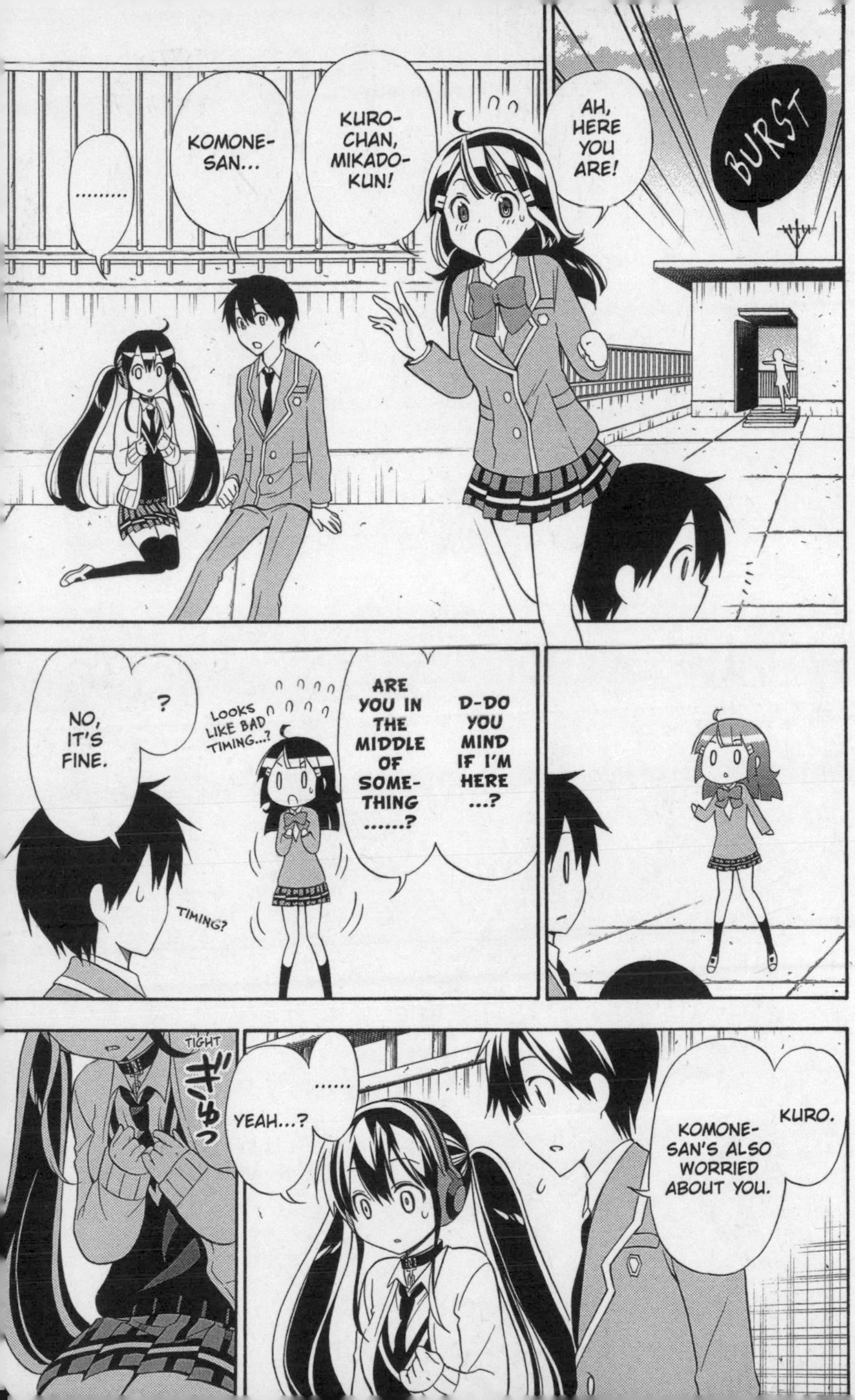

BURST
AH, HERE YOU ARE!
KURO-CHAN, MIKADO-KUN!
KOMONE-SAN...
....
D-DO YOU MIND IF I'M HERE ...?
ARE YOU IN THE MIDDLE OF SOME-THING ......?
LOOKS LIKE BAD TIMING...?
?
NO, IT'S FINE.
TIMING?
KURO.
KOMONE-SAN'S ALSO WORRIED ABOUT YOU.
......
YEAH...?
TIGHT
ぎゅっ

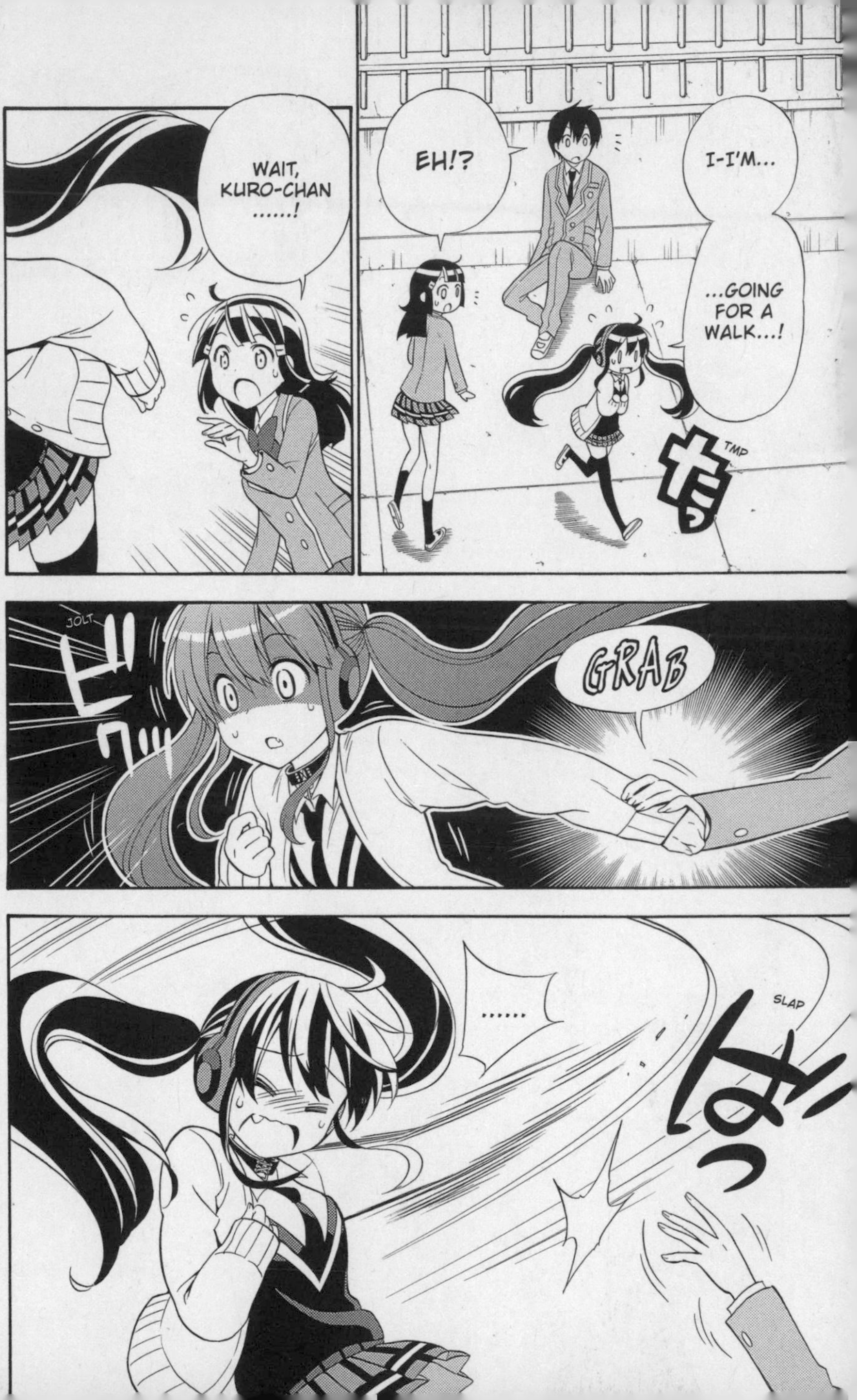
I-I'M... ...GOING FOR A WALK...!
EH!?
TMP
WAIT, KURO-CHAN ......!
GRAB
JOLT
SLAP
......

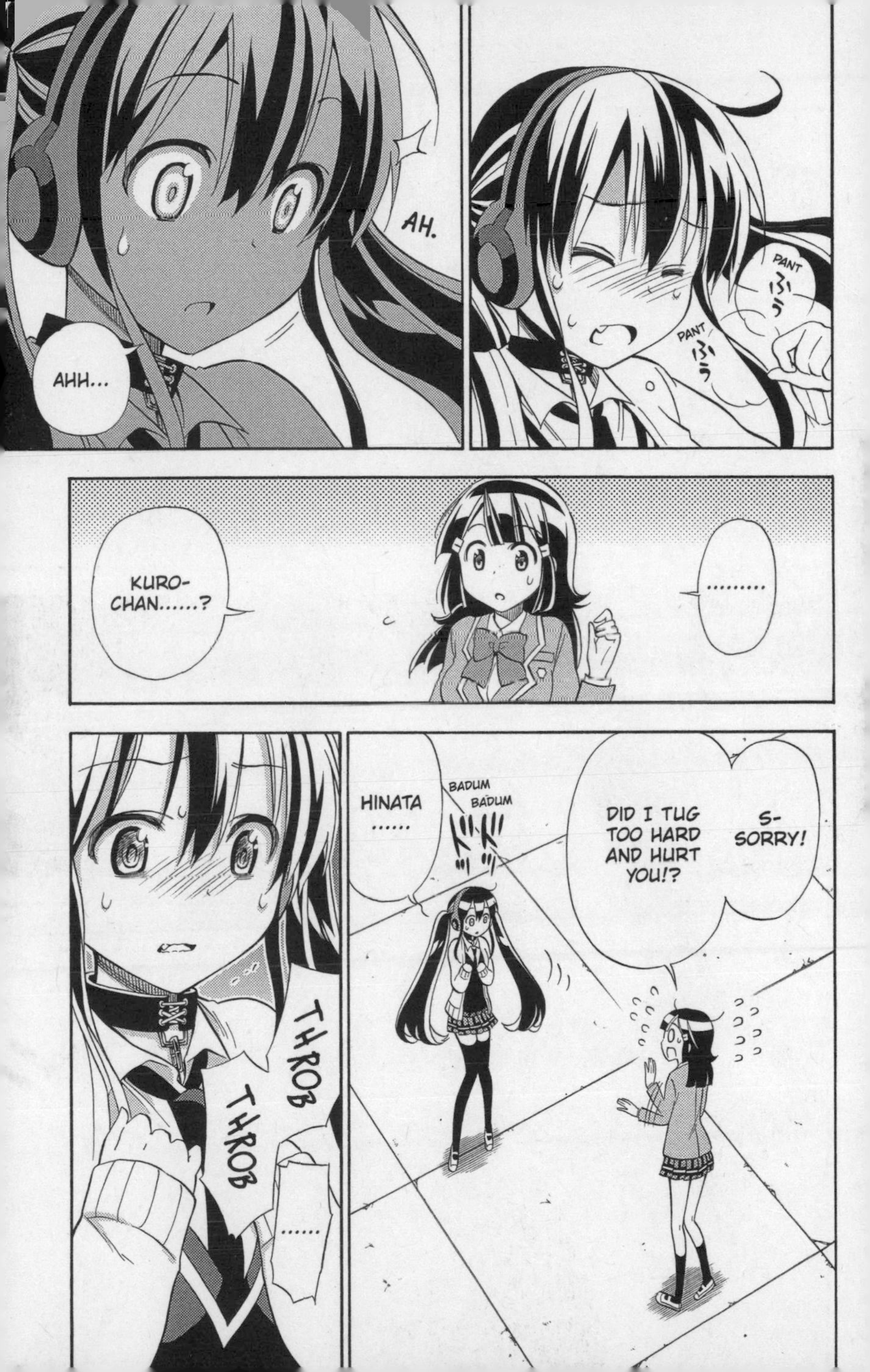
PANT
ふぅ
PANT
ふぅ
AH.
AHH...
....
KURO-CHAN......?
S-SORRY!
DID I TUG TOO HARD AND HURT YOU!?
BADUM
BADUM
ドッドッ
HINATA ......
THROB
THROB
......

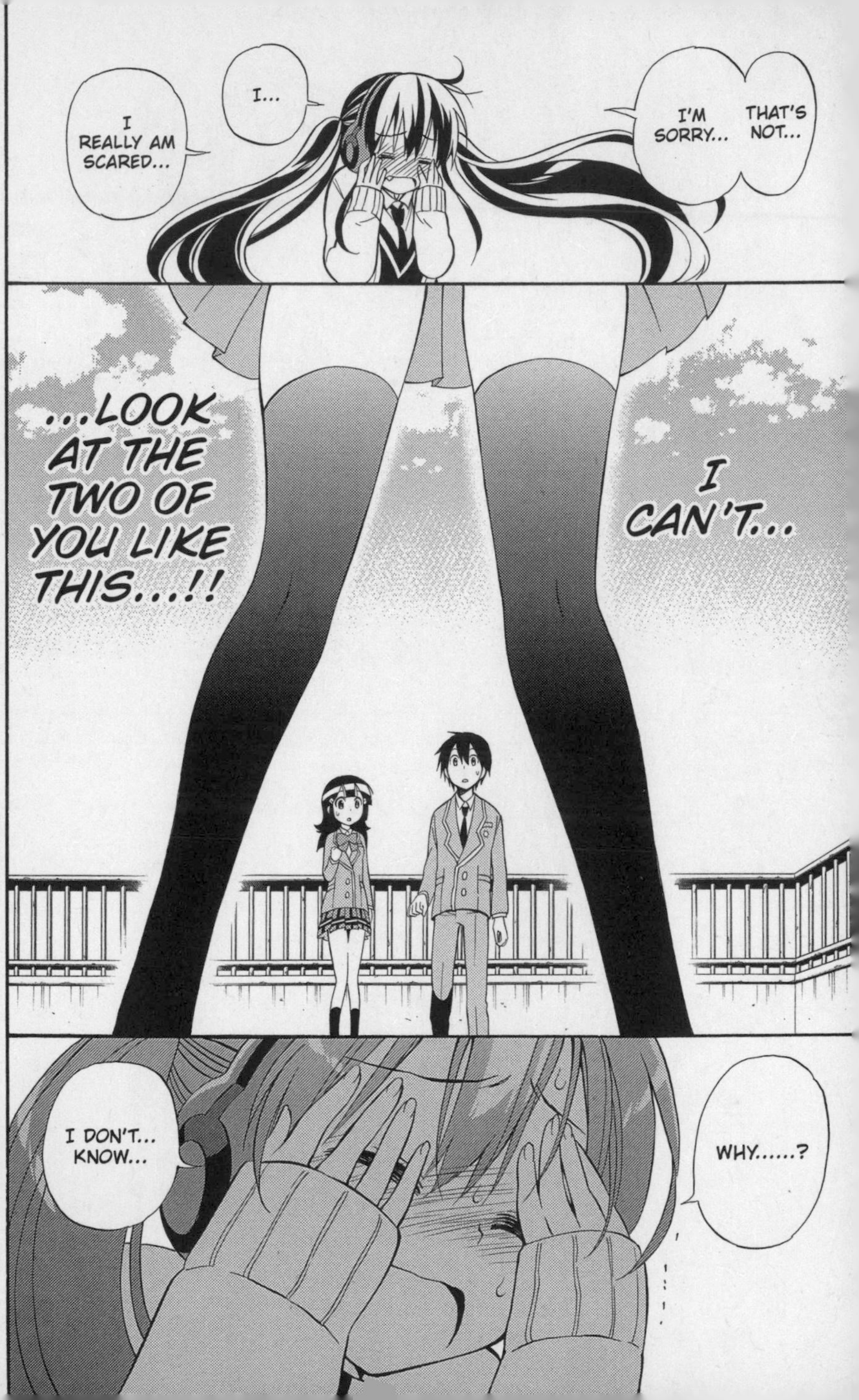
THAT'S NOT...
I'M SORRY...
I...
I REALLY AM SCARED...
I CAN'T...
...LOOK AT THE TWO OF YOU LIKE THIS...!!
WHY......?
I DON'T... KNOW...

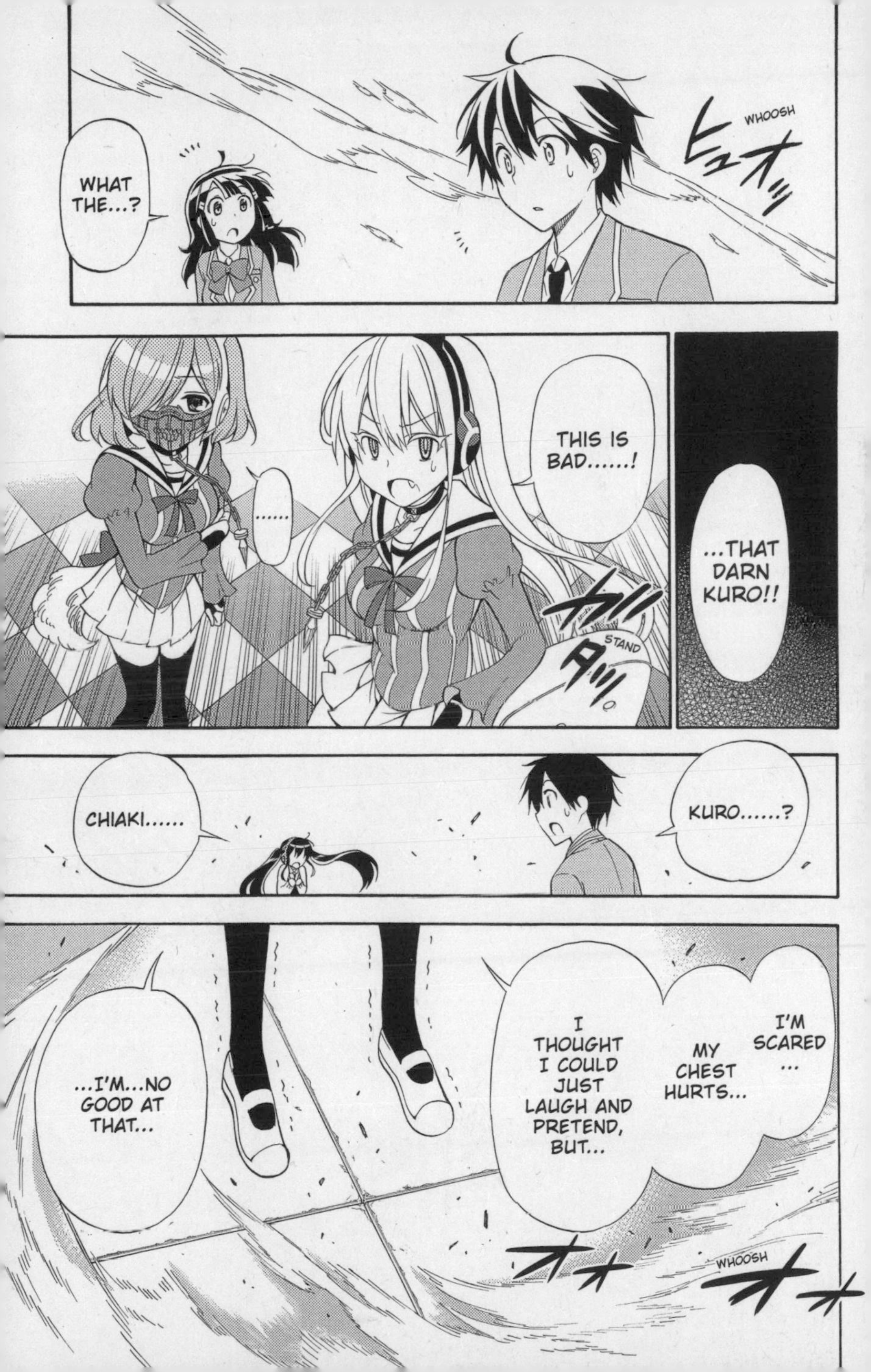
WHOOSH
WHAT THE...?
...THAT DARN KURO!!
THIS IS BAD......!
STAND
......
KURO......?
CHIAKI......
I'M SCARED...
MY CHEST HURTS...
I THOUGHT I COULD JUST LAUGH AND PRETEND, BUT...
...I'M...NO GOOD AT THAT...
WHOOSH

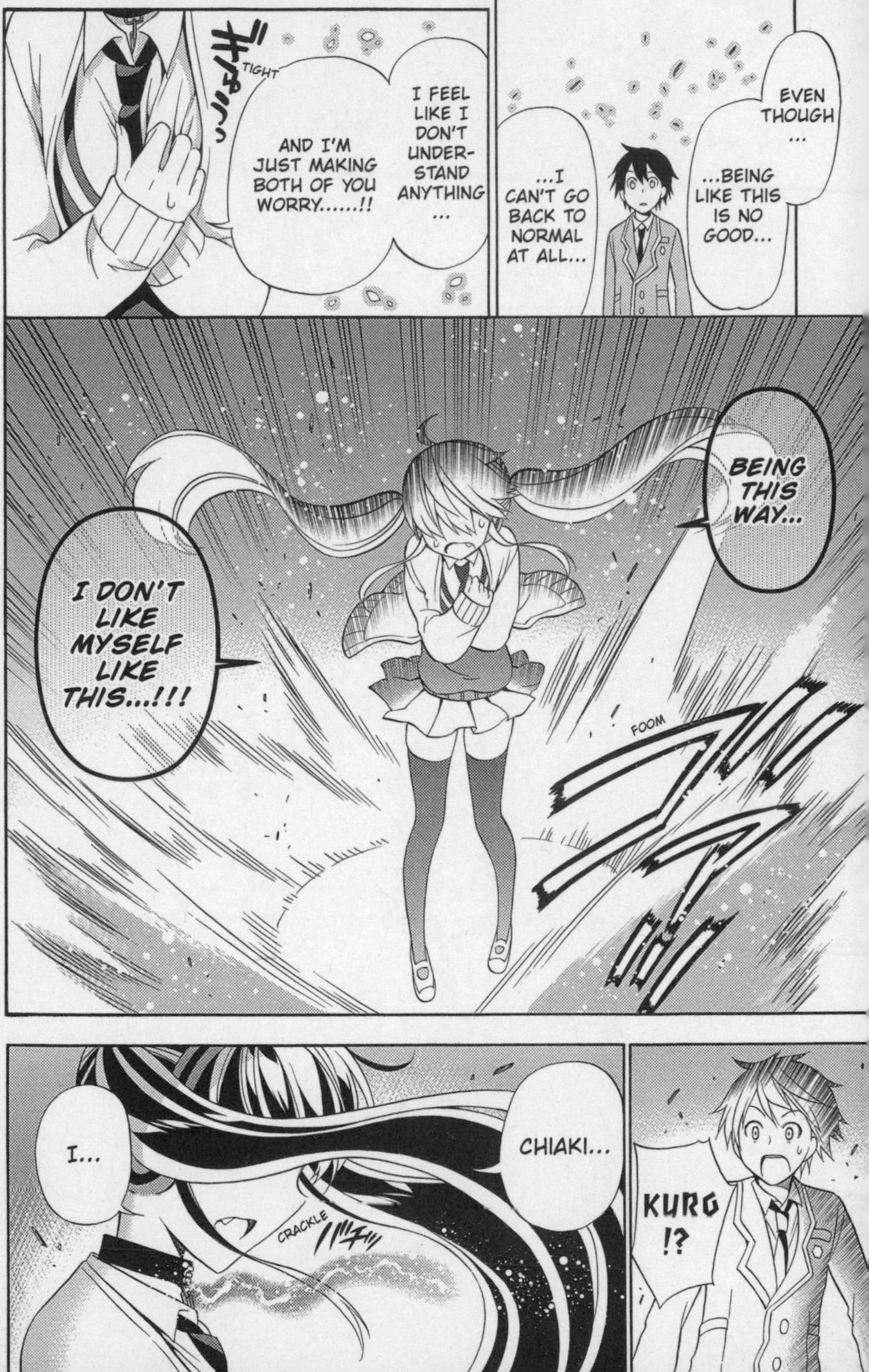
EVEN THOUGH...
...BEING LIKE THIS IS NO GOOD...
...I CAN'T GO BACK TO NORMAL AT ALL...
TIGHT
I FEEL LIKE I DON'T UNDER-STAND ANYTHING...
AND I'M JUST MAKING BOTH OF YOU WORRY......!!
BEING THIS WAY...
I DON'T LIKE MYSELF LIKE THIS...!!!
FOOM
KURG !?
CHIAKI...
I...
CRACKLE

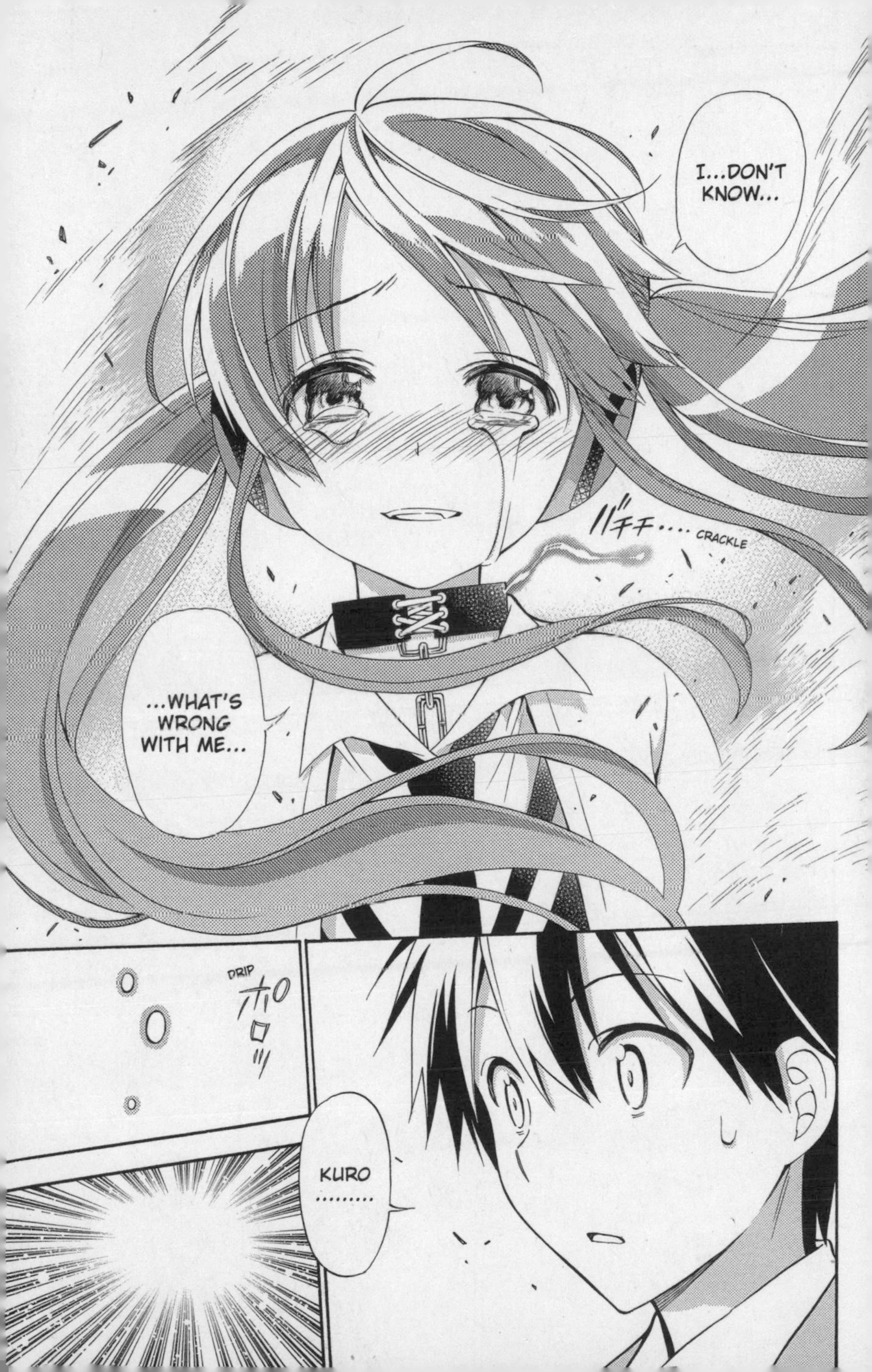
I...DON'T KNOW...
バチチ.... CRACKLE
...WHAT'S WRONG WITH ME...
KURO ....
ポロッ DRIP

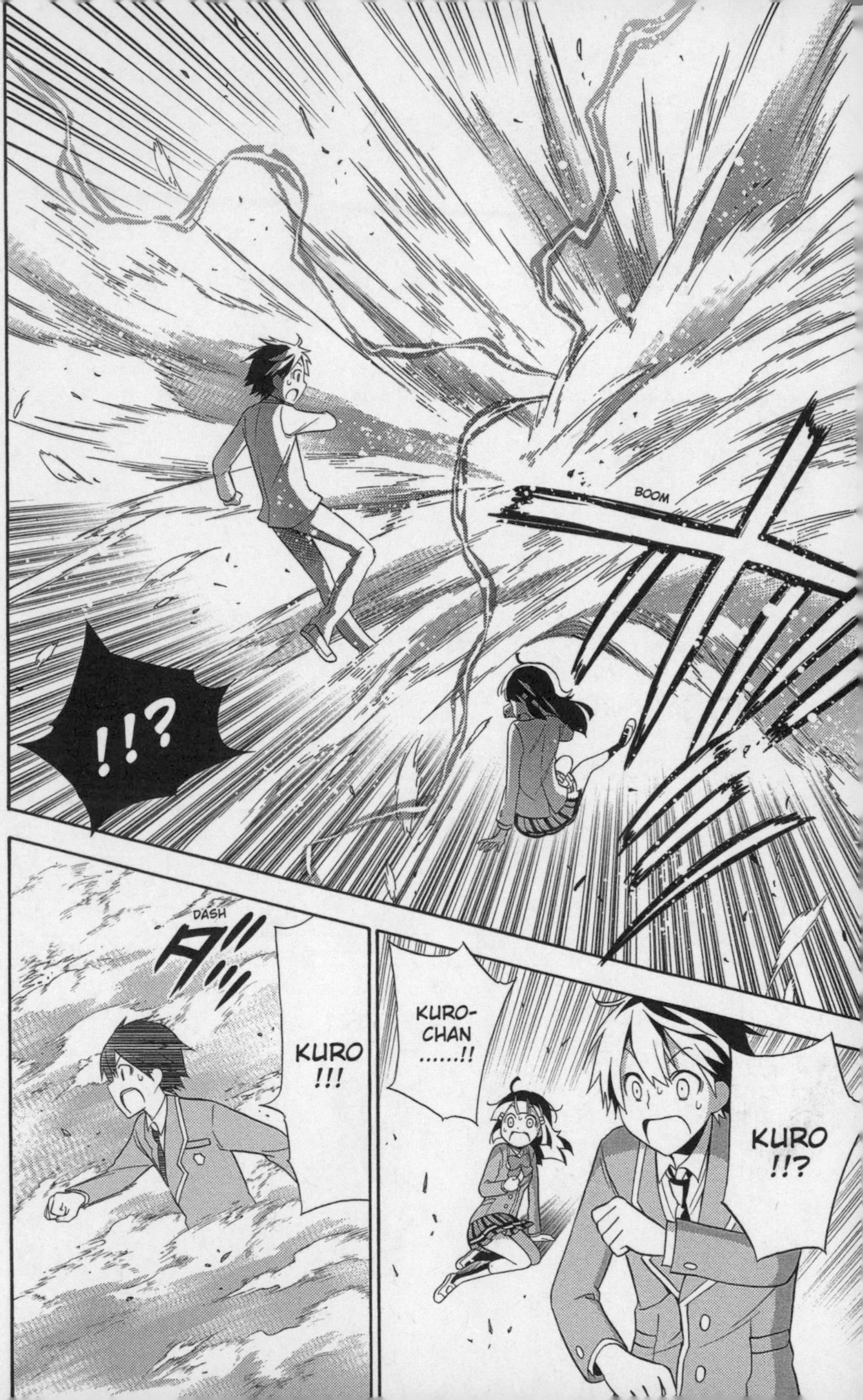
BOOM
!!?
KURO-CHAN ......!!
KURO !!?
DASH
KURO !!!

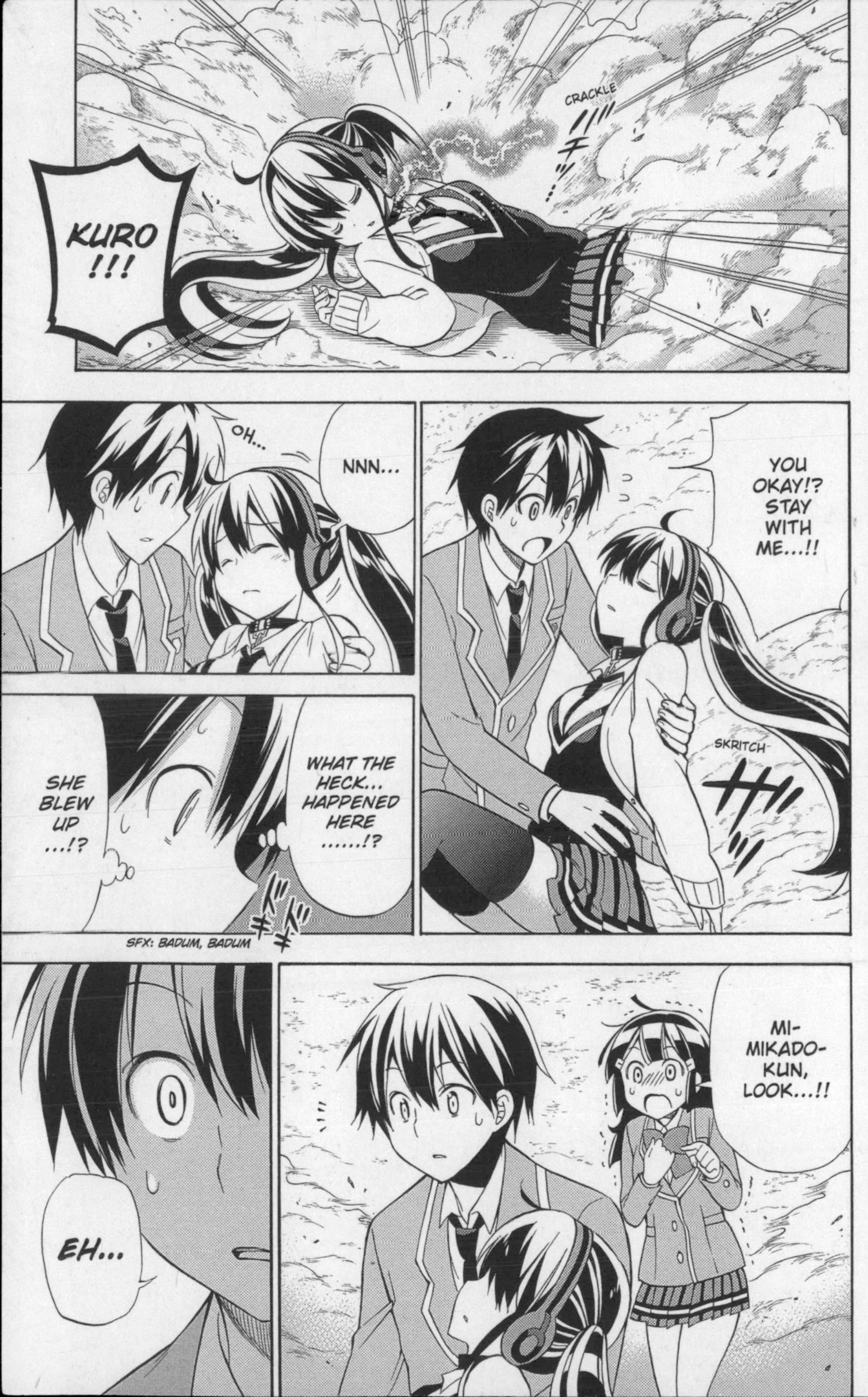
CRACKLE
KURO !!!
YOU OKAY!? STAY WITH ME...!!
SKRITCH
NNN...
OH...
WHAT THE HECK... HAPPENED HERE ......!?
SHE BLEW UP ...!?
SFX: BADUM, BADUM
MI-MIKADO-KUN, LOOK...!!
EH...

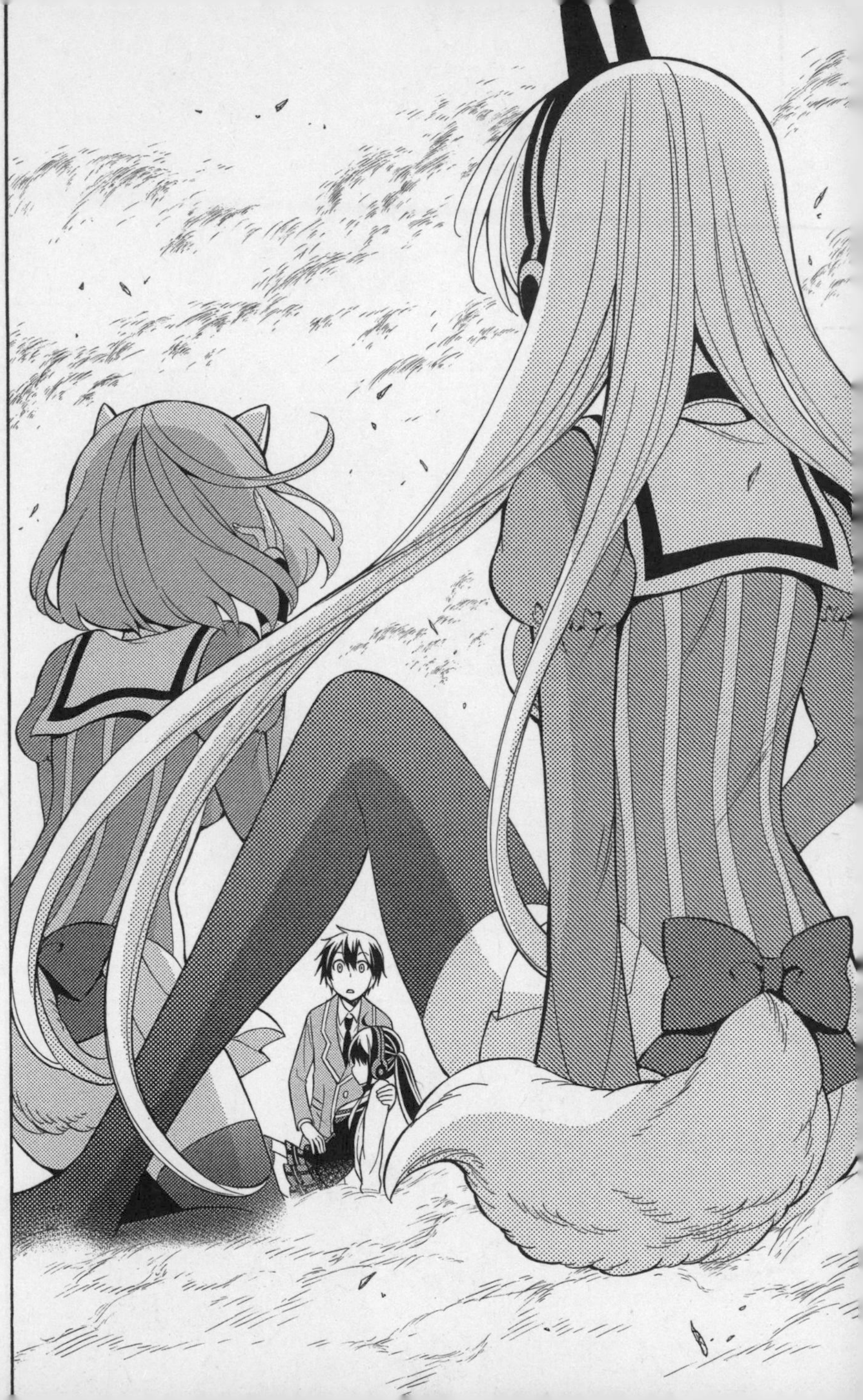

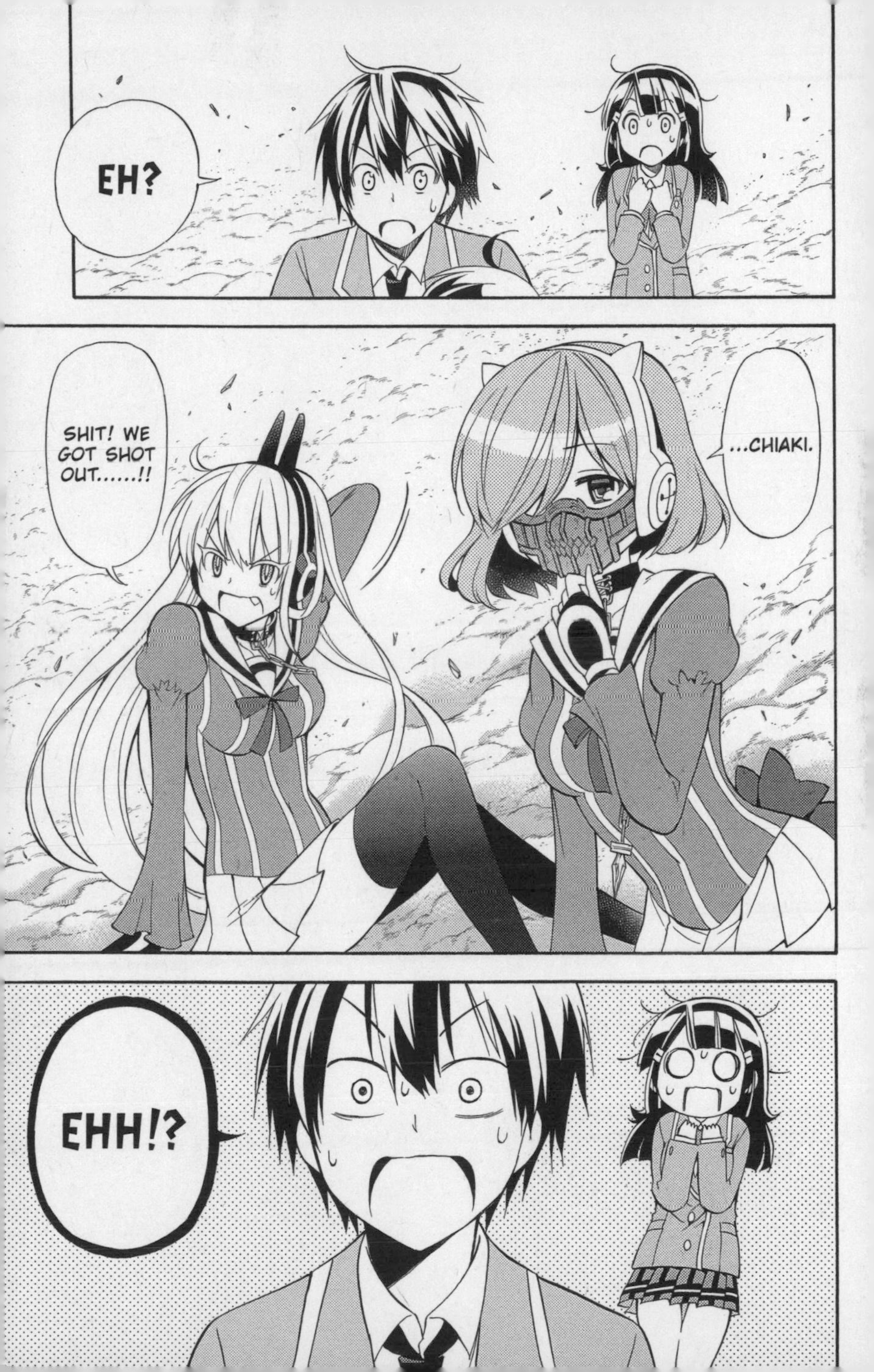
EH?
...CHIAKI.
SHIT! WE GOT SHOT OUT......!!
EHH!?

TODAY'S CERBERUS

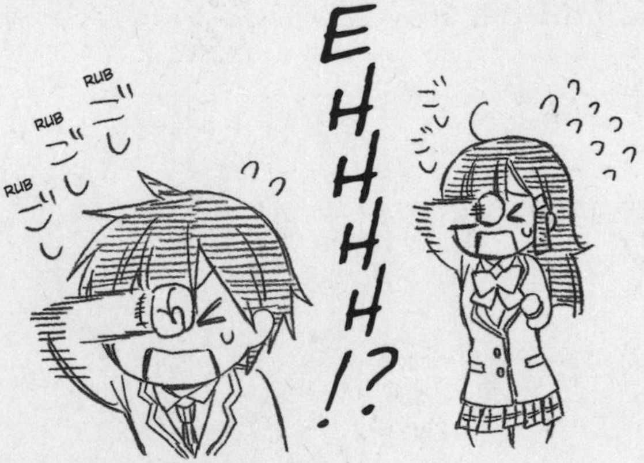
EHHHH!?
RUB
RUB
RUB

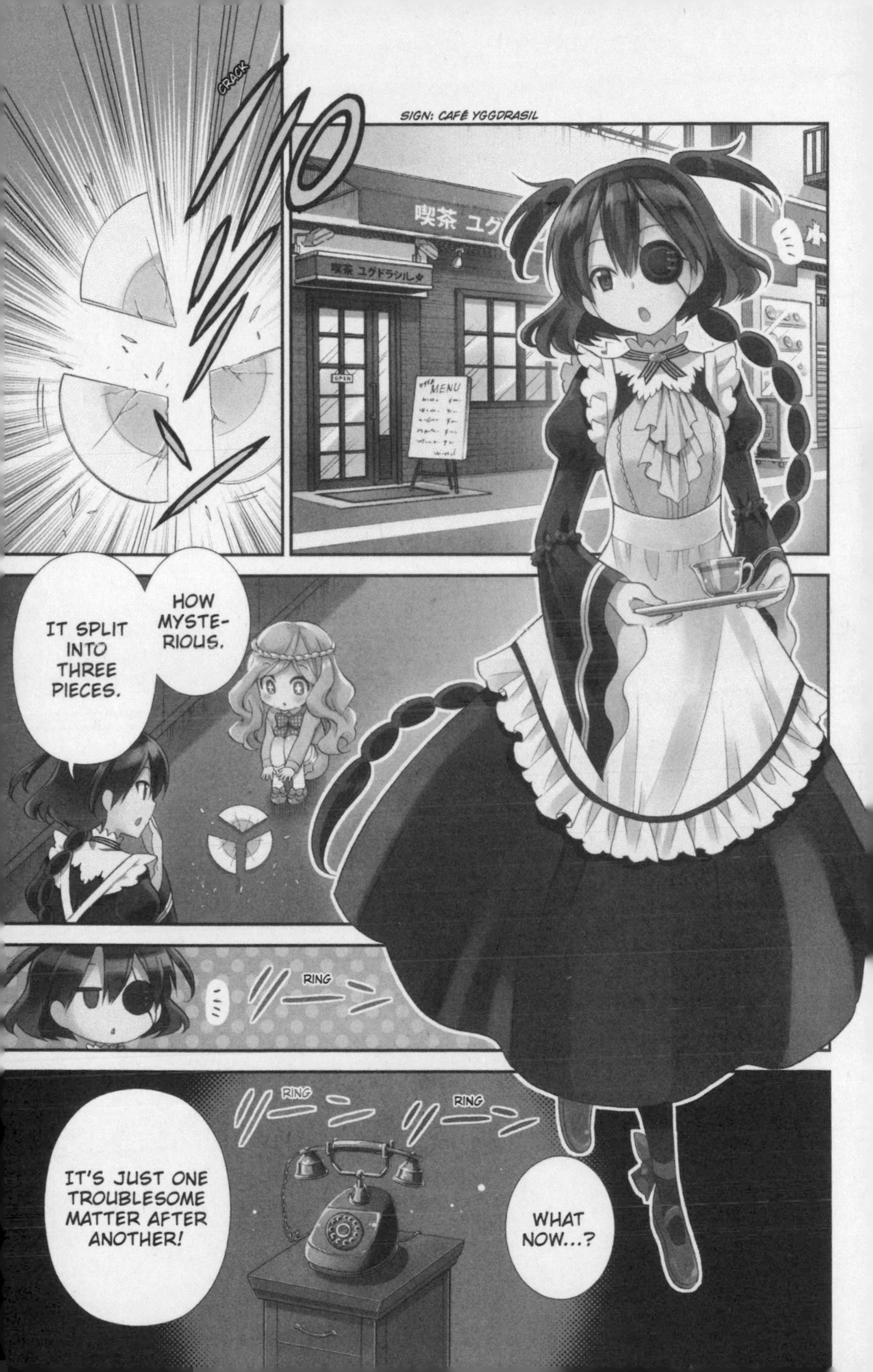
SIGN: CAFÉ YGGDRASIL
...
CRACK
HOW MYSTERIOUS.
IT SPLIT INTO THREE PIECES.
RING
...
RING
RING
WHAT NOW...?
IT'S JUST ONE TROUBLESOME MATTER AFTER ANOTHER!

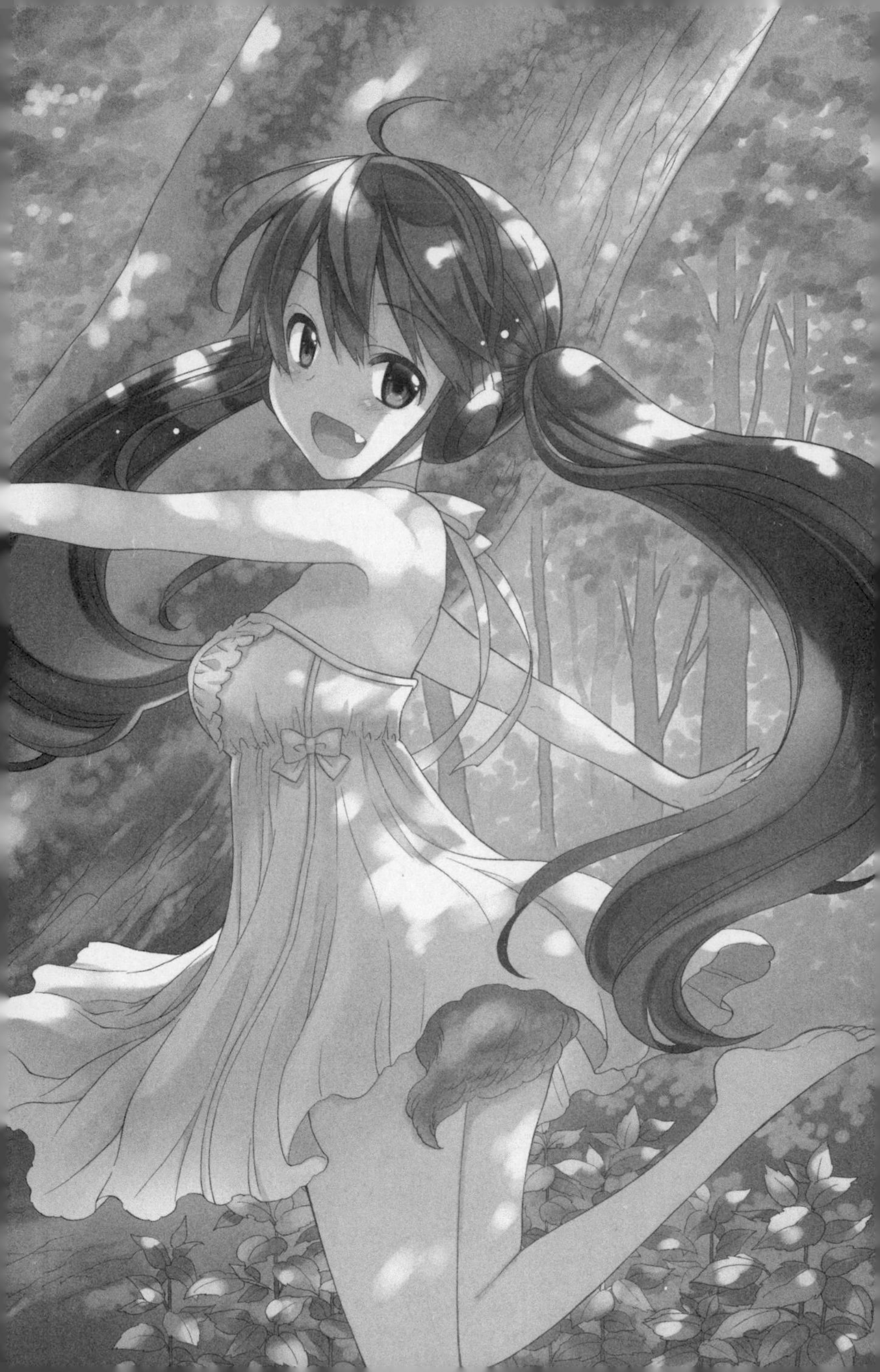

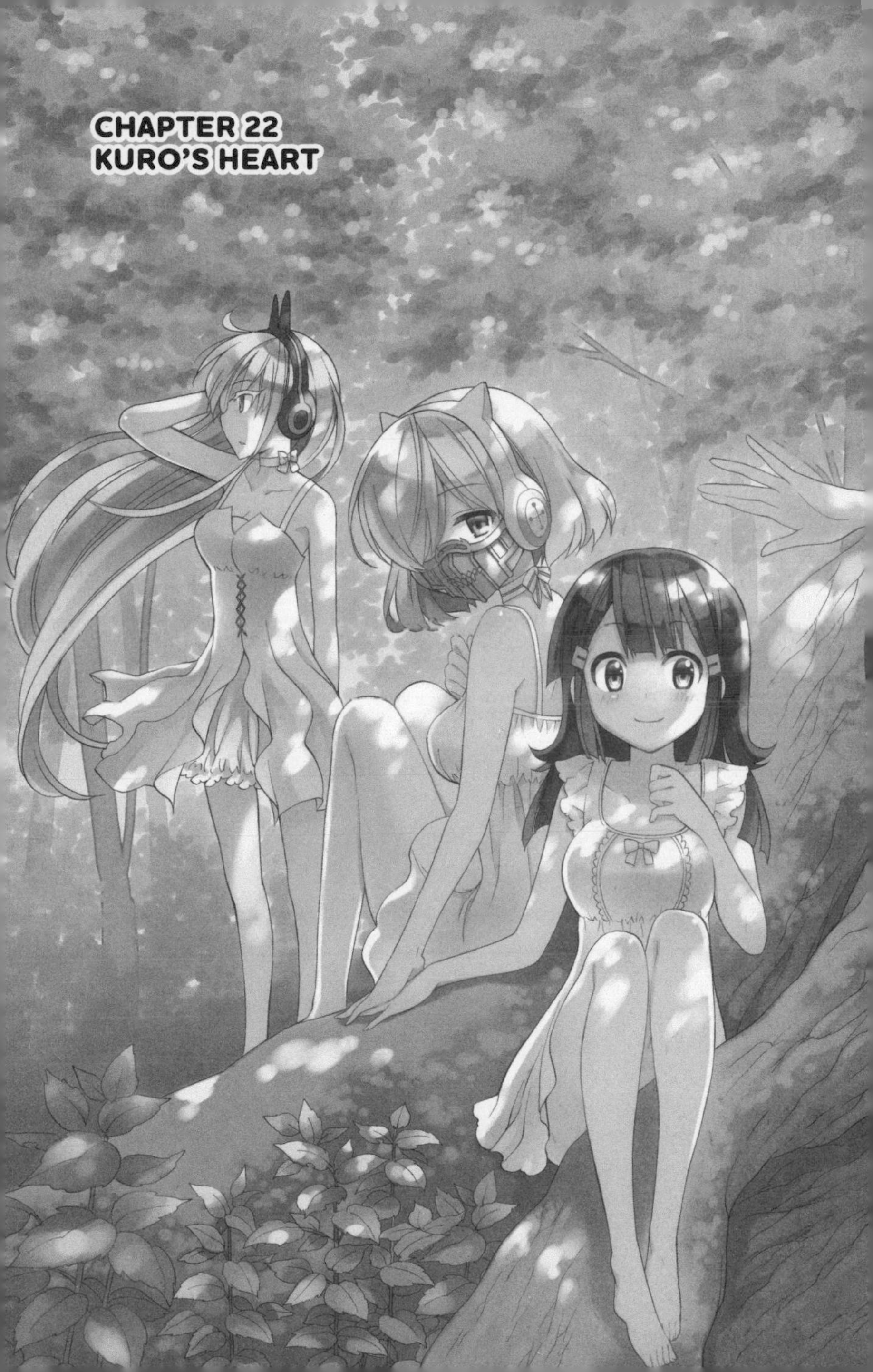
CHAPTER 22
KURO'S HEART

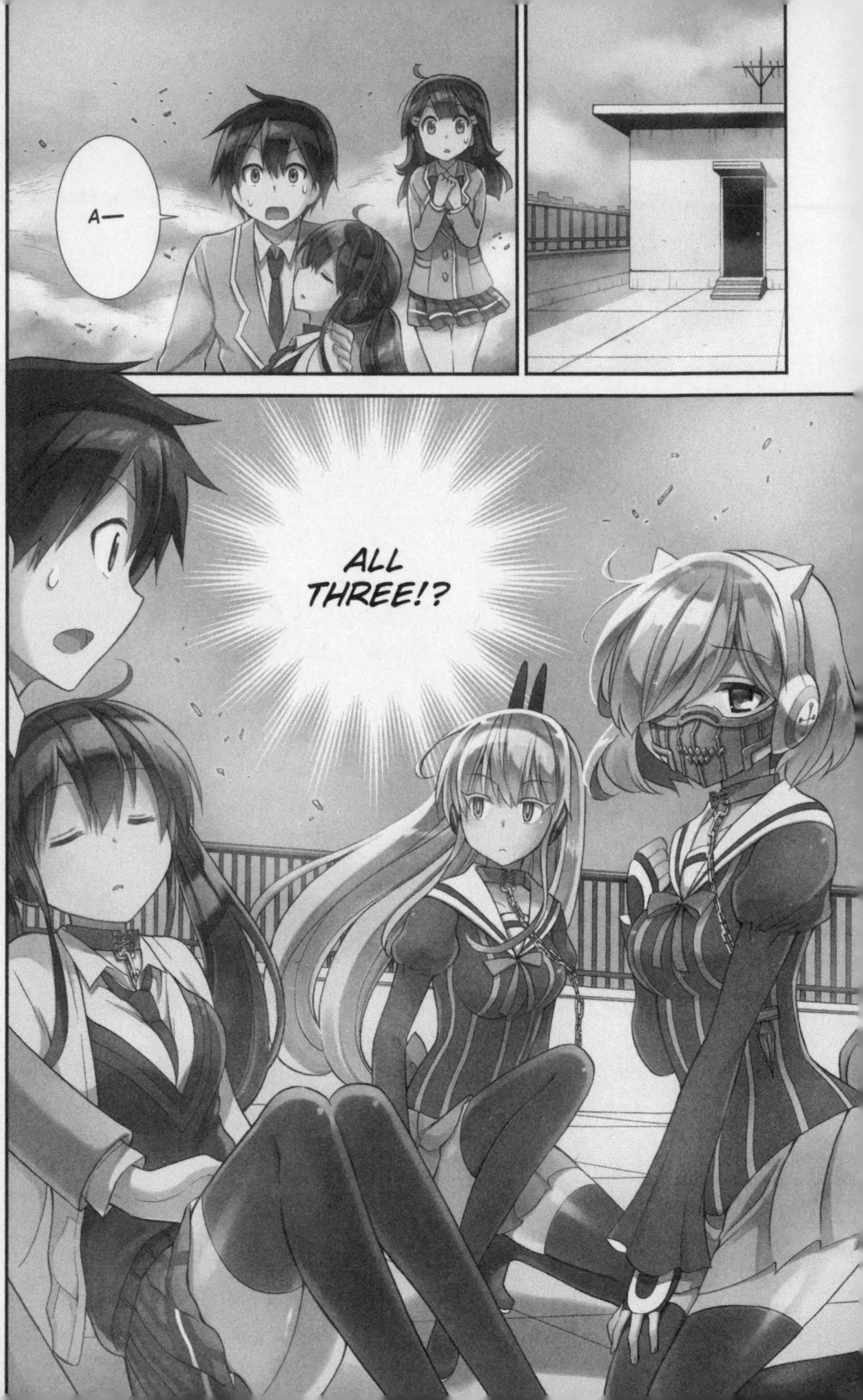
A—
ALL THREE!?

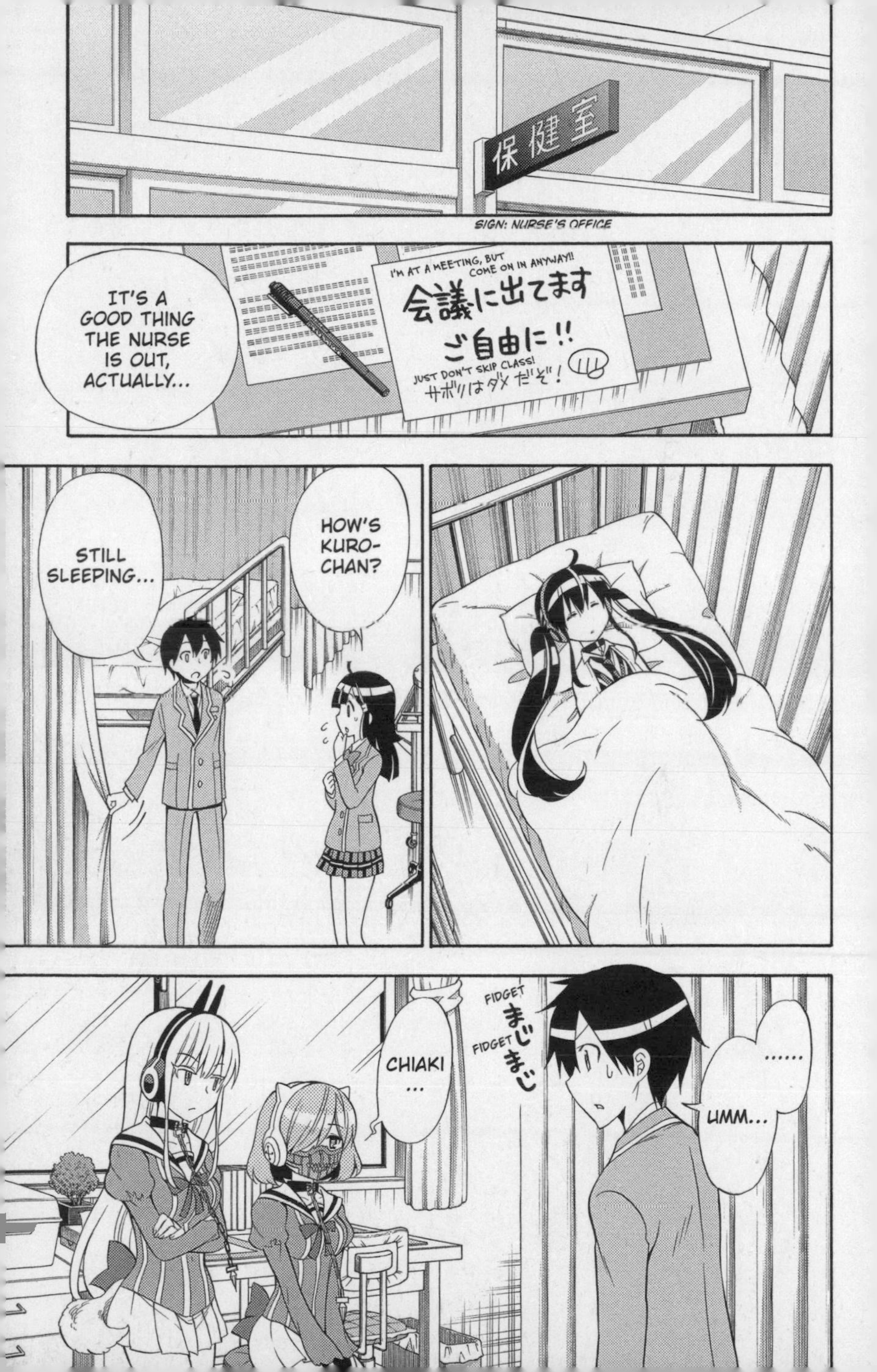
保健室
SIGN: NURSE'S OFFICE
I'M AT A MEETING, BUT COME ON IN ANYWAY!!
会議に出てます
ご自由に!!
JUST DON'T SKIP CLASS!
サボりはダメだぞ!
IT'S A GOOD THING THE NURSE IS OUT, ACTUALLY...
HOW'S KURO-CHAN?
STILL SLEEPING...
...... UMM...
FIDGET まじまじ FIDGET
CHIAKI ...

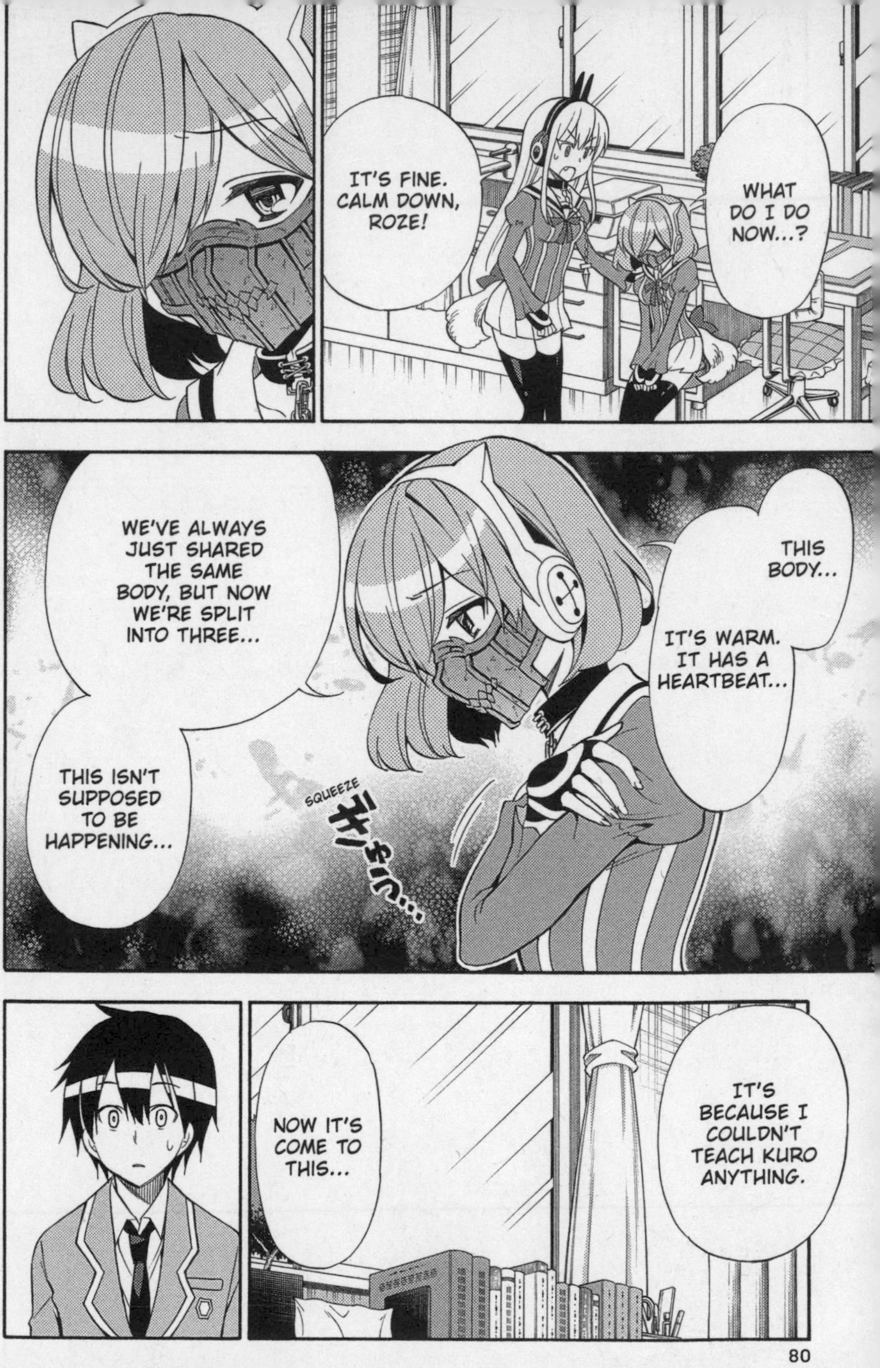
WHAT DO I DO NOW...?
IT'S FINE. CALM DOWN, ROZE!
THIS BODY...
IT'S WARM. IT HAS A HEARTBEAT...
WE'VE ALWAYS JUST SHARED THE SAME BODY, BUT NOW WE'RE SPLIT INTO THREE...
SQUEEZE
THIS ISN'T SUPPOSED TO BE HAPPENING...
IT'S BECAUSE I COULDN'T TEACH KURO ANYTHING.
NOW IT'S COME TO THIS...

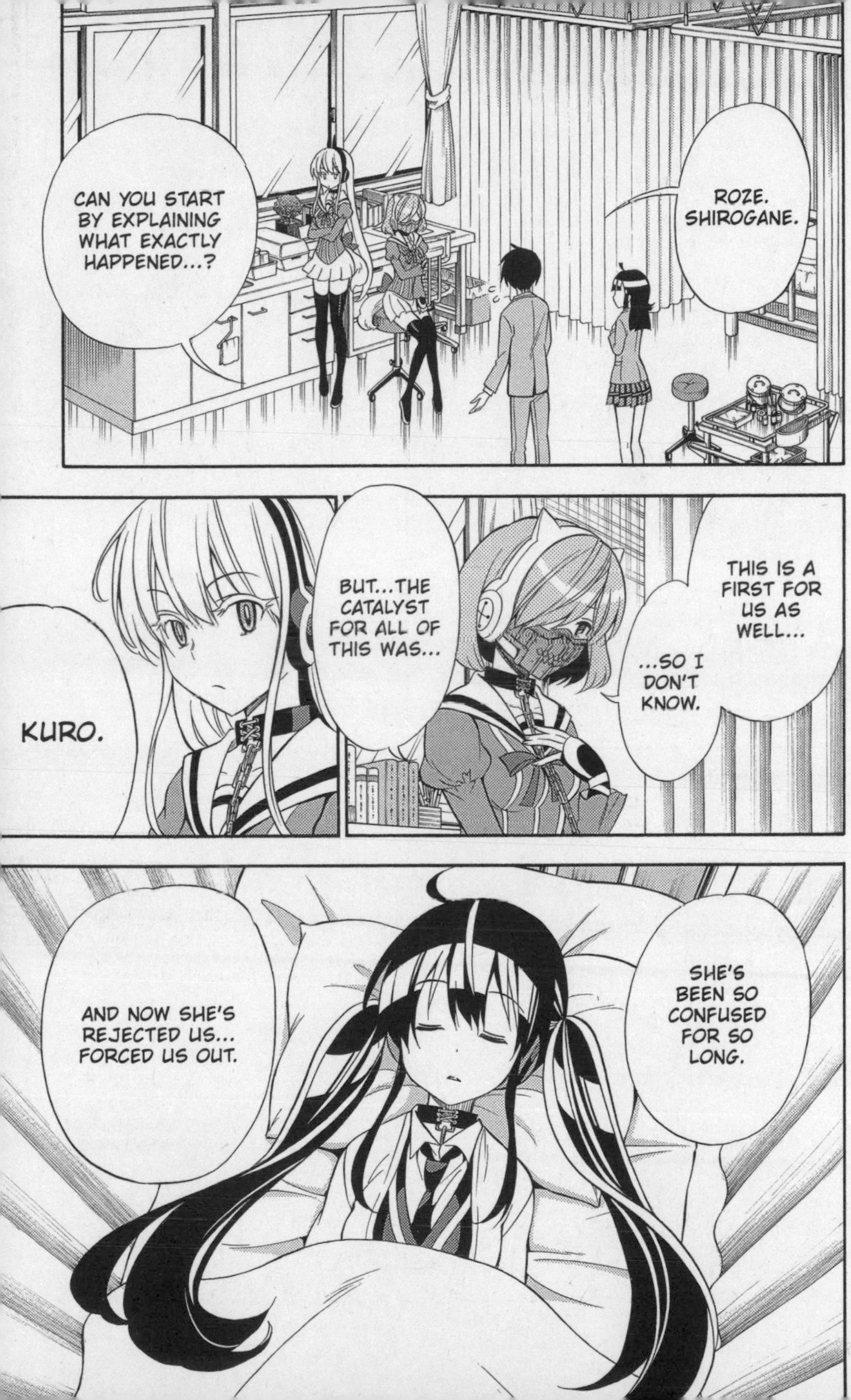
ROZE. SHIROGANE.
CAN YOU START BY EXPLAINING WHAT EXACTLY HAPPENED...?
THIS IS A FIRST FOR US AS WELL...
...SO I DON'T KNOW.
BUT...THE CATALYST FOR ALL OF THIS WAS...
KURO.
SHE'S BEEN SO CONFUSED FOR SO LONG.
AND NOW SHE'S REJECTED US... FORCED US OUT.

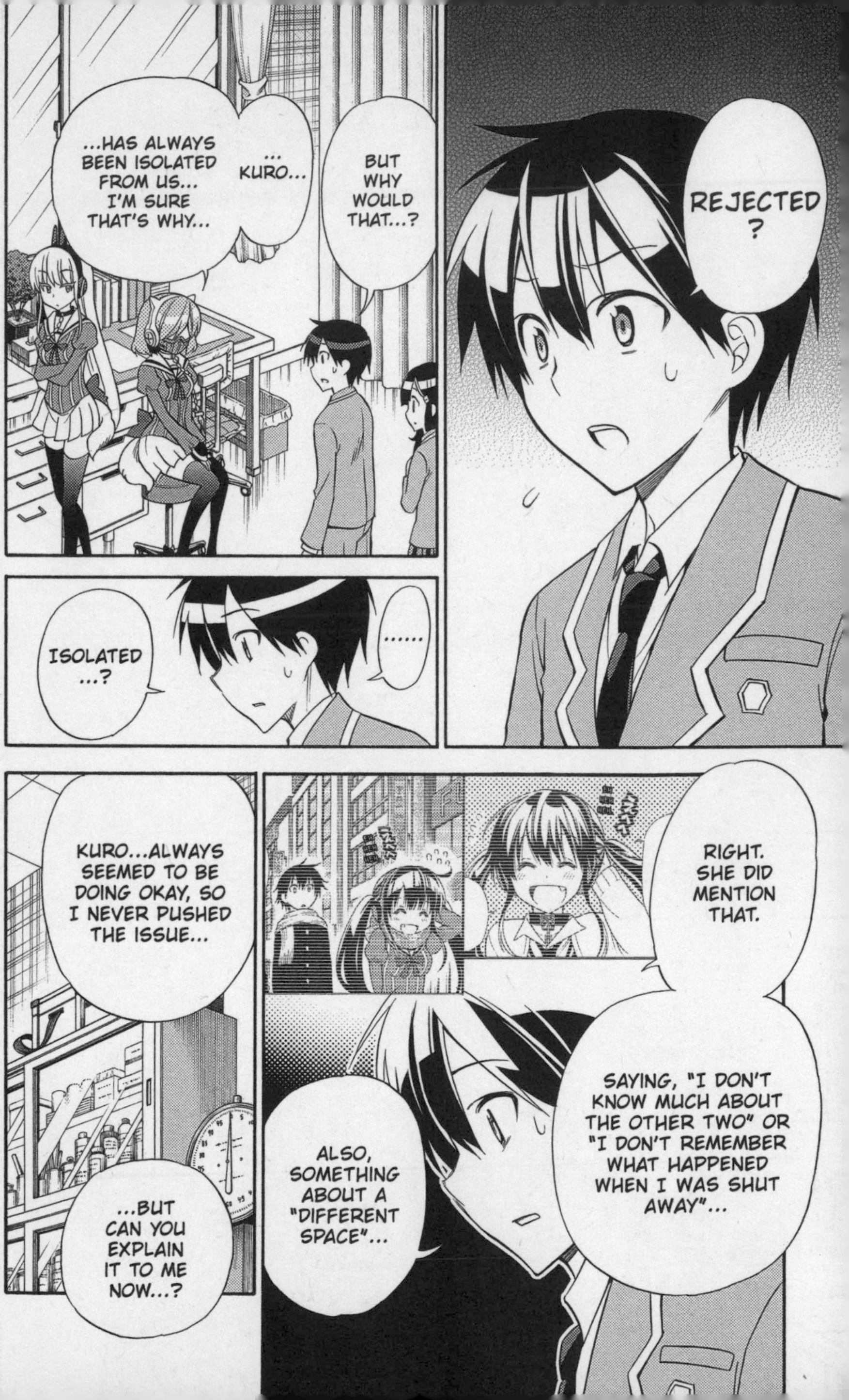
REJECTED?
BUT WHY WOULD THAT...?
... KURO...
...HAS ALWAYS BEEN ISOLATED FROM US... I'M SURE THAT'S WHY...
......
ISOLATED ...?
RIGHT. SHE DID MENTION THAT.
SAYING, "I DON'T KNOW MUCH ABOUT THE OTHER TWO" OR "I DON'T REMEMBER WHAT HAPPENED WHEN I WAS SHUT AWAY"...
ALSO, SOMETHING ABOUT A "DIFFERENT SPACE"...
KURO...ALWAYS SEEMED TO BE DOING OKAY, SO I NEVER PUSHED THE ISSUE...
...BUT CAN YOU EXPLAIN IT TO ME NOW...?

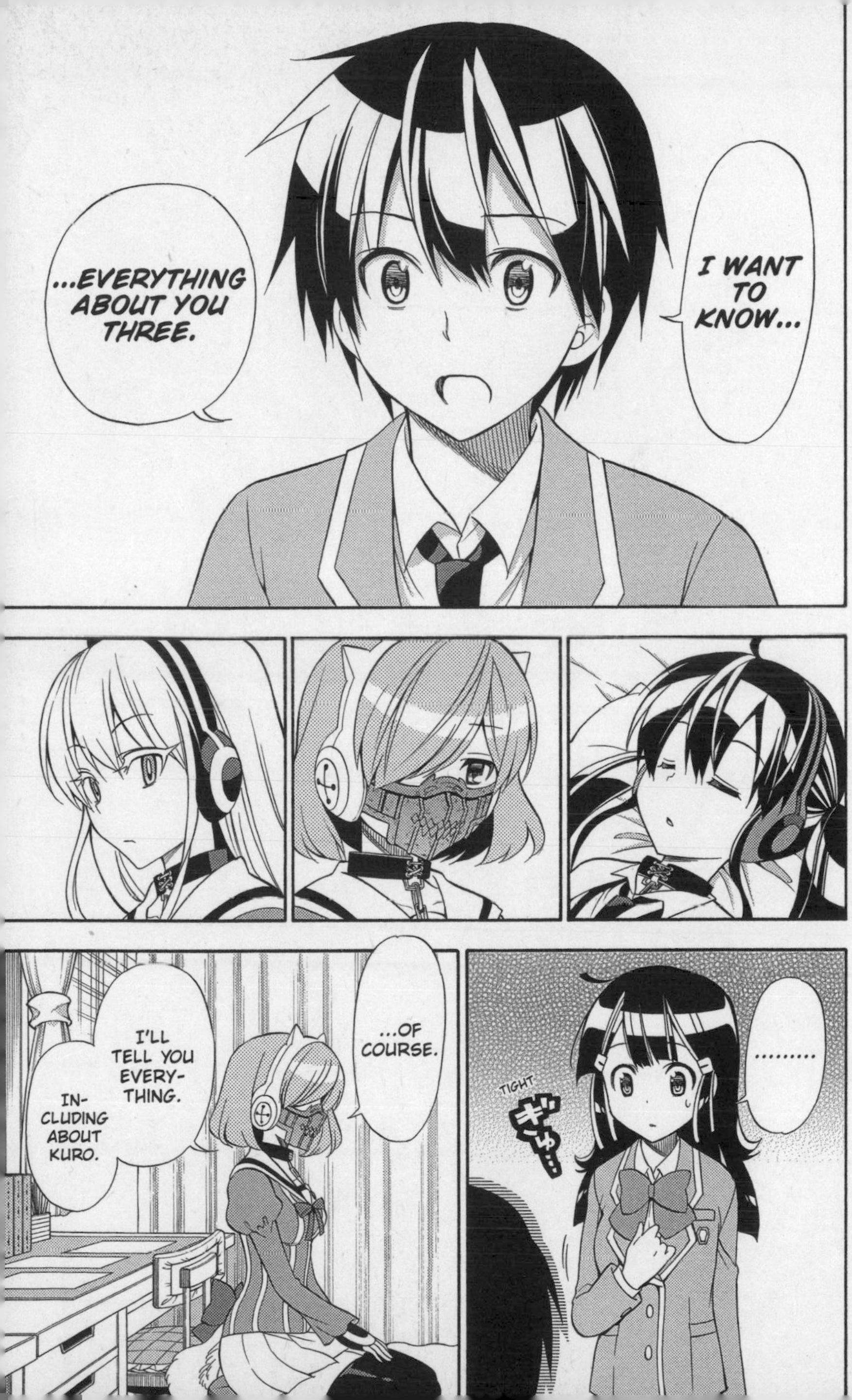
I WANT TO KNOW...
...EVERYTHING ABOUT YOU THREE.
....
TIGHT
...OF COURSE.
I'LL TELL YOU EVERY-THING.
IN-CLUDING ABOUT KURO.

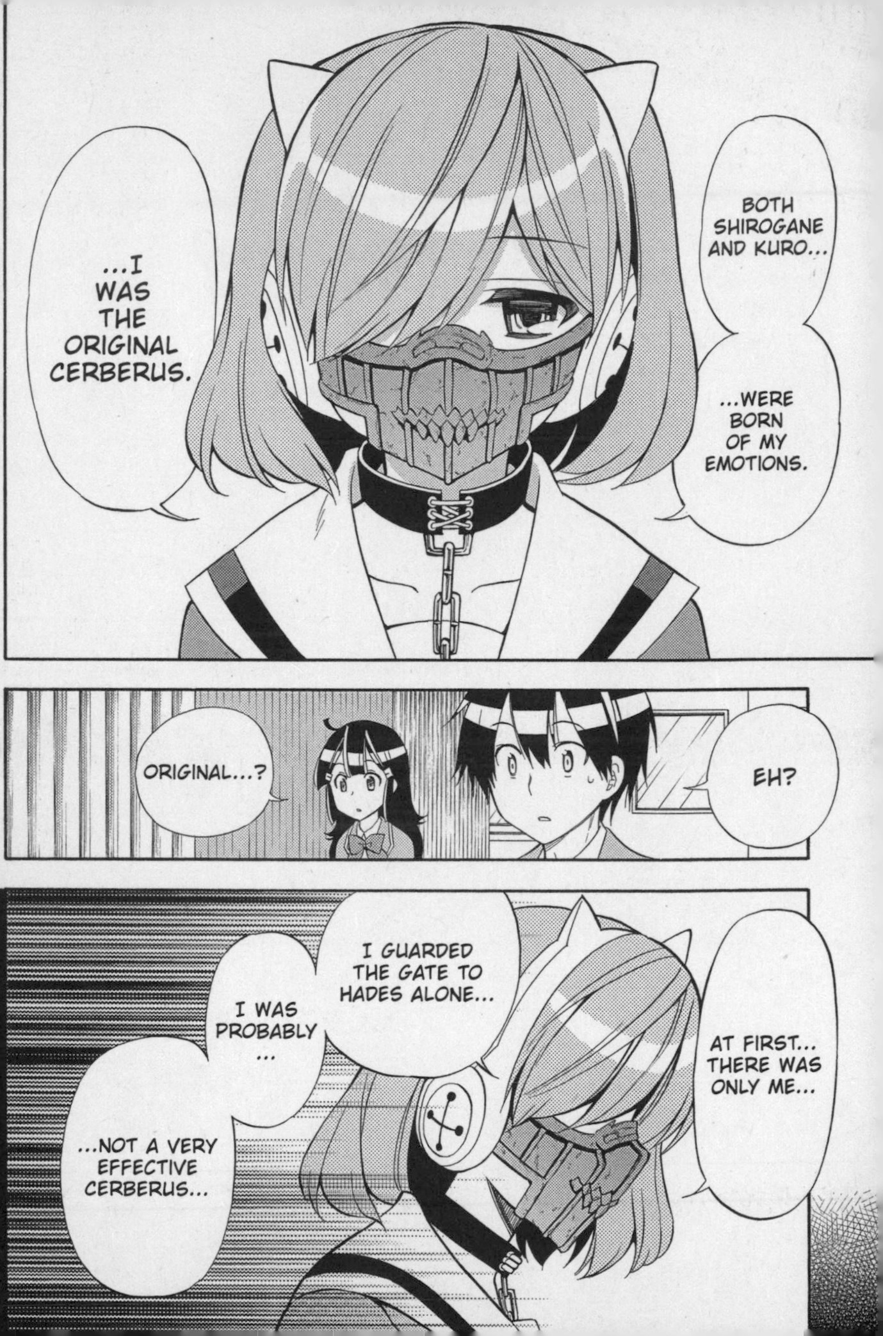
BOTH SHIROGANE AND KURO...
...WERE BORN OF MY EMOTIONS.
...I WAS THE ORIGINAL CERBERUS.
EH?
ORIGINAL...?
AT FIRST... THERE WAS ONLY ME...
I GUARDED THE GATE TO HADES ALONE...
I WAS PROBABLY ...
...NOT A VERY EFFECTIVE CERBERUS...

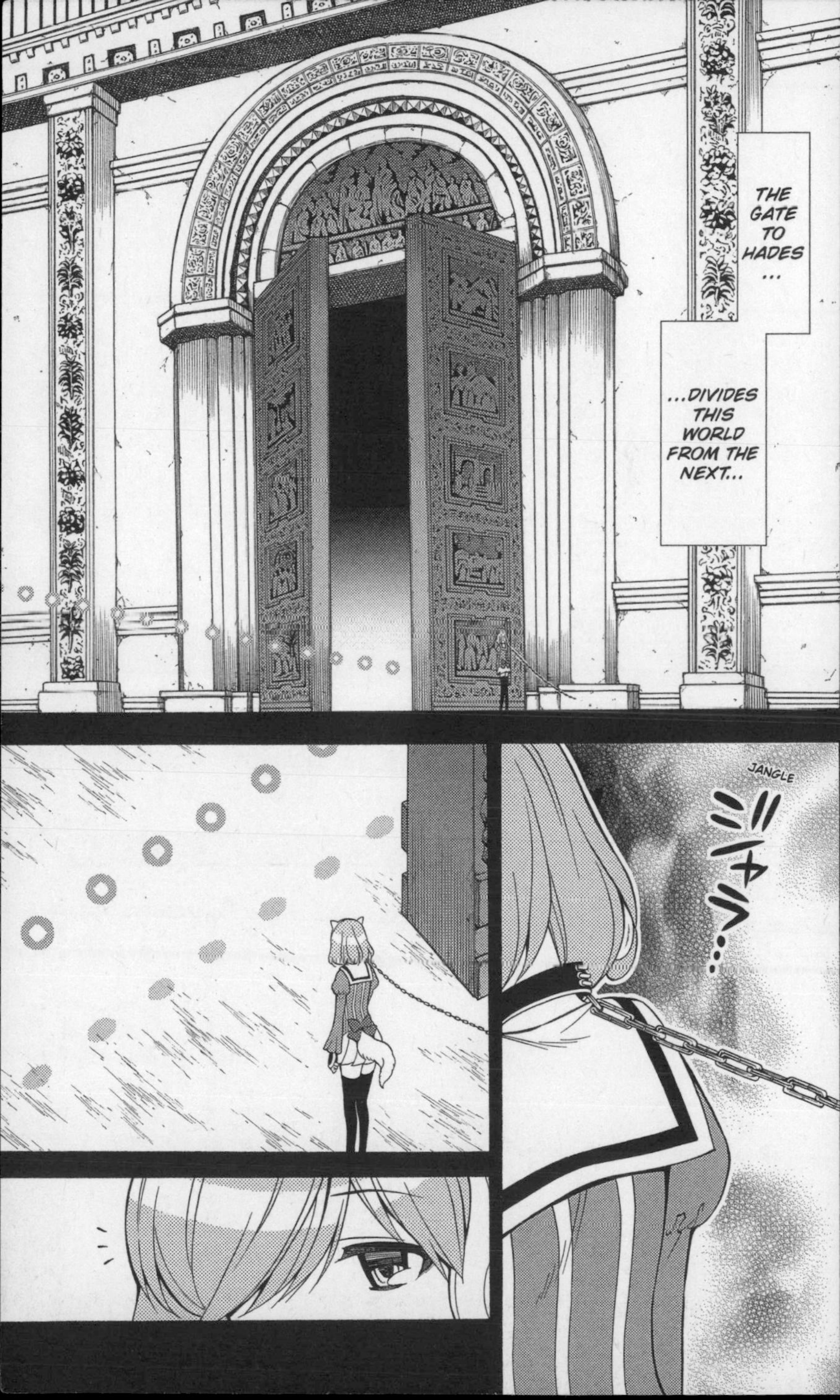
THE GATE TO HADES ...
...DIVIDES THIS WORLD FROM THE NEXT...
JANGLE
ジャラ…

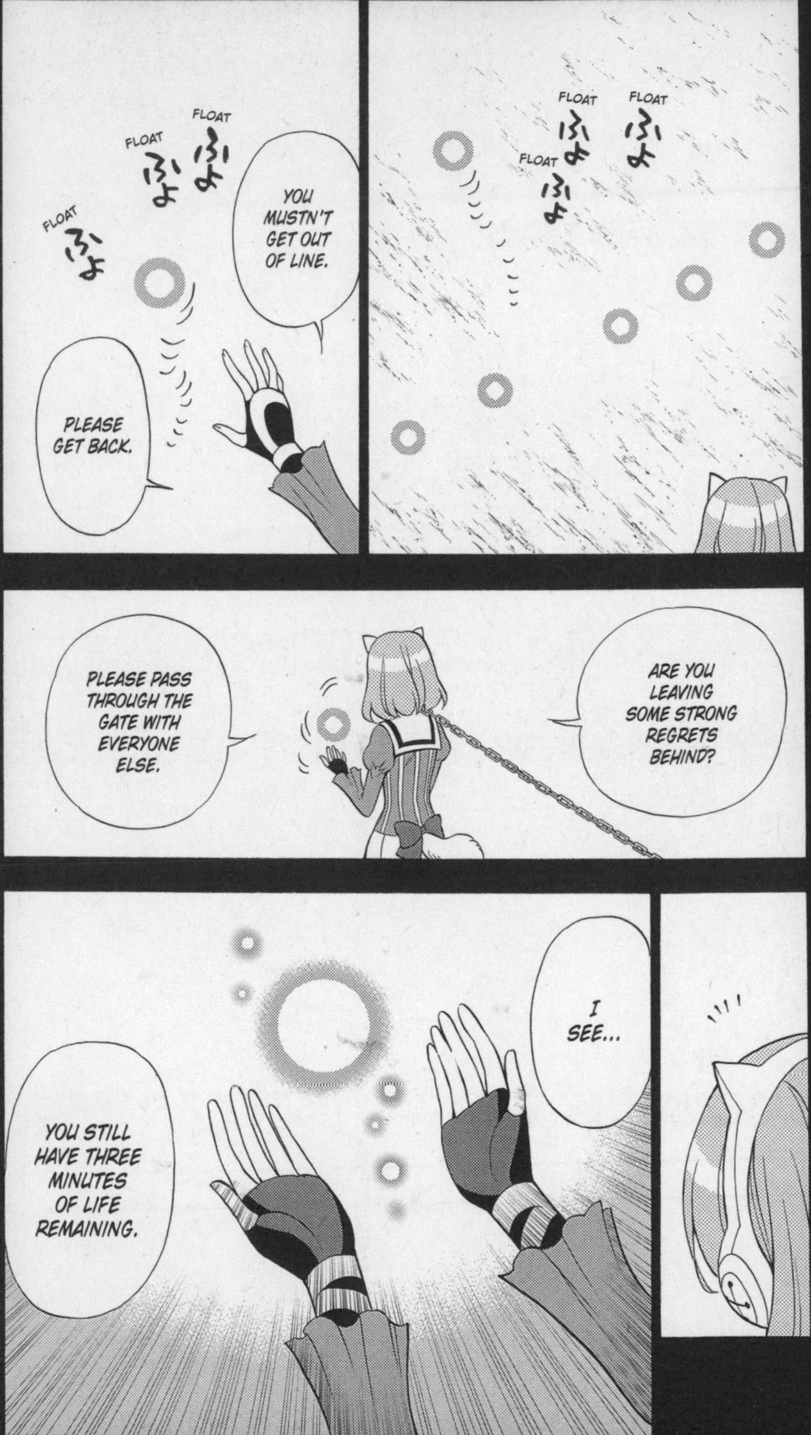
FLOAT ふよ
FLOAT ふよ
FLOAT ふよ
YOU MUSTN'T GET OUT OF LINE.
FLOAT ふよ
FLOAT ふよ
FLOAT ふよ
PLEASE GET BACK.
ARE YOU LEAVING SOME STRONG REGRETS BEHIND?
PLEASE PASS THROUGH THE GATE WITH EVERYONE ELSE.
I SEE...
YOU STILL HAVE THREE MINUTES OF LIFE REMAINING.

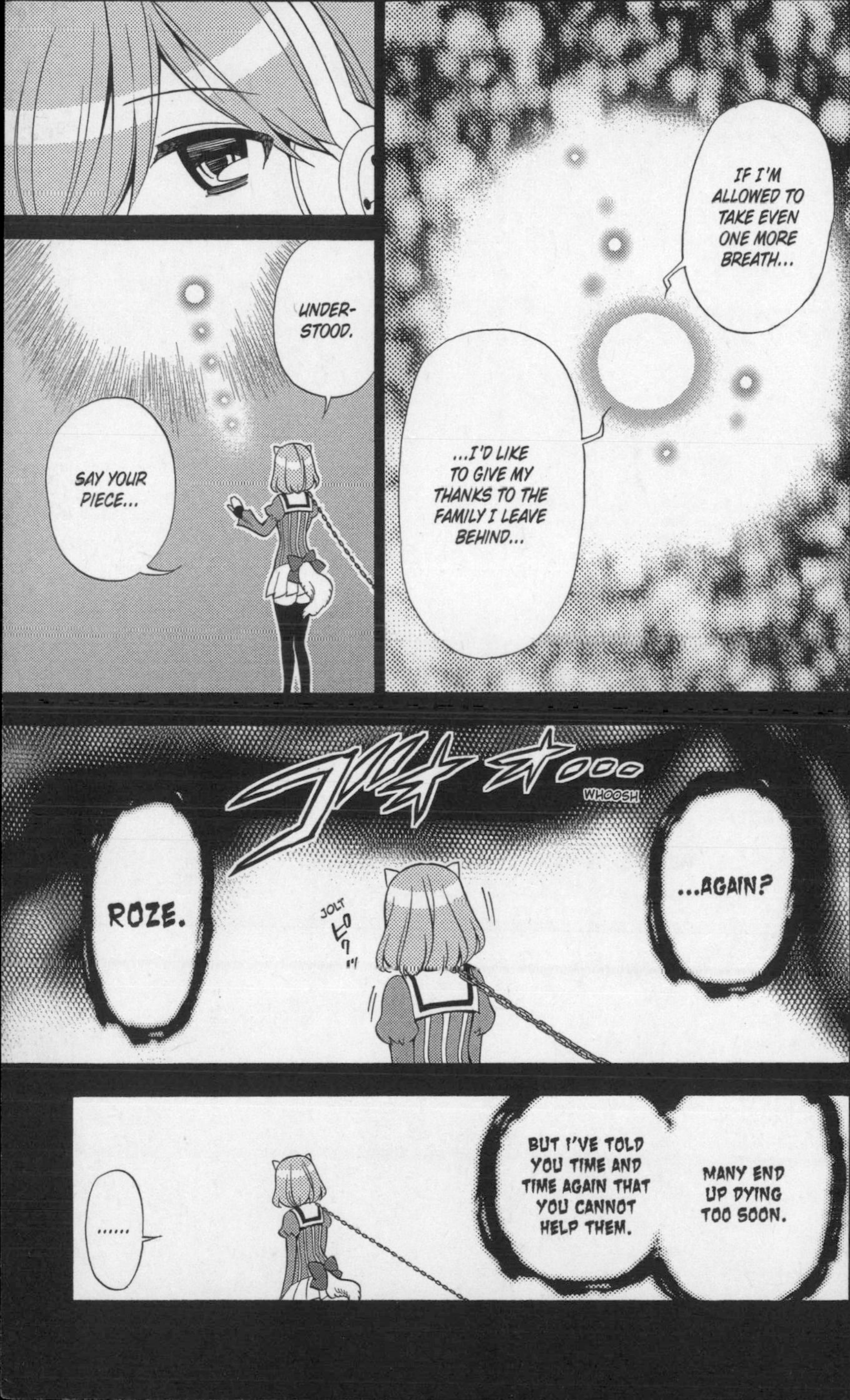
IF I'M ALLOWED TO TAKE EVEN ONE MORE BREATH...
...I'D LIKE TO GIVE MY THANKS TO THE FAMILY I LEAVE BEHIND...
UNDER-STOOD.
SAY YOUR PIECE...
WHOOSH
...AGAIN?
ROZE.
JOLT
MANY END UP DYING TOO SOON.
BUT I'VE TOLD YOU TIME AND TIME AGAIN THAT YOU CANNOT HELP THEM.
......

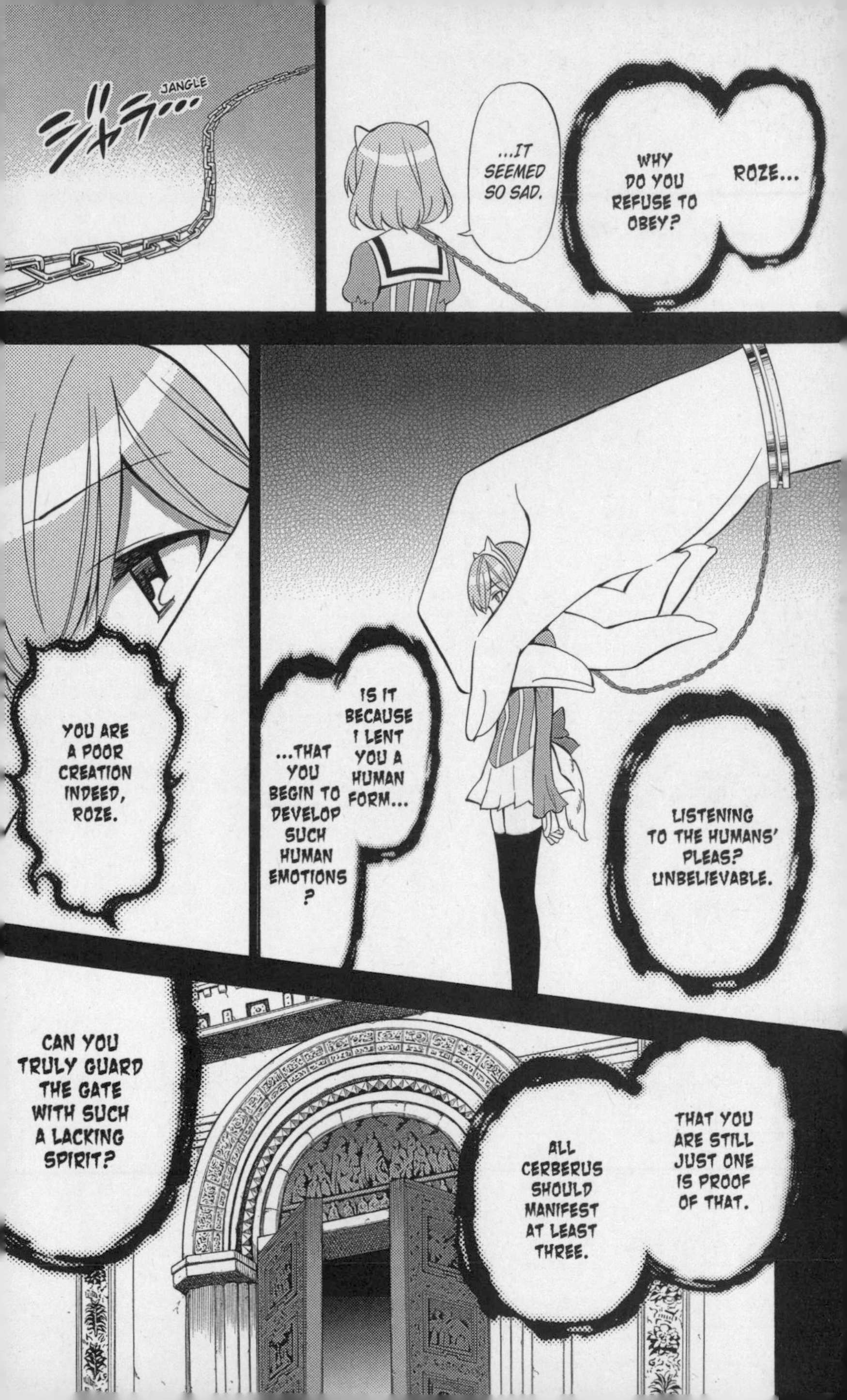
ROZE...
WHY DO YOU REFUSE TO OBEY?
...IT SEEMED SO SAD.
ジャラ...
JANGLE
LISTENING TO THE HUMANS' PLEAS? UNBELIEVABLE.
IS IT BECAUSE I LENT YOU A HUMAN FORM...
...THAT YOU BEGIN TO DEVELOP SUCH HUMAN EMOTIONS?
YOU ARE A POOR CREATION INDEED, ROZE.
ALL CERBERUS SHOULD MANIFEST AT LEAST THREE.
THAT YOU ARE STILL JUST ONE IS PROOF OF THAT.
CAN YOU TRULY GUARD THE GATE WITH SUCH A LACKING SPIRIT?

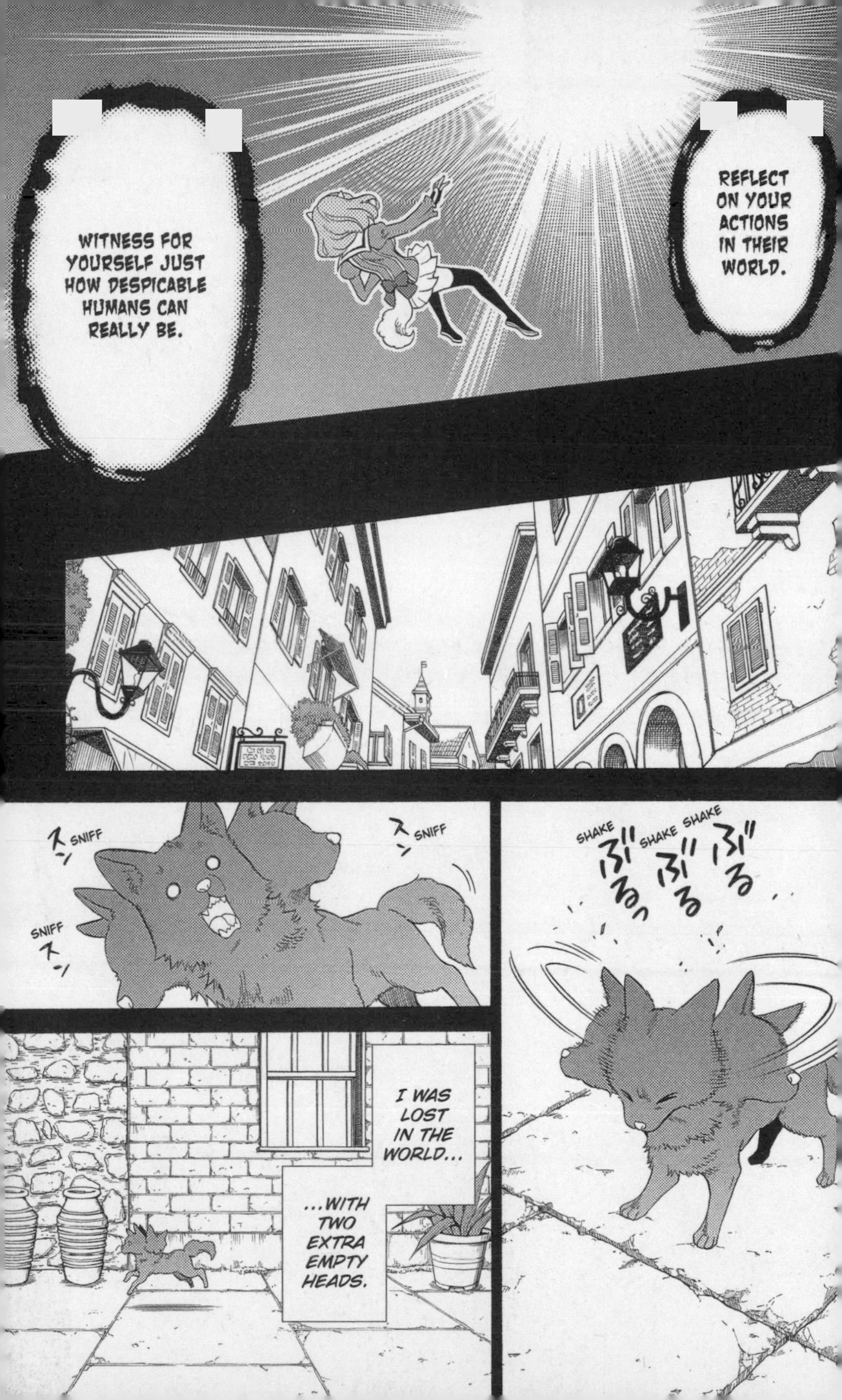
REFLECT ON YOUR ACTIONS IN THEIR WORLD.
WITNESS FOR YOURSELF JUST HOW DESPICABLE HUMANS CAN REALLY BE.
SHAKE SHAKE SHAKE
ぶる ぶる ぶるっ
SNIFF
SNIFF
SNIFF
I WAS LOST IN THE WORLD...
...WITH TWO EXTRA EMPTY HEADS.

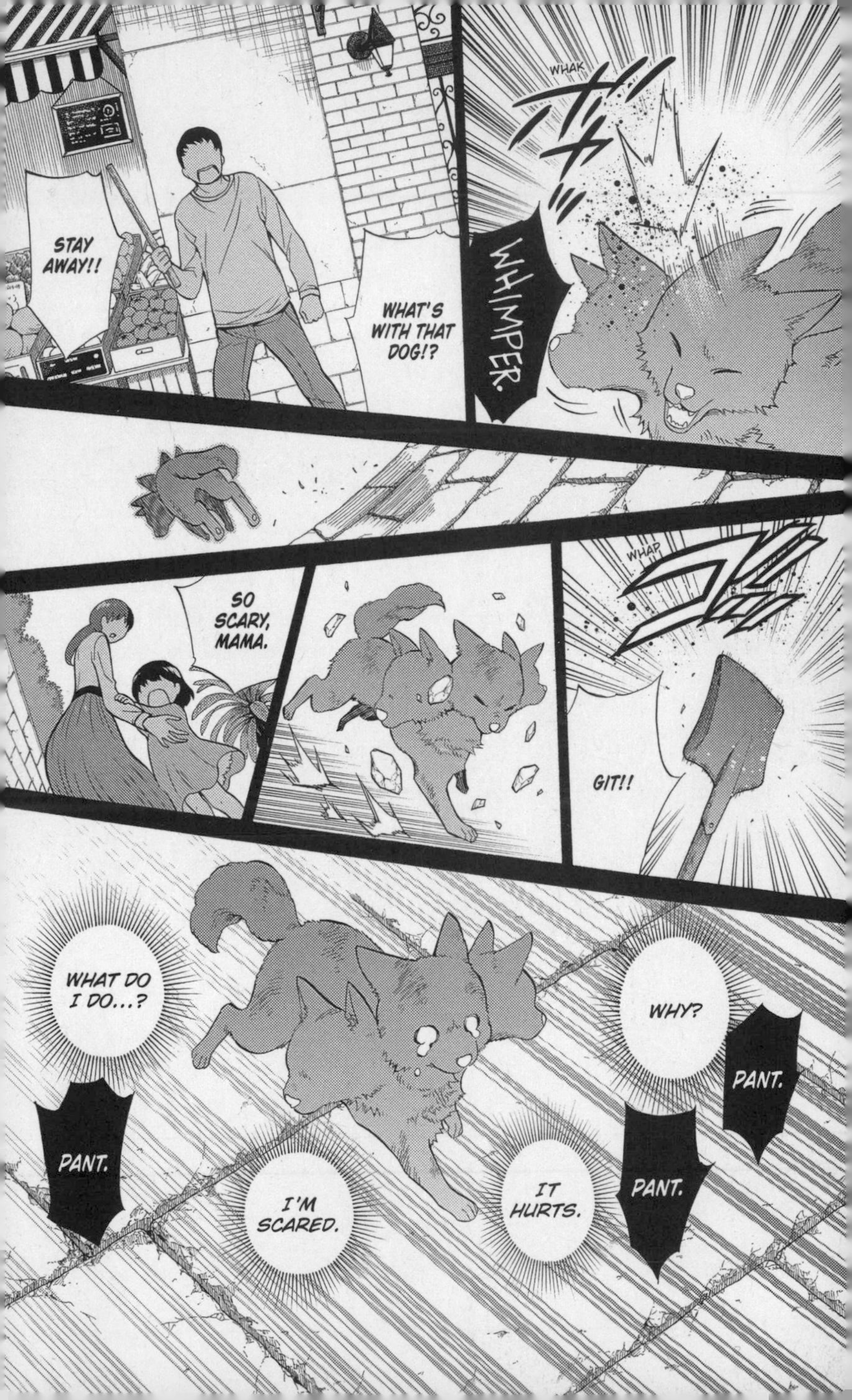
WHAK
WHIMPER.
WHAT'S WITH THAT DOG!?
STAY AWAY!!
WHAP
GIT!!
SO SCARY, MAMA.
WHY?
PANT.
PANT.
IT HURTS.
I'M SCARED.
WHAT DO I DO...?
PANT.

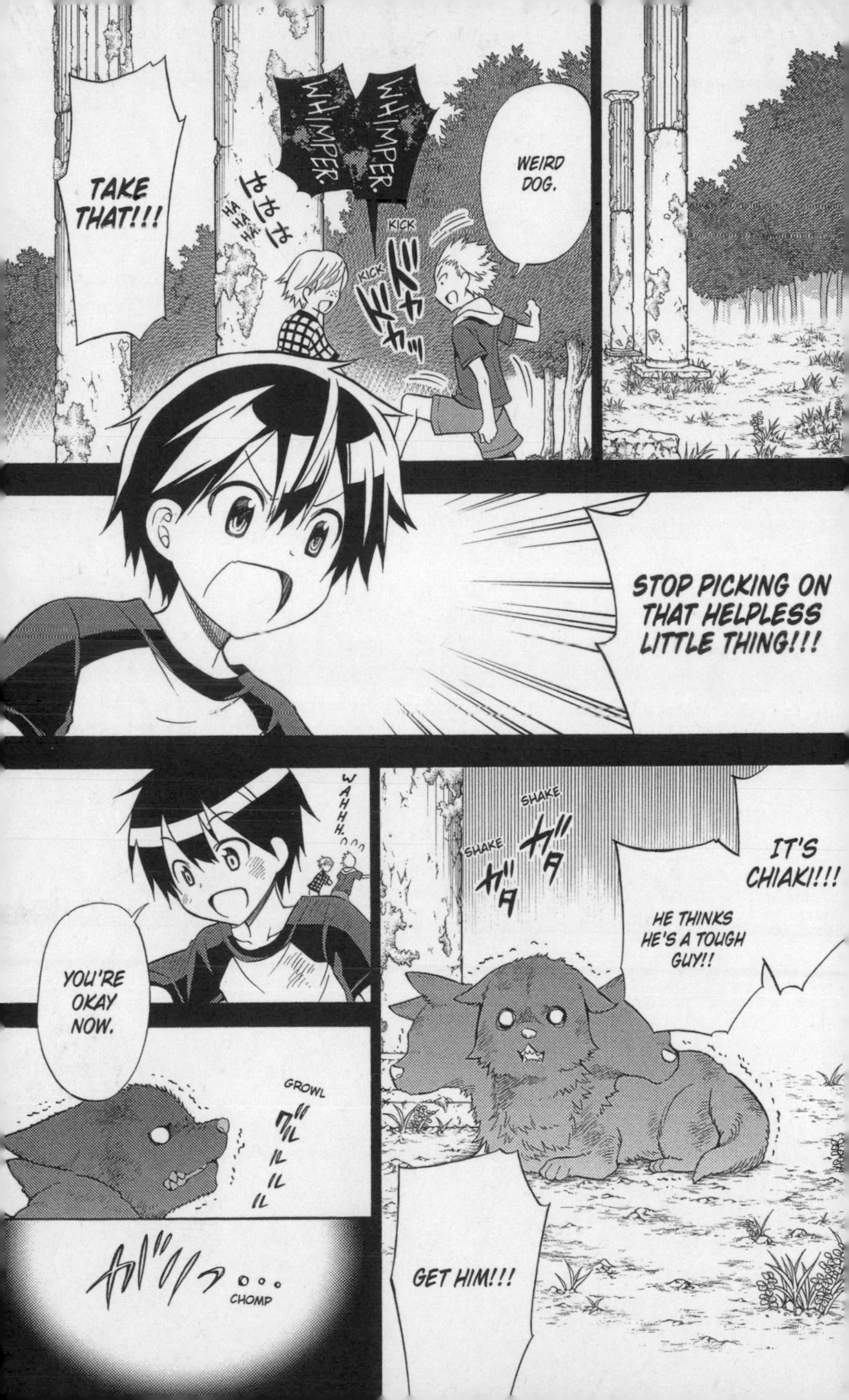
WEIRD DOG.
WHIMPER. WHIMPER.
KICK KICK
HA HA HA
TAKE THAT!!!
STOP PICKING ON THAT HELPLESS LITTLE THING!!!
IT'S CHIAKI!!!
HE THINKS HE'S A TOUGH GUY!!
SHAKE SHAKE
GET HIM!!!
WAHHH...
YOU'RE OKAY NOW.
GROWL
CHOMP

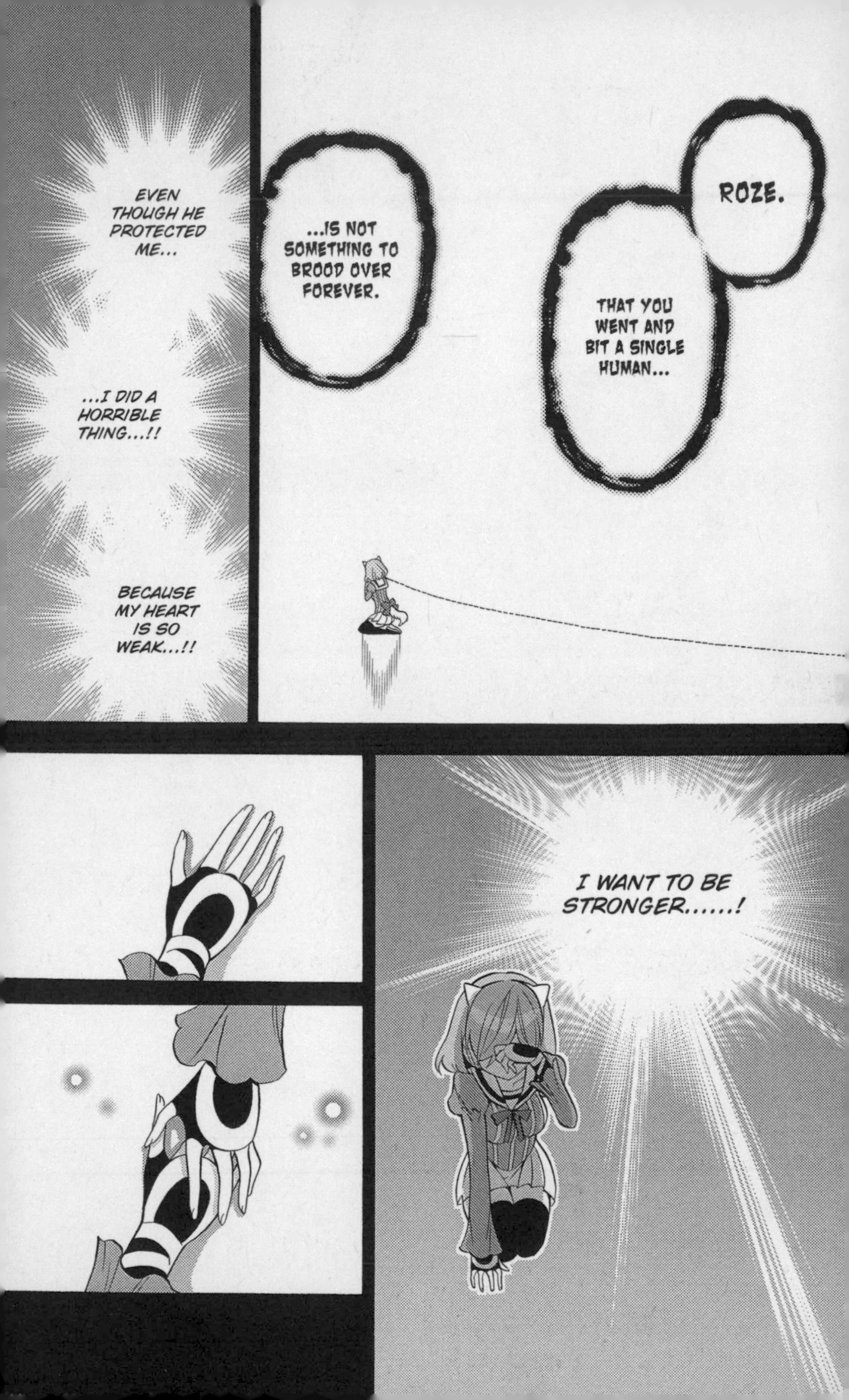
ROZE.
THAT YOU WENT AND BIT A SINGLE HUMAN...
...IS NOT SOMETHING TO BROOD OVER FOREVER.
EVEN THOUGH HE PROTECTED ME...
...I DID A HORRIBLE THING...!!
BECAUSE MY HEART IS SO WEAK...!!
I WANT TO BE STRONGER......!

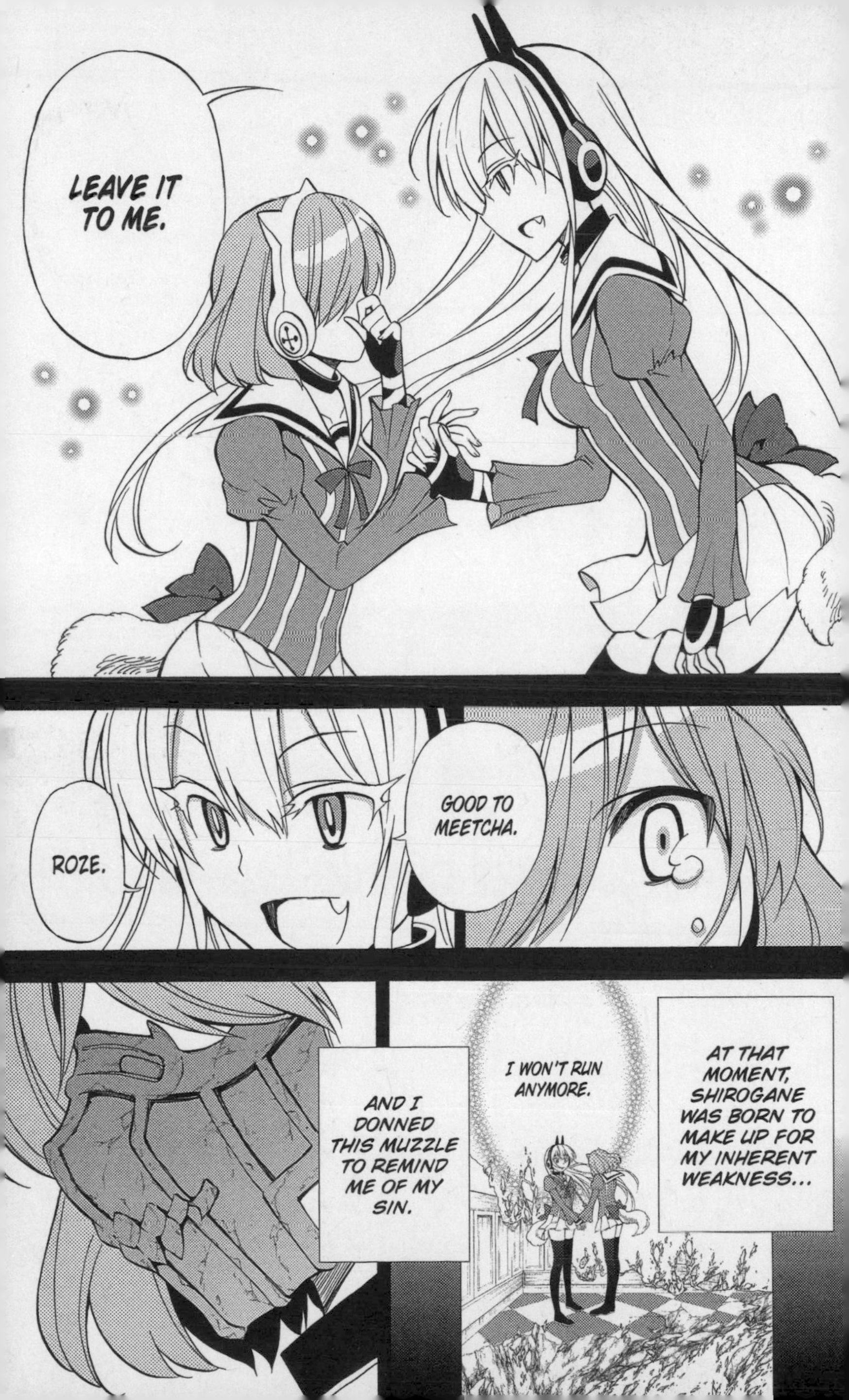
LEAVE IT TO ME.
GOOD TO MEETCHA.
ROZE.
AT THAT MOMENT, SHIROGANE WAS BORN TO MAKE UP FOR MY INHERENT WEAKNESS...
I WON'T RUN ANYMORE.
AND I DONNED THIS MUZZLE TO REMIND ME OF MY SIN.

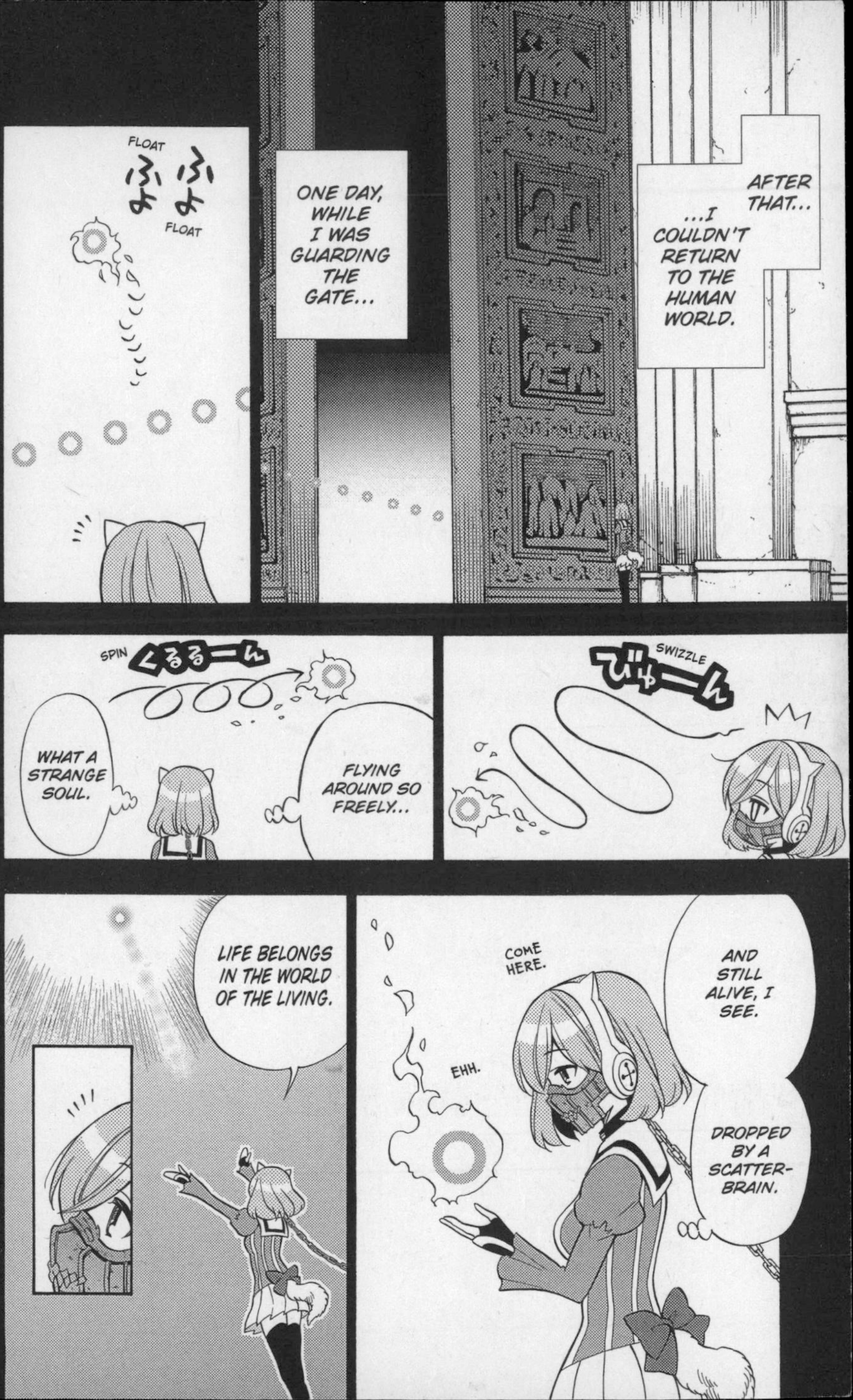
AFTER THAT...
...I COULDN'T RETURN TO THE HUMAN WORLD.
ONE DAY, WHILE I WAS GUARDING THE GATE...
FLOAT
ふよ
ふよ
FLOAT
SWIZZLE
びゅーん
SPIN
くるるーん
FLYING AROUND SO FREELY...
WHAT A STRANGE SOUL.
AND STILL ALIVE, I SEE.
DROPPED BY A SCATTER-BRAIN.
COME HERE.
EHH.
LIFE BELONGS IN THE WORLD OF THE LIVING.

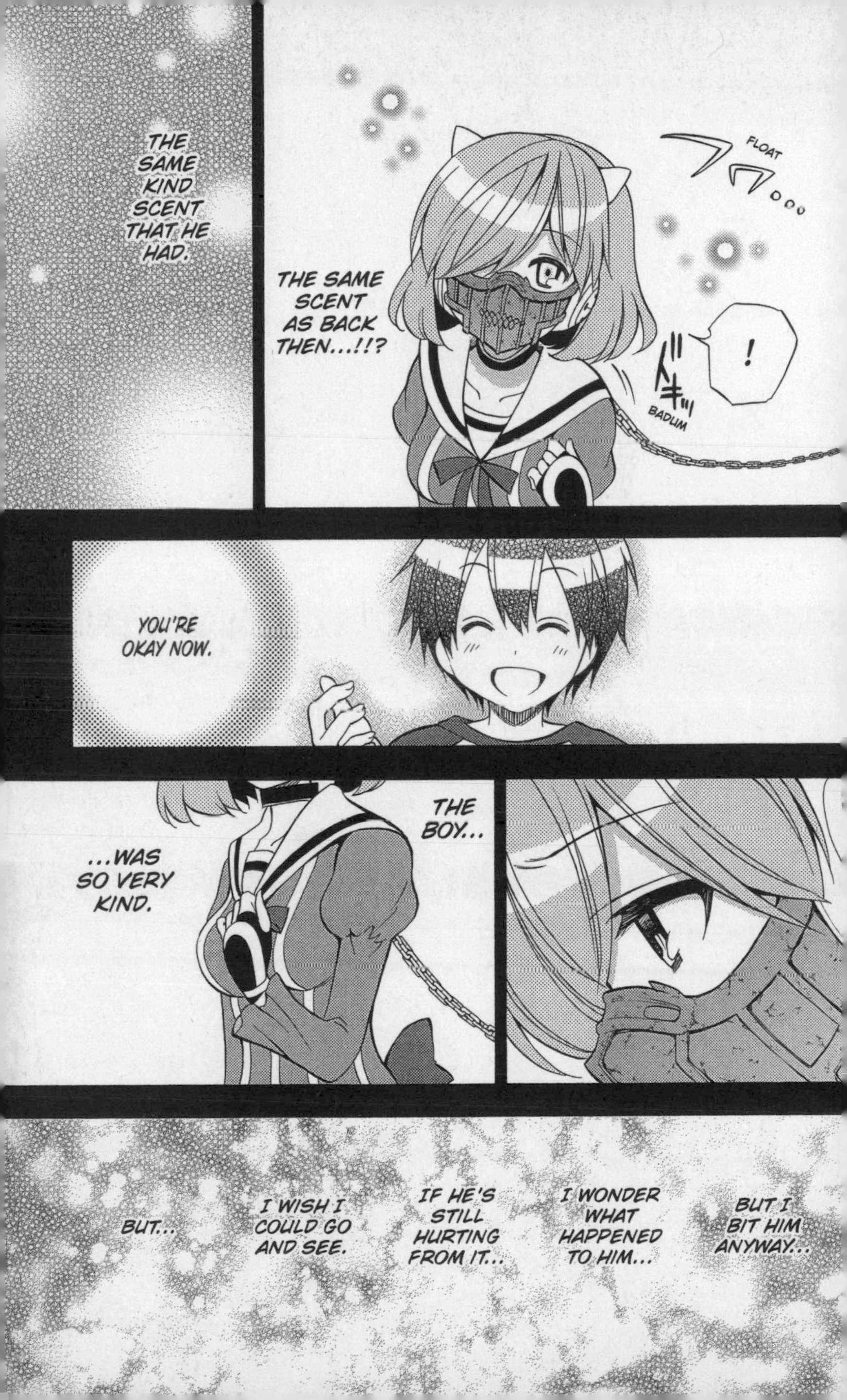
FLOAT
!
BADUM
THE SAME SCENT AS BACK THEN...!!?
THE SAME KIND SCENT THAT HE HAD.
YOU'RE OKAY NOW.
THE BOY...
...WAS SO VERY KIND.
BUT I BIT HIM ANYWAY...
I WONDER WHAT HAPPENED TO HIM...
IF HE'S STILL HURTING FROM IT...
I WISH I COULD GO AND SEE.
BUT...

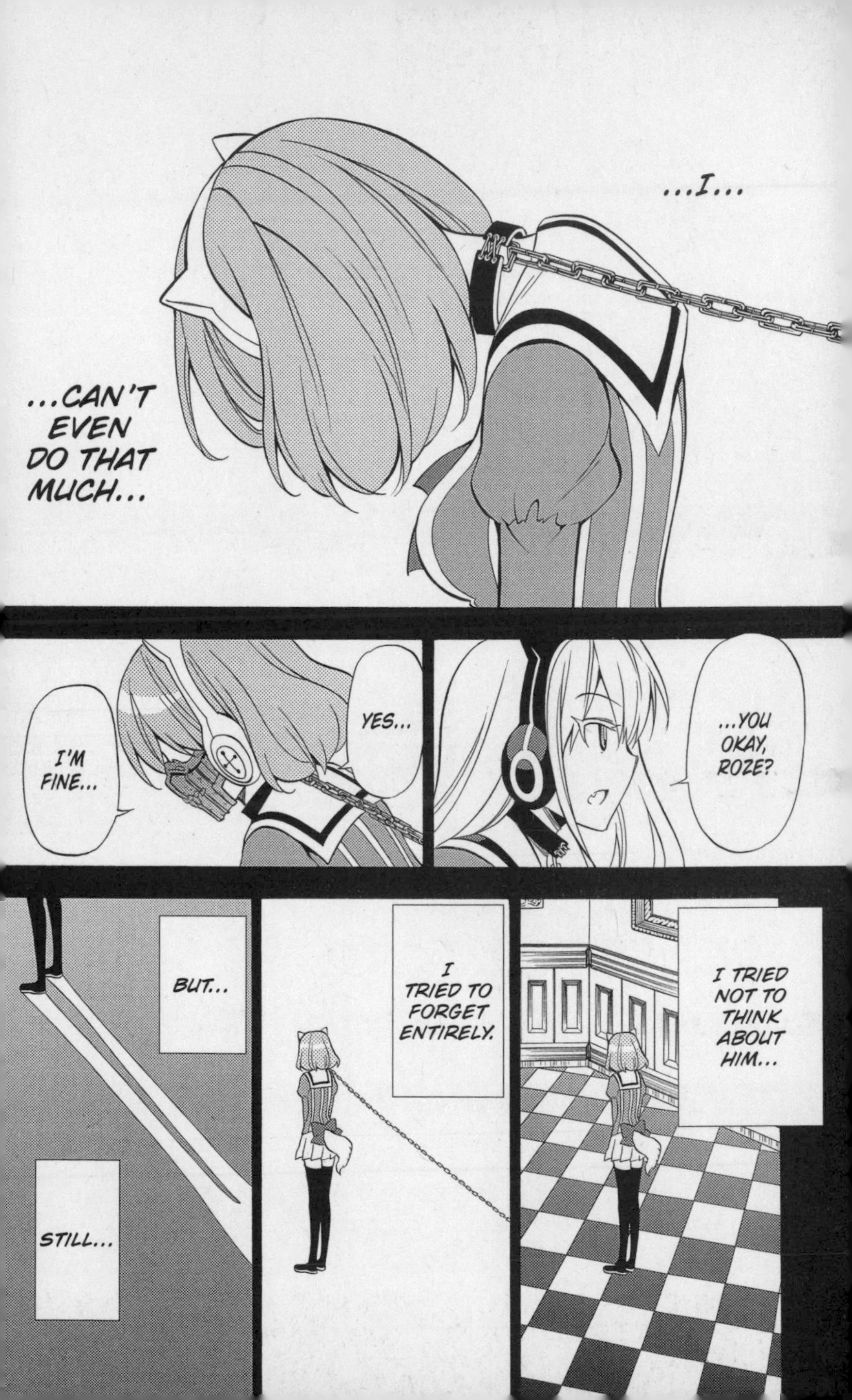
...I...
...CAN'T EVEN DO THAT MUCH...
...YOU OKAY, ROZE?
YES...
I'M FINE...
I TRIED NOT TO THINK ABOUT HIM...
I TRIED TO FORGET ENTIRELY.
BUT...
STILL...

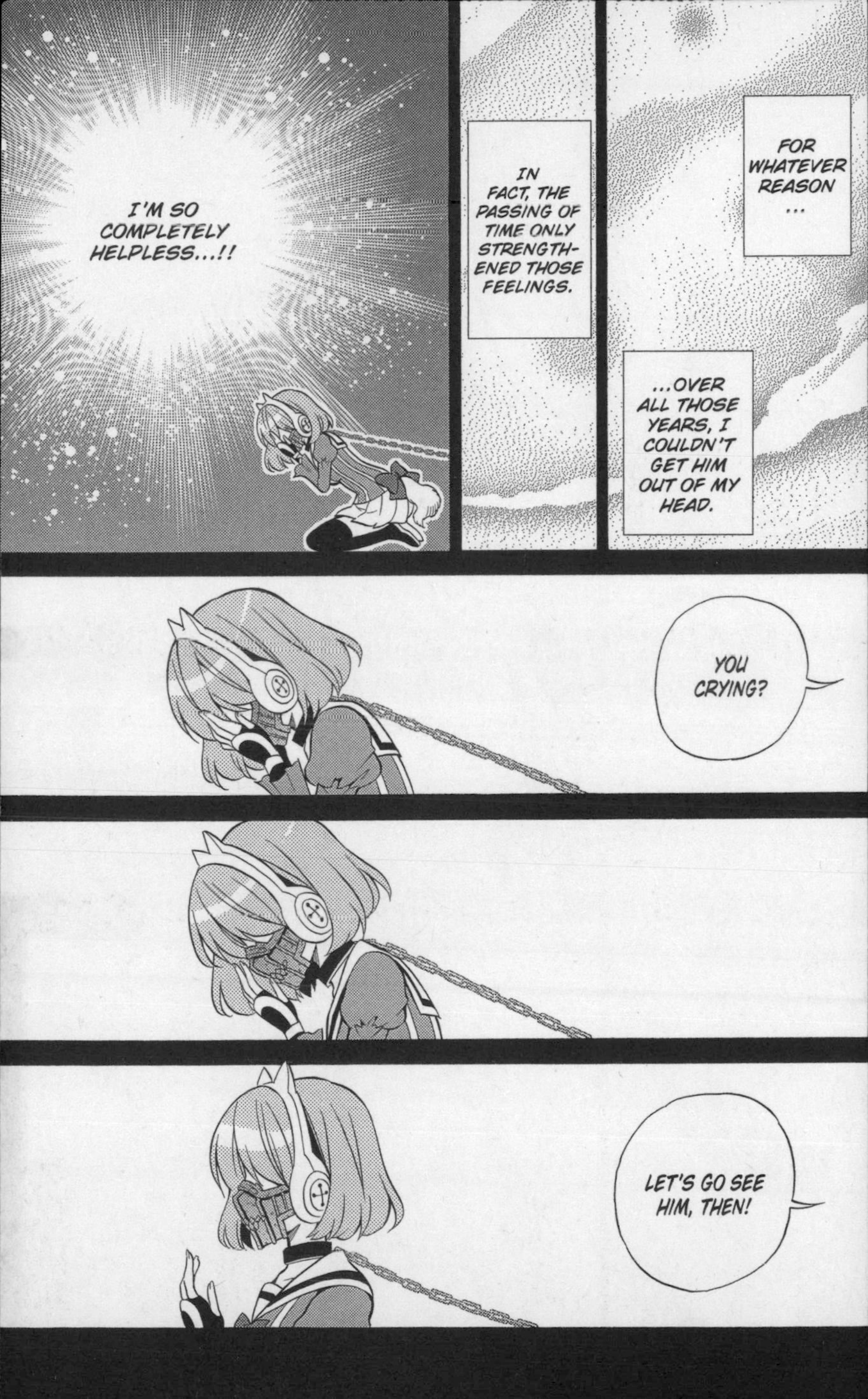
FOR WHATEVER REASON ...
...OVER ALL THOSE YEARS, I COULDN'T GET HIM OUT OF MY HEAD.
IN FACT, THE PASSING OF TIME ONLY STRENGTH-ENED THOSE FEELINGS.
I'M SO COMPLETELY HELPLESS...!!
YOU CRYING?
LET'S GO SEE HIM, THEN!

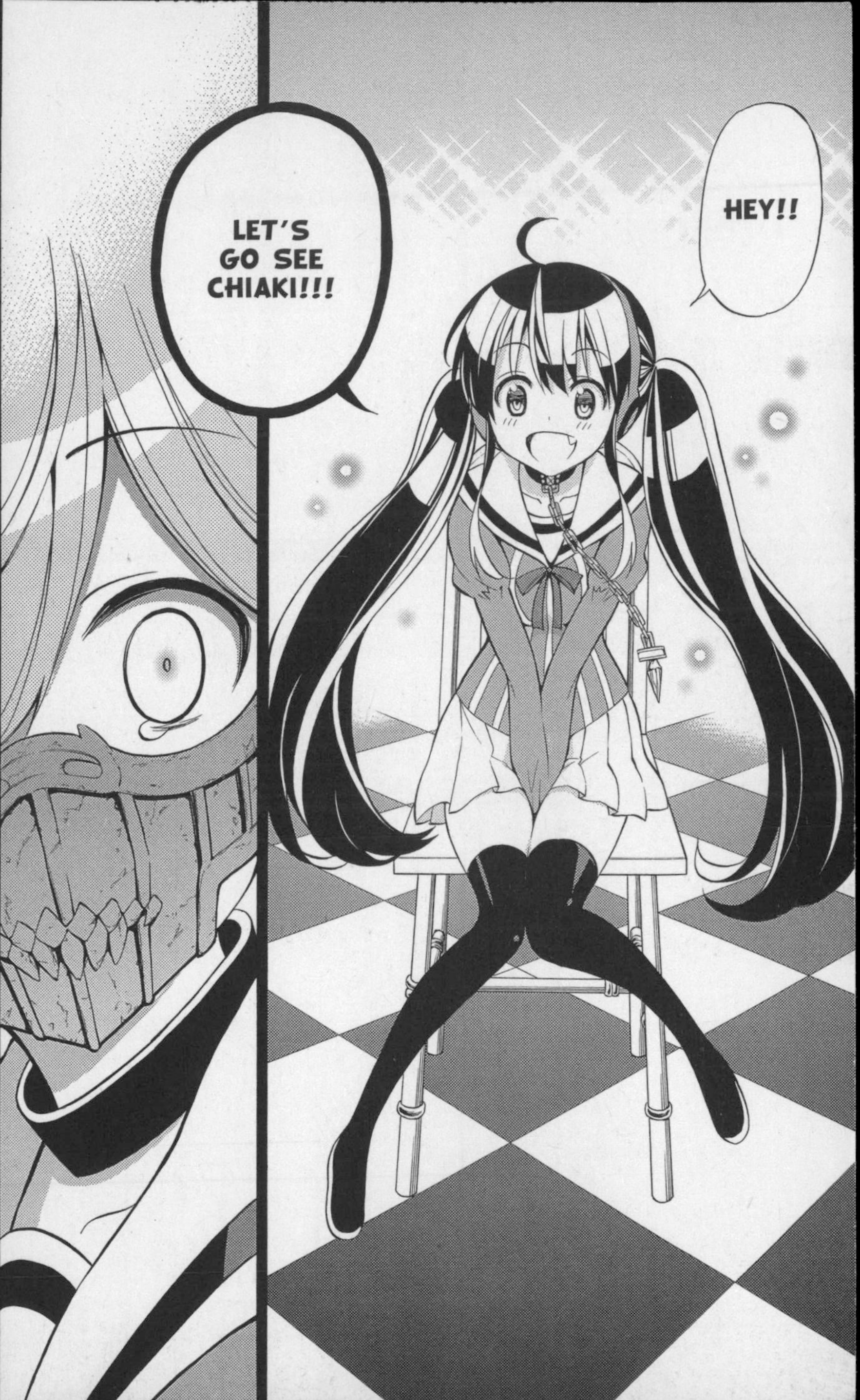
HEY!!
LET'S GO SEE CHIAKI!!!

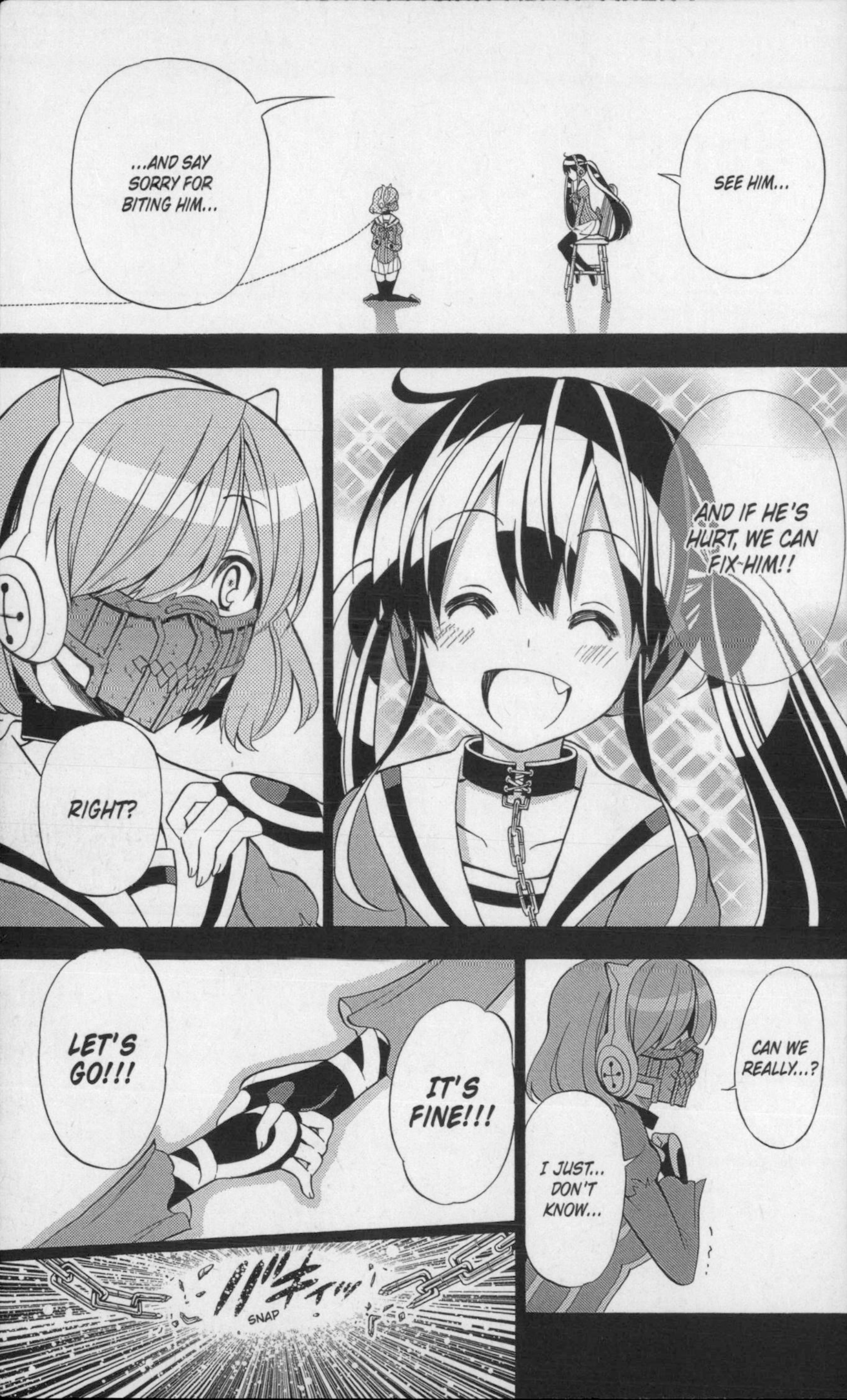
SEE HIM...
...AND SAY SORRY FOR BITING HIM...
AND IF HE'S HURT, WE CAN FIX HIM!!
RIGHT?
CAN WE REALLY...?
I JUST... DON'T KNOW...
IT'S FINE!!!
LET'S GO!!!
SNAP

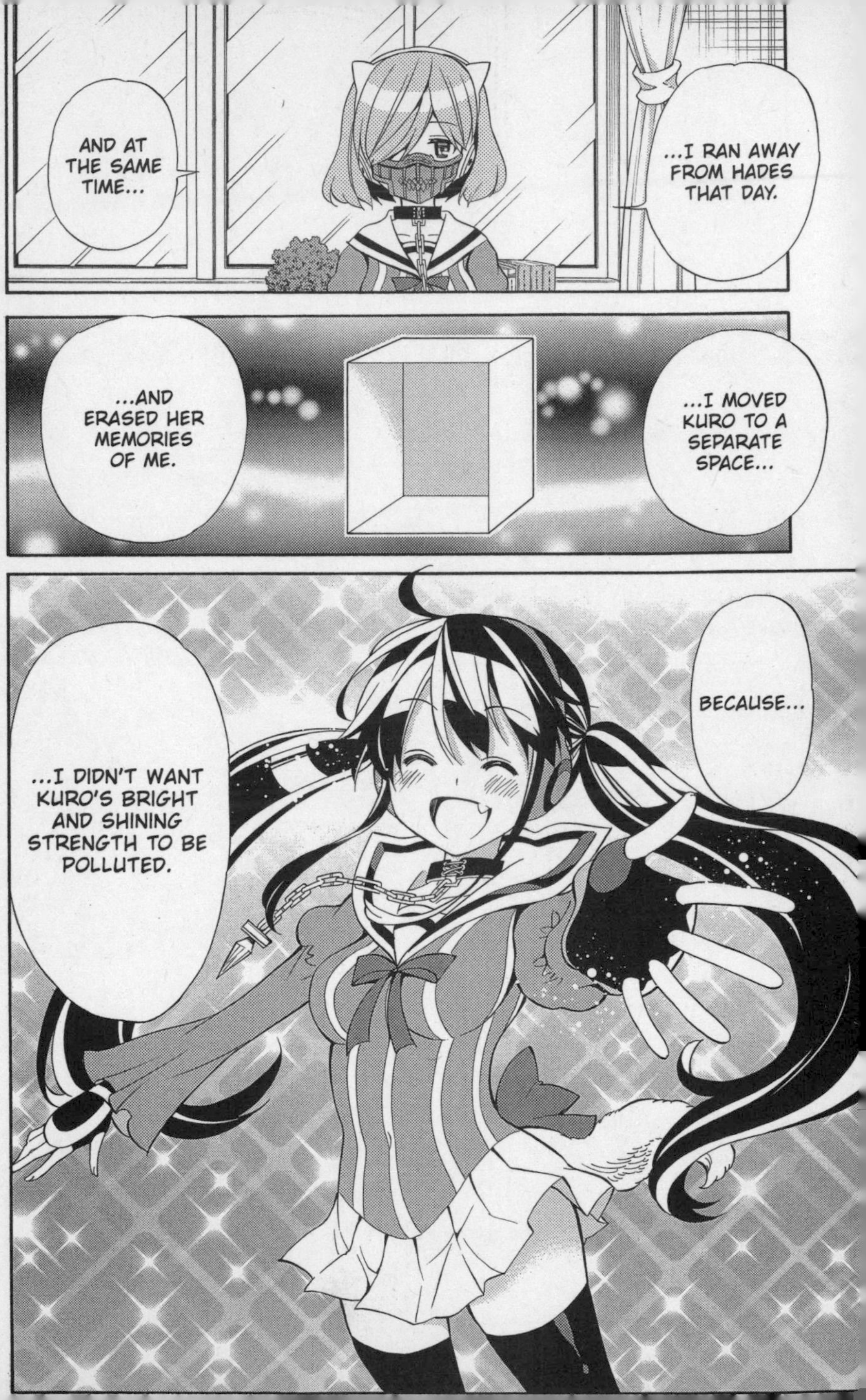
...I RAN AWAY FROM HADES THAT DAY.
AND AT THE SAME TIME...
...I MOVED KURO TO A SEPARATE SPACE...
...AND ERASED HER MEMORIES OF ME.
BECAUSE...
...I DIDN'T WANT KURO'S BRIGHT AND SHINING STRENGTH TO BE POLLUTED.

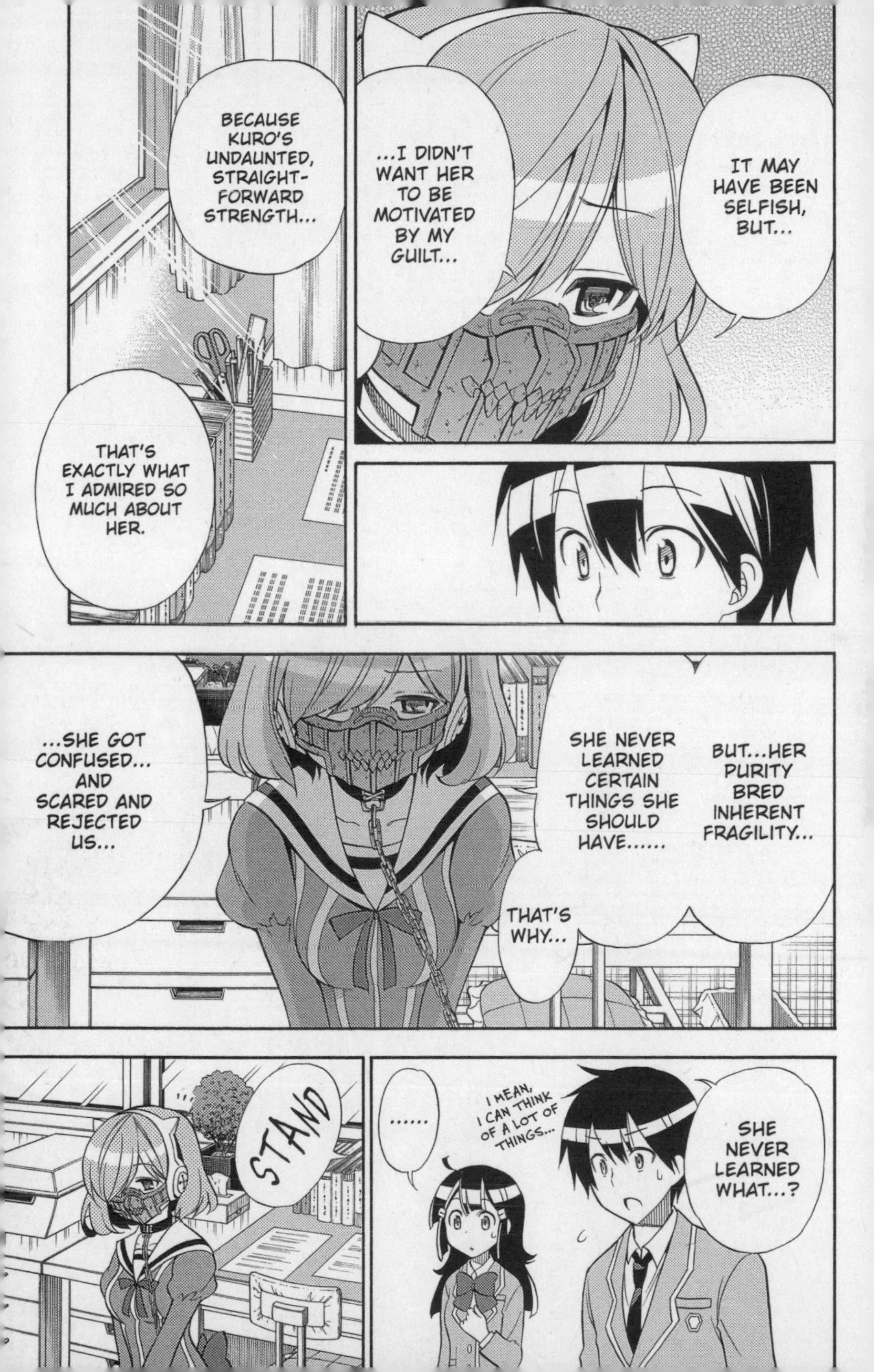
IT MAY HAVE BEEN SELFISH, BUT...
...I DIDN'T WANT HER TO BE MOTIVATED BY MY GUILT...
BECAUSE KURO'S UNDAUNTED, STRAIGHT-FORWARD STRENGTH...
THAT'S EXACTLY WHAT I ADMIRED SO MUCH ABOUT HER.
BUT...HER PURITY BRED INHERENT FRAGILITY...
SHE NEVER LEARNED CERTAIN THINGS SHE SHOULD HAVE......
THAT'S WHY...
...SHE GOT CONFUSED... AND SCARED AND REJECTED US...
SHE NEVER LEARNED WHAT...?
I MEAN, I CAN THINK OF A LOT OF THINGS...
......
STAND

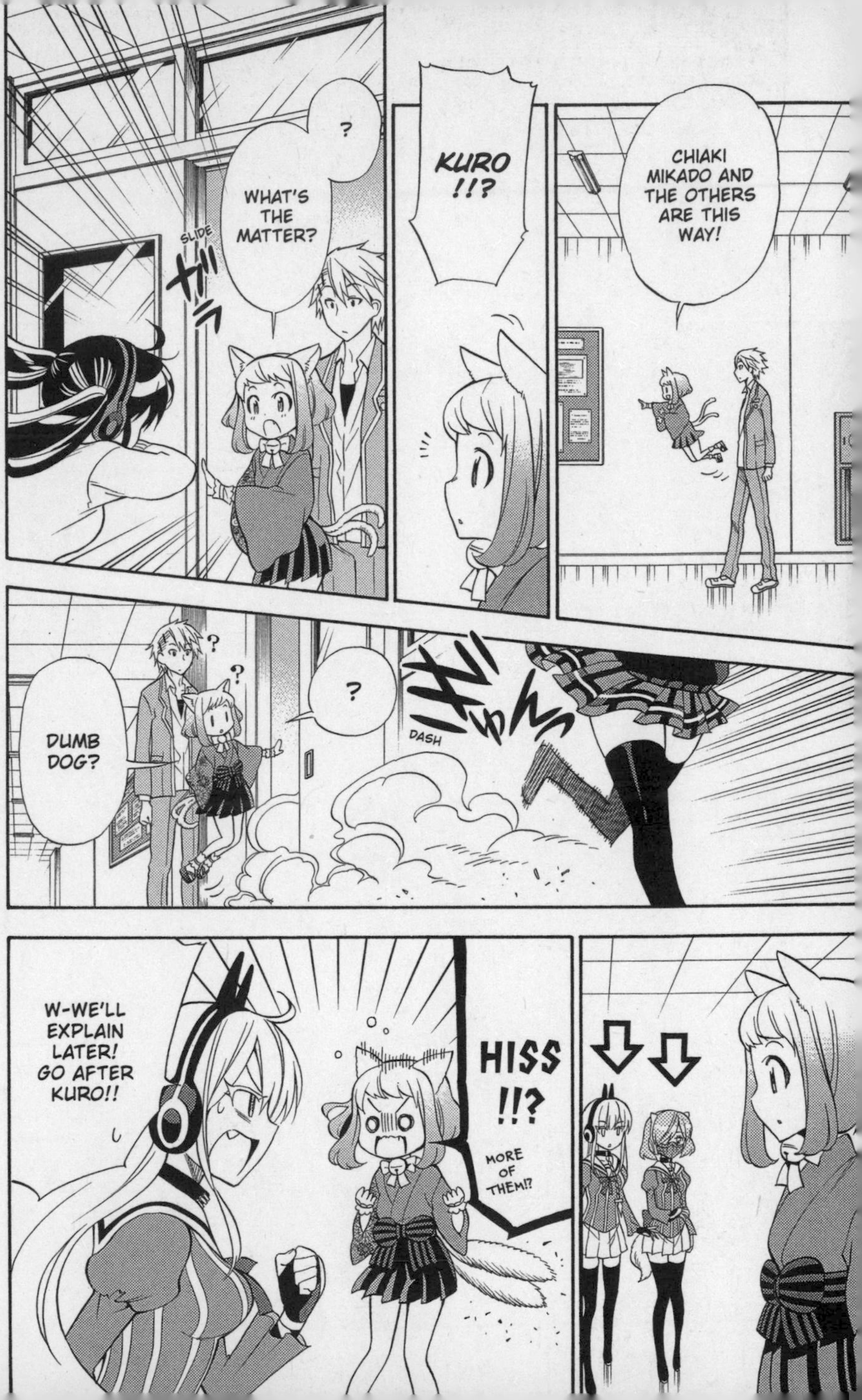
CHIAKI MIKADO AND THE OTHERS ARE THIS WAY!
KURO!!?
?
WHAT'S THE MATTER?
SLIDE
DASH
?
DUMB DOG?
HISS!!?
MORE OF THEM!?
W-WE'LL EXPLAIN LATER! GO AFTER KURO!!

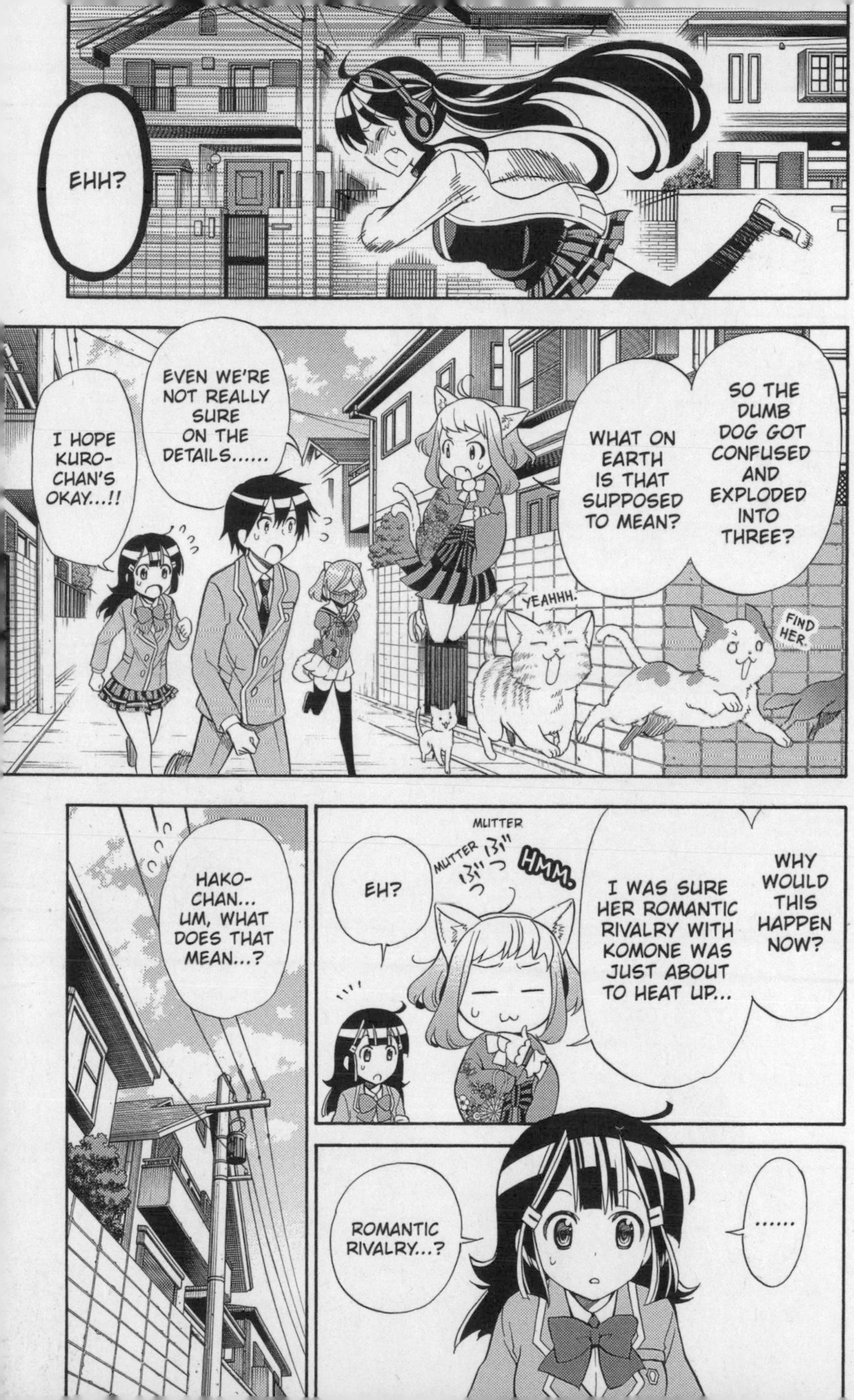
EHH?
SO THE DUMB DOG GOT CONFUSED AND EXPLODED INTO THREE?
WHAT ON EARTH IS THAT SUPPOSED TO MEAN?
EVEN WE'RE NOT REALLY SURE ON THE DETAILS......
I HOPE KURO-CHAN'S OKAY...!!
FIND HER.
YEAHHH.
WHY WOULD THIS HAPPEN NOW?
I WAS SURE HER ROMANTIC RIVALRY WITH KOMONE WAS JUST ABOUT TO HEAT UP...
HMM.
MUTTER
MUTTER
EH?
......
ROMANTIC RIVALRY...?
HAKO-CHAN... UM, WHAT DOES THAT MEAN...?

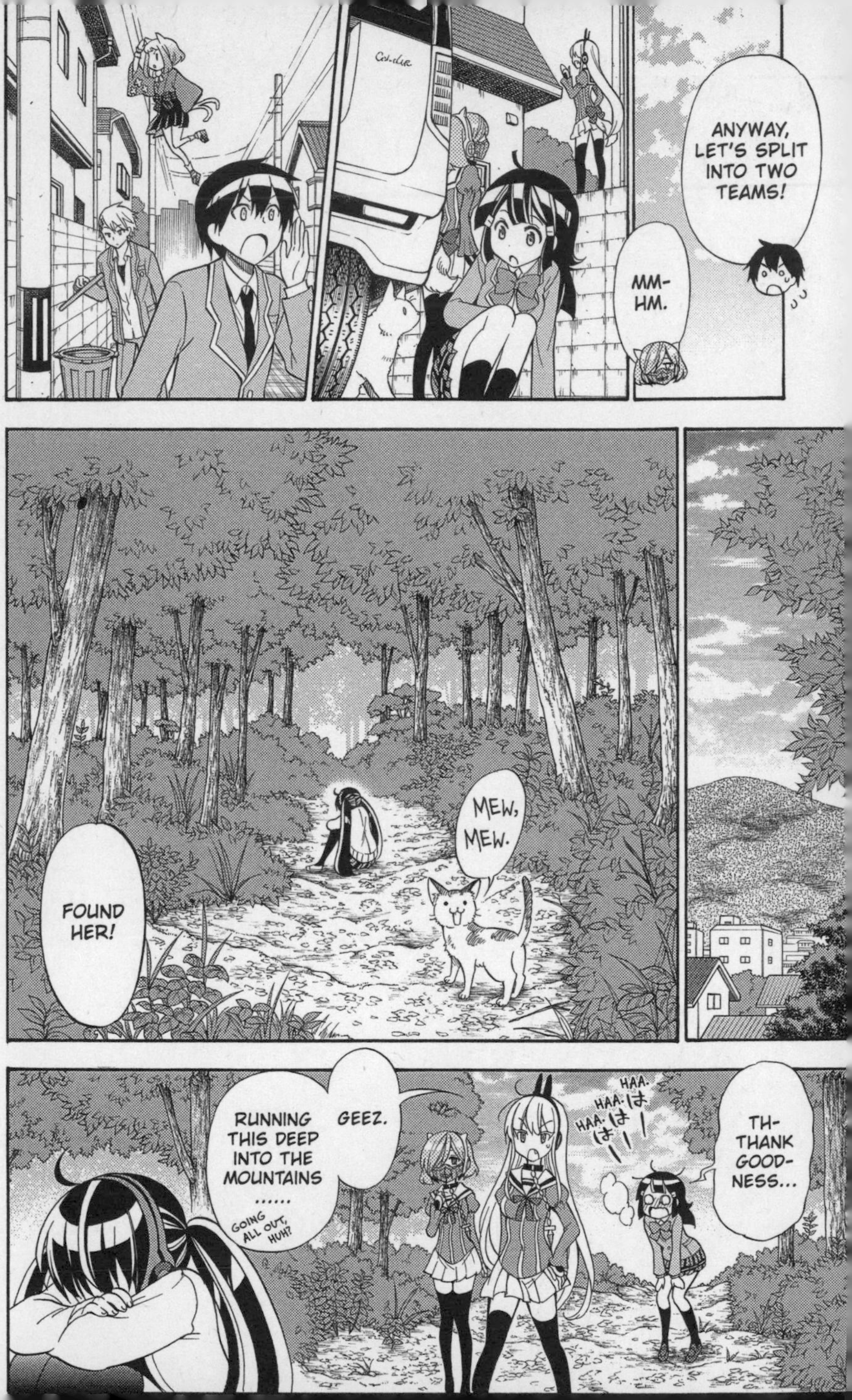
ANYWAY, LET'S SPLIT INTO TWO TEAMS!
MM-HM.
MEW, MEW.
FOUND HER!
TH-THANK GOOD-NESS...
HAA. は ー HAA. は ー HAA. は ー
GEEZ.
RUNNING THIS DEEP INTO THE MOUNTAINS ......
GOING ALL OUT, HUH?

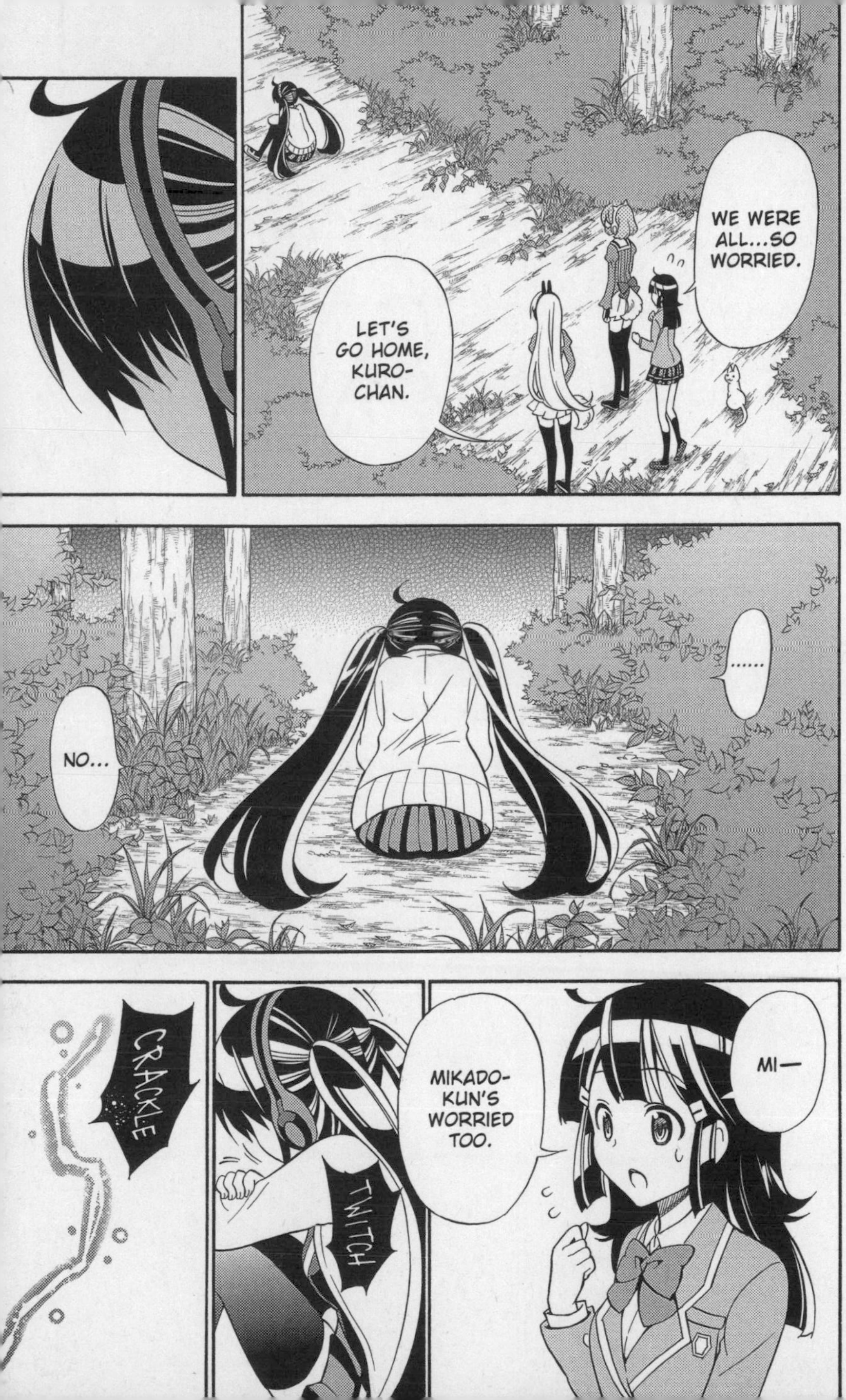
WE WERE ALL...SO WORRIED.
LET'S GO HOME, KURO-CHAN.
......
NO...
MI—
MIKADO-KUN'S WORRIED TOO.
TWITCH
CRACKLE

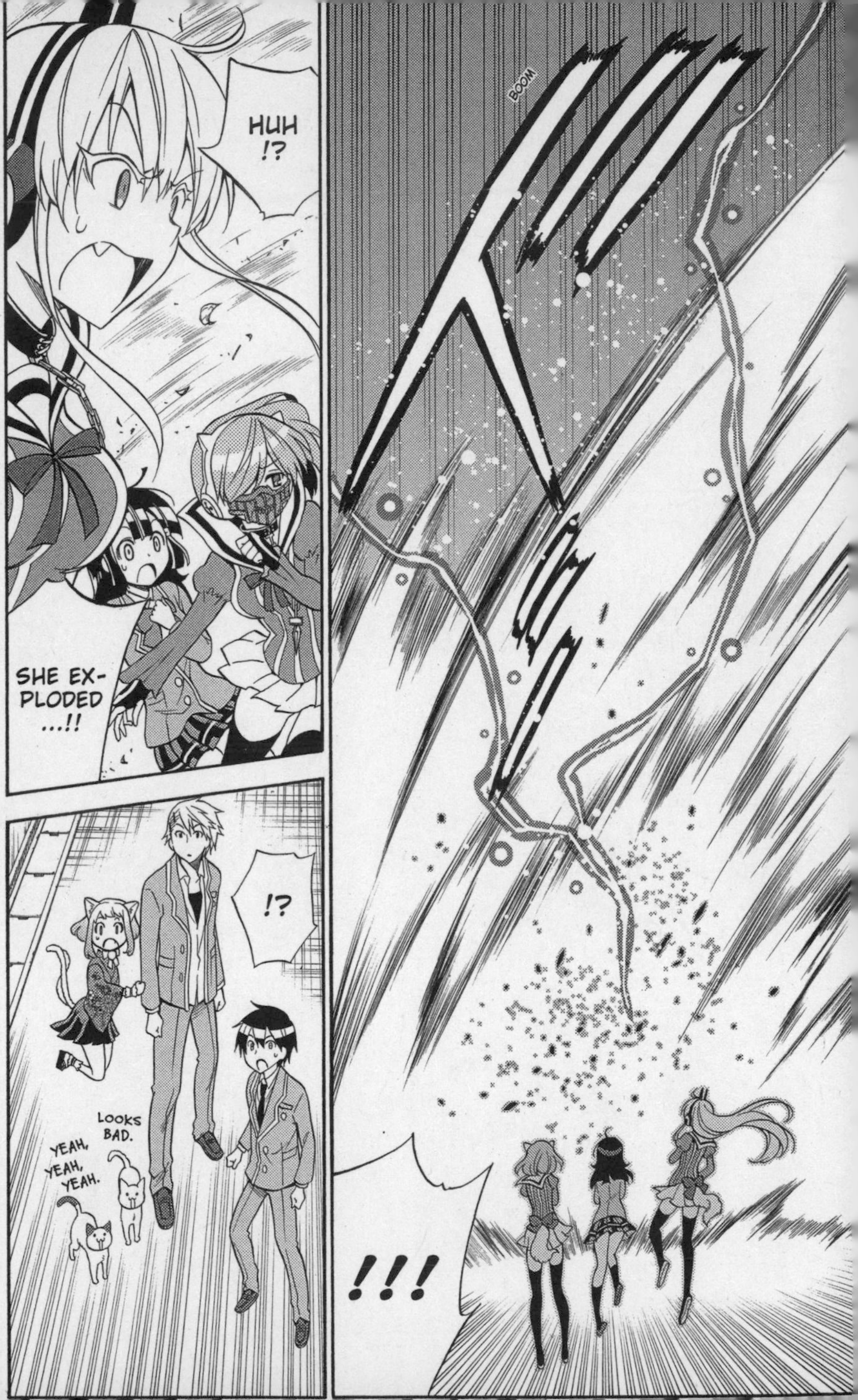
BOOM
!!!
HUH!?
SHE EX-PLODED ...!!
!?
LOOKS BAD.
YEAH, YEAH, YEAH.

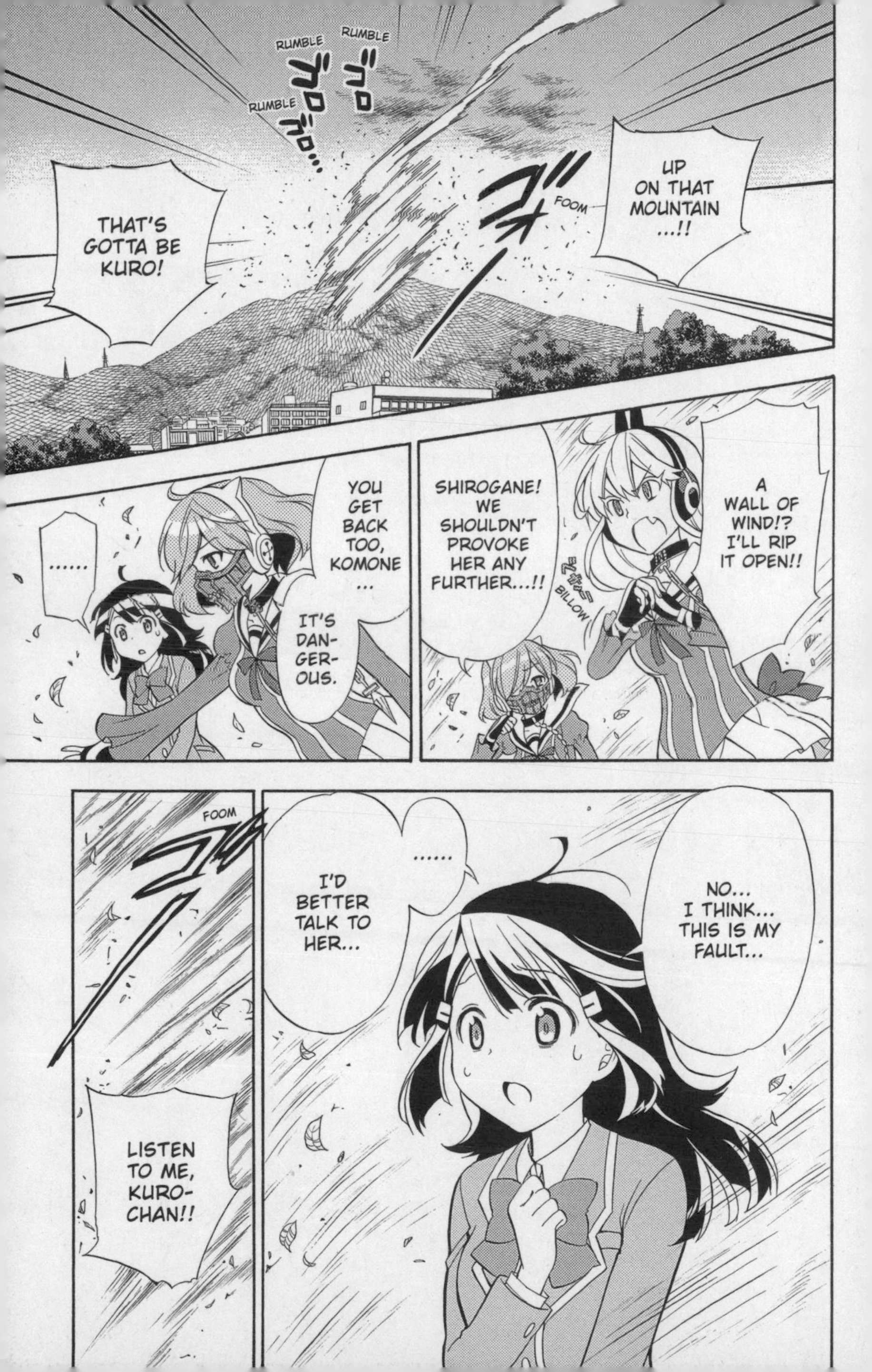
RUMBLE
RUMBLE
RUMBLE
UP ON THAT MOUNTAIN ...!!
FOOM
THAT'S GOTTA BE KURO!
A WALL OF WIND!? I'LL RIP IT OPEN!!
SHIROGANE! WE SHOULDN'T PROVOKE HER ANY FURTHER...!!
BILLOW
YOU GET BACK TOO, KOMONE ...
IT'S DAN-GER-OUS.
......
NO... I THINK... THIS IS MY FAULT...
......
I'D BETTER TALK TO HER...
FOOM
LISTEN TO ME, KURO-CHAN!!

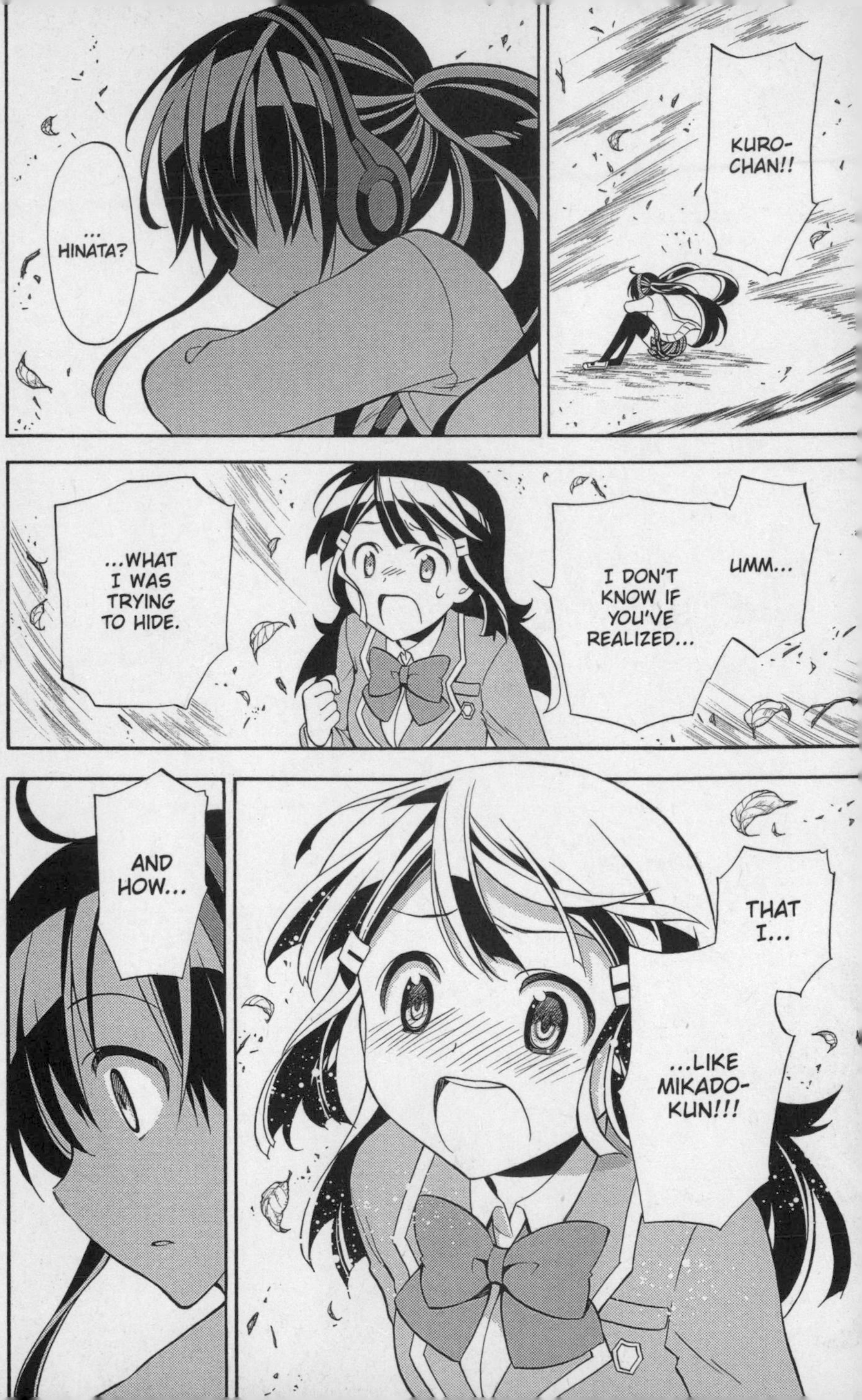
KURO-CHAN!!
... HINATA?
UMM...
I DON'T KNOW IF YOU'VE REALIZED...
...WHAT I WAS TRYING TO HIDE.
THAT I...
...LIKE MIKADO-KUN!!!
AND HOW...

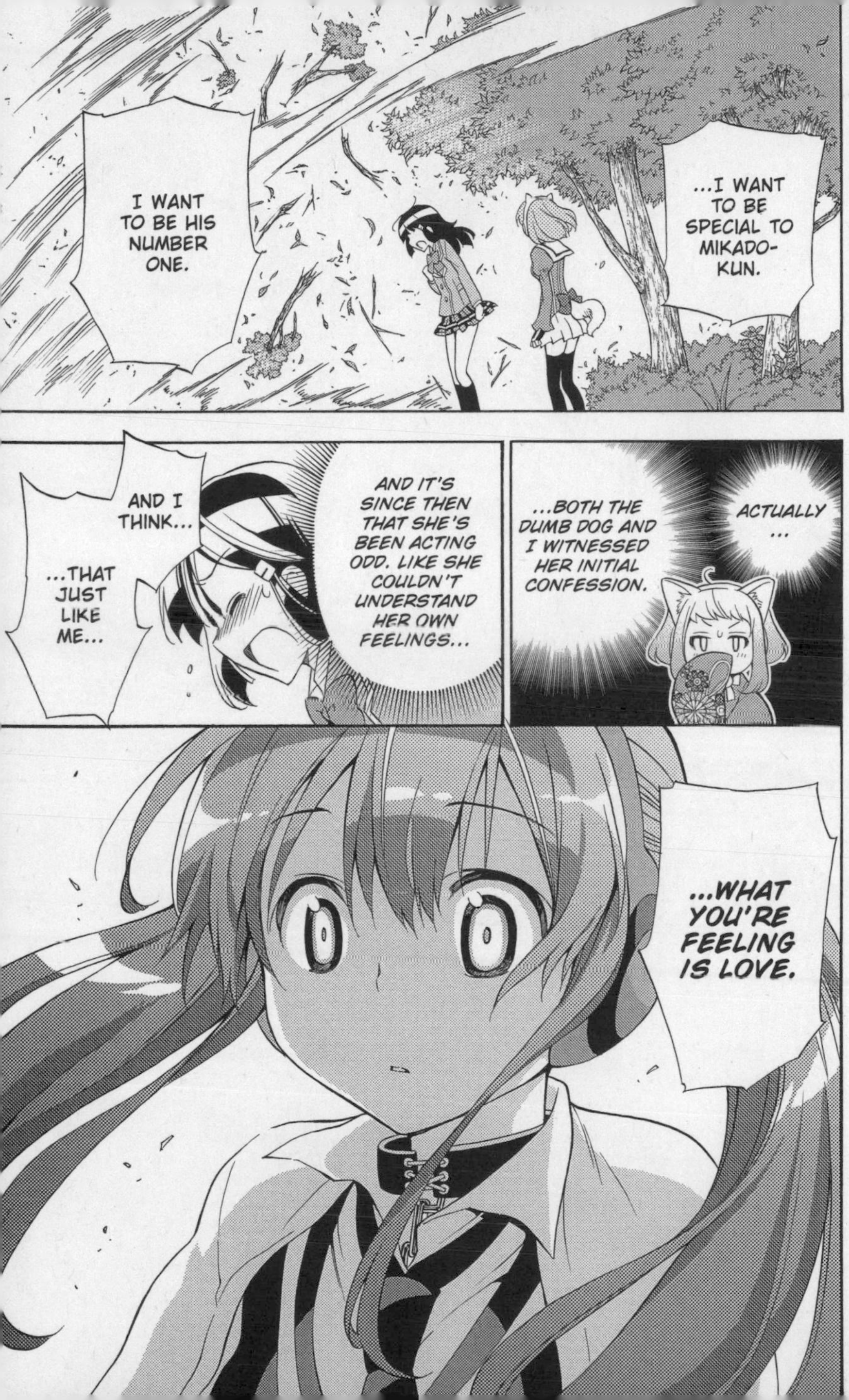
...I WANT TO BE SPECIAL TO MIKADO-KUN.
I WANT TO BE HIS NUMBER ONE.
ACTUALLY...
...BOTH THE DUMB DOG AND I WITNESSED HER INITIAL CONFESSION.
AND IT'S SINCE THEN THAT SHE'S BEEN ACTING ODD. LIKE SHE COULDN'T UNDERSTAND HER OWN FEELINGS...
AND I THINK...
...THAT JUST LIKE ME...
...WHAT YOU'RE FEELING IS LOVE.

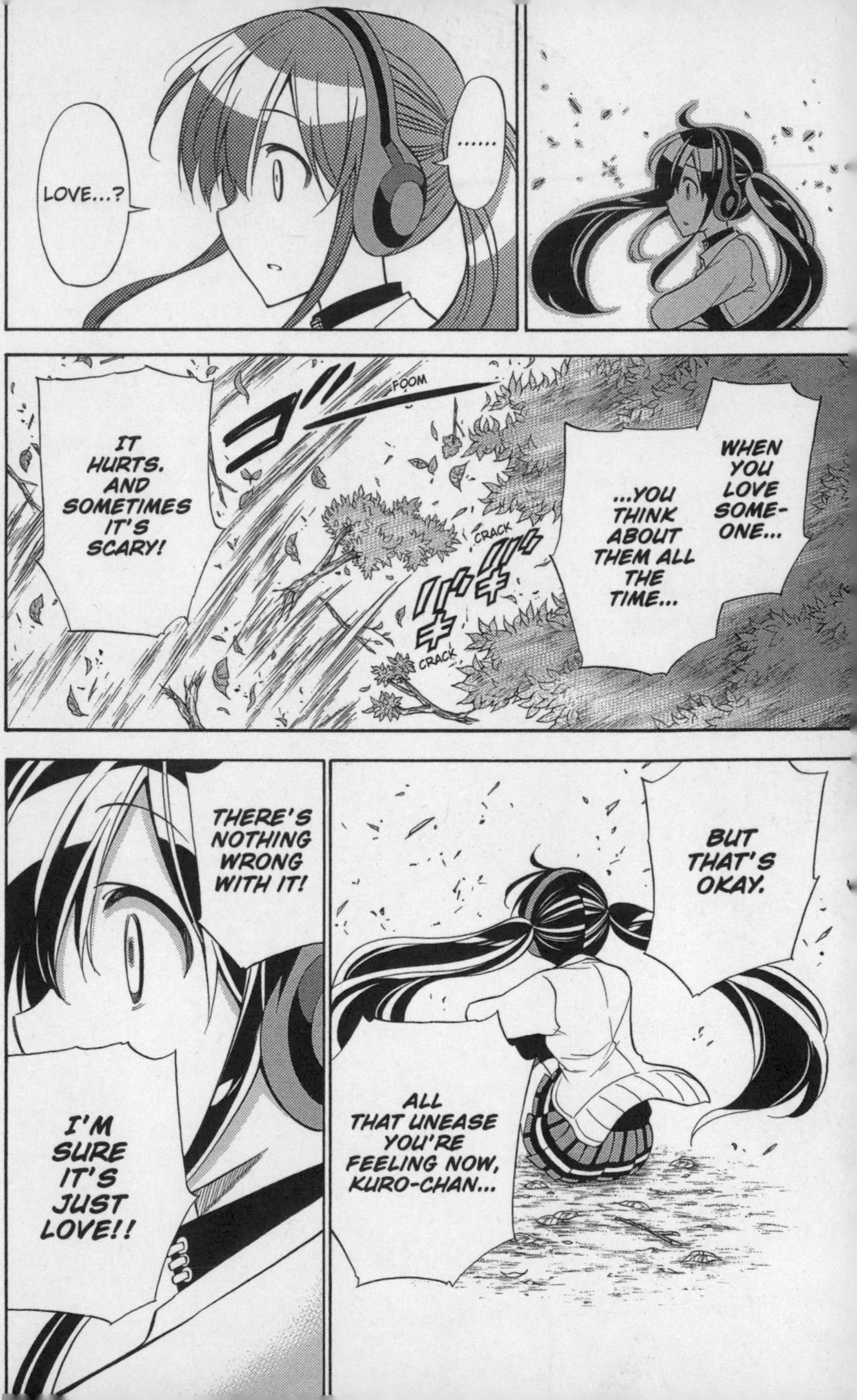
......
LOVE...?
WHEN YOU LOVE SOMEONE...
FOOM
...YOU THINK ABOUT THEM ALL THE TIME...
CRACK
CRACK
IT HURTS. AND SOMETIMES IT'S SCARY!
BUT THAT'S OKAY.
ALL THAT UNEASE YOU'RE FEELING NOW, KURO-CHAN...
THERE'S NOTHING WRONG WITH IT!
I'M SURE IT'S JUST LOVE!!

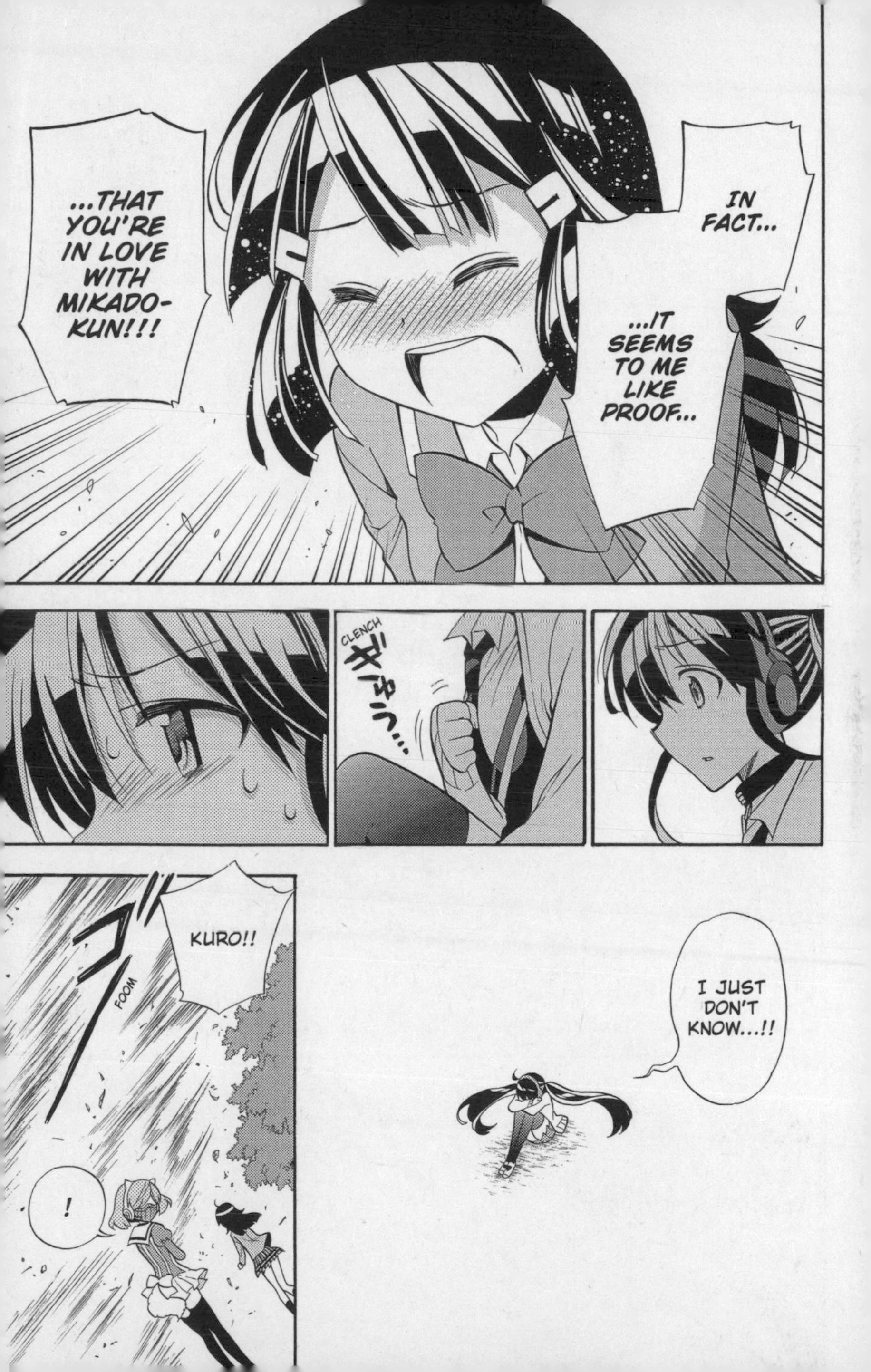
IN FACT...
...IT SEEMS TO ME LIKE PROOF...
...THAT YOU'RE IN LOVE WITH MIKADO-KUN!!!
CLENCH
I JUST DON'T KNOW...!!
KURO!!
FOOM
!

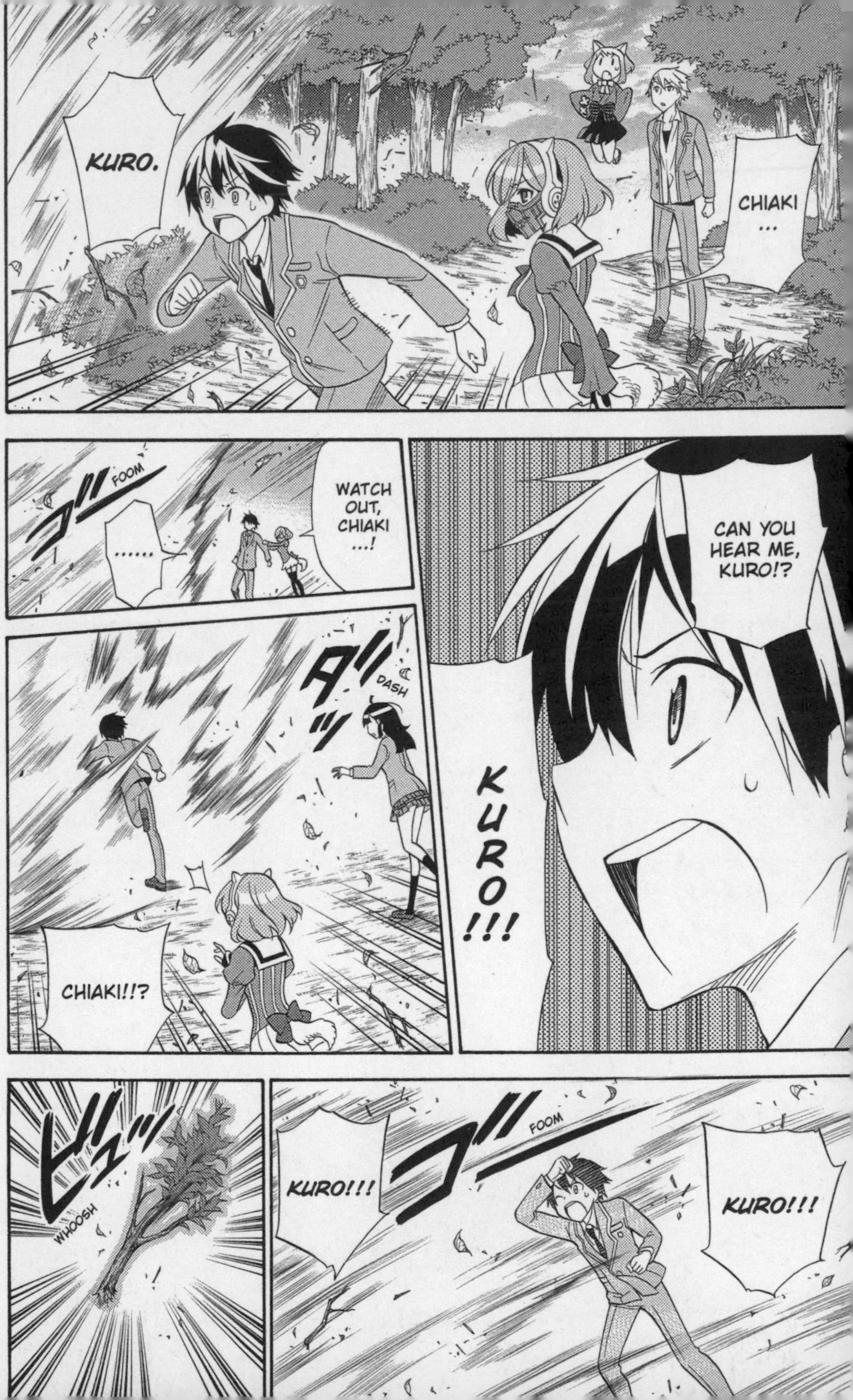
CHIAKI ...
KURO.
CAN YOU HEAR ME, KURO!?
KURO!!!
WATCH OUT, CHIAKI ...!
FOOM
......
DASH
CHIAKI!!?
KURO!!!
FOOM
KURO!!!
WHOOSH

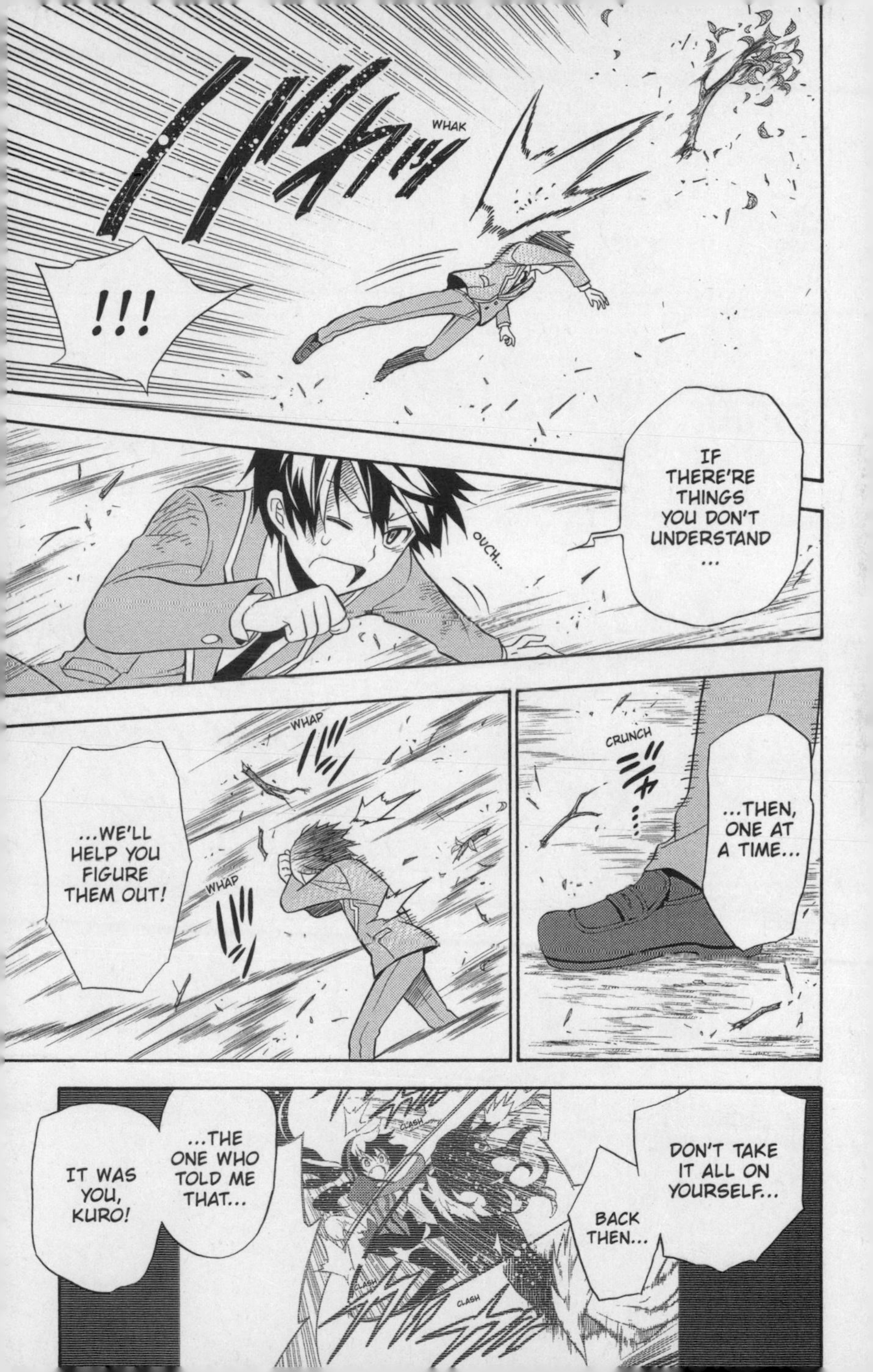
WHAK
!!!
IF THERE'RE THINGS YOU DON'T UNDERSTAND ...
OUCH...
CRUNCH
...THEN, ONE AT A TIME...
WHAP
WHAP
...WE'LL HELP YOU FIGURE THEM OUT!
DON'T TAKE IT ALL ON YOURSELF...
BACK THEN...
CLASH
...THE ONE WHO TOLD ME THAT...
IT WAS YOU, KURO!
CLASH
CLASH

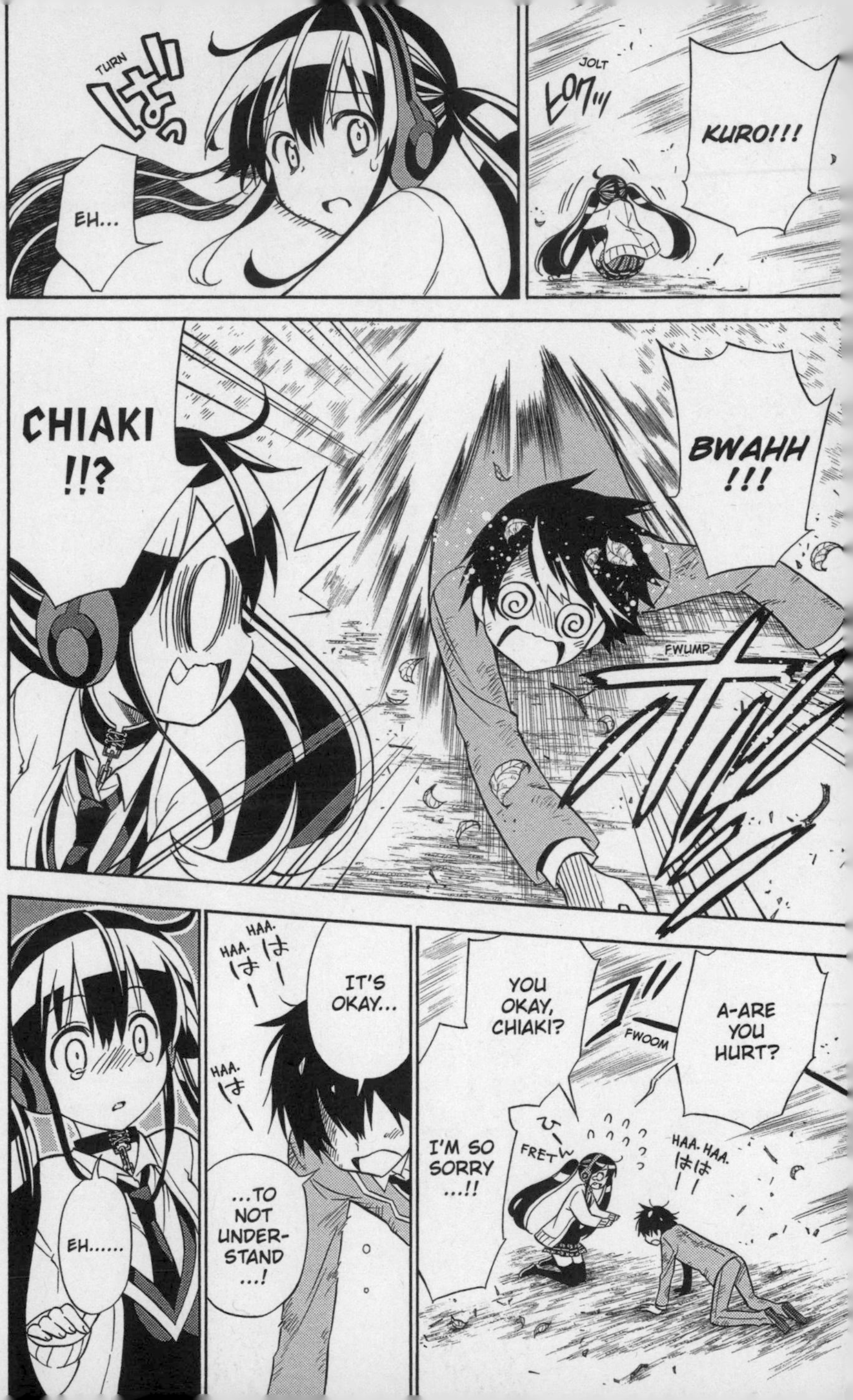
JOLT
KURO!!!
TURN
EH...
BWAHH !!!
FWUMP
CHIAKI !!?
A-ARE YOU HURT?
YOU OKAY, CHIAKI?
FWOOM
HAA. HAA.
FRET
I'M SO SORRY ...!!
HAA. HAA.
IT'S OKAY...
HAA.
...TO NOT UNDER-STAND ...!
EH......

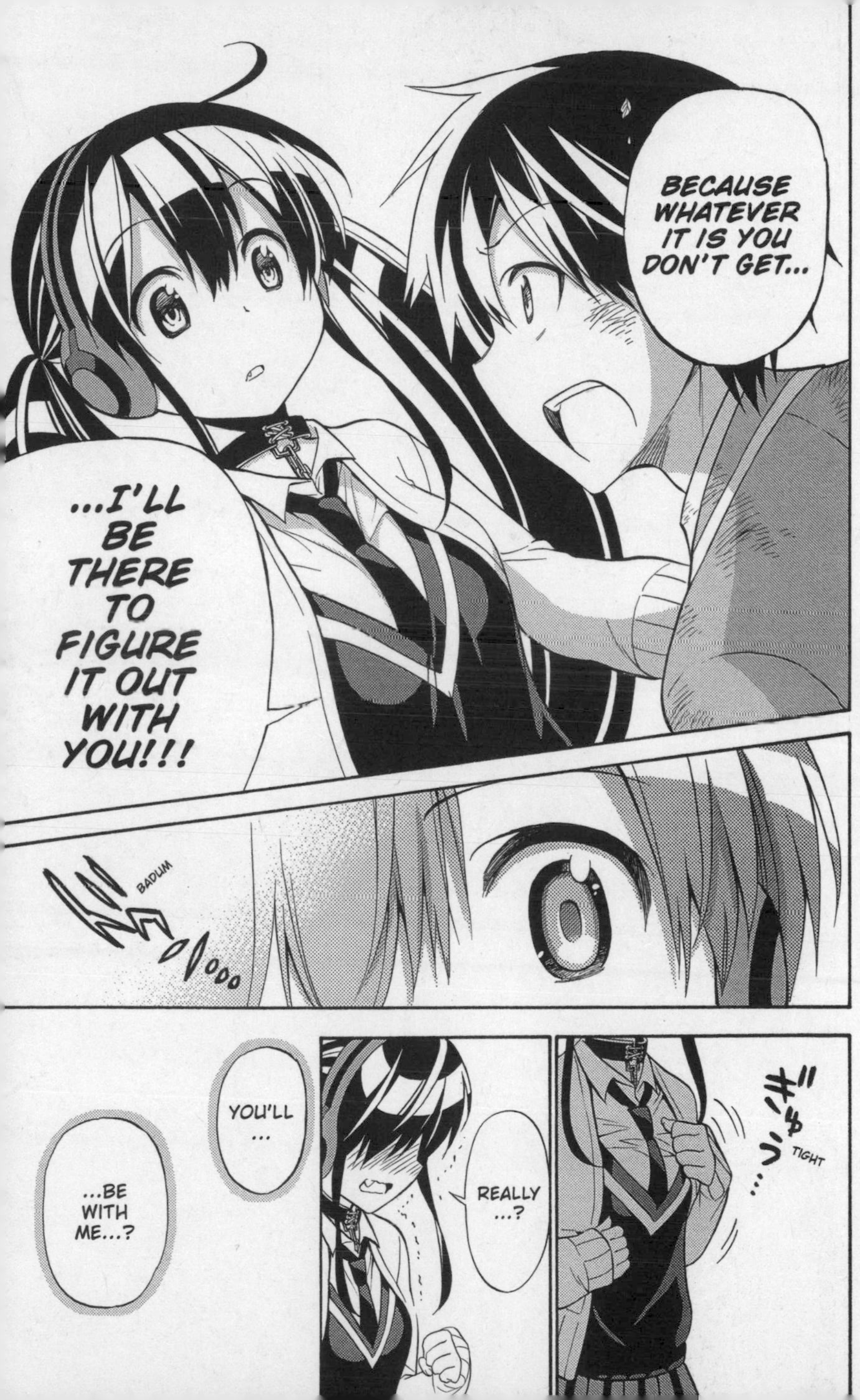
BECAUSE WHATEVER IT IS YOU DON'T GET...
...I'LL BE THERE TO FIGURE IT OUT WITH YOU!!!
BADUM
TIGHT
REALLY ...?
YOU'LL ...
...BE WITH ME...?

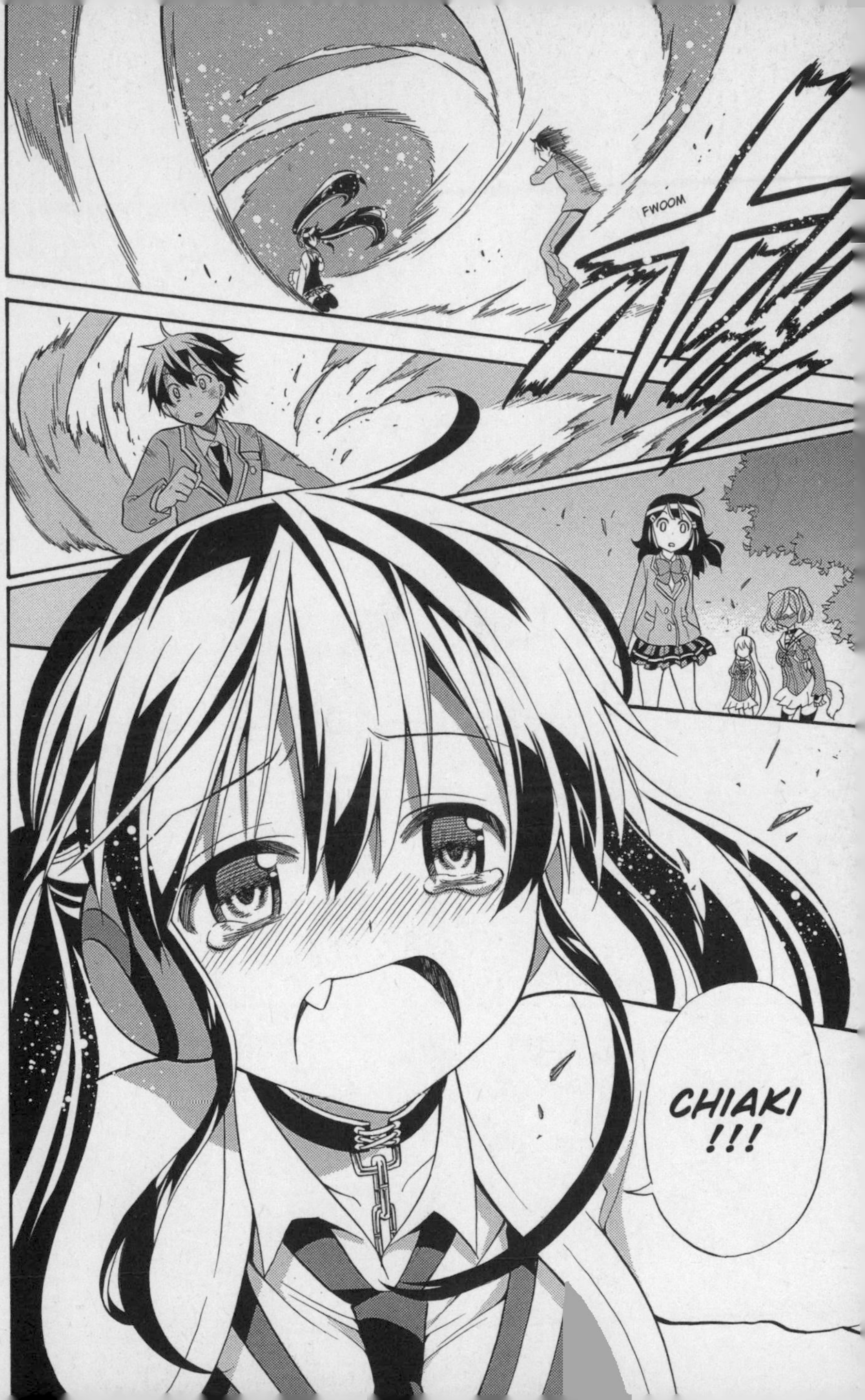
FWOOM
CHIAKI
!!!

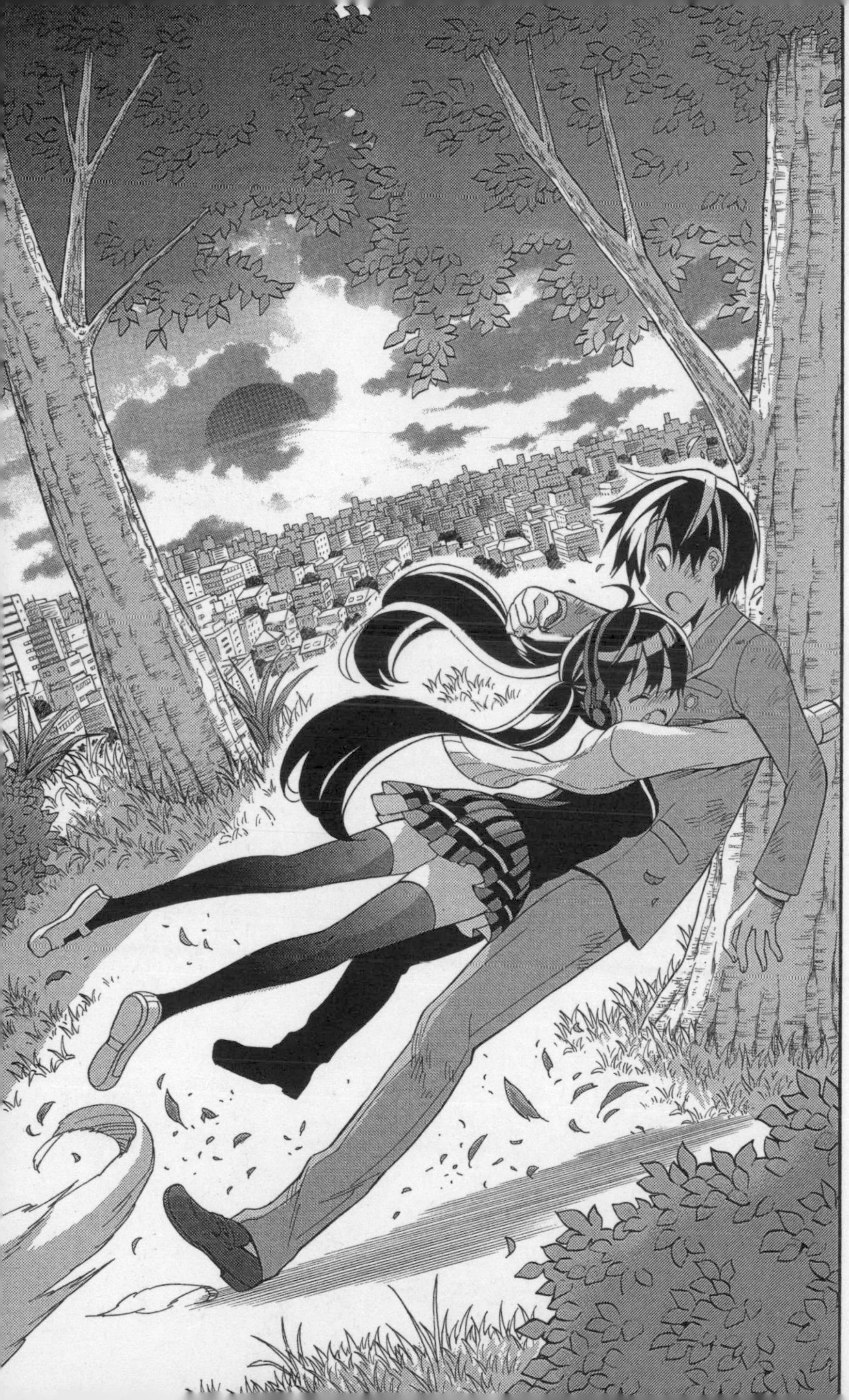

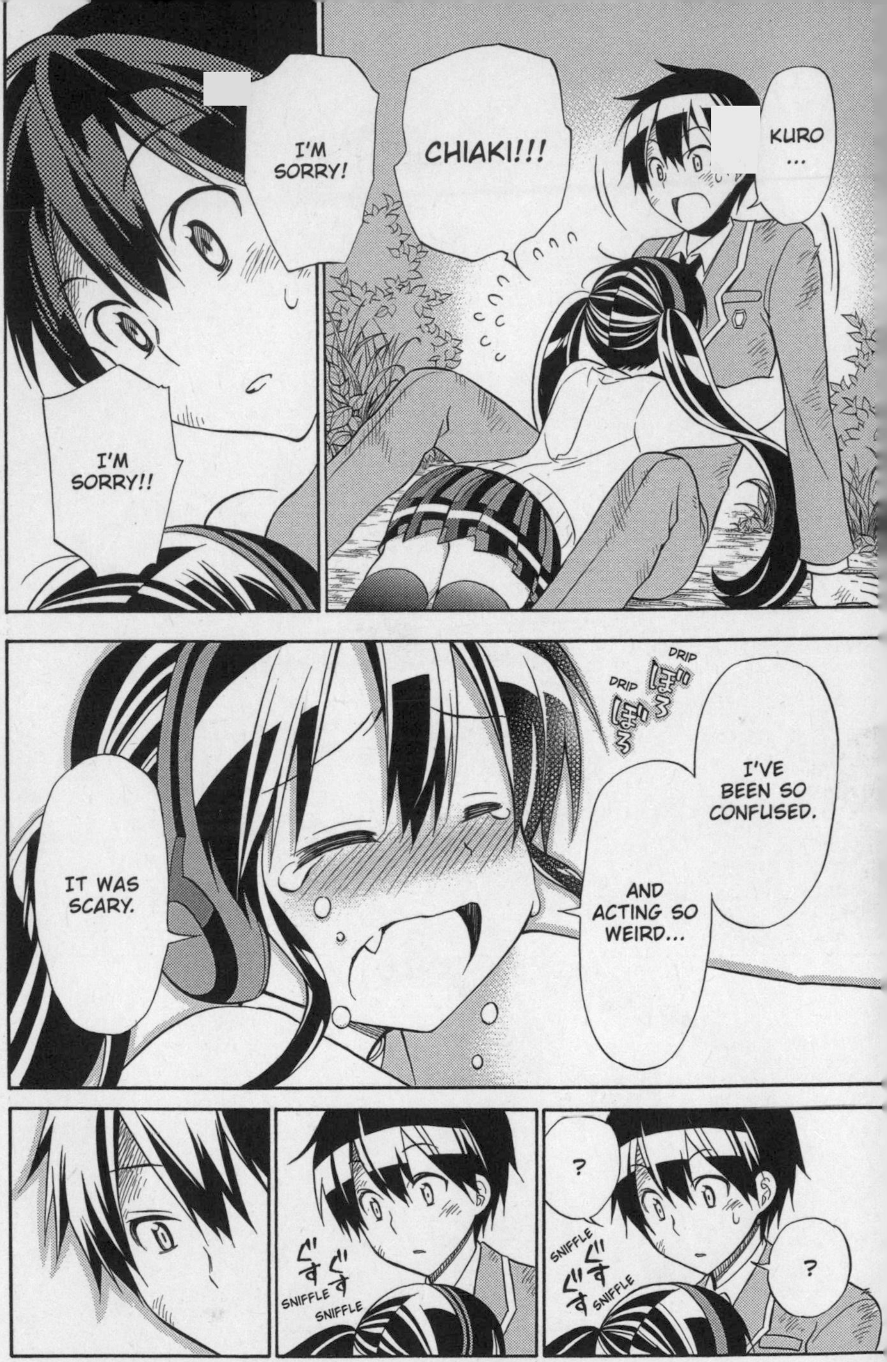
KURO...
CHIAKI!!!
I'M SORRY!
I'M SORRY!!
DRIP
ぼろ
DRIP
ぼろ
I'VE BEEN SO CONFUSED.
AND ACTING SO WEIRD...
IT WAS SCARY.
?
SNIFFLE
ぐす
ぐす
SNIFFLE
?
ぐす
ぐす
SNIFFLE
SNIFFLE

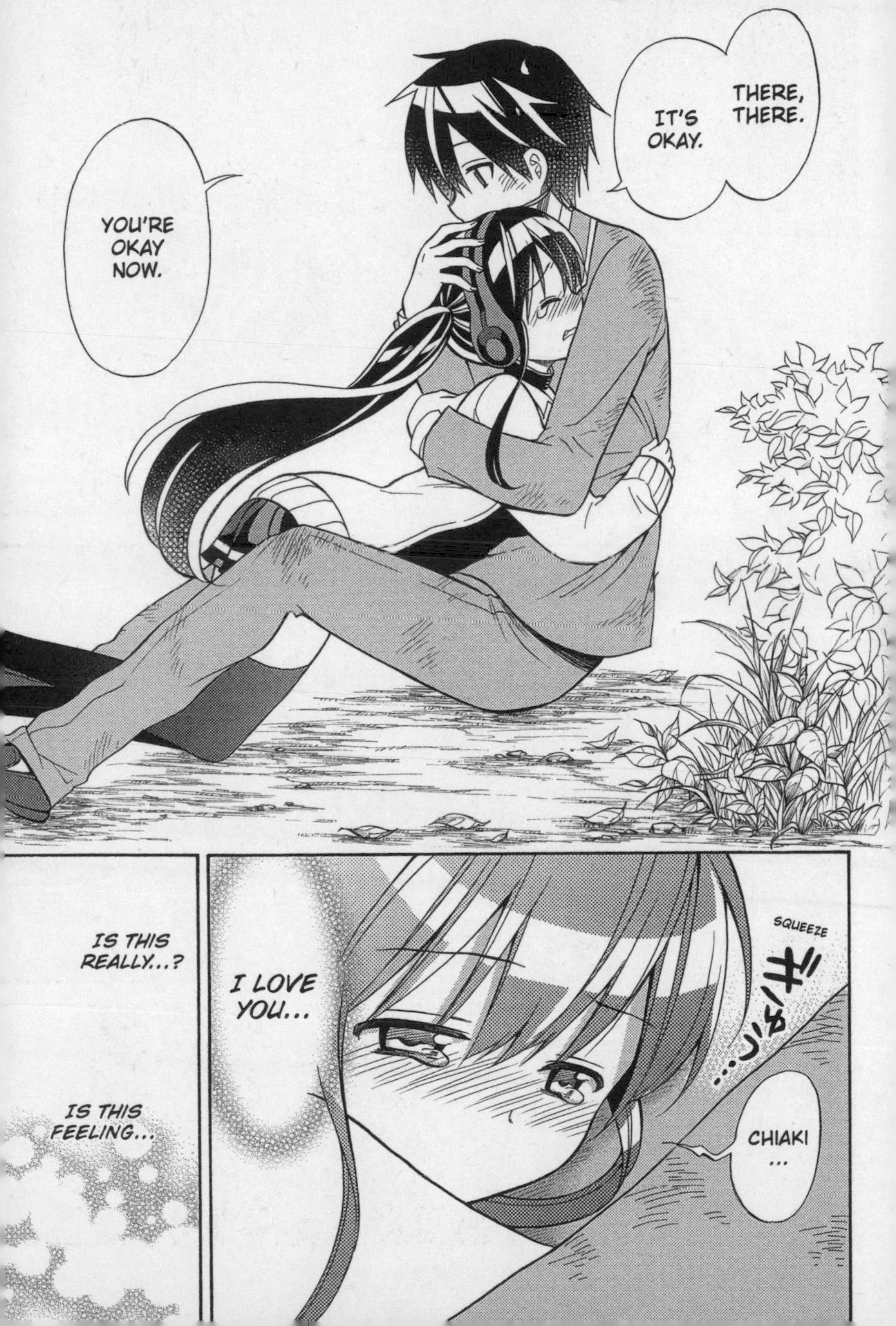
THERE, THERE.
IT'S OKAY.
YOU'RE OKAY NOW.
SQUEEZE
ギュッ…
I LOVE YOU…
CHIAKI …
IS THIS REALLY…?
IS THIS FEELING…

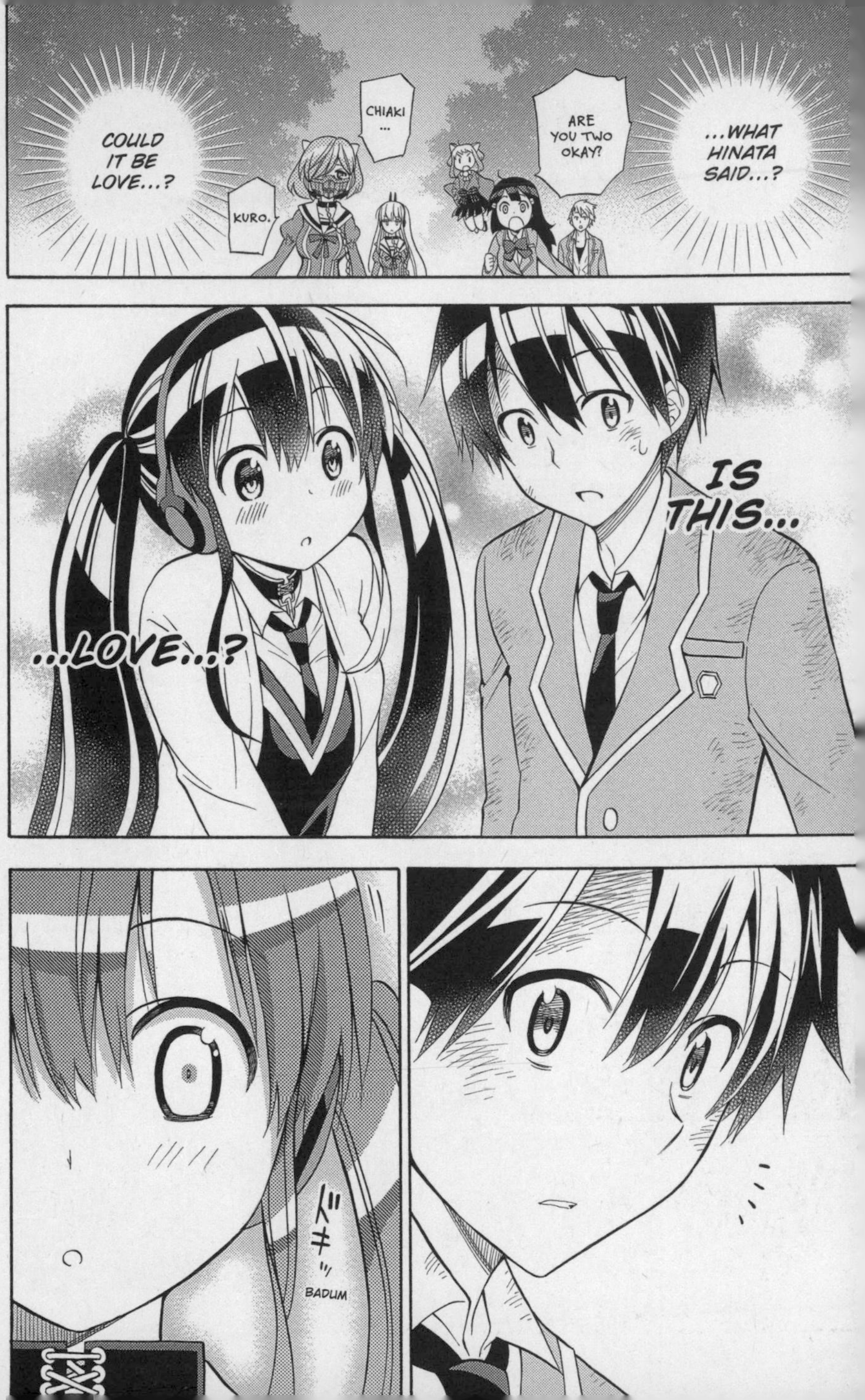
...WHAT HINATA SAID...?
ARE YOU TWO OKAY?
CHIAKI ...
KURO.
COULD IT BE LOVE...?
IS THIS...
...LOVE...?
ドキッ
BADUM

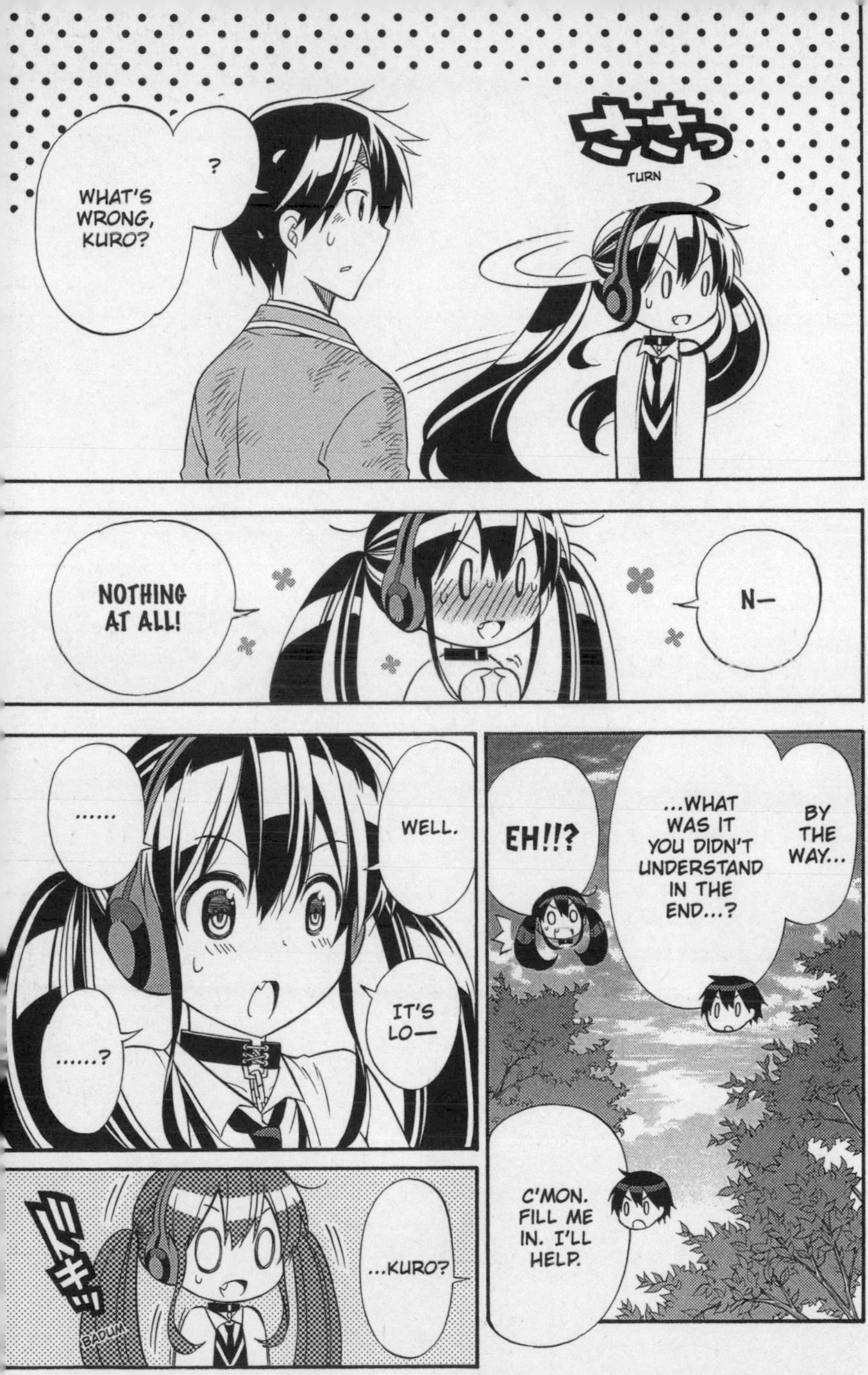
ささっ
TURN
?
WHAT'S WRONG, KURO?
N—
NOTHING AT ALL!
BY THE WAY...
...WHAT WAS IT YOU DIDN'T UNDERSTAND IN THE END...?
EH!!?
C'MON. FILL ME IN. I'LL HELP.
WELL.
......
IT'S LO—
......?
...KURO?
ドキッ
BADUM

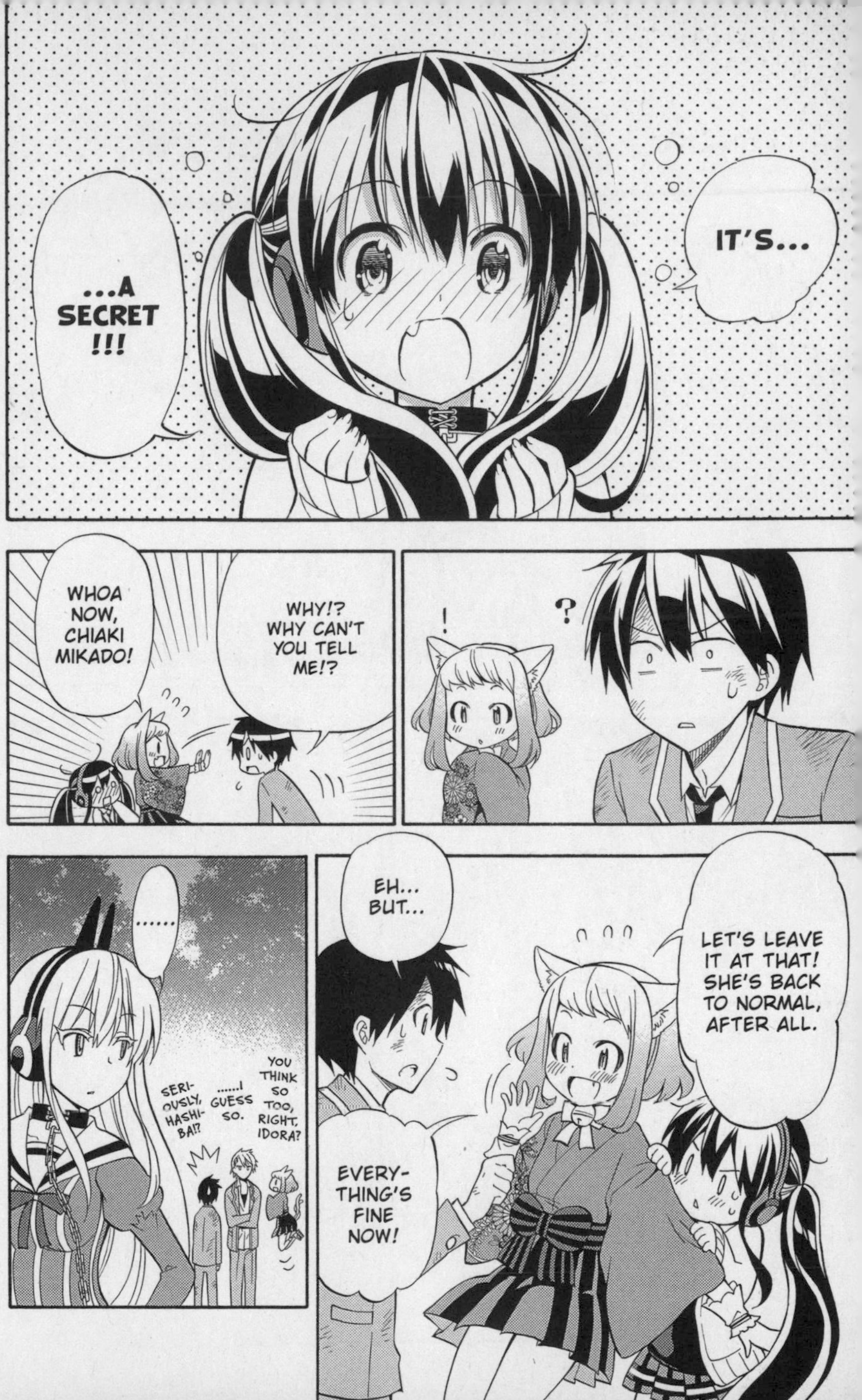
IT'S...
...A SECRET!!!
!
?
WHY!? WHY CAN'T YOU TELL ME!?
WHOA NOW, CHIAKI MIKADO!
LET'S LEAVE IT AT THAT! SHE'S BACK TO NORMAL, AFTER ALL.
EH... BUT...
EVERY-THING'S FINE NOW!
......
YOU THINK SO TOO, RIGHT, IDORA?
......I GUESS SO.
SERI-OUSLY, HASHI-BA!?

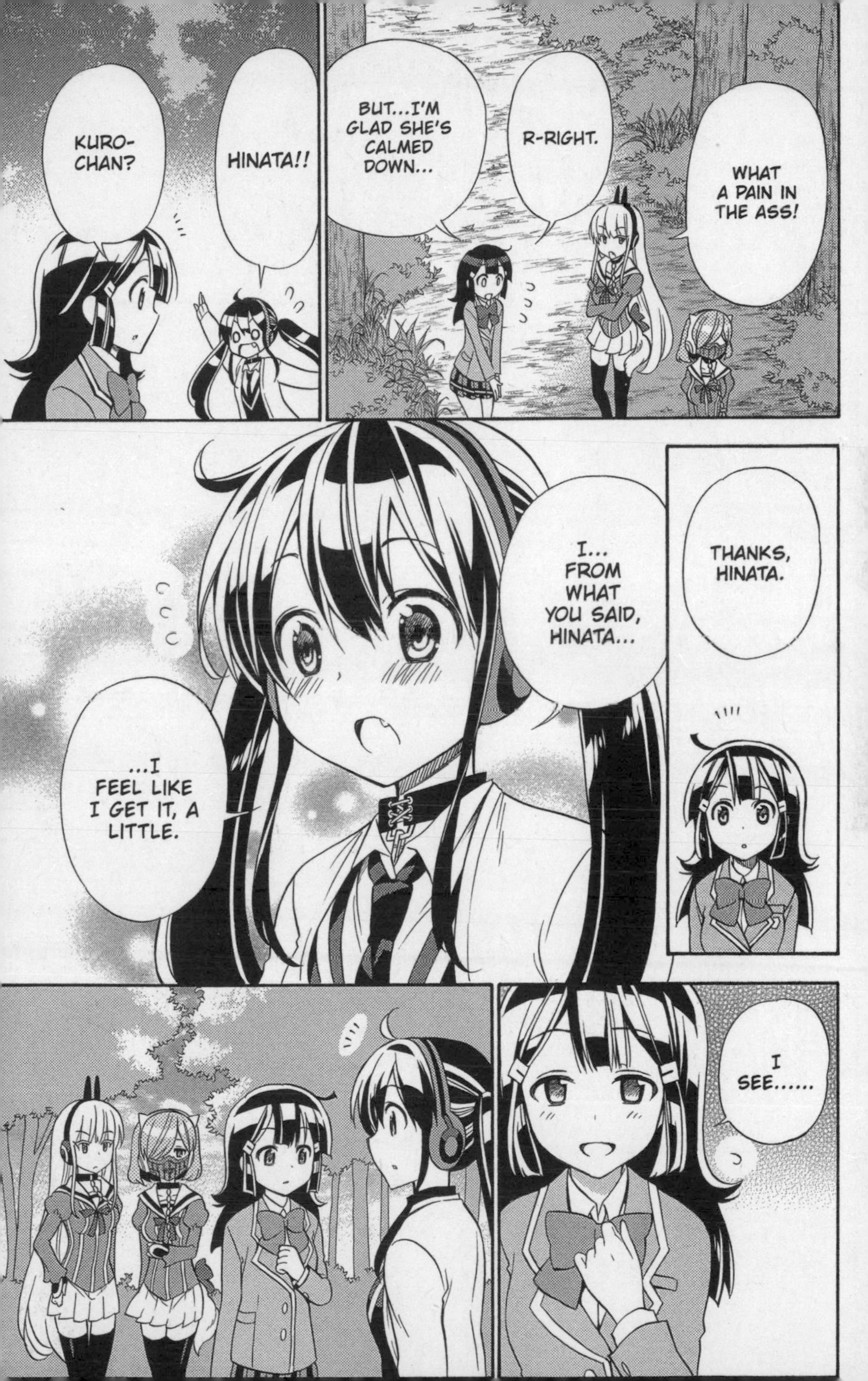
WHAT A PAIN IN THE ASS!
R-RIGHT.
BUT...I'M GLAD SHE'S CALMED DOWN...
HINATA!!
KURO-CHAN?
THANKS, HINATA.
I... FROM WHAT YOU SAID, HINATA...
...I FEEL LIKE I GET IT, A LITTLE.
I SEE......

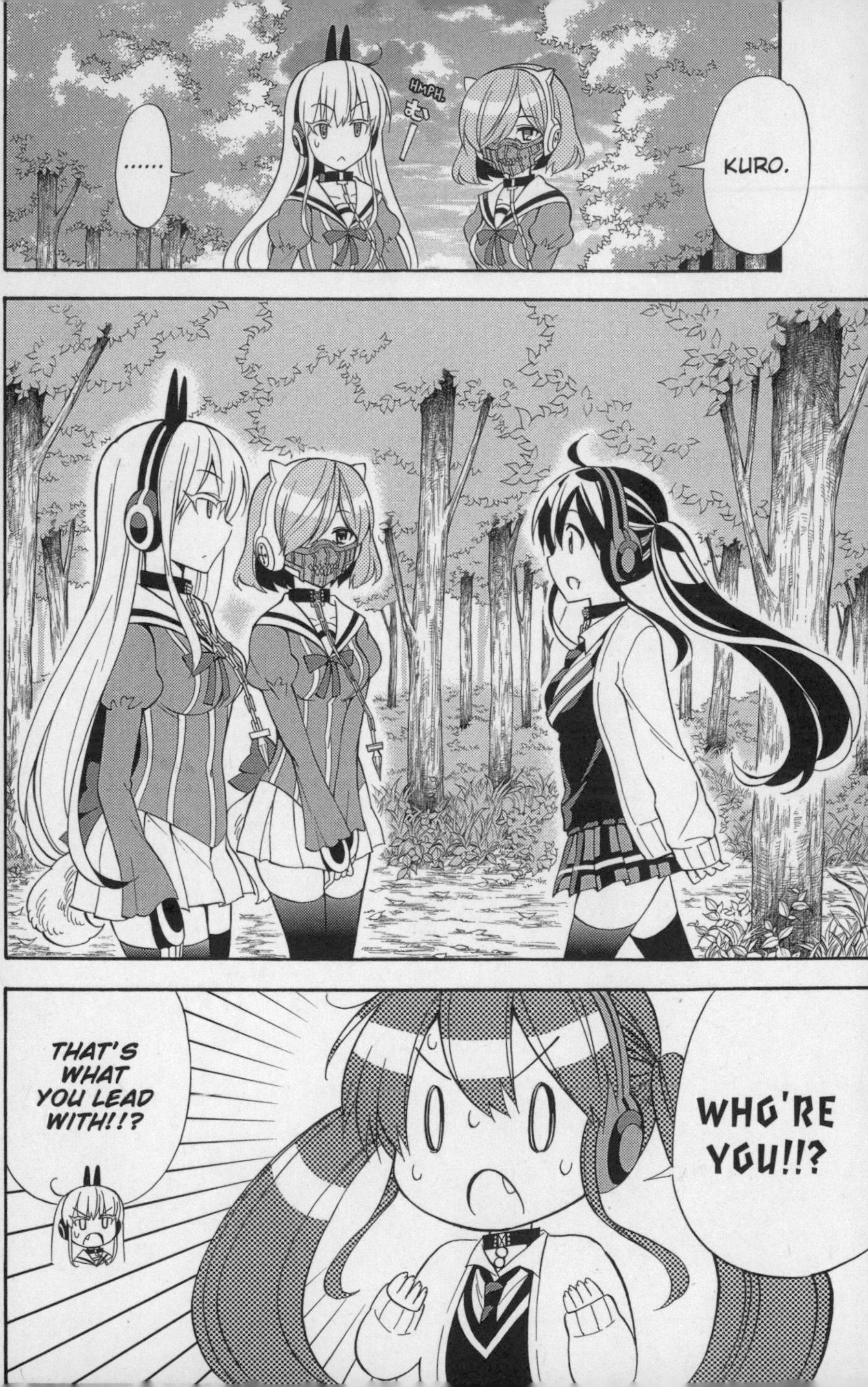
KURO.
HMPH.
むっ
......
WHO'RE YOU!!?
THAT'S WHAT YOU LEAD WITH!!?

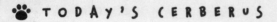 **TODAY'S CERBERUS**

LET'S
START...

...WITH
A HUG.

TODAY'S CERBERUS 🐾

AND NOW A HUG FROM ME.

SHIROGANE. SHIROGANE.

THIS WAY NOW.

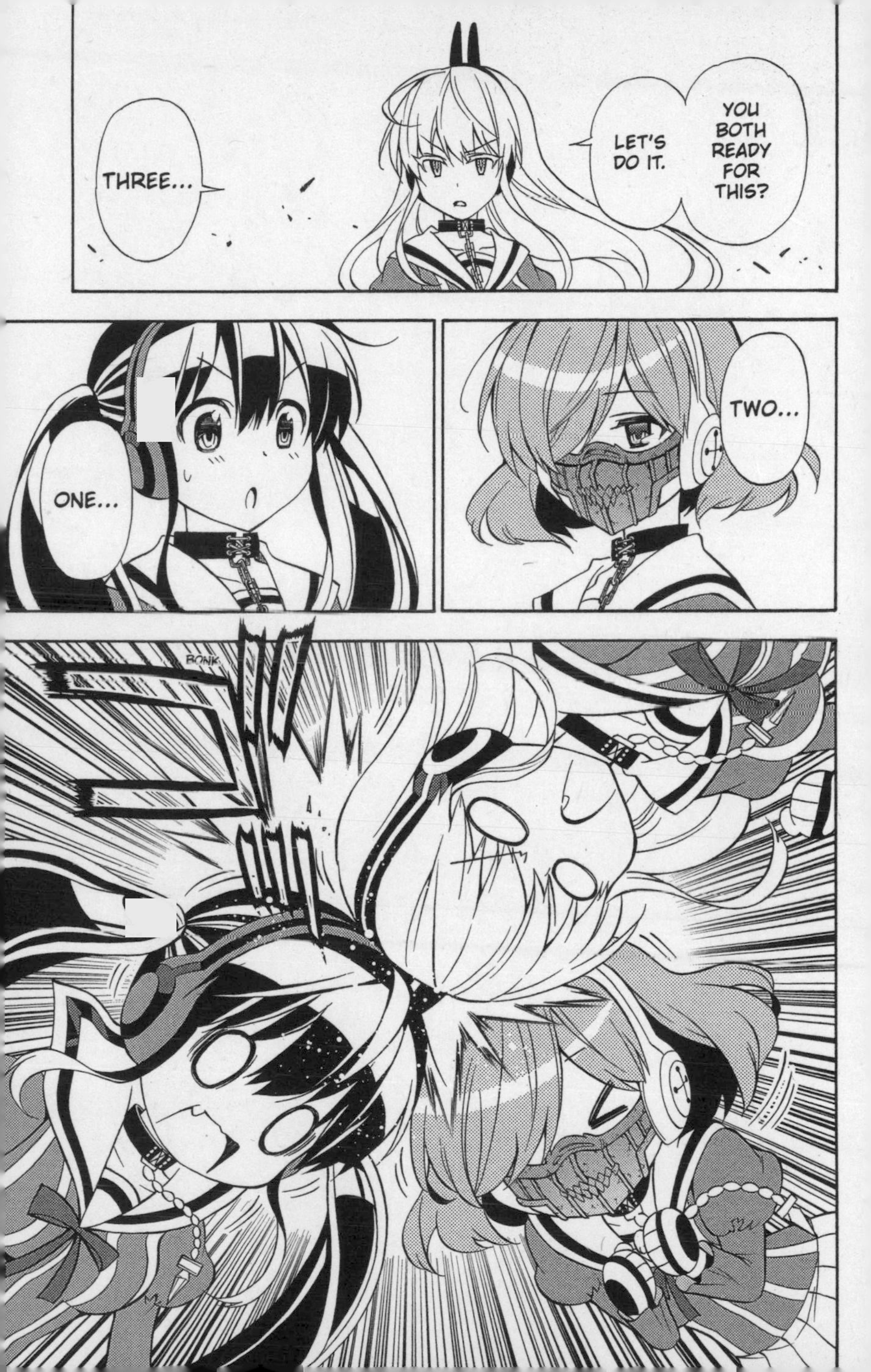
YOU BOTH READY FOR THIS?
LET'S DO IT.
THREE...
TWO...
ONE...
BONK

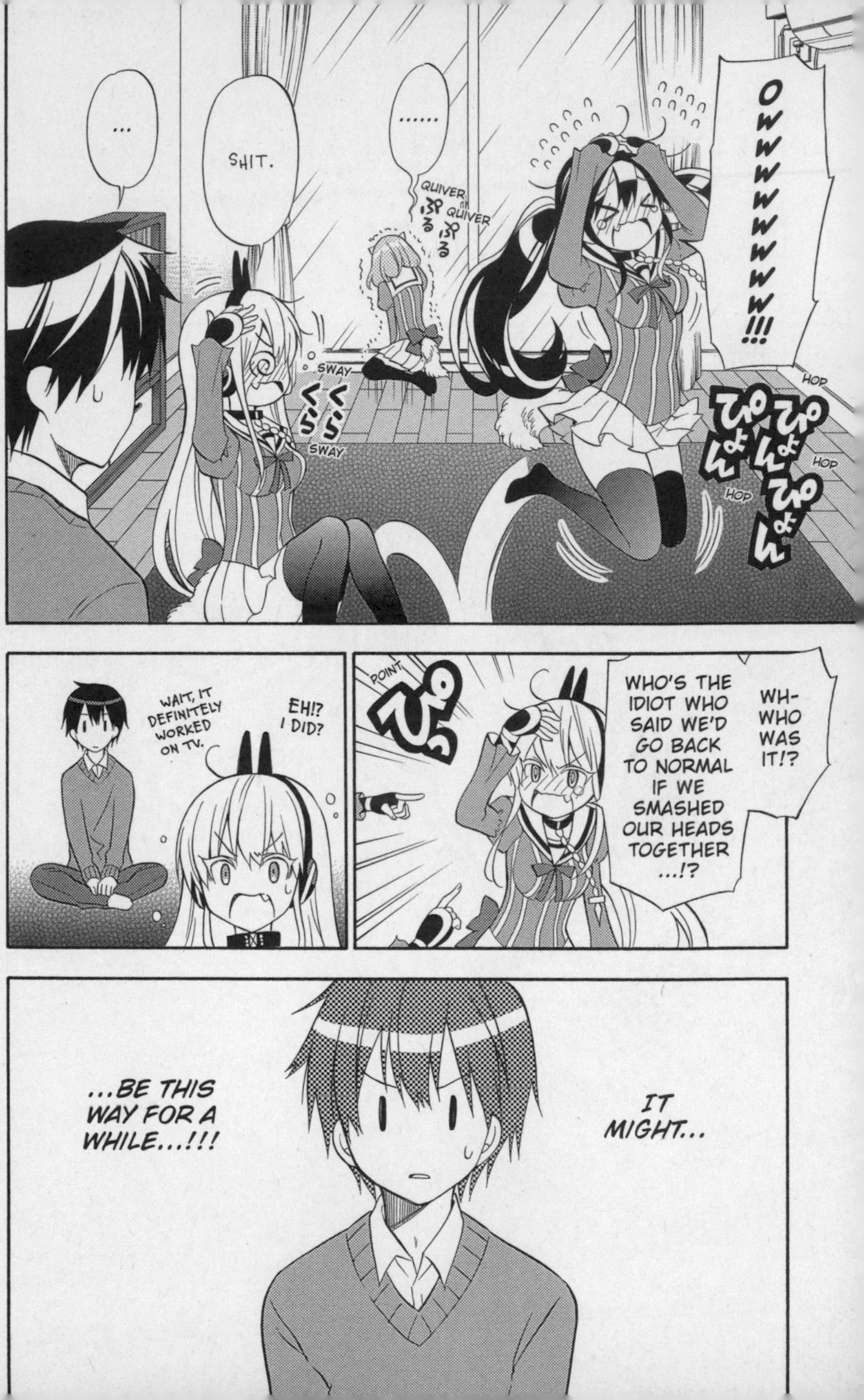
OWWWWWWWW!!!
HOP ぴょん HOP ぴょん HOP ぴょん ぴょん
......
QUIVER ぷる QUIVER ぷる
SHIT.
...
SWAY くら SWAY くら
WH-WHO WAS IT!?
WHO'S THE IDIOT WHO SAID WE'D GO BACK TO NORMAL IF WE SMASHED OUR HEADS TOGETHER ...!?
POINT ぴっ
EH!? I DID?
WAIT, IT DEFINITELY WORKED ON TV.
IT MIGHT...
...BE THIS WAY FOR A WHILE...!!!

CHAPTER 23
ALL THREE, TOGETHER

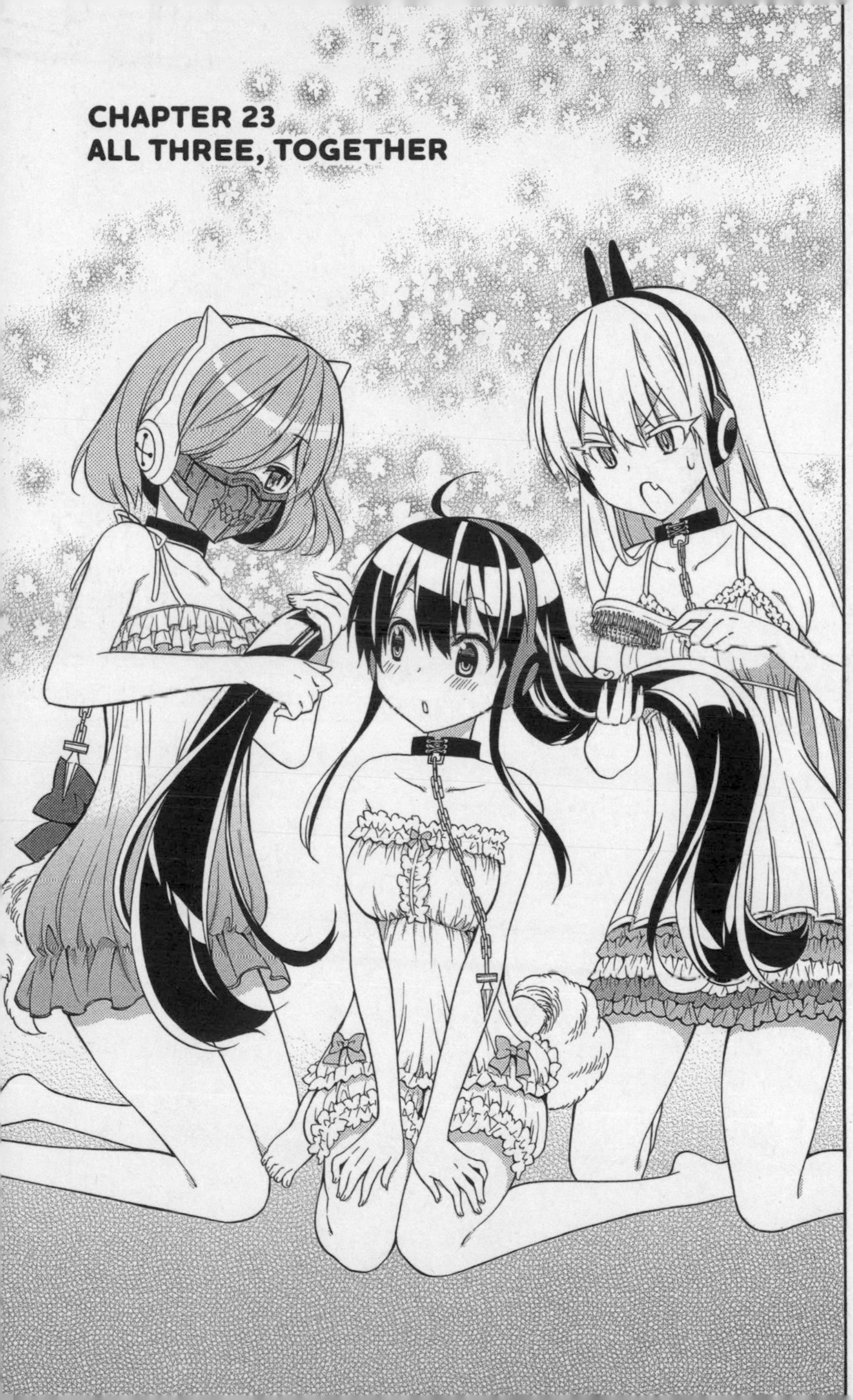

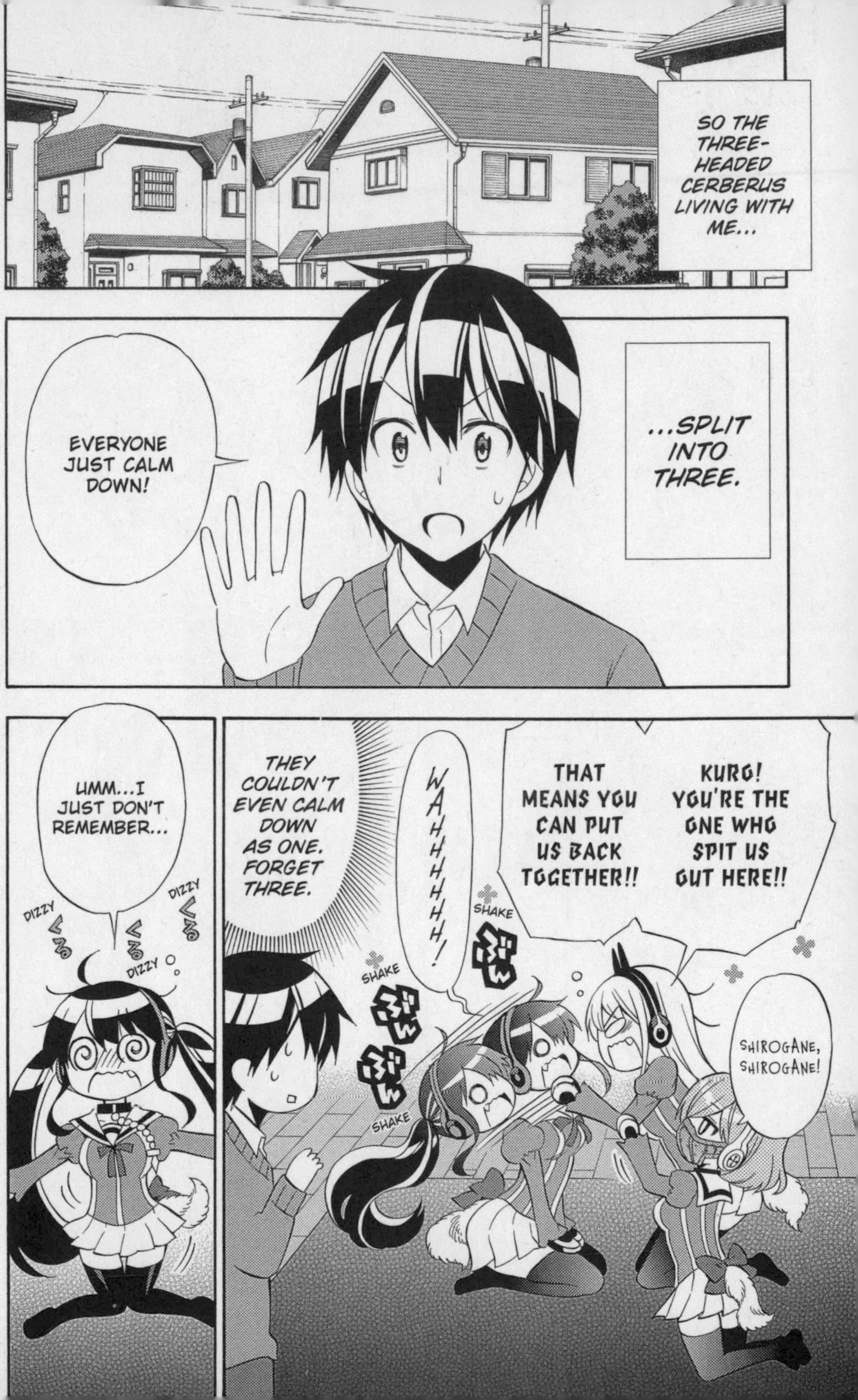
SO THE THREE-HEADED CERBERUS LIVING WITH ME...
...SPLIT INTO THREE.
EVERYONE JUST CALM DOWN!
KURO! YOU'RE THE ONE WHO SPIT US OUT HERE!!
THAT MEANS YOU CAN PUT US BACK TOGETHER!!
SHIROGANE, SHIROGANE!
SHAKE
WAHHHHHHH!
SHAKE
SHAKE
THEY COULDN'T EVEN CALM DOWN AS ONE. FORGET THREE.
UMM...I JUST DON'T REMEMBER...
DIZZY
DIZZY
DIZZY

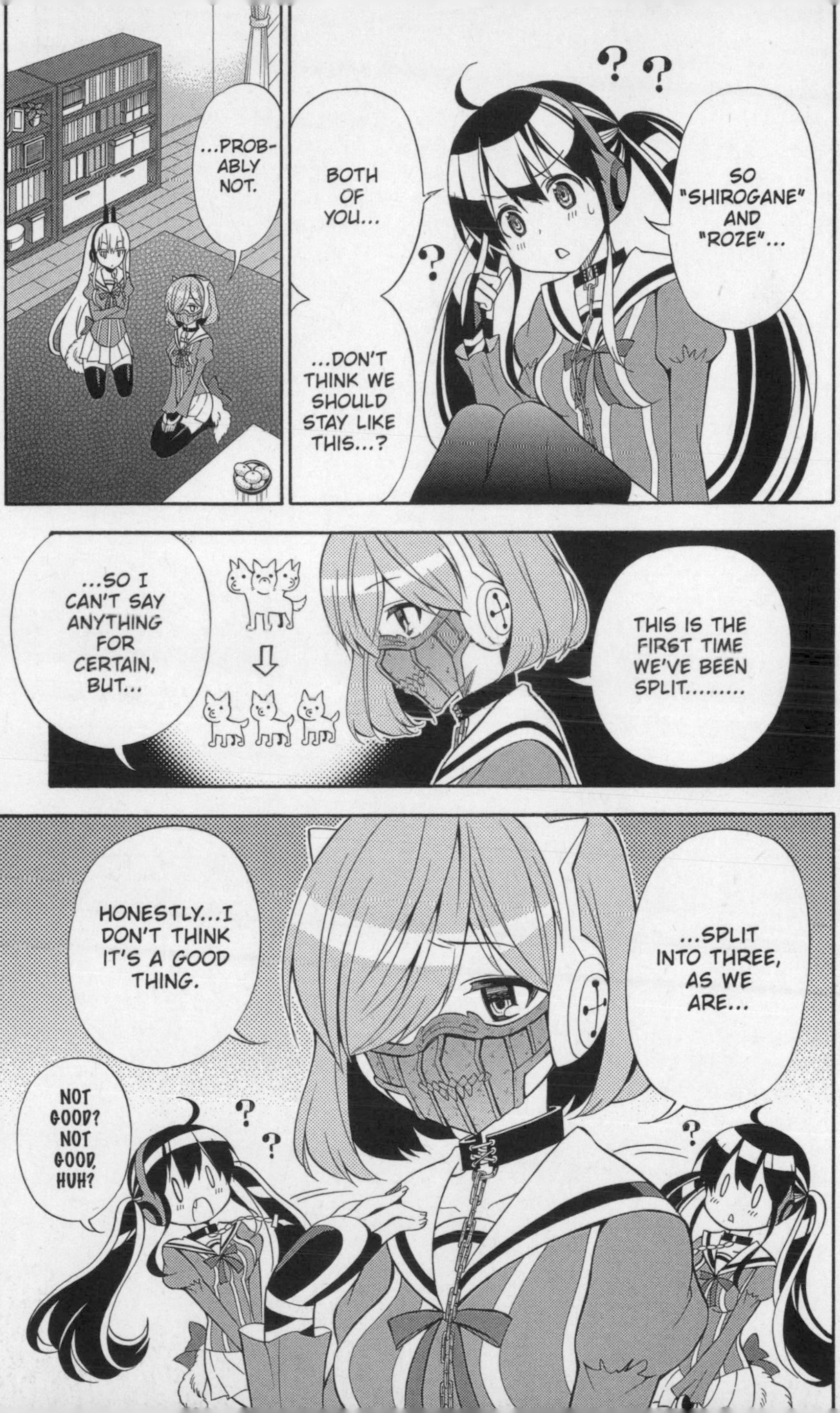
SO "SHIROGANE" AND "ROZE"...
BOTH OF YOU...
...DON'T THINK WE SHOULD STAY LIKE THIS...?
...PROBABLY NOT.
THIS IS THE FIRST TIME WE'VE BEEN SPLIT.........
...SO I CAN'T SAY ANYTHING FOR CERTAIN, BUT...
...SPLIT INTO THREE, AS WE ARE...
HONESTLY...I DON'T THINK IT'S A GOOD THING.
NOT GOOD? NOT GOOD, HUH?

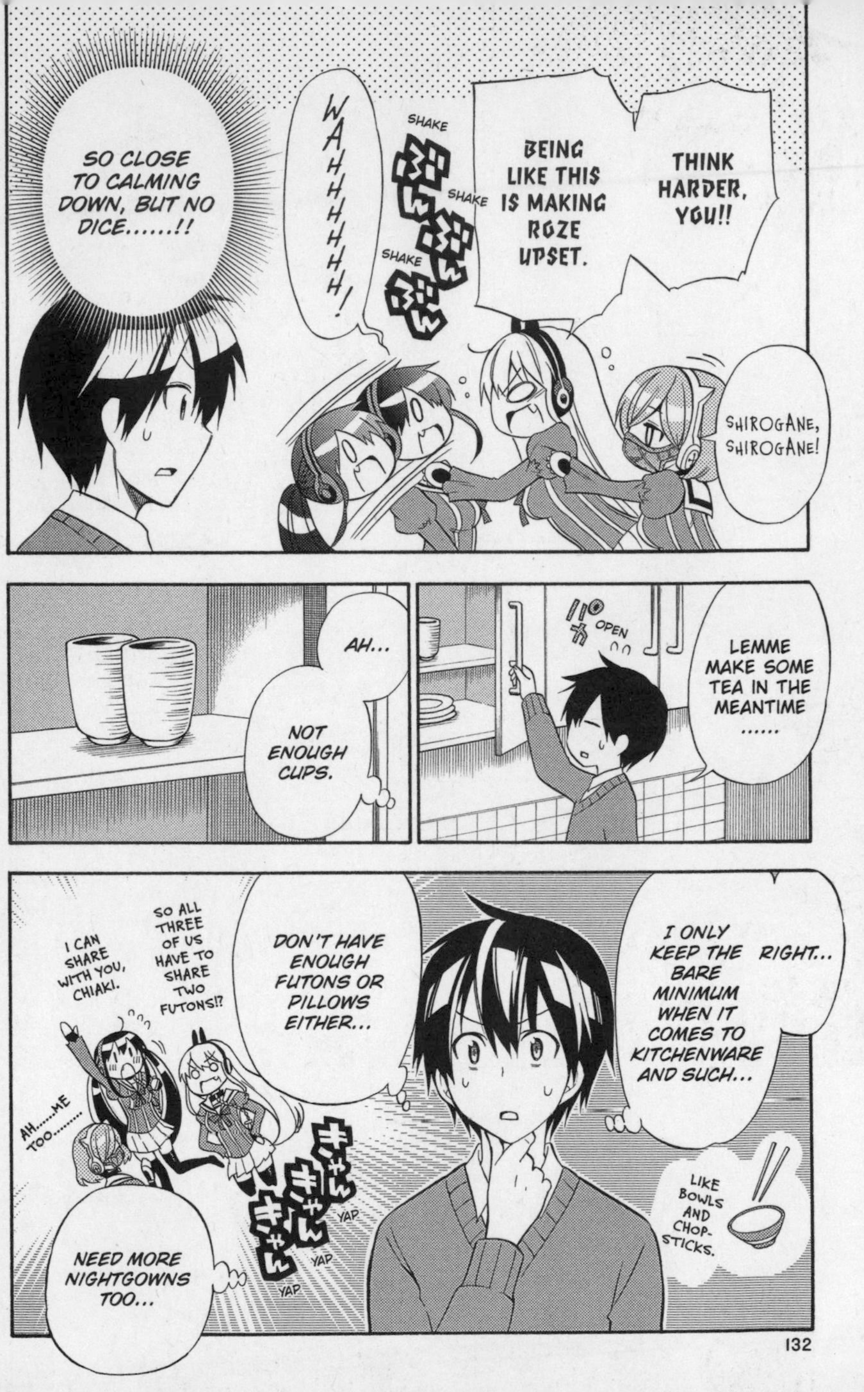
THINK HARDER, YOU!!
BEING LIKE THIS IS MAKING ROZE UPSET.
SHIROGANE, SHIROGANE!
SHAKE
SHAKE
SHAKE
WAHHHHHHH!
SO CLOSE TO CALMING DOWN, BUT NO DICE......!!
OPEN
LEMME MAKE SOME TEA IN THE MEANTIME ......
AH...
NOT ENOUGH CUPS.
RIGHT...
I ONLY KEEP THE BARE MINIMUM WHEN IT COMES TO KITCHENWARE AND SUCH...
LIKE BOWLS AND CHOP-STICKS.
DON'T HAVE ENOUGH FUTONS OR PILLOWS EITHER...
SO ALL THREE OF US HAVE TO SHARE TWO FUTONS!?
I CAN SHARE WITH YOU, CHIAKI.
YAP
YAP
YAP
AH......ME TOO.........
NEED MORE NIGHTGOWNS TOO...

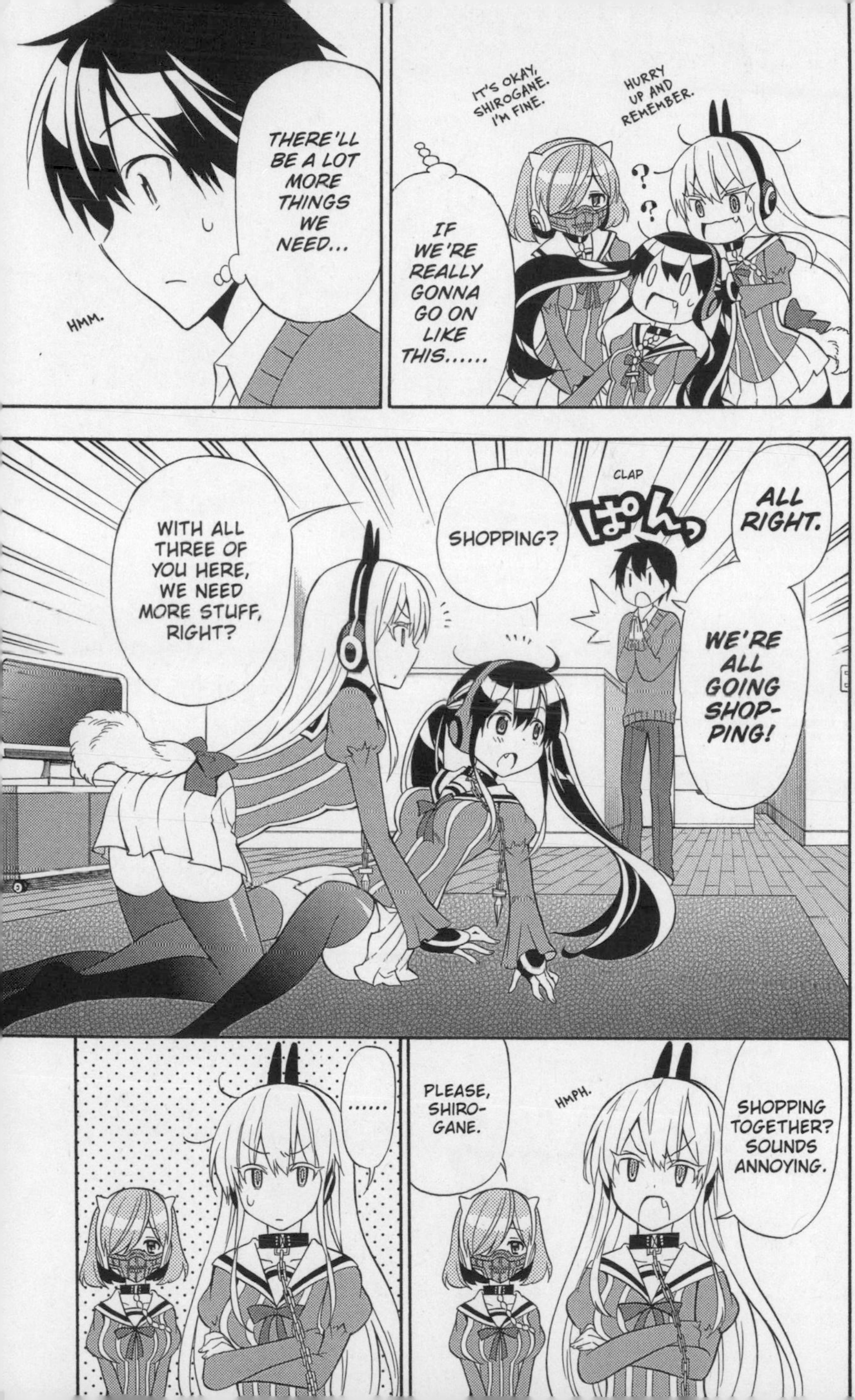
HURRY UP AND REMEMBER.
IT'S OKAY, SHIROGANE. I'M FINE.
??
IF WE'RE REALLY GONNA GO ON LIKE THIS......
THERE'LL BE A LOT MORE THINGS WE NEED...
HMM.
ALL RIGHT.
CLAP
ぱんっ
WE'RE ALL GOING SHOP-PING!
SHOPPING?
WITH ALL THREE OF YOU HERE, WE NEED MORE STUFF, RIGHT?
SHOPPING TOGETHER? SOUNDS ANNOYING.
HMPH.
PLEASE, SHIRO-GANE.
......

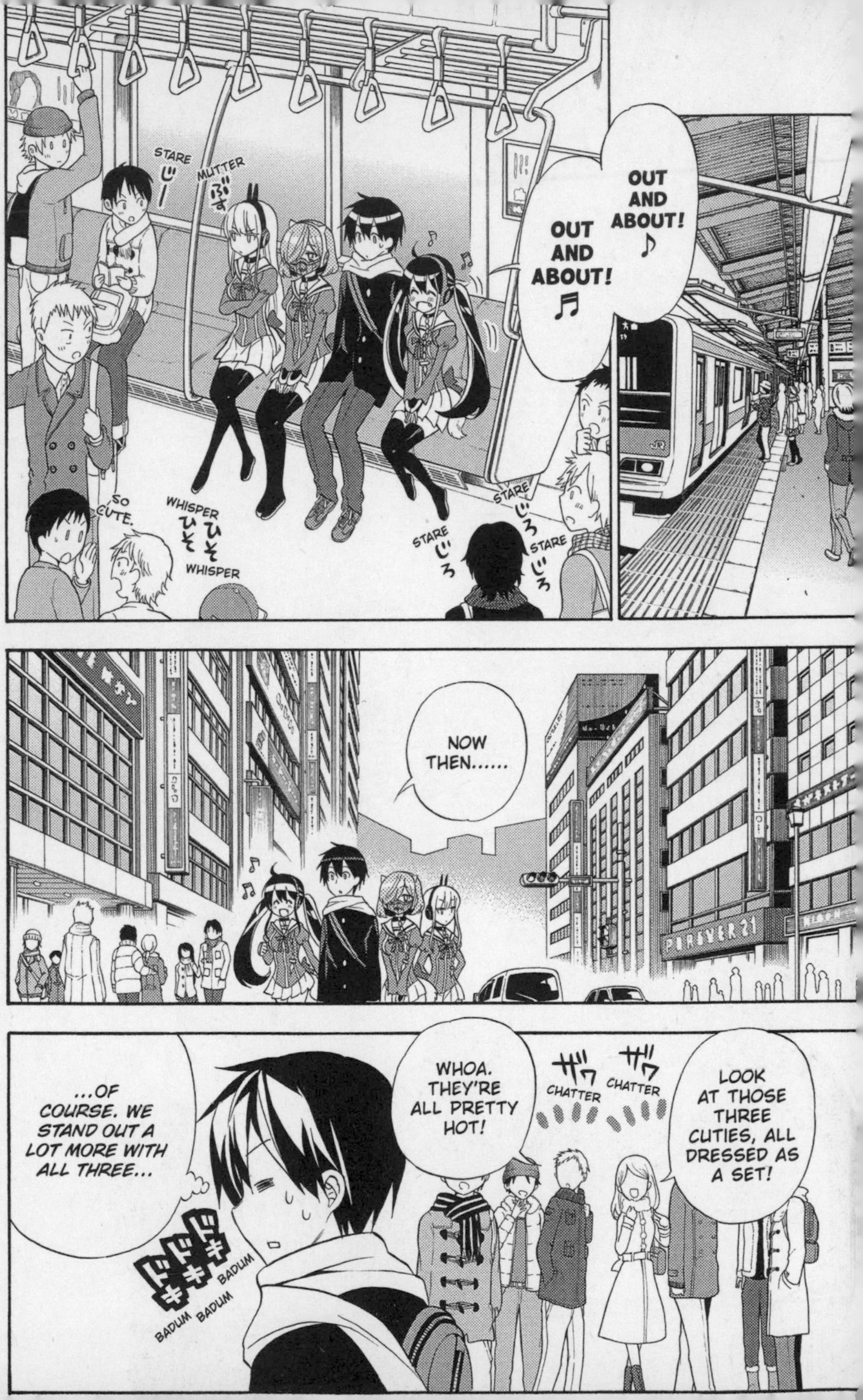
OUT AND ABOUT! ♪
OUT AND ABOUT! ♬
STARE じー
MUTTER ぶす
STARE じろ
STARE じろ
STARE じろ
WHISPER ひそ ひそ WHISPER
SO CUTE.
NOW THEN......
LOOK AT THOSE THREE CUTIES, ALL DRESSED AS A SET!
ザワ CHATTER
ザワ CHATTER
WHOA. THEY'RE ALL PRETTY HOT!
...OF COURSE. WE STAND OUT A LOT MORE WITH ALL THREE...
ドキ ドキ ドキ
BADUM BADUM BADUM

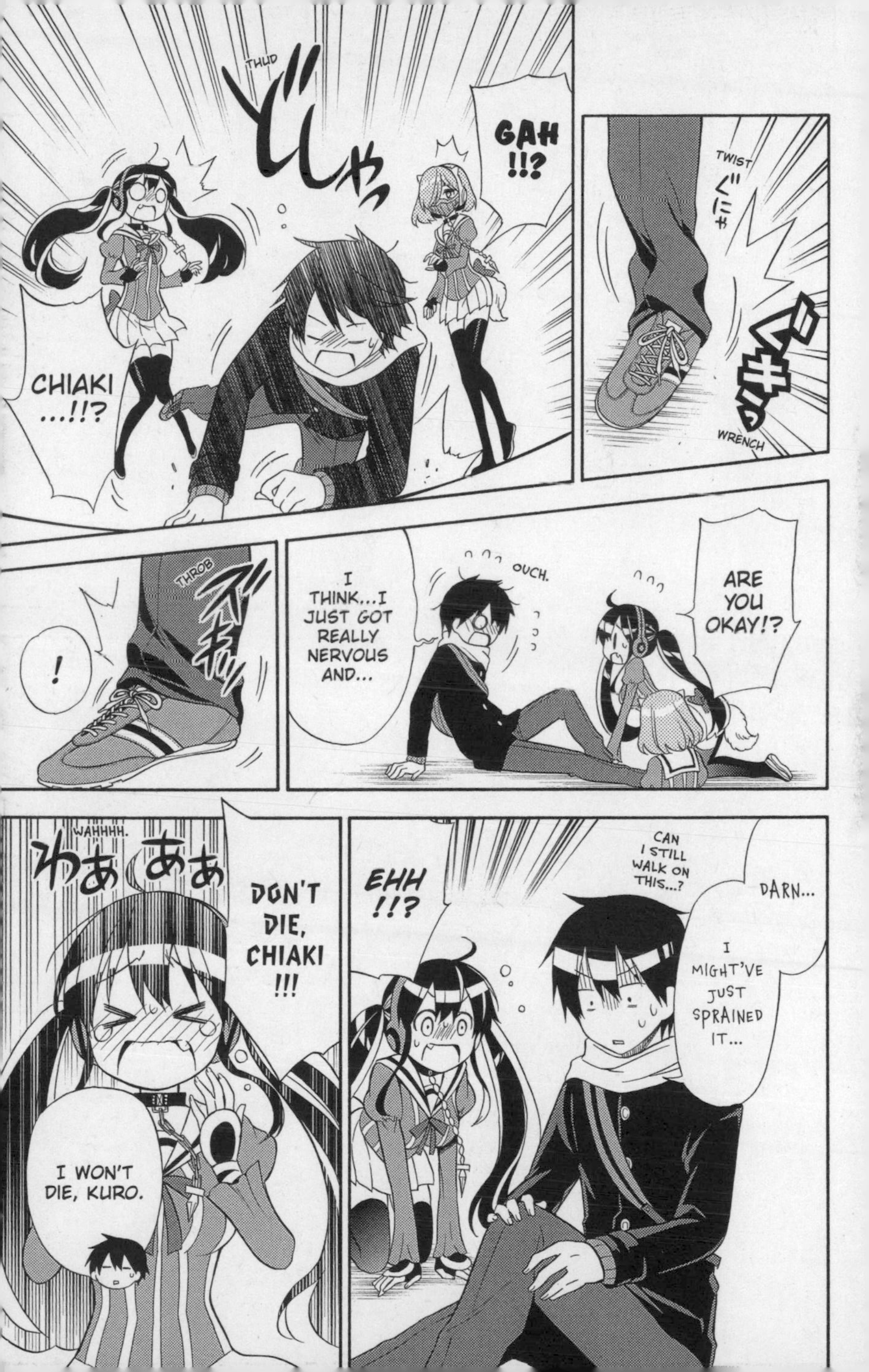

TWIST
ぐにゃ
WRENCH
THUD
どしゃっ
GAH !!?
CHIAKI ...!!?
ARE YOU OKAY!?
OUCH.
I THINK...I JUST GOT REALLY NERVOUS AND...
THROB
!
DARN...
I MIGHT'VE JUST SPRAINED IT...
CAN I STILL WALK ON THIS...?
EHH !!?
DON'T DIE, CHIAKI !!!
WAHHHH.
わあ
I WON'T DIE, KURO.

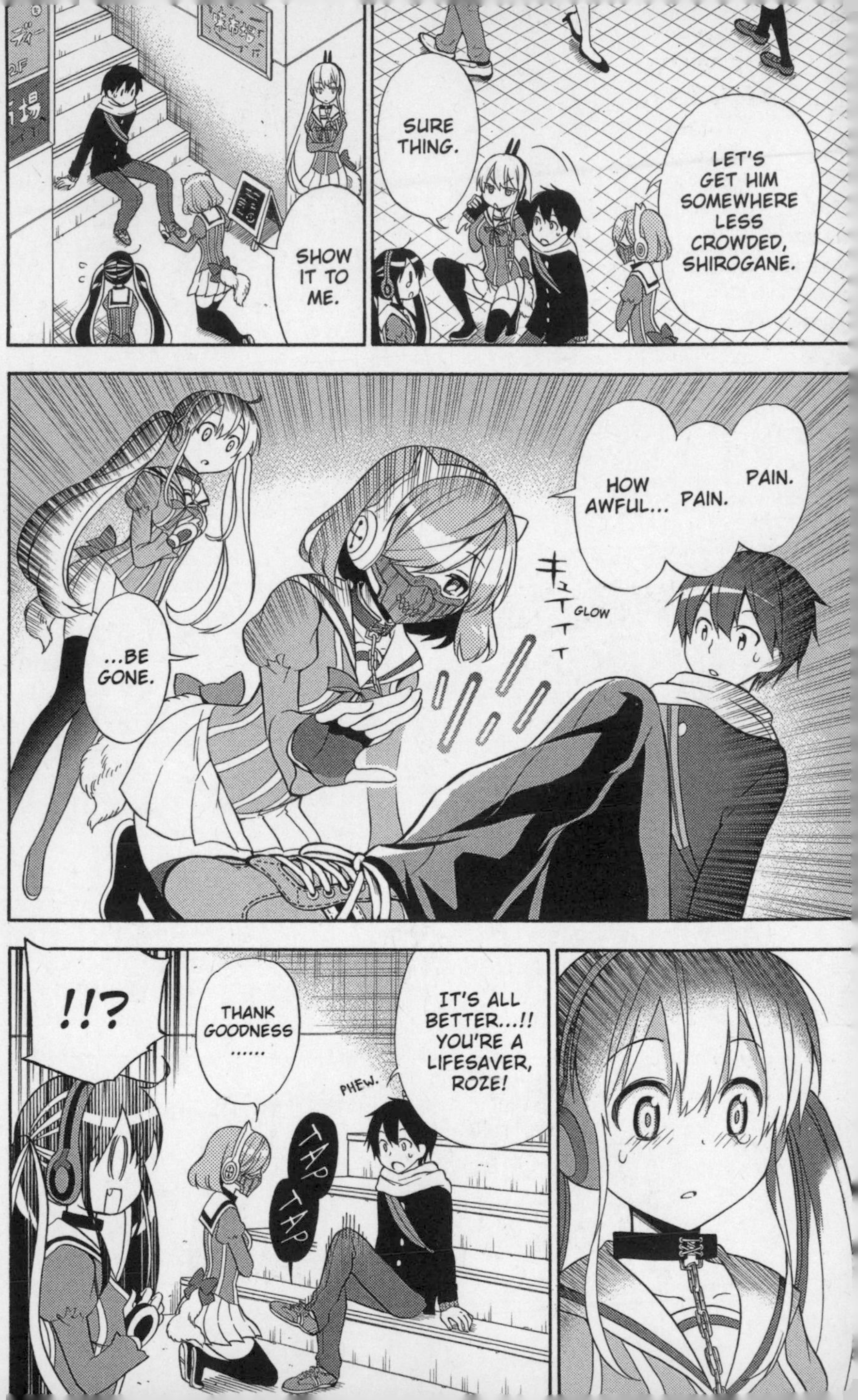
LET'S GET HIM SOMEWHERE LESS CROWDED, SHIROGANE.
SURE THING.
SHOW IT TO ME.
HOW AWFUL... PAIN. PAIN.
GLOW
...BE GONE.
IT'S ALL BETTER...!! YOU'RE A LIFESAVER, ROZE!
PHEW.
TAP TAP
THANK GOODNESS ......
!!?

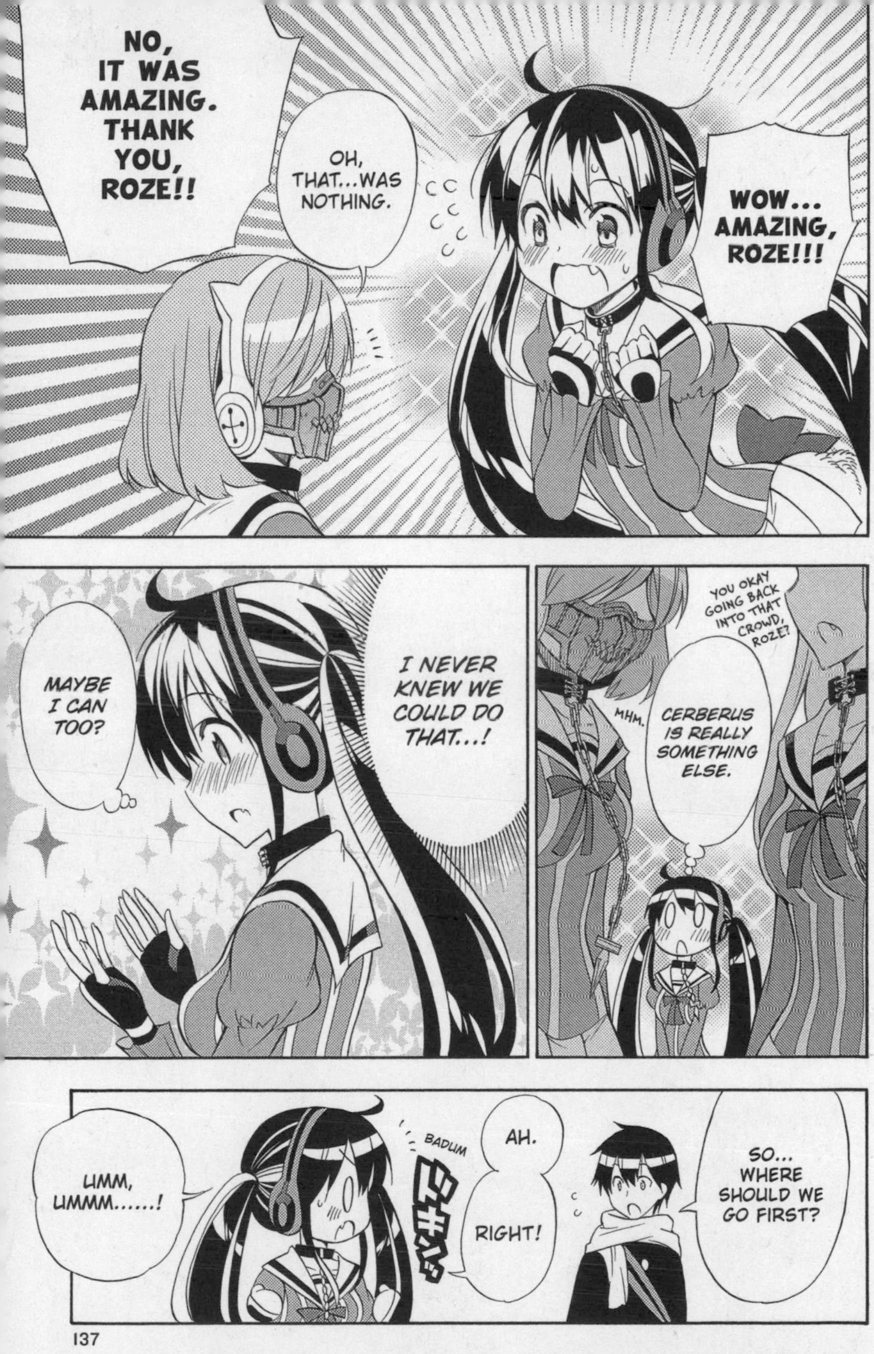
WOW... AMAZING, ROZE!!!
OH, THAT...WAS NOTHING.
NO, IT WAS AMAZING. THANK YOU, ROZE!!
YOU OKAY GOING BACK INTO THAT CROWD, ROZE?
CERBERUS IS REALLY SOMETHING ELSE.
MHM.
I NEVER KNEW WE COULD DO THAT...!
MAYBE I CAN TOO?
SO... WHERE SHOULD WE GO FIRST?
AH.
RIGHT!
BADUM
UMM, UMMM......!

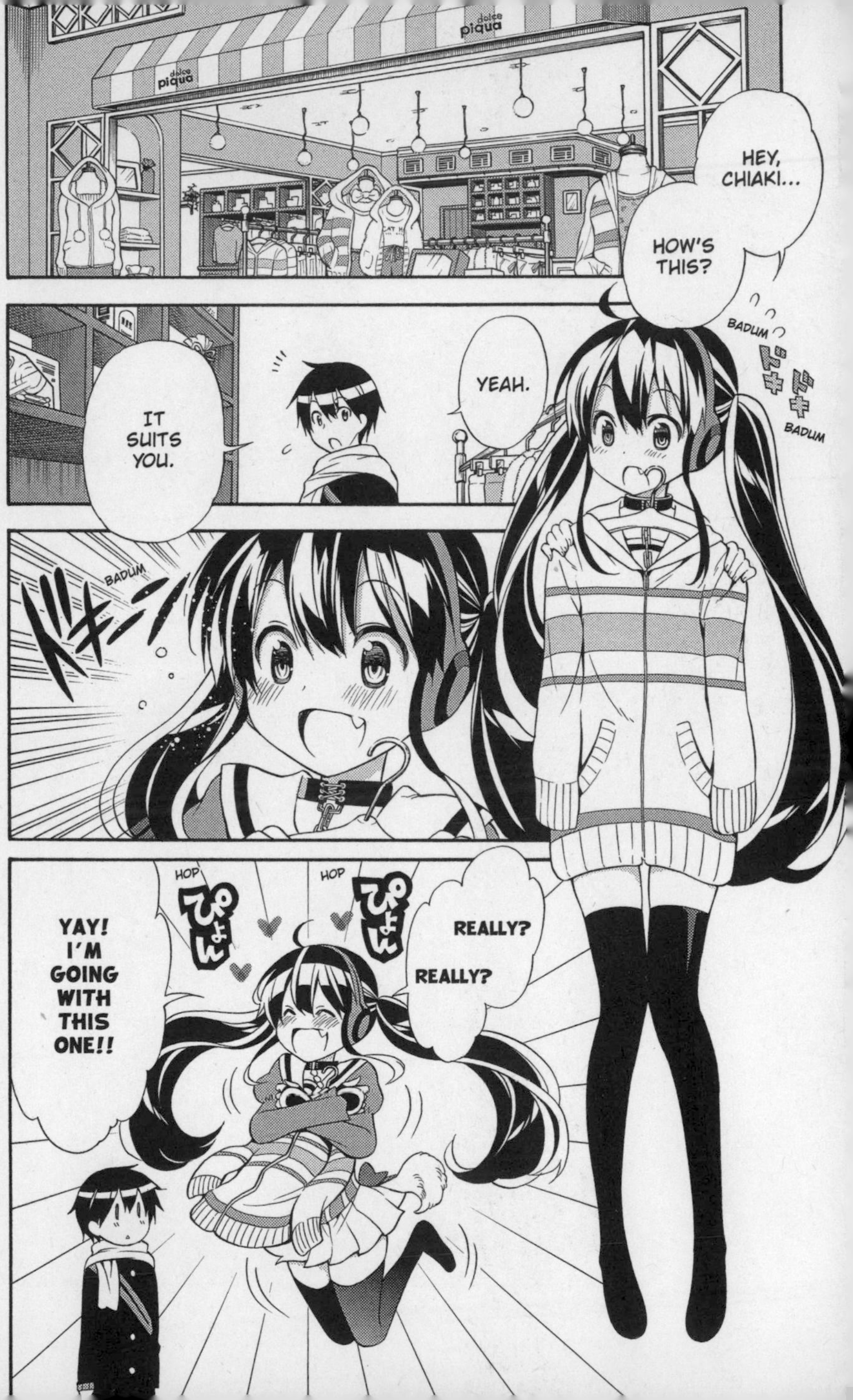
dolce piqua
dolce piqua
HEY, CHIAKI...
HOW'S THIS?
BADUM
ドキドキ
BADUM
YEAH.
IT SUITS YOU.
BADUM
ドキーン
REALLY?
REALLY?
HOP
ぴょん
HOP
ぴょん
YAY! I'M GOING WITH THIS ONE!!

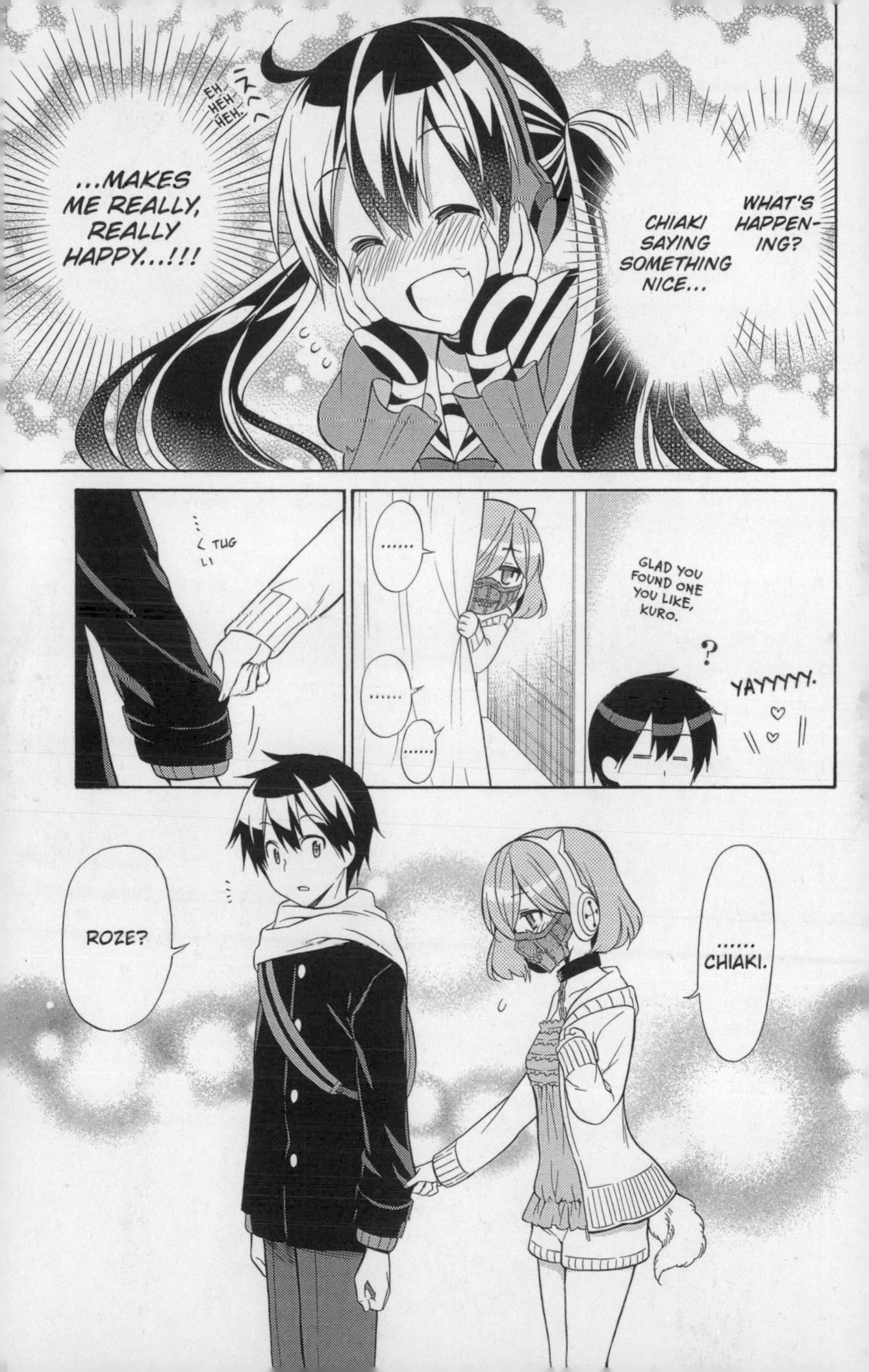
WHAT'S HAPPEN-ING?
CHIAKI SAYING SOMETHING NICE...
EH HEH HEH.
...MAKES ME REALLY, REALLY HAPPY...!!!
GLAD YOU FOUND ONE YOU LIKE, KURO.
?
YAYYYYY.
......
......
......
TUG
......CHIAKI.
ROZE?

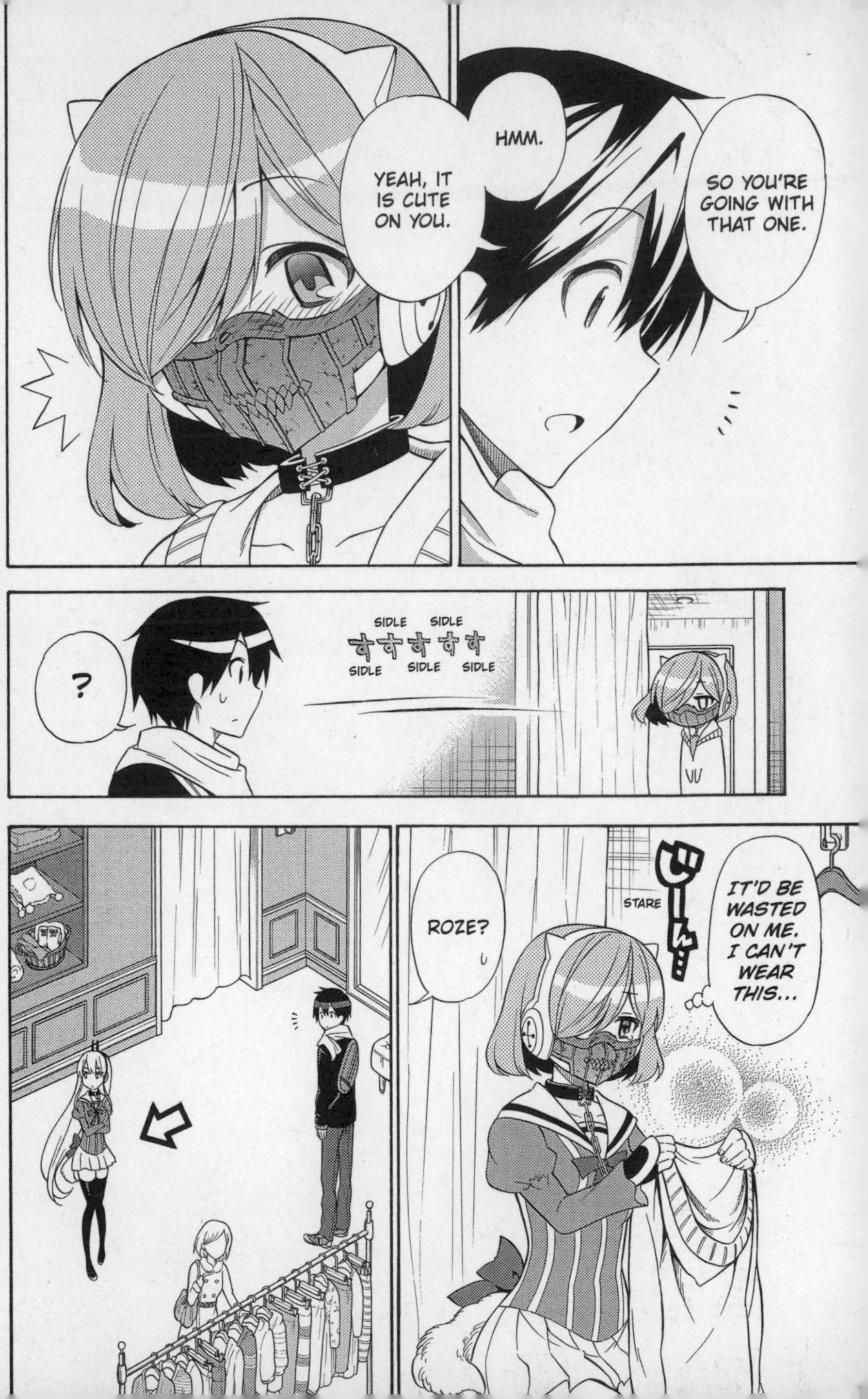
SO YOU'RE GOING WITH THAT ONE.
HMM.
YEAH, IT IS CUTE ON YOU.
SIDLE SIDLE
すすすすす
SIDLE SIDLE SIDLE
?
IT'D BE WASTED ON ME. I CAN'T WEAR THIS...
STARE
ROZE?

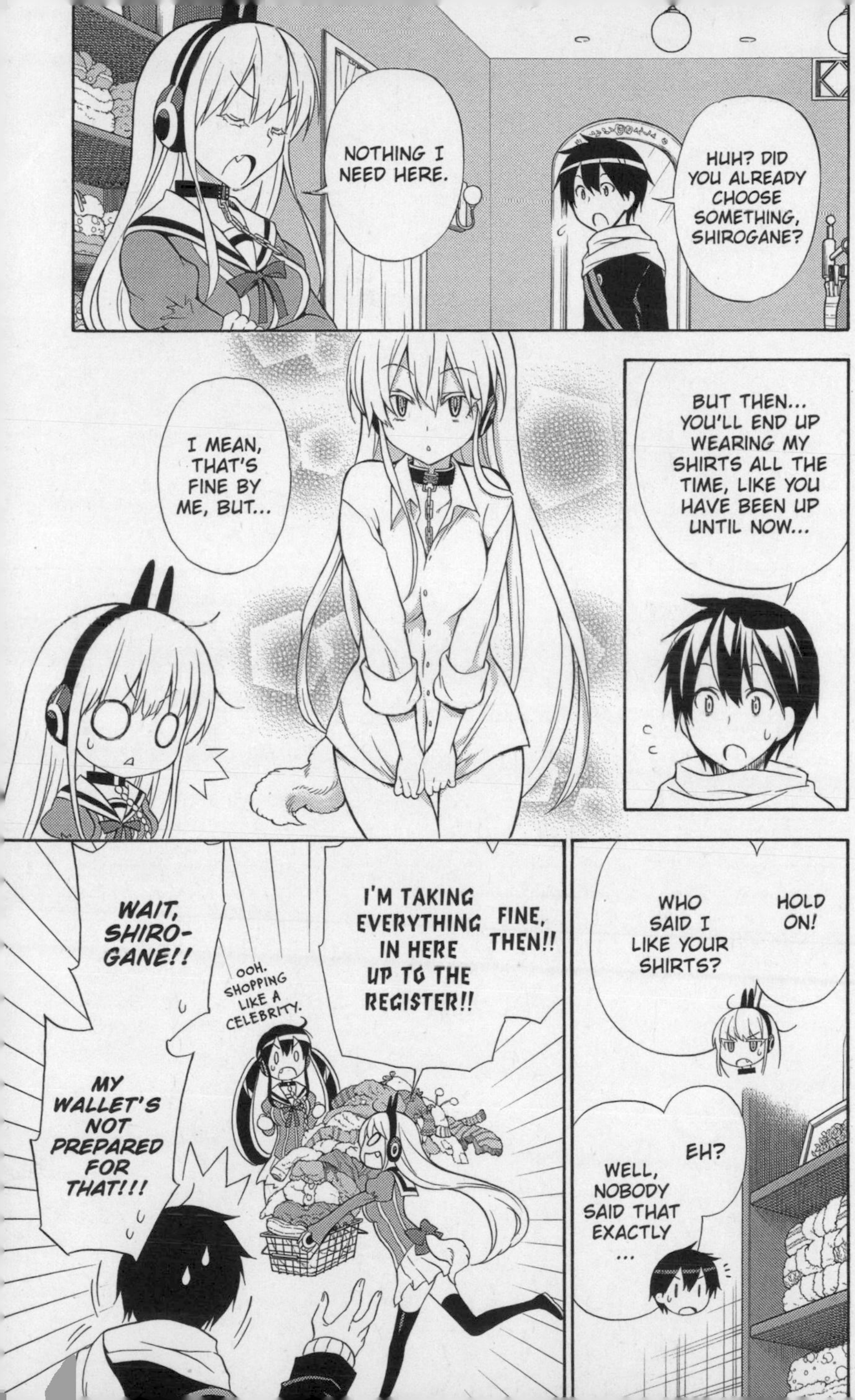
HUH? DID YOU ALREADY CHOOSE SOMETHING, SHIROGANE?
NOTHING I NEED HERE.
BUT THEN... YOU'LL END UP WEARING MY SHIRTS ALL THE TIME, LIKE YOU HAVE BEEN UP UNTIL NOW...
I MEAN, THAT'S FINE BY ME, BUT...
HOLD ON!
WHO SAID I LIKE YOUR SHIRTS?
EH?
WELL, NOBODY SAID THAT EXACTLY ...
FINE, THEN!!
I'M TAKING EVERYTHING IN HERE UP TO THE REGISTER!!
OOH. SHOPPING LIKE A CELEBRITY.
WAIT, SHIRO-GANE!!
MY WALLET'S NOT PREPARED FOR THAT!!!

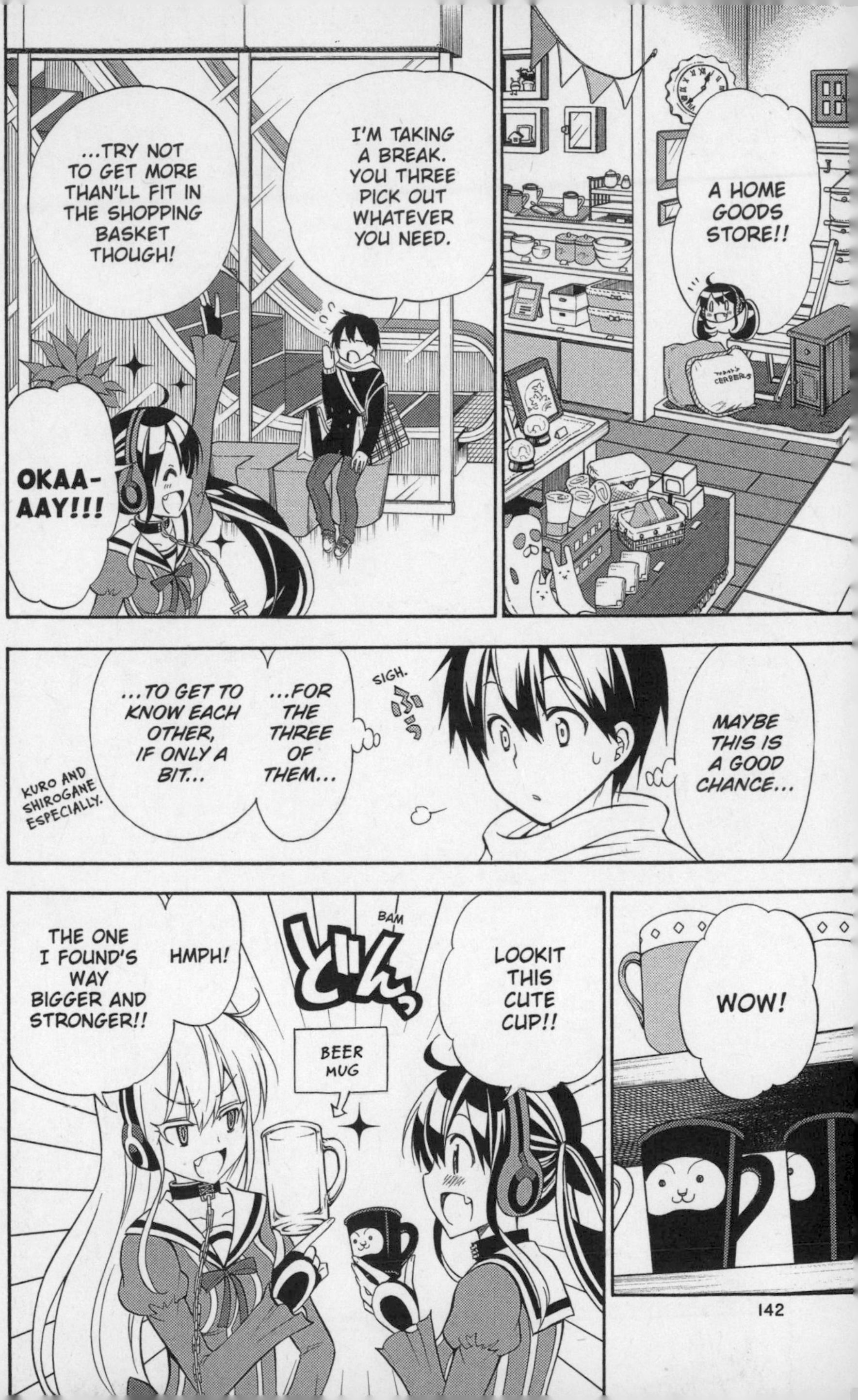
A HOME GOODS STORE!!
I'M TAKING A BREAK. YOU THREE PICK OUT WHATEVER YOU NEED.
...TRY NOT TO GET MORE THAN'LL FIT IN THE SHOPPING BASKET THOUGH!
OKAA-AAY!!!
MAYBE THIS IS A GOOD CHANCE...
SIGH.
...FOR THE THREE OF THEM...
...TO GET TO KNOW EACH OTHER, IF ONLY A BIT...
KURO AND SHIROGANE ESPECIALLY.
WOW!
LOOKIT THIS CUTE CUP!!
BAM
HMPH!
THE ONE I FOUND'S WAY BIGGER AND STRONGER!!
BEER MUG

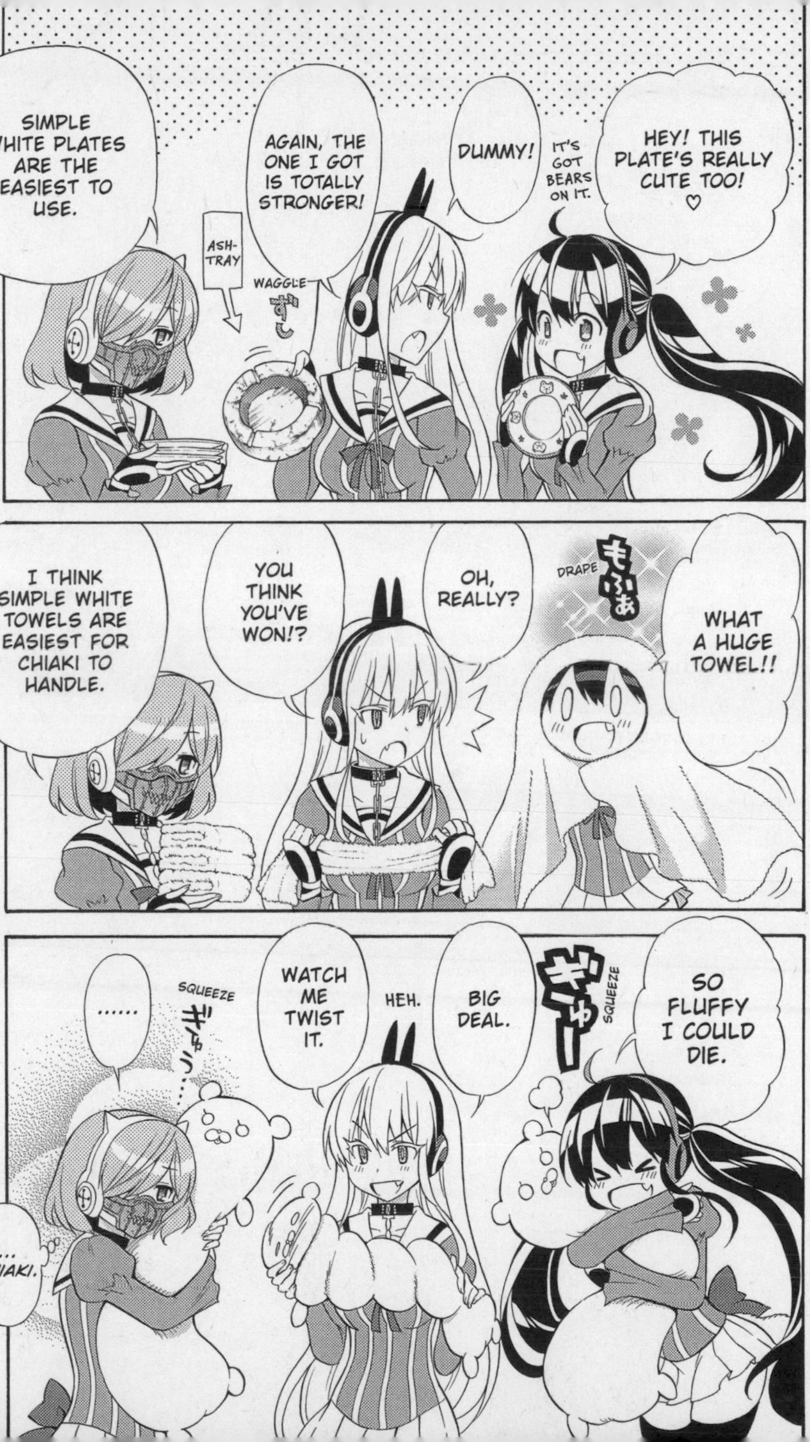
HEY! THIS PLATE'S REALLY CUTE TOO! ♡
IT'S GOT BEARS ON IT.
DUMMY!
AGAIN, THE ONE I GOT IS TOTALLY STRONGER!
WAGGLE
ASH-TRAY
SIMPLE WHITE PLATES ARE THE EASIEST TO USE.
WHAT A HUGE TOWEL!!
DRAPE
OH, REALLY?
YOU THINK YOU'VE WON!?
I THINK SIMPLE WHITE TOWELS ARE EASIEST FOR CHIAKI TO HANDLE.
SO FLUFFY I COULD DIE.
SQUEEZE
BIG DEAL.
HEH.
WATCH ME TWIST IT.
SQUEEZE
......
...CHIAKI.

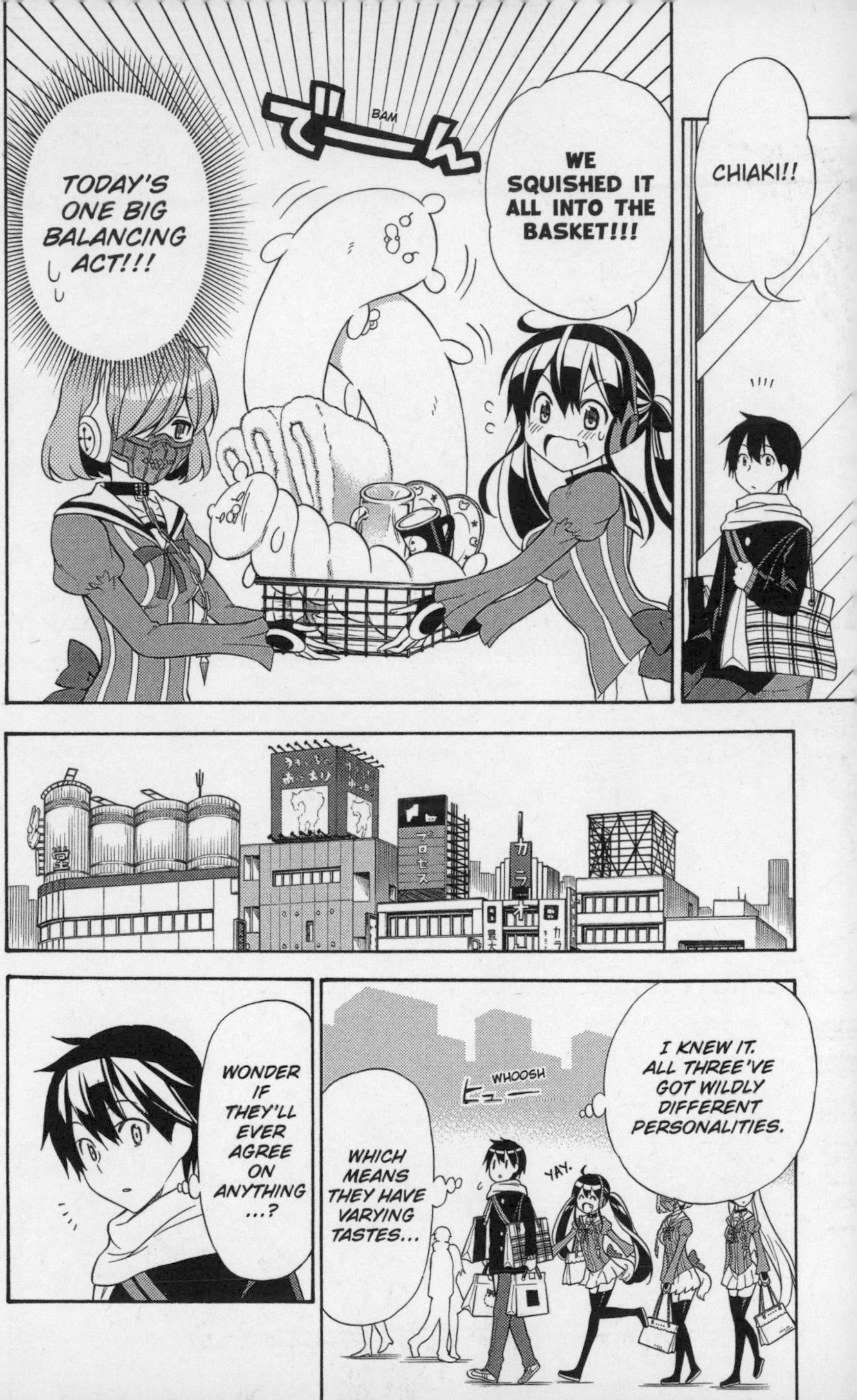
CHIAKI!!
WE SQUISHED IT ALL INTO THE BASKET!!!
BAM
TODAY'S ONE BIG BALANCING ACT!!!
I KNEW IT. ALL THREE'VE GOT WILDLY DIFFERENT PERSONALITIES.
WHOOSH
YAY.
WHICH MEANS THEY HAVE VARYING TASTES...
WONDER IF THEY'LL EVER AGREE ON ANYTHING ...?

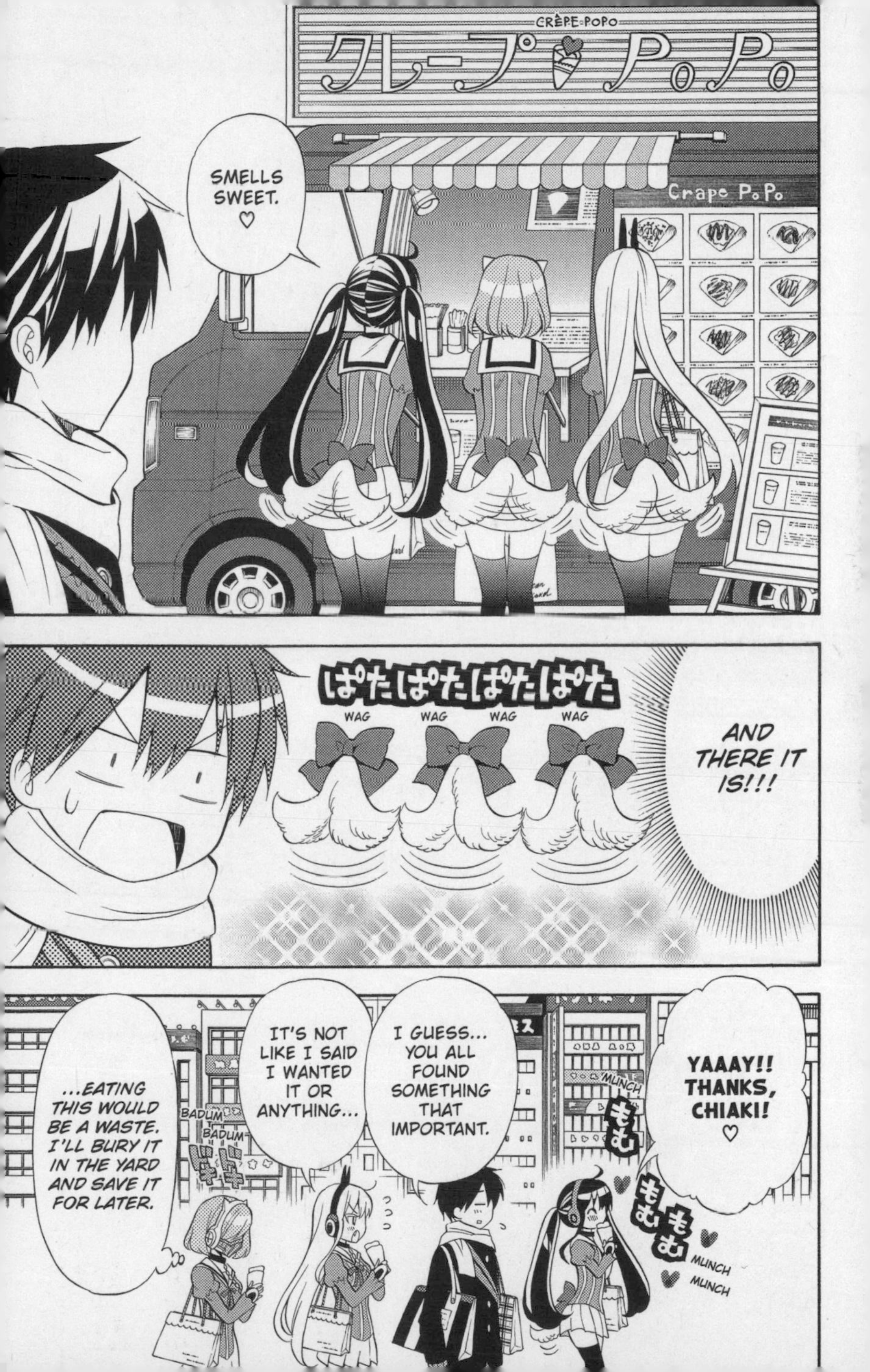
CRÊPE POPO
クレープ♥PoPo
Crape PoPo
SMELLS SWEET. ♡
AND THERE IT IS!!!
ぱたぱたぱたぱた
WAG WAG WAG WAG
YAAAY!! THANKS, CHIAKI! ♡
MUNCH
もむ
もむもむ
MUNCH MUNCH
I GUESS... YOU ALL FOUND SOMETHING THAT IMPORTANT.
IT'S NOT LIKE I SAID I WANTED IT OR ANYTHING...
BADUM BADUM
...EATING THIS WOULD BE A WASTE. I'LL BURY IT IN THE YARD AND SAVE IT FOR LATER.

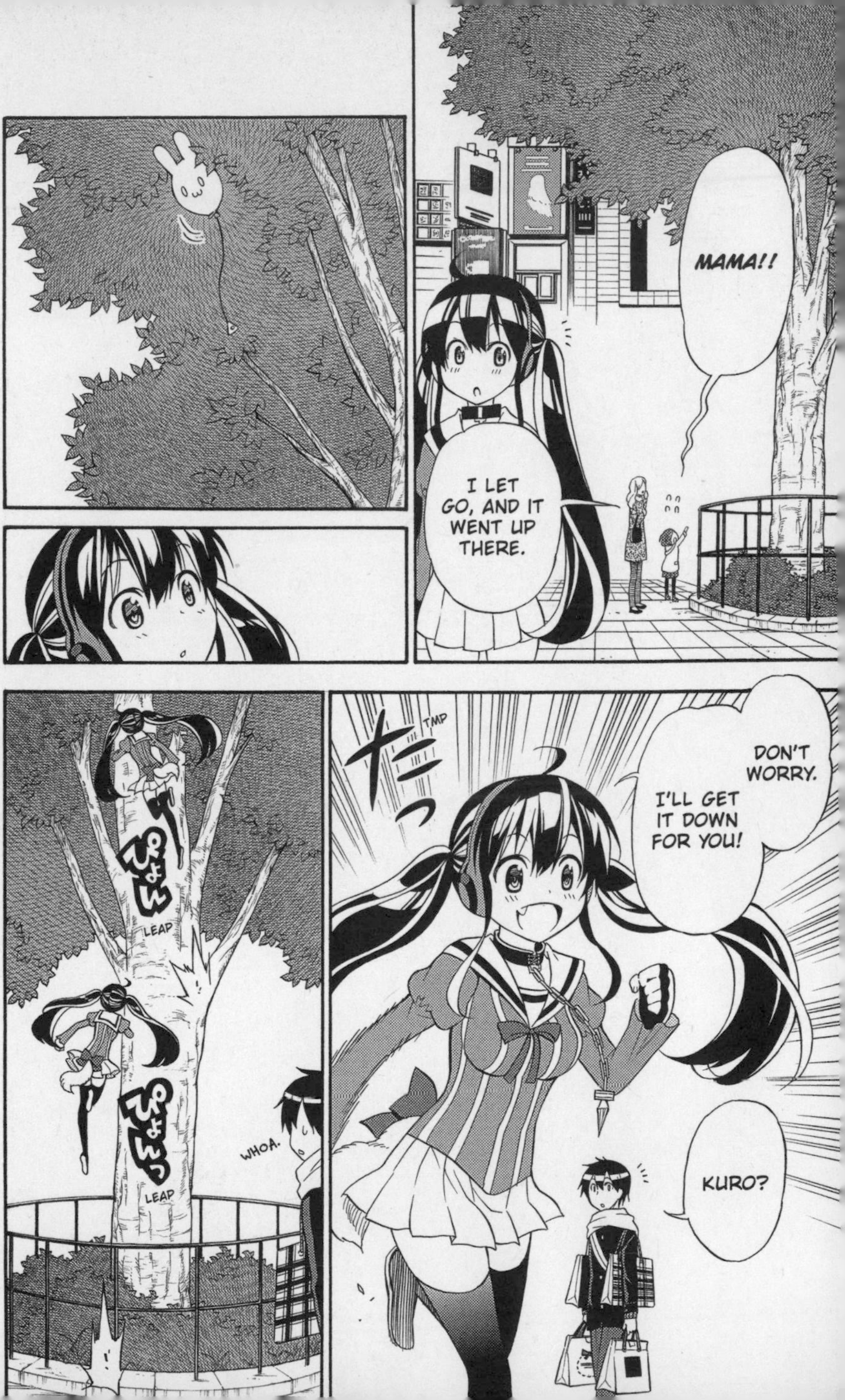
MAMA!!
I LET GO, AND IT WENT UP THERE.
TMP
DON'T WORRY.
I'LL GET IT DOWN FOR YOU!
KURO?
LEAP
LEAP
WHOA.

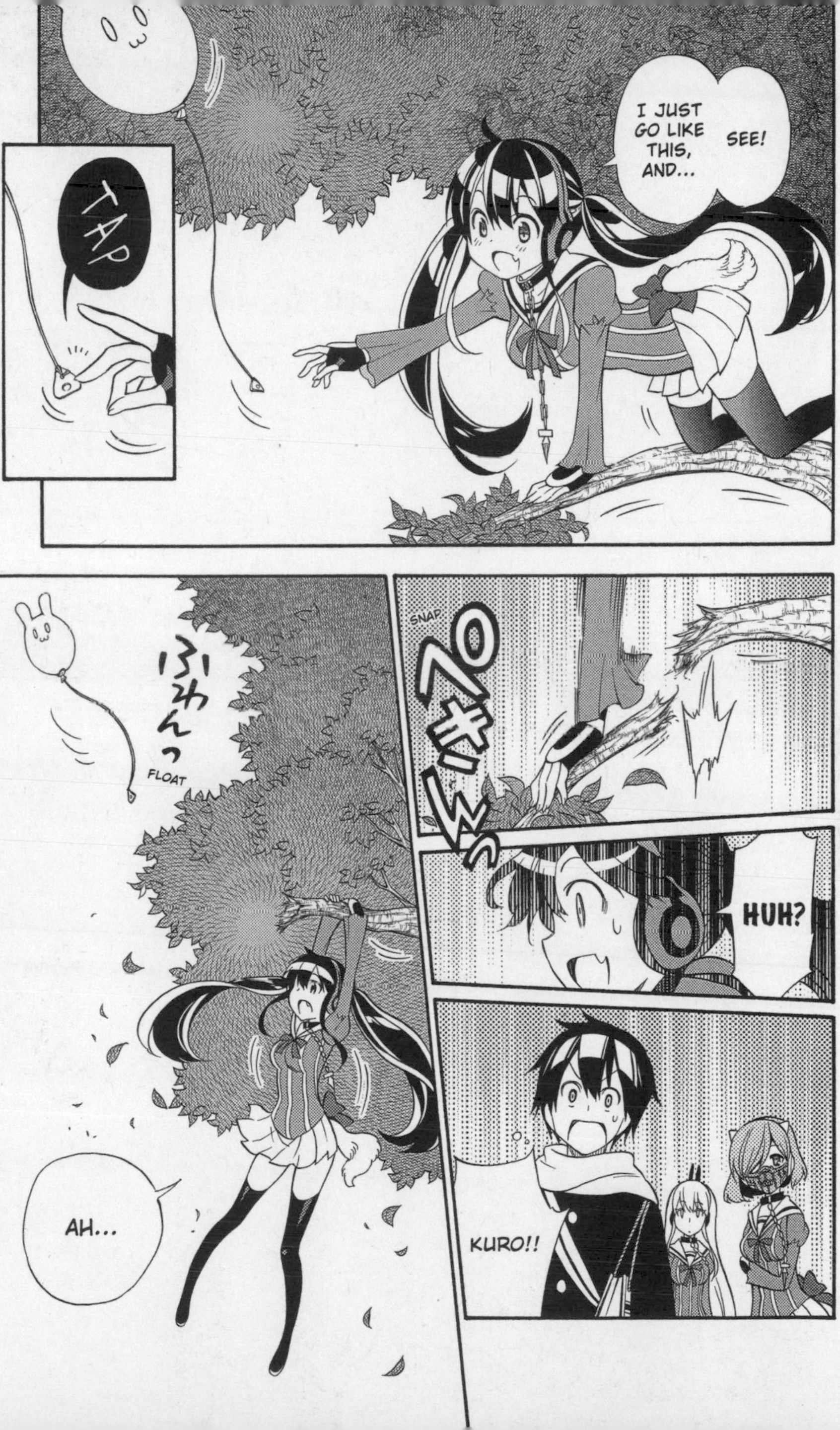
I JUST GO LIKE THIS, AND...
SEE!
TAP
SNAP
ぺきぃっ
HUH?
KURO!!
ふわんっ
FLOAT
AH...

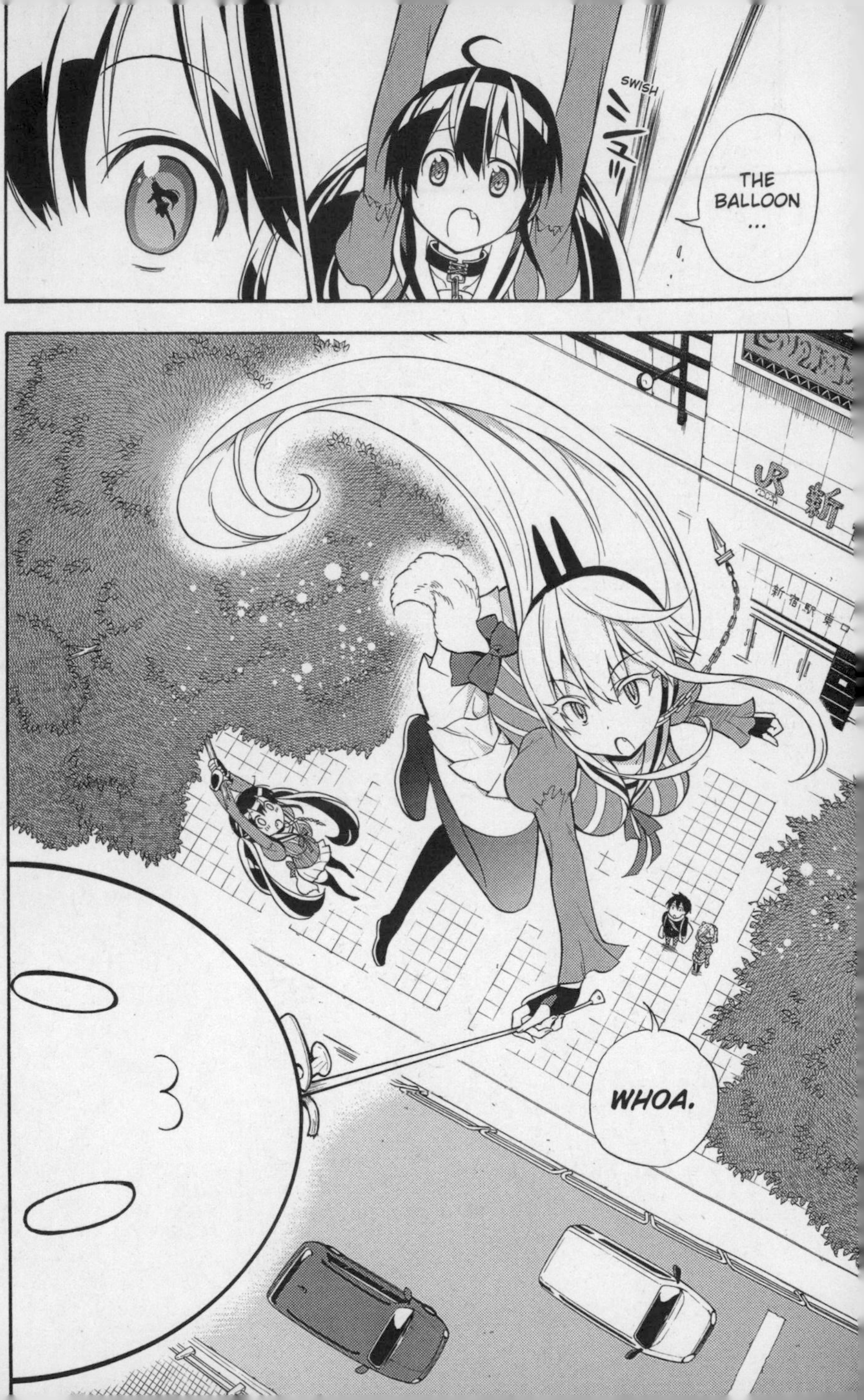
THE BALLOON ...
SWISH
新宿駅東口
WHOA.

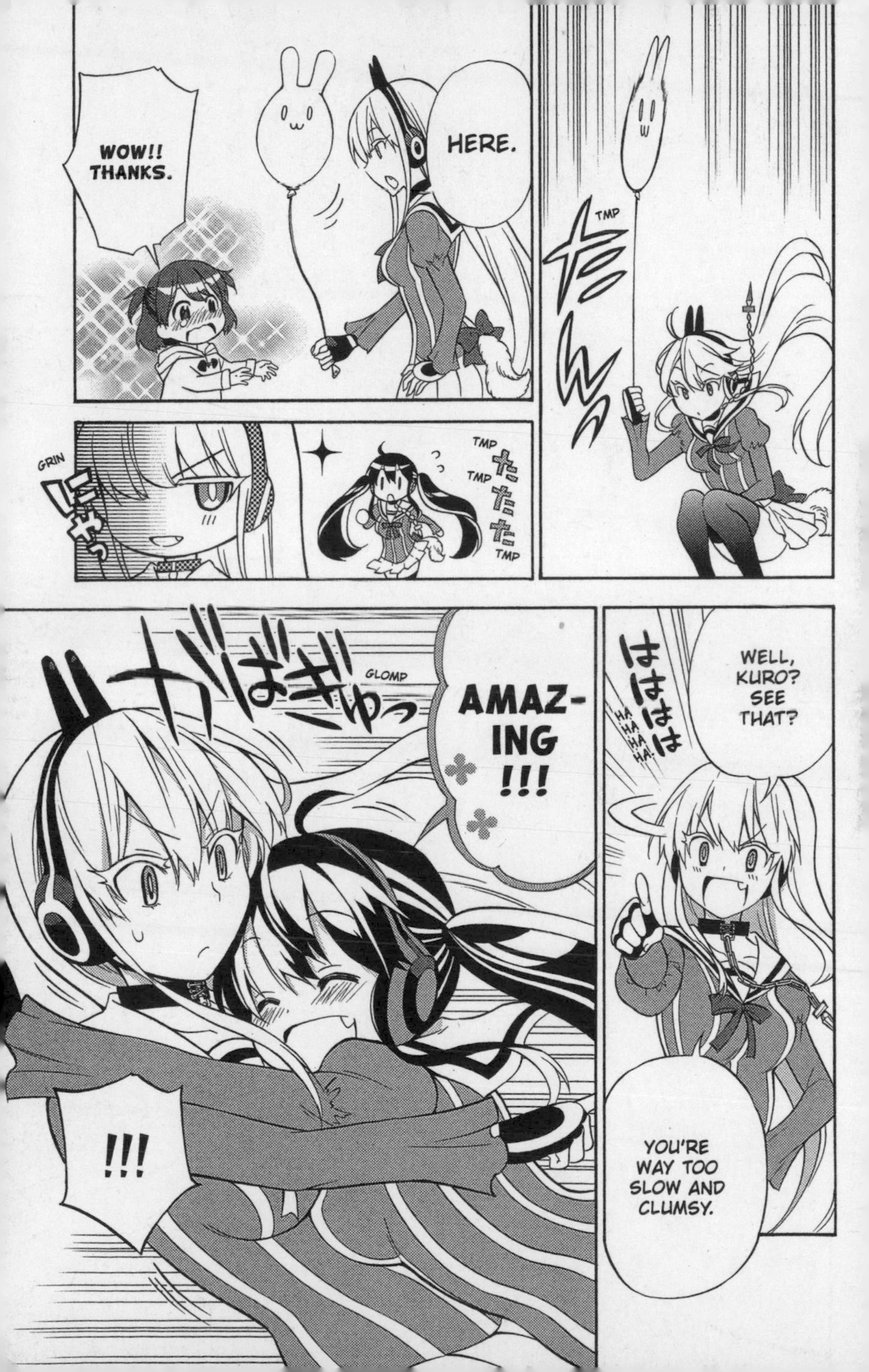
TMP
たんっ
HERE.
WOW!! THANKS.
TMP TMP TMP
たたた
GRIN
にやっ
WELL, KURO? SEE THAT?
ははは
HA HA HA HA!
YOU'RE WAY TOO SLOW AND CLUMSY.
AMAZ-ING!!!
GLOMP
がばぎゅっ
!!!

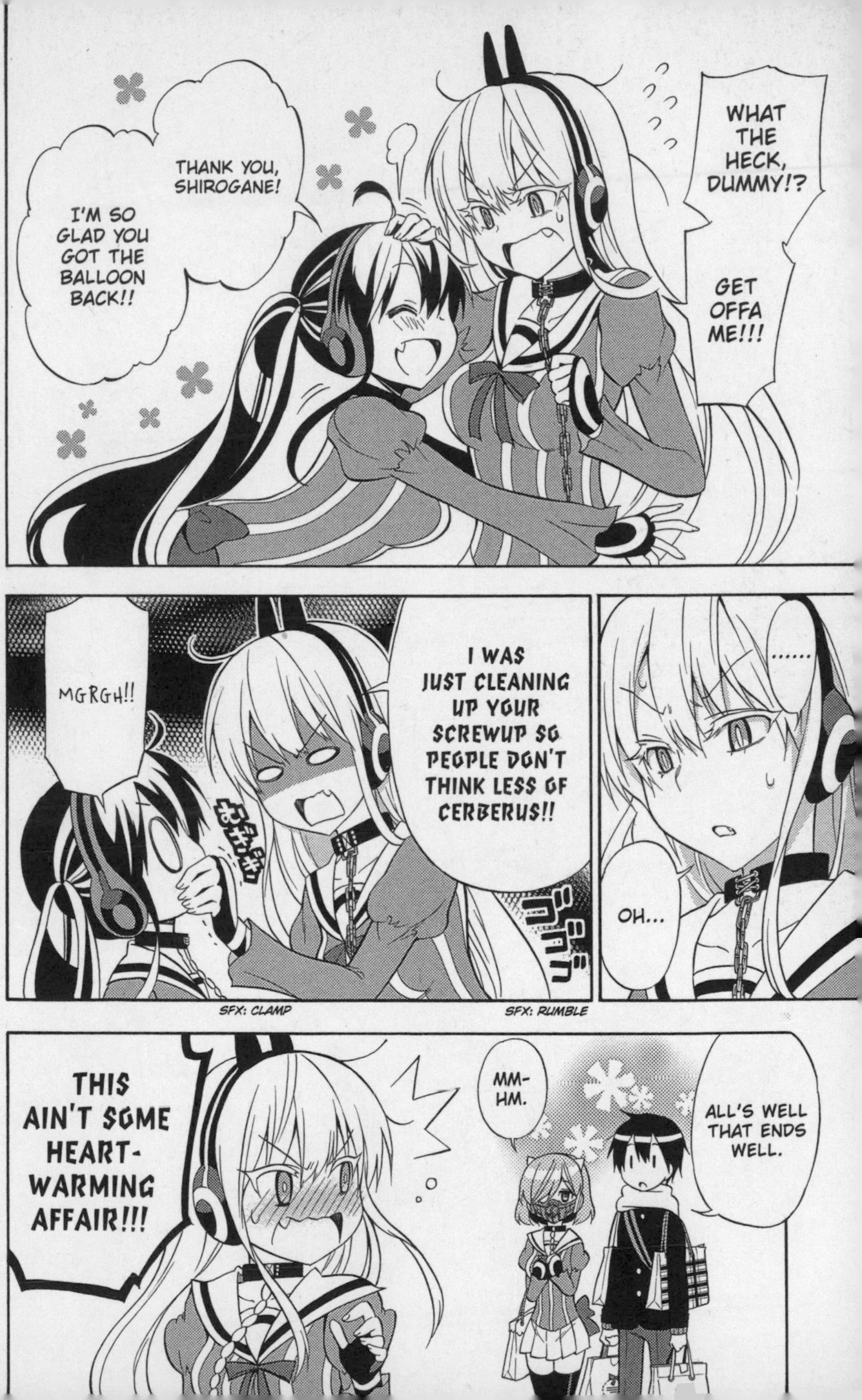
WHAT THE HECK, DUMMY!? GET OFFA ME!!!
THANK YOU, SHIROGANE! I'M SO GLAD YOU GOT THE BALLOON BACK!!
......
OH...
I WAS JUST CLEANING UP YOUR SCREWUP SO PEOPLE DON'T THINK LESS OF CERBERUS!!
MGRGH!!
SFX: RUMBLE
SFX: CLAMP
ALL'S WELL THAT ENDS WELL.
MM-HM.
THIS AIN'T SOME HEART-WARMING AFFAIR!!!

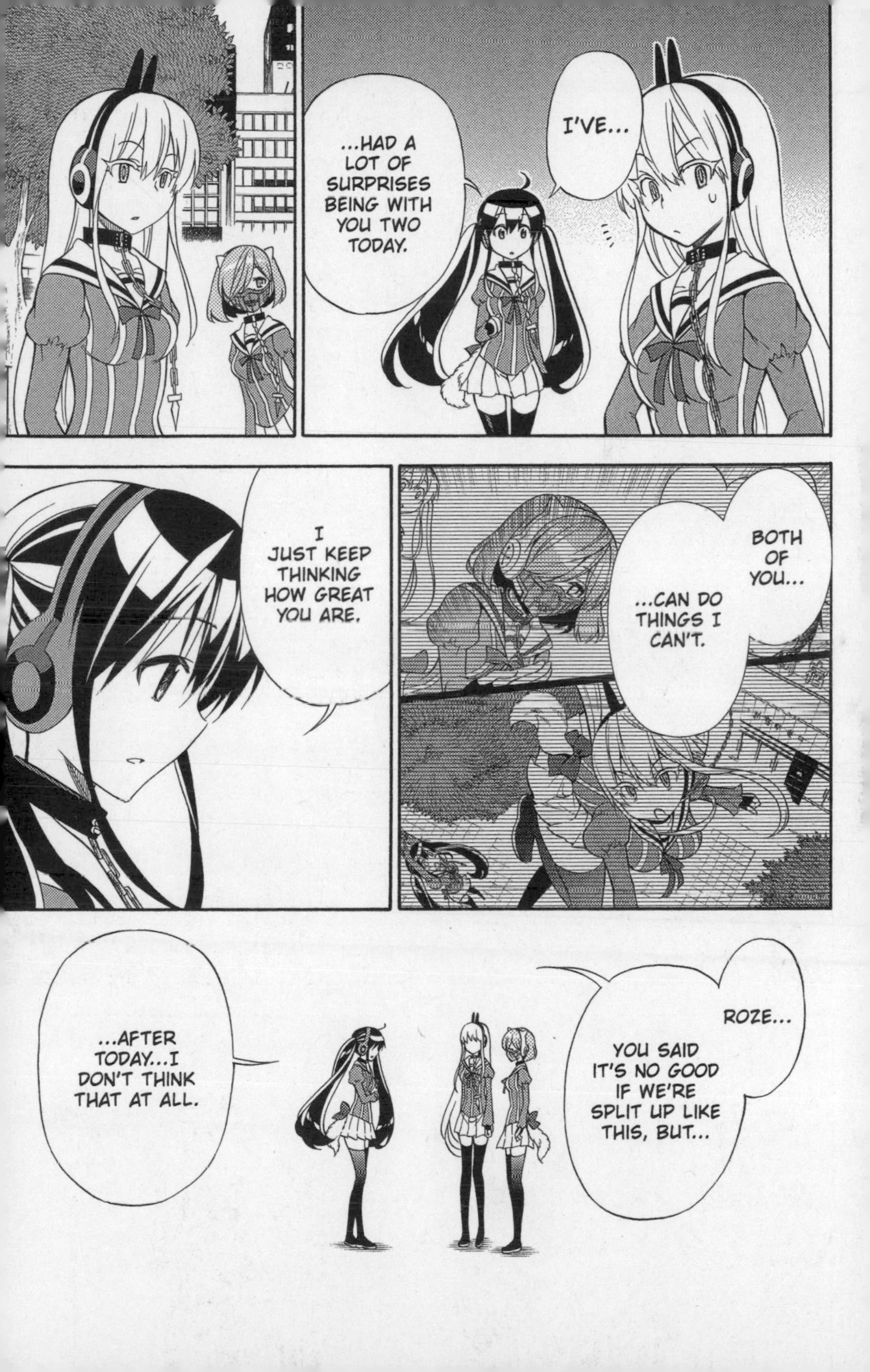
I'VE...
...HAD A LOT OF SURPRISES BEING WITH YOU TWO TODAY.
BOTH OF YOU...
...CAN DO THINGS I CAN'T.
I JUST KEEP THINKING HOW GREAT YOU ARE.
ROZE...
YOU SAID IT'S NO GOOD IF WE'RE SPLIT UP LIKE THIS, BUT...
...AFTER TODAY...I DON'T THINK THAT AT ALL.

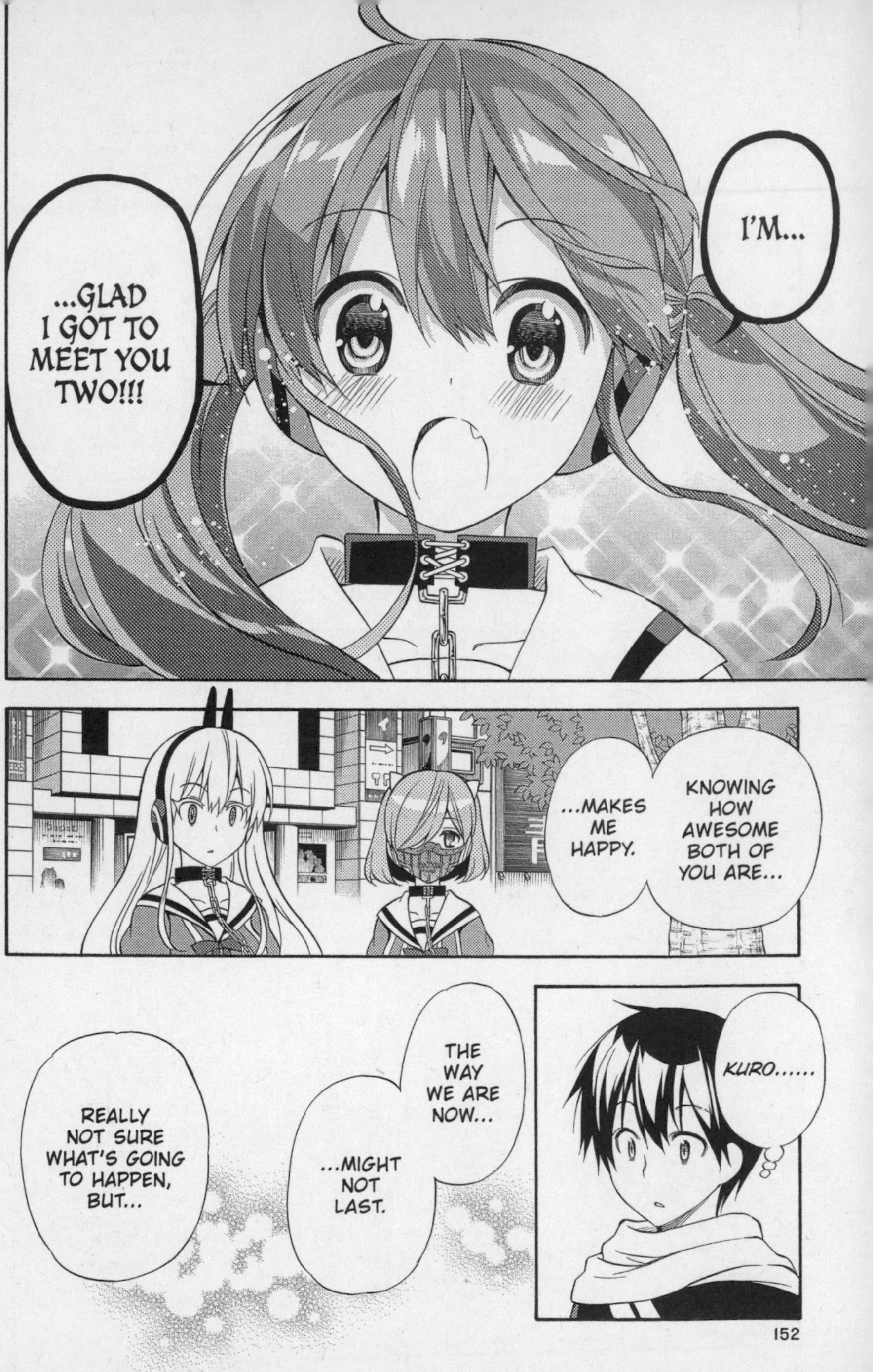
I'M...
...GLAD I GOT TO MEET YOU TWO!!!
KNOWING HOW AWESOME BOTH OF YOU ARE...
...MAKES ME HAPPY.
KURO......
THE WAY WE ARE NOW...
...MIGHT NOT LAST.
REALLY NOT SURE WHAT'S GOING TO HAPPEN, BUT...

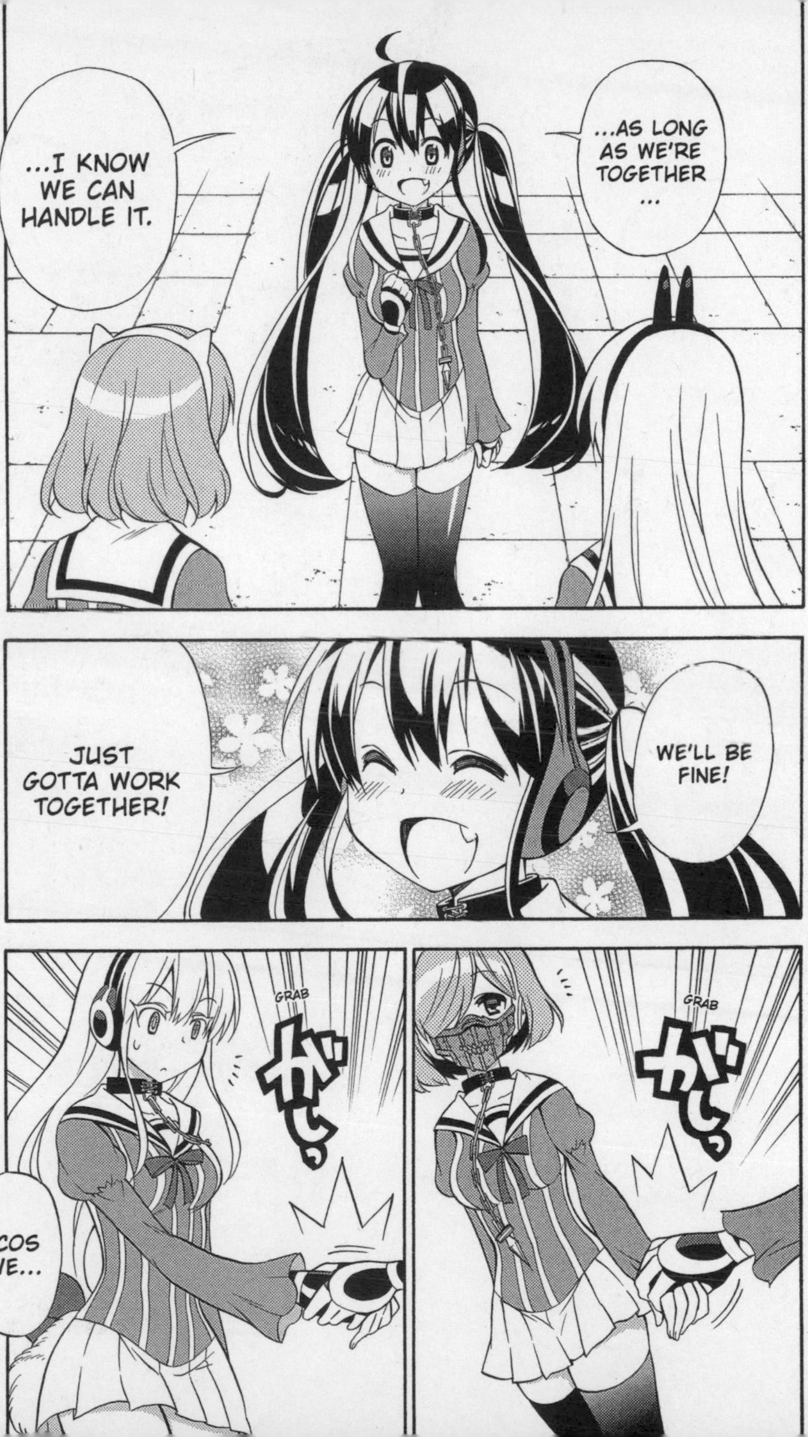
...AS LONG AS WE'RE TOGETHER ...
...I KNOW WE CAN HANDLE IT.
WE'LL BE FINE!
JUST GOTTA WORK TOGETHER!
GRAB
がしっ
GRAB
がしっ
'COS WE...

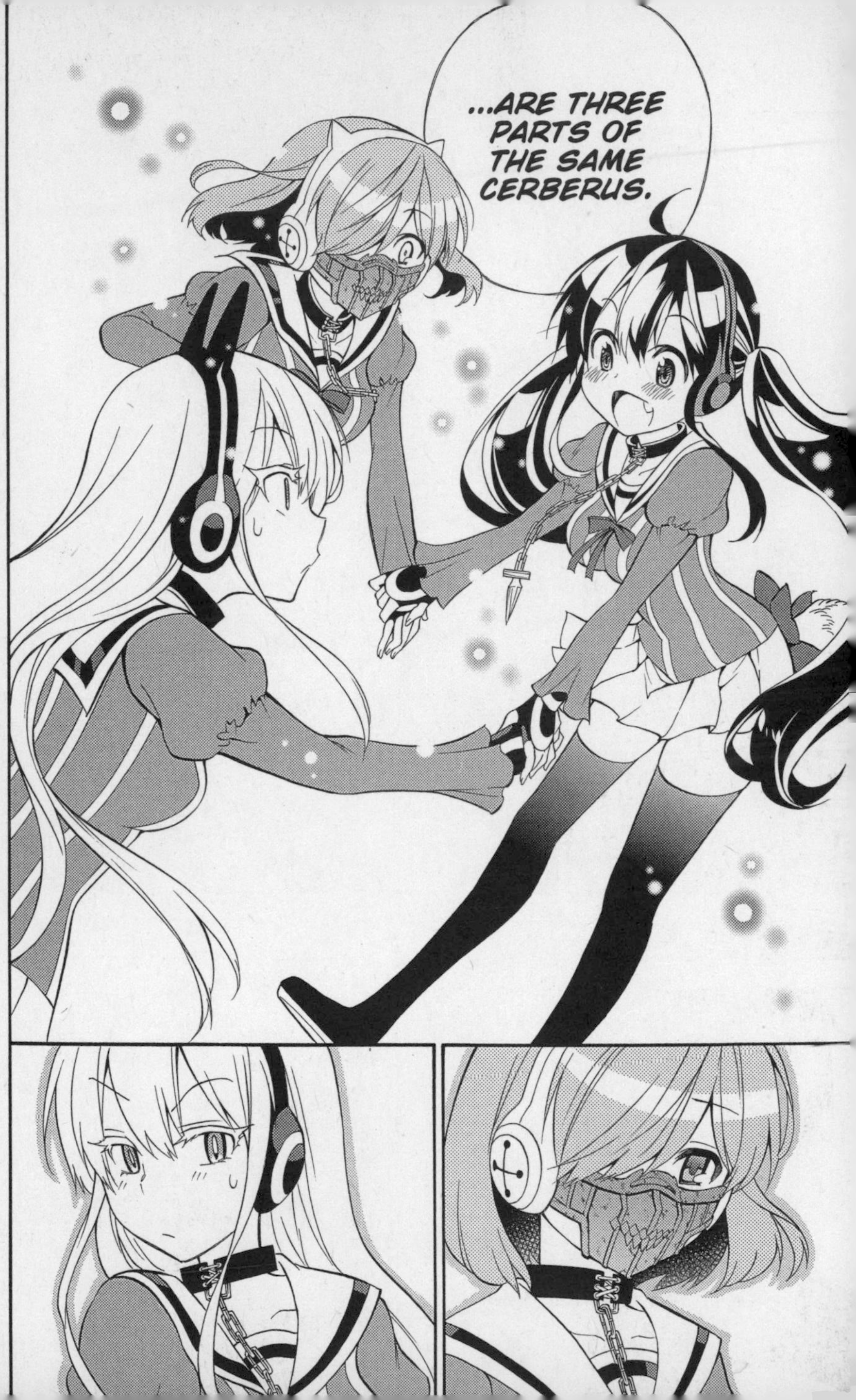
...ARE THREE PARTS OF THE SAME CERBERUS.

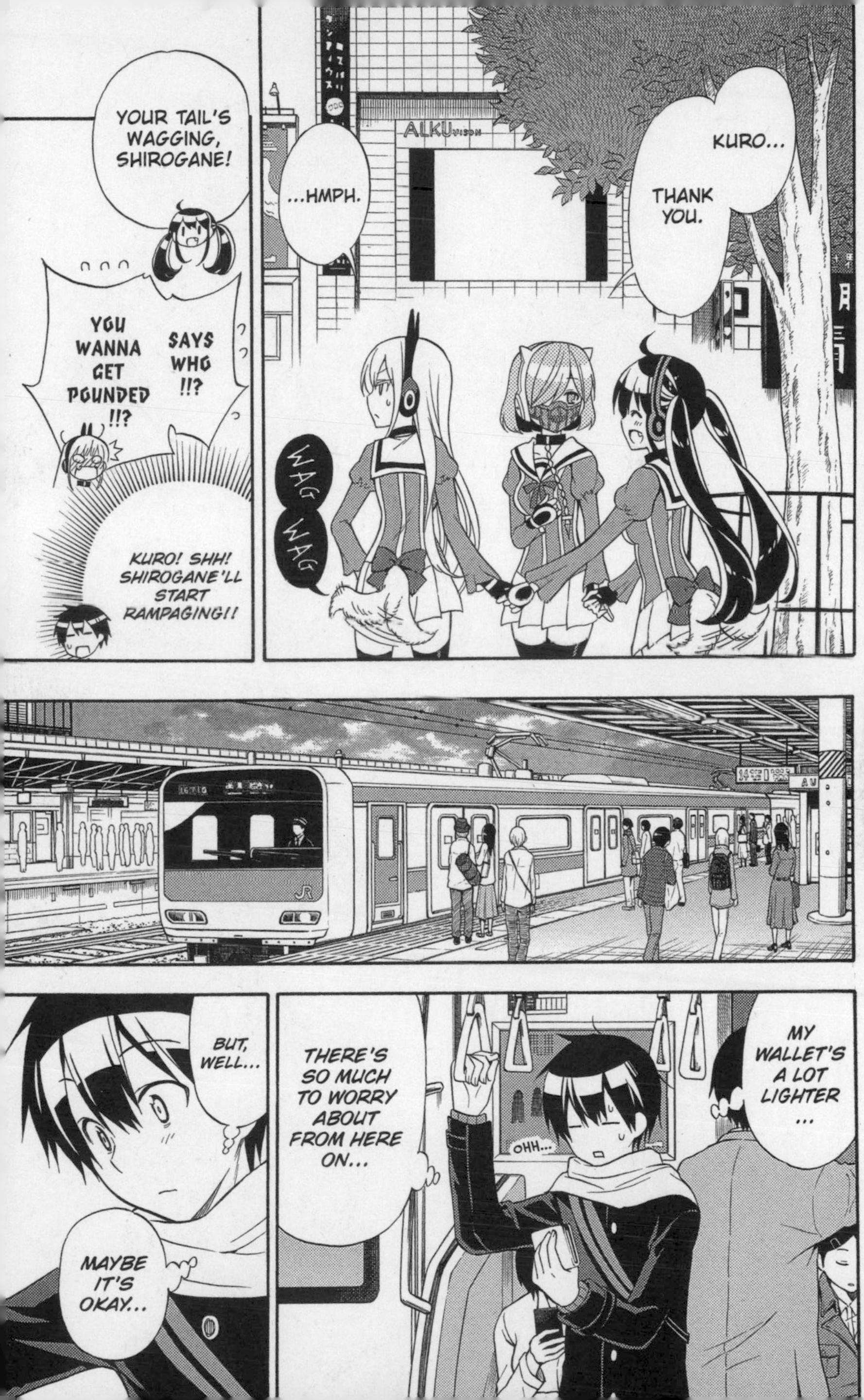
KURO...
THANK YOU.
...HMPH.
WAG WAG
YOUR TAIL'S WAGGING, SHIROGANE!
SAYS WHO!!?
YOU WANNA GET POUNDED!!?
KURO! SHH! SHIROGANE'LL START RAMPAGING!!
MY WALLET'S A LOT LIGHTER...
OHH...
THERE'S SO MUCH TO WORRY ABOUT FROM HERE ON...
BUT, WELL...
MAYBE IT'S OKAY...

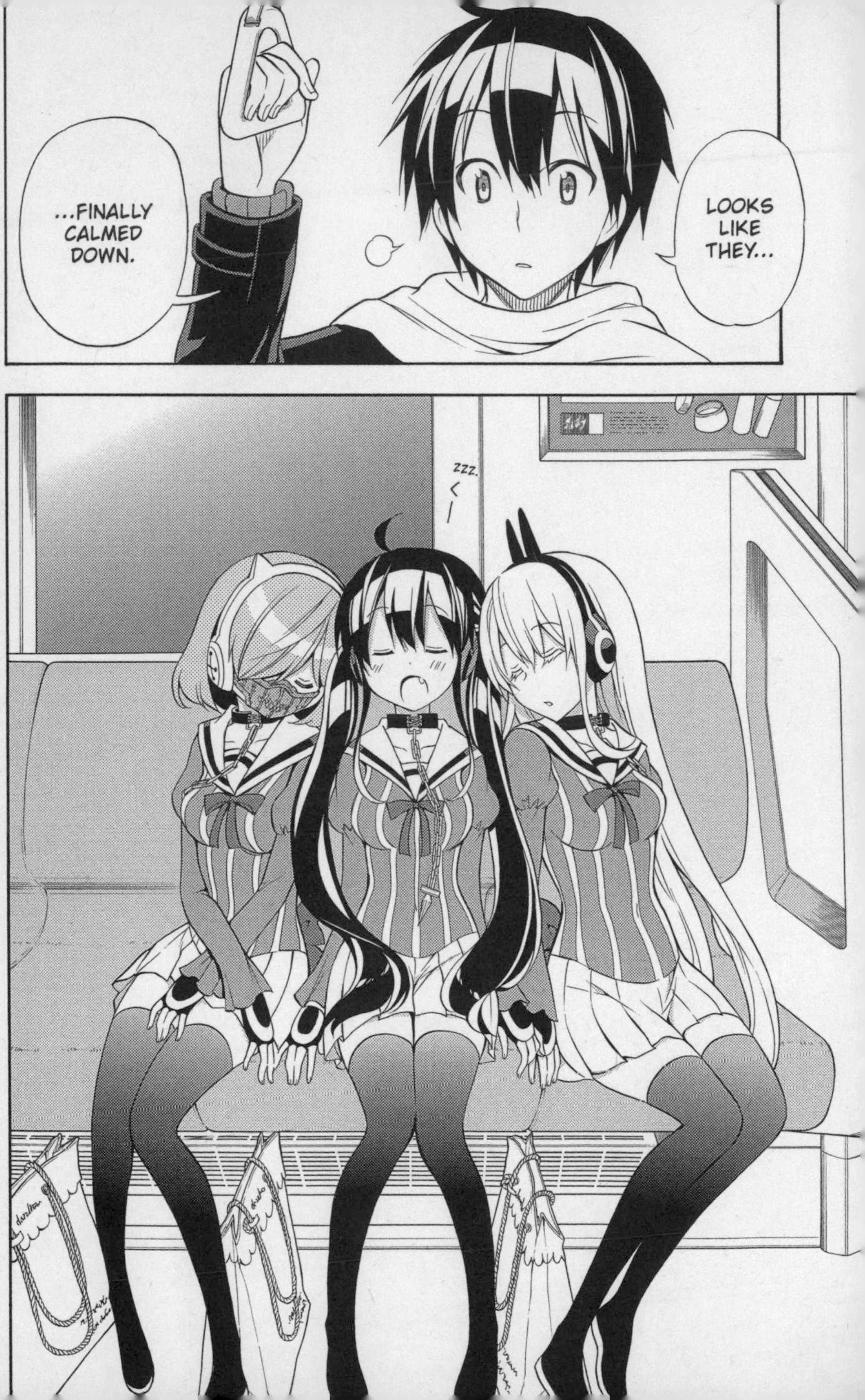
LOOKS LIKE THEY...
...FINALLY CALMED DOWN.
ZZZ.

🐾 TODAY'S CERBERUS

BREATHE
BREATHE すや
すや

NO
PROBLEM
USING
THIS GUY
AS A
PILLOW

TODAY'S CERBERUS

IF BIG SIS WERE TO FIND OUT
OH MY! ♡ HE'S GOT THREE NOW? HE WAS SO LONELY HE WENT AND GOT A HAREM?
EXCITED

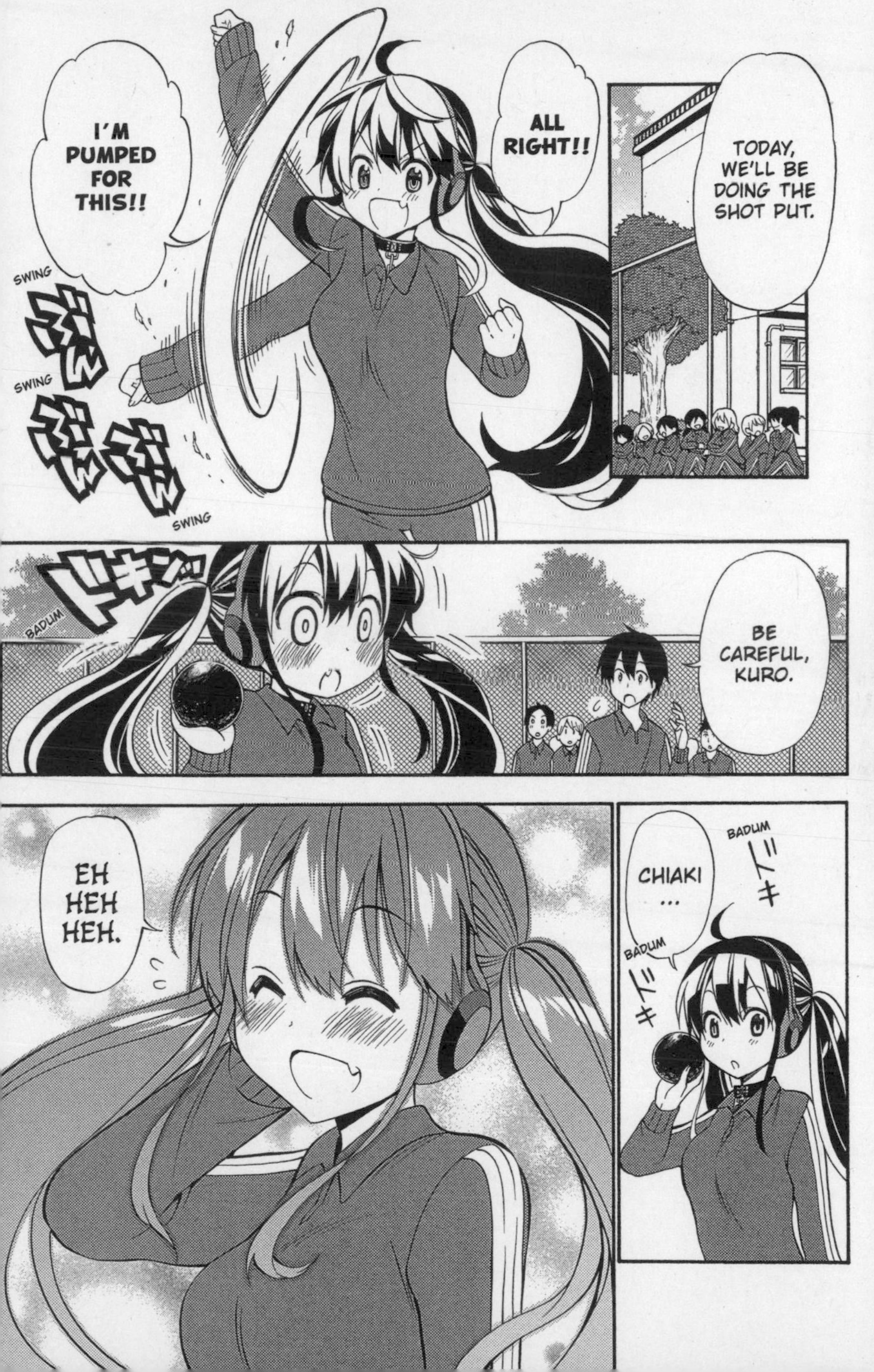
TODAY, WE'LL BE DOING THE SHOT PUT.
ALL RIGHT!!
I'M PUMPED FOR THIS!!
SWING
SWING
SWING
BE CAREFUL, KURO.
BADUM
BADUM
CHIAKI ...
BADUM
EH HEH HEH.

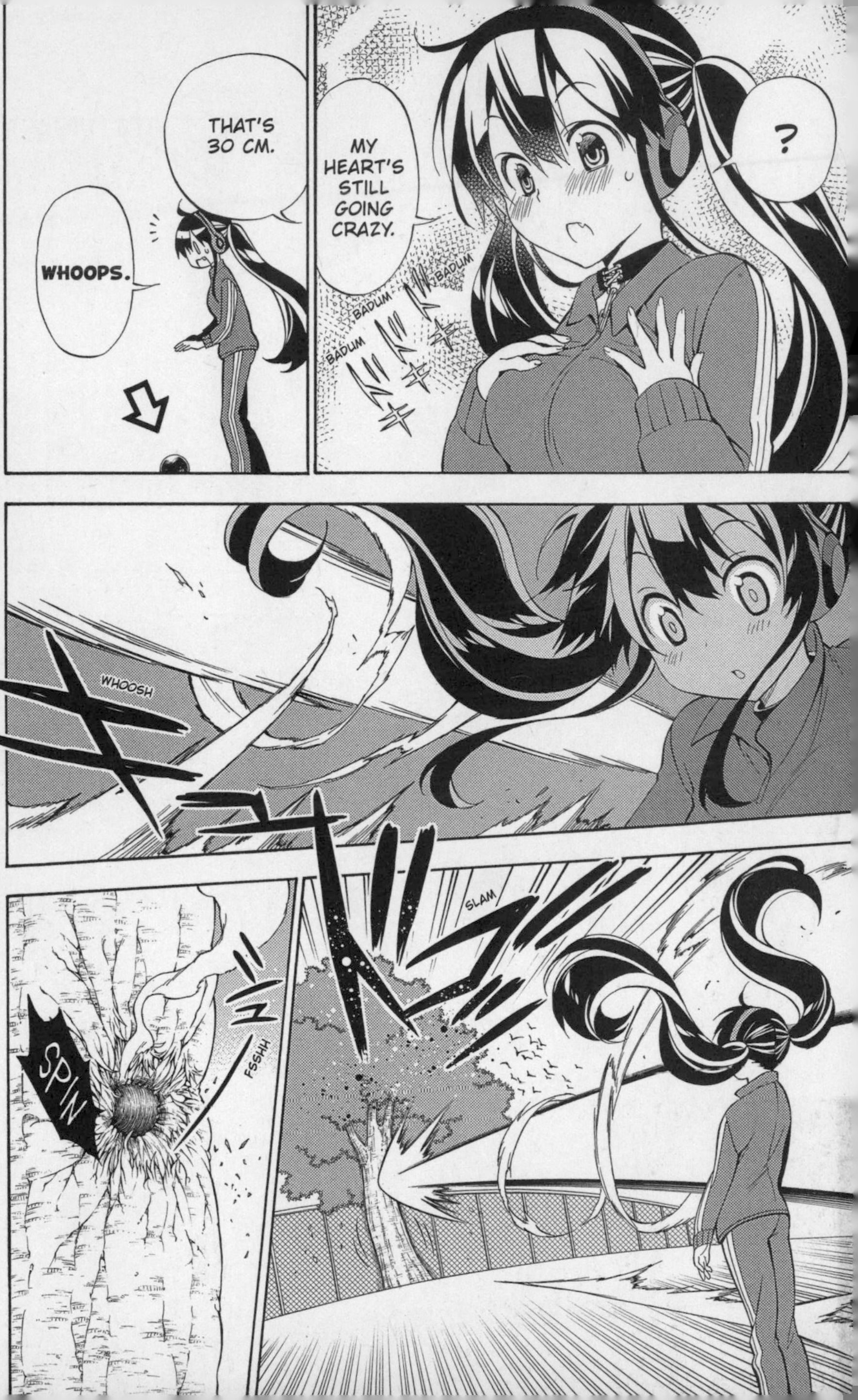
?
MY HEART'S STILL GOING CRAZY.
BADUM
BADUM
BADUM
THAT'S 30 CM.
WHOOPS.
WHOOSH
SLAM
SPIN
FSSHH

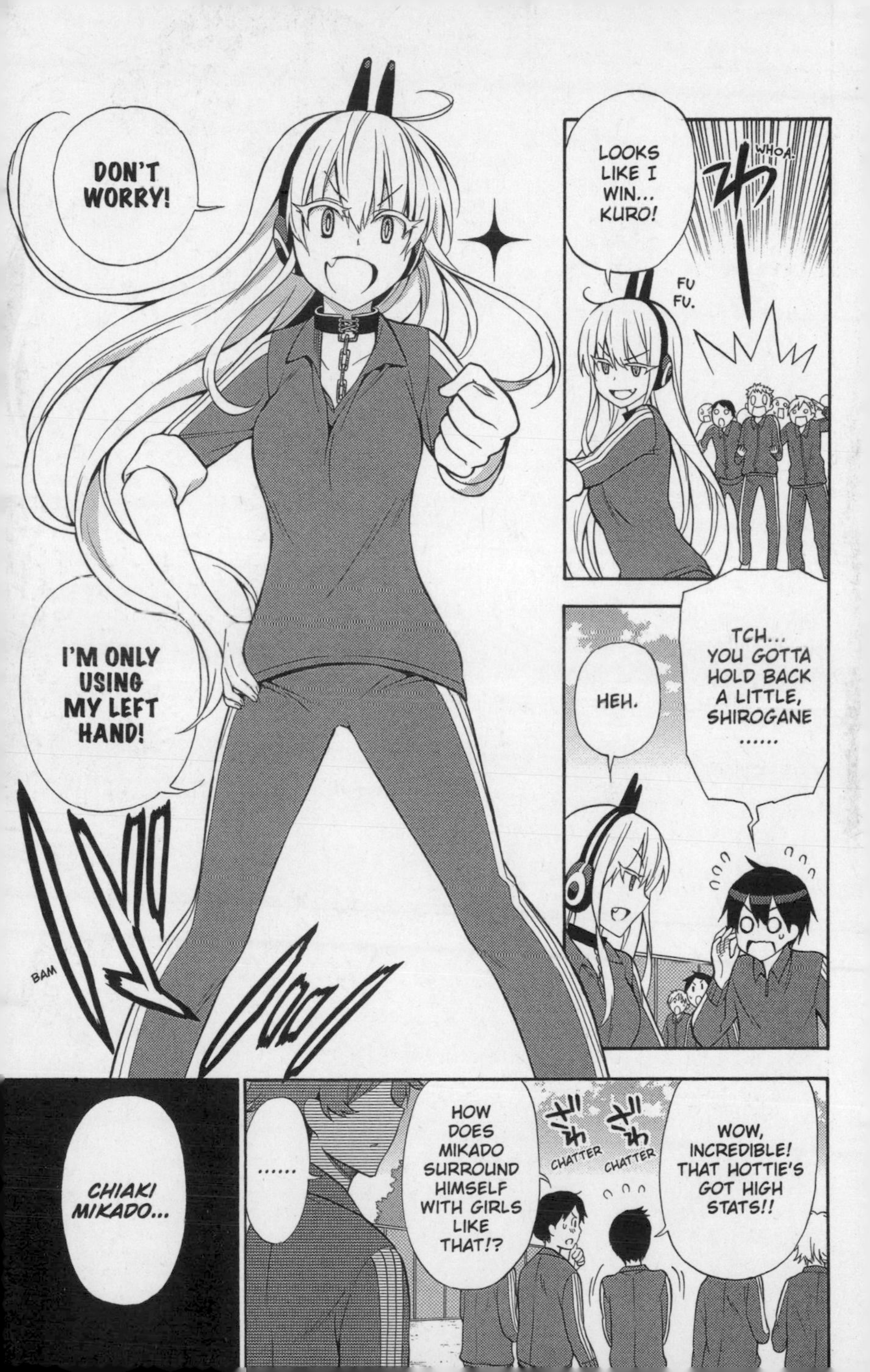
WHOA.
LOOKS LIKE I WIN... KURO!
FU FU.
TCH... YOU GOTTA HOLD BACK A LITTLE, SHIROGANE ......
HEH.
DON'T WORRY!
I'M ONLY USING MY LEFT HAND!
BAM
WOW, INCREDIBLE! THAT HOTTIE'S GOT HIGH STATS!!
ざわ CHATTER
ざわ CHATTER
HOW DOES MIKADO SURROUND HIMSELF WITH GIRLS LIKE THAT!?
......
CHIAKI MIKADO...

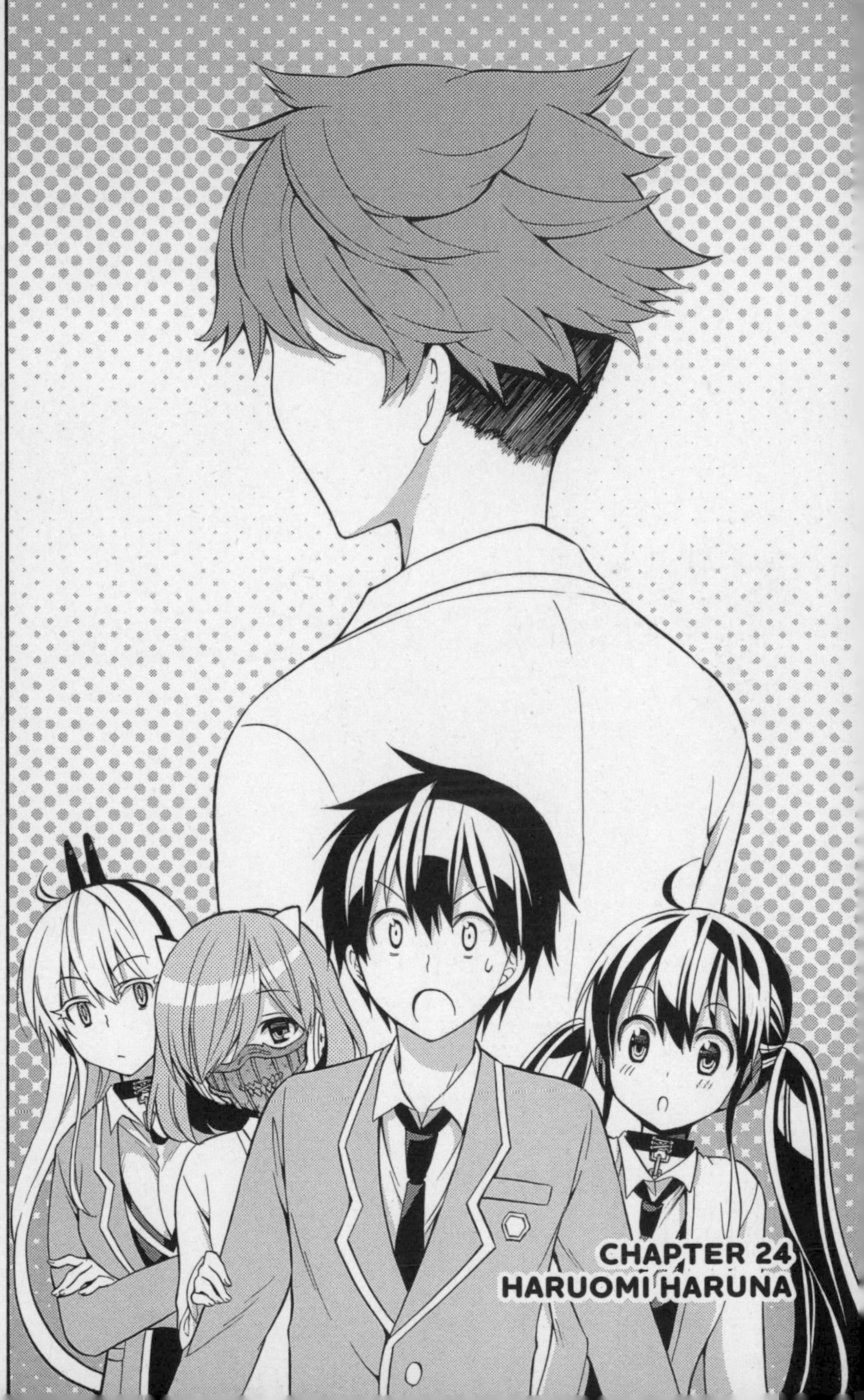
CHAPTER 24
HARUOMI HARUNA

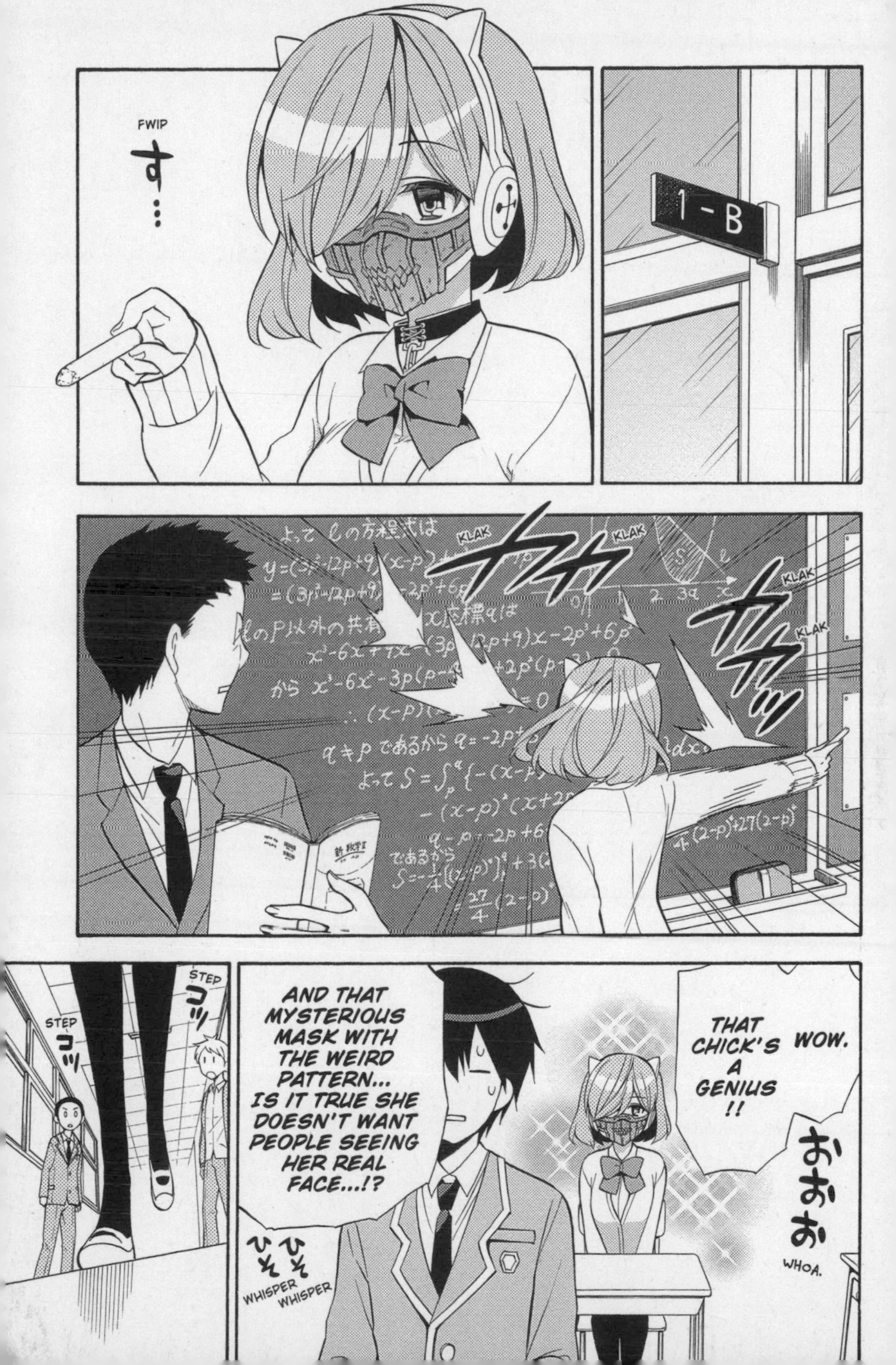
1-B
FWIP
す…
KLAK
カ
KLAK
カ
KLAK
カ
KLAK
カッ
WOW.
THAT CHICK'S A GENIUS!!
おおお
WHOA.
AND THAT MYSTERIOUS MASK WITH THE WEIRD PATTERN... IS IT TRUE SHE DOESN'T WANT PEOPLE SEEING HER REAL FACE...!?
ひそ ひそ
WHISPER WHISPER
STEP
コツ
STEP
コツ

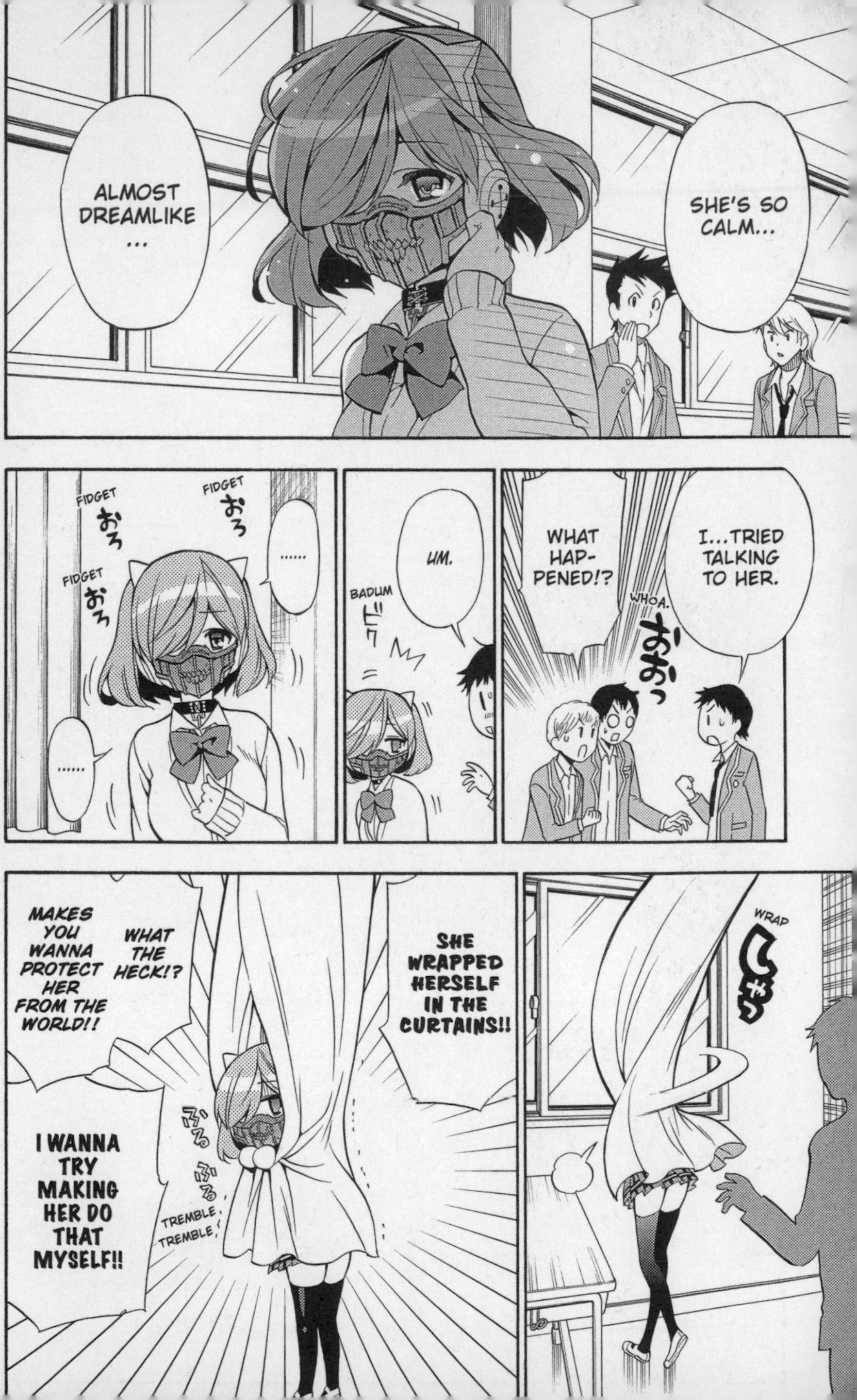
SHE'S SO CALM...
ALMOST DREAMLIKE ...
I...TRIED TALKING TO HER.
WHAT HAP-PENED!?
WHOA. おおっ
UM.
BADUM ビク
FIDGET おろ
FIDGET おろ
FIDGET おろ
......
......
WRAP しゅっ
SHE WRAPPED HERSELF IN THE CURTAINS!!
WHAT THE HECK!?
MAKES YOU WANNA PROTECT HER FROM THE WORLD!!
I WANNA TRY MAKING HER DO THAT MYSELF!!
TREMBLE TREMBLE ぷるぷる

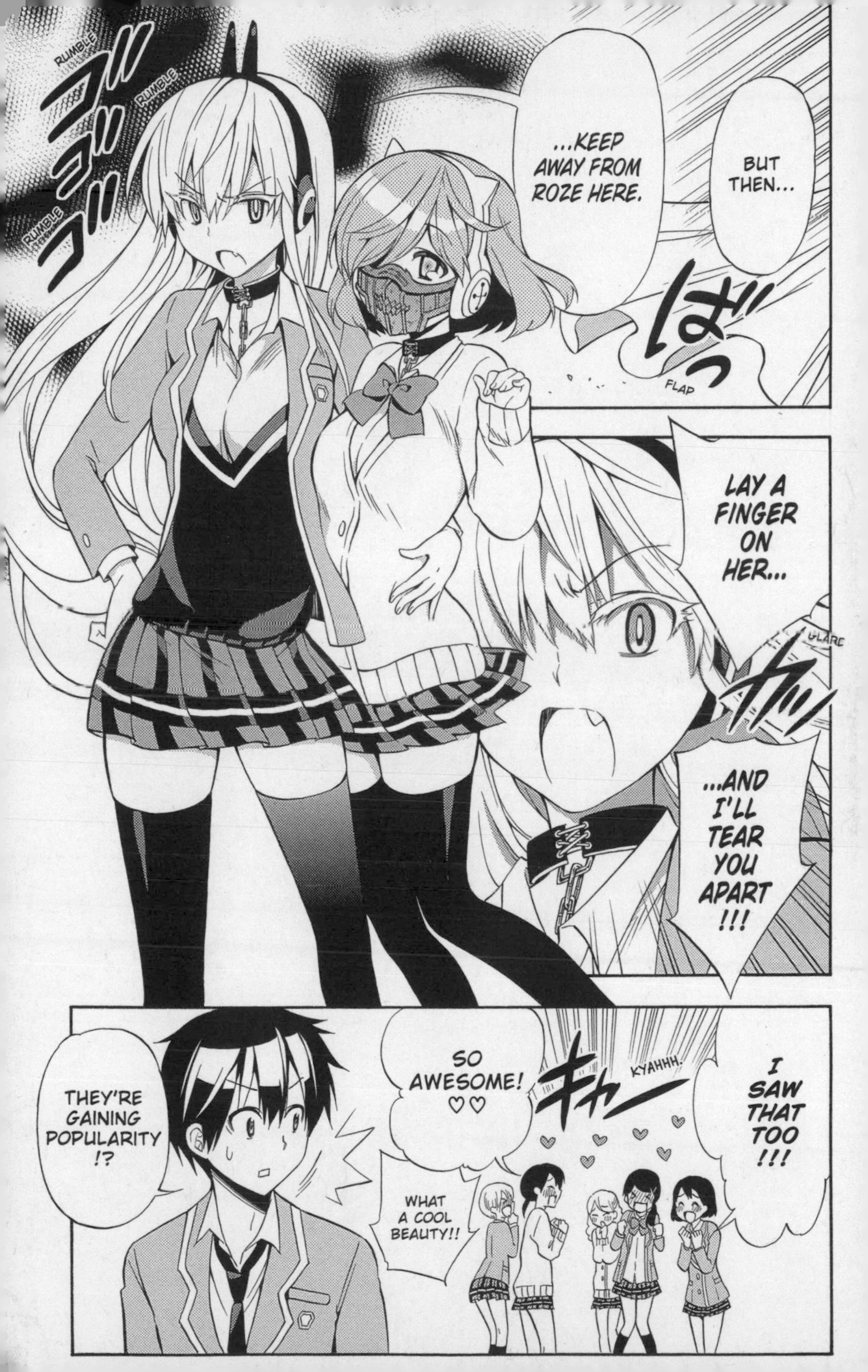
BUT THEN...
...KEEP AWAY FROM ROZE HERE.
FLAP
RUMBLE
RUMBLE
RUMBLE
LAY A FINGER ON HER...
GLARE
...AND I'LL TEAR YOU APART!!!
I SAW THAT TOO!!!
KYAHHH.
SO AWESOME! ♡♡
WHAT A COOL BEAUTY!!
THEY'RE GAINING POPULARITY!?

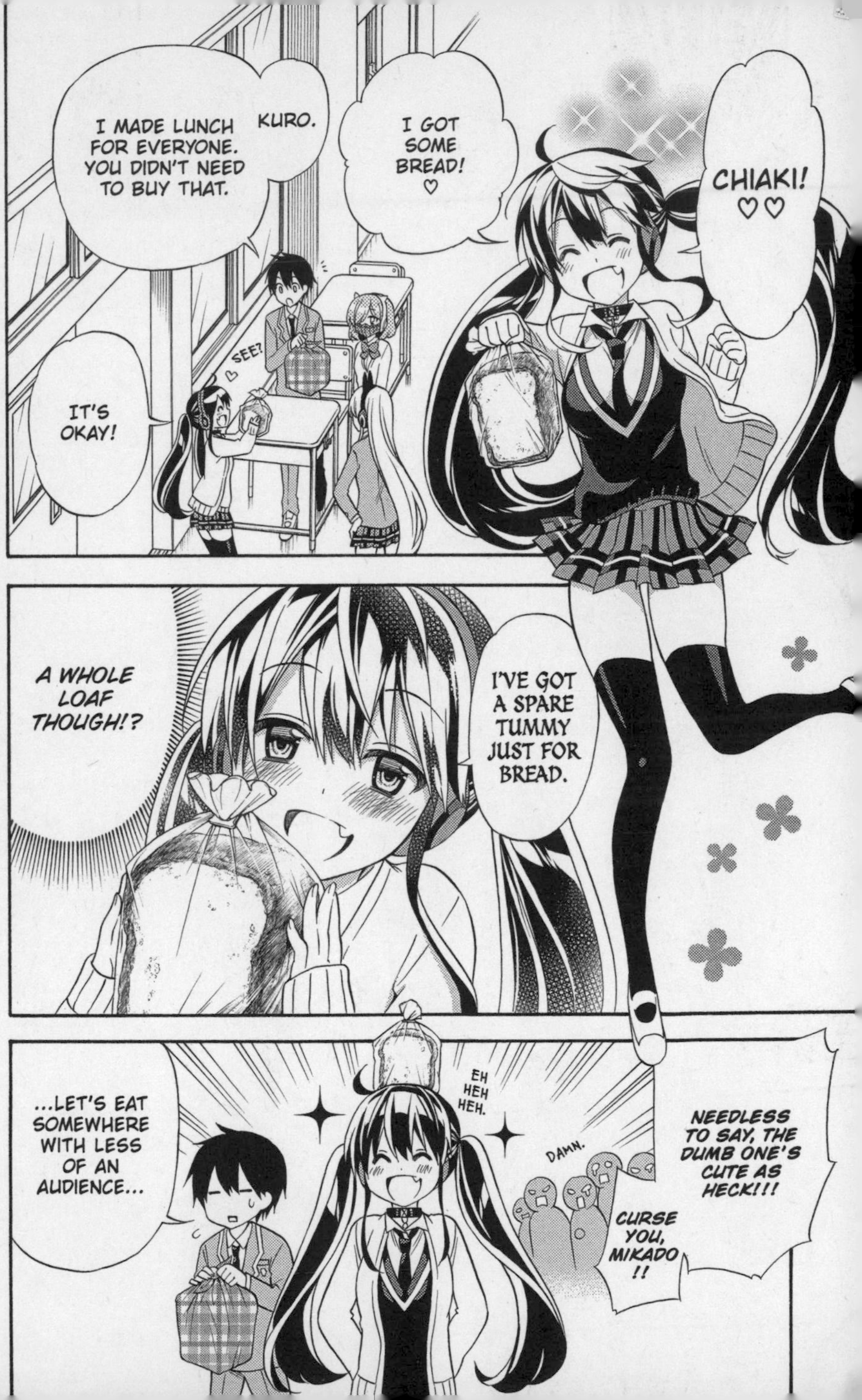
CHIAKI! ♡♡
I GOT SOME BREAD! ♡
KURO.
I MADE LUNCH FOR EVERYONE. YOU DIDN'T NEED TO BUY THAT.
SEE? ♡
IT'S OKAY!
I'VE GOT A SPARE TUMMY JUST FOR BREAD.
A WHOLE LOAF THOUGH!?
NEEDLESS TO SAY, THE DUMB ONE'S CUTE AS HECK!!!
CURSE YOU, MIKADO !!
DAMN.
EH HEH HEH.
...LET'S EAT SOMEWHERE WITH LESS OF AN AUDIENCE...

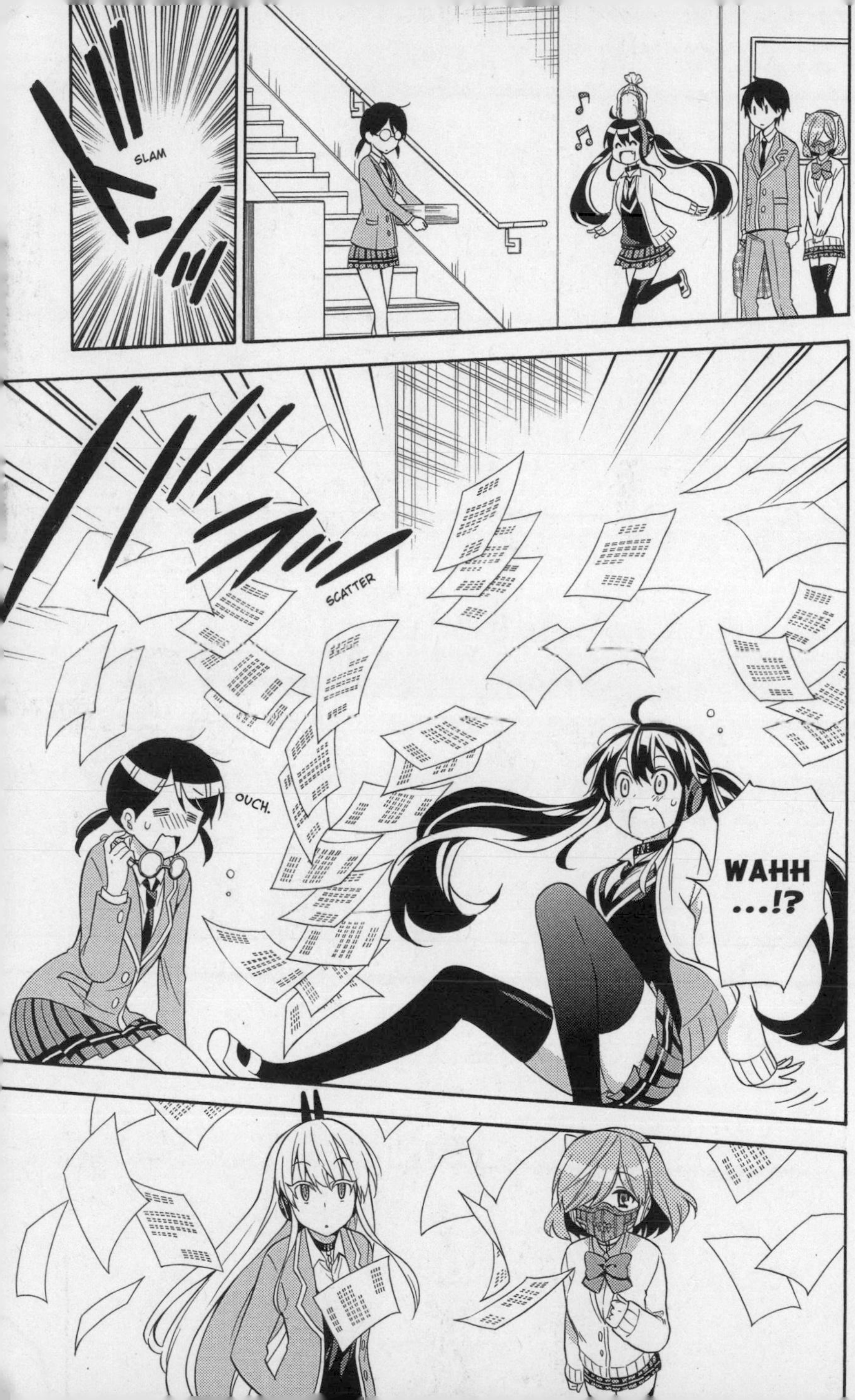
SLAM
SCATTER
WAHH ...!?
OUCH.

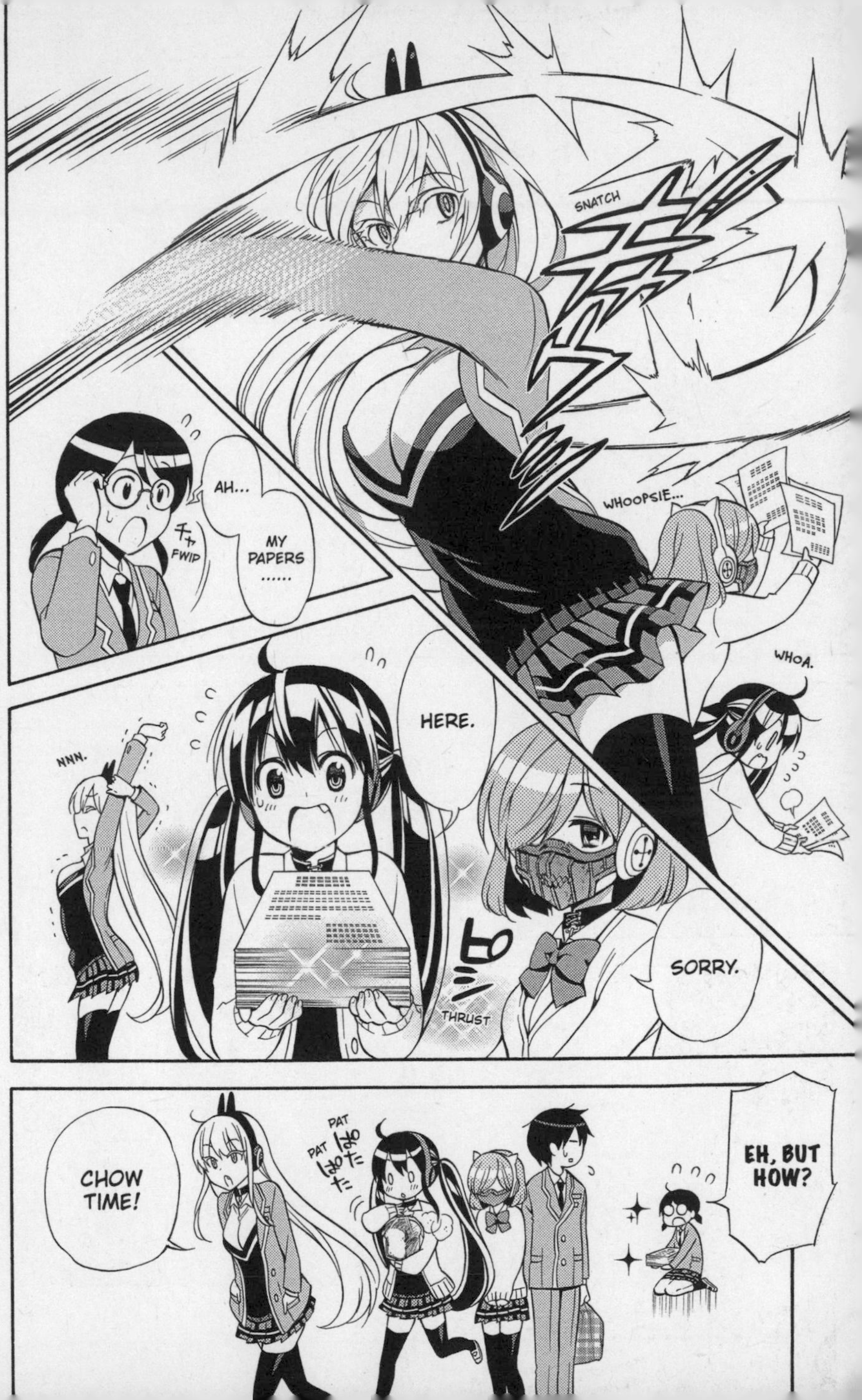
SNATCH
WHOOPSIE...
WHOA.
AH...
MY PAPERS ......
チャ
FWIP
SORRY.
THRUST
HERE.
NNN.
EH, BUT HOW?
PAT PAT
ぱたぱた
CHOW TIME!

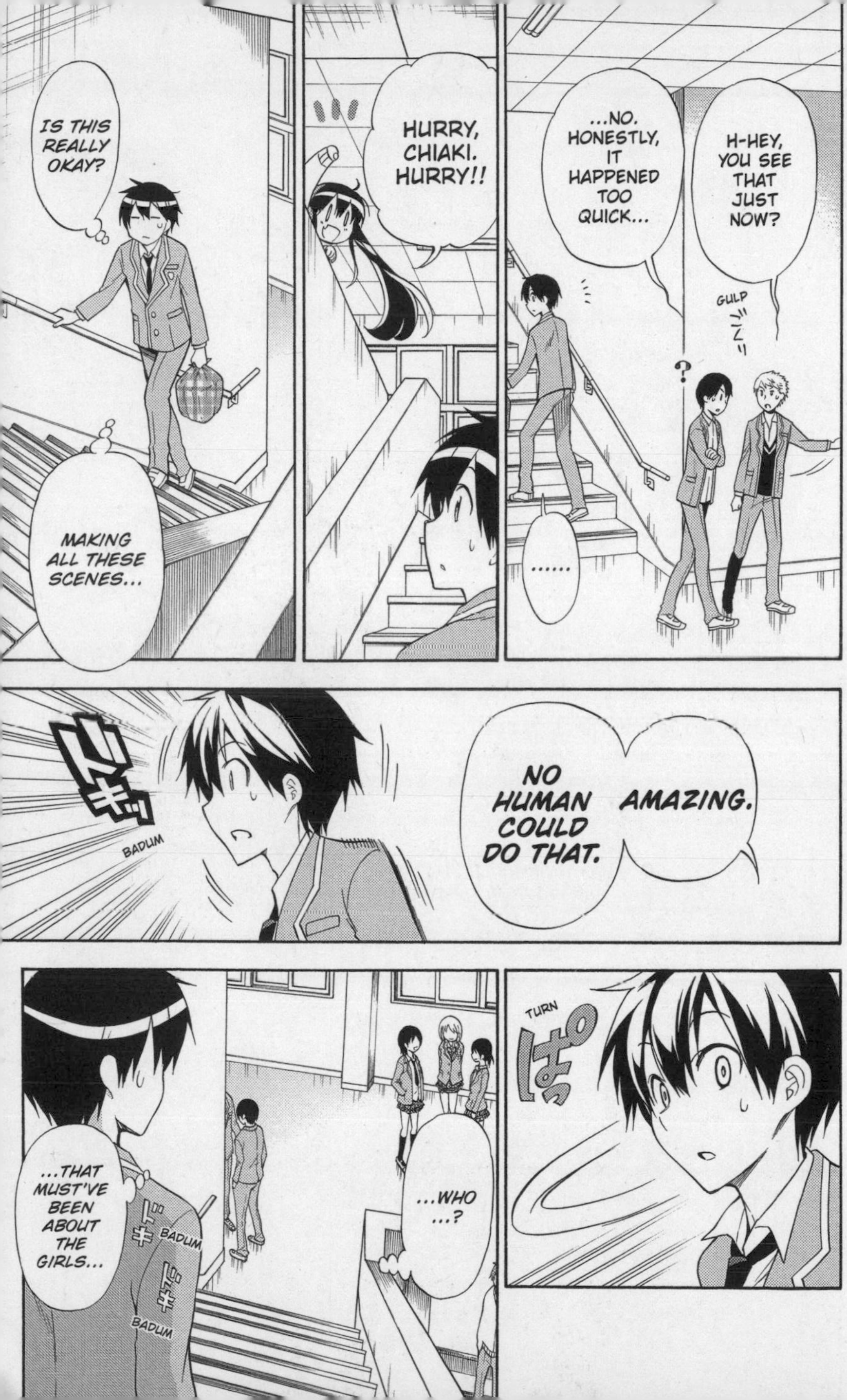
H-HEY, YOU SEE THAT JUST NOW?
GULP
...NO. HONESTLY, IT HAPPENED TOO QUICK...
......
HURRY, CHIAKI. HURRY!!
IS THIS REALLY OKAY?
MAKING ALL THESE SCENES...
AMAZING.
NO HUMAN COULD DO THAT.
BADUM
TURN
...WHO ...?
...THAT MUST'VE BEEN ABOUT THE GIRLS...
BADUM
BADUM

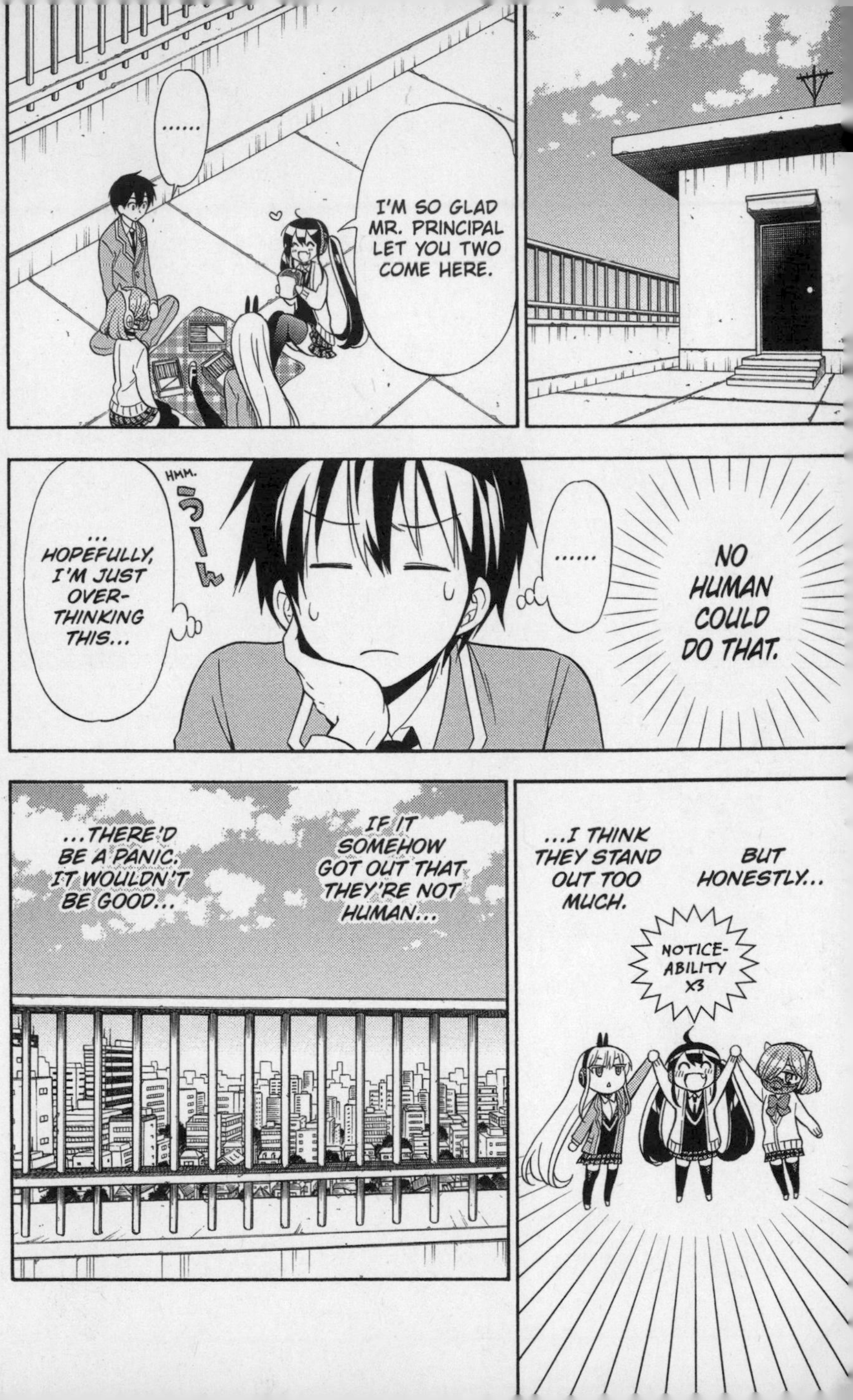
I'M SO GLAD MR. PRINCIPAL LET YOU TWO COME HERE.
......
NO HUMAN COULD DO THAT.
......
HMM.
うーん
...HOPEFULLY, I'M JUST OVER-THINKING THIS...
BUT HONESTLY...
...I THINK THEY STAND OUT TOO MUCH.
NOTICE-ABILITY X3
IF IT SOMEHOW GOT OUT THAT THEY'RE NOT HUMAN...
...THERE'D BE A PANIC. IT WOULDN'T BE GOOD...

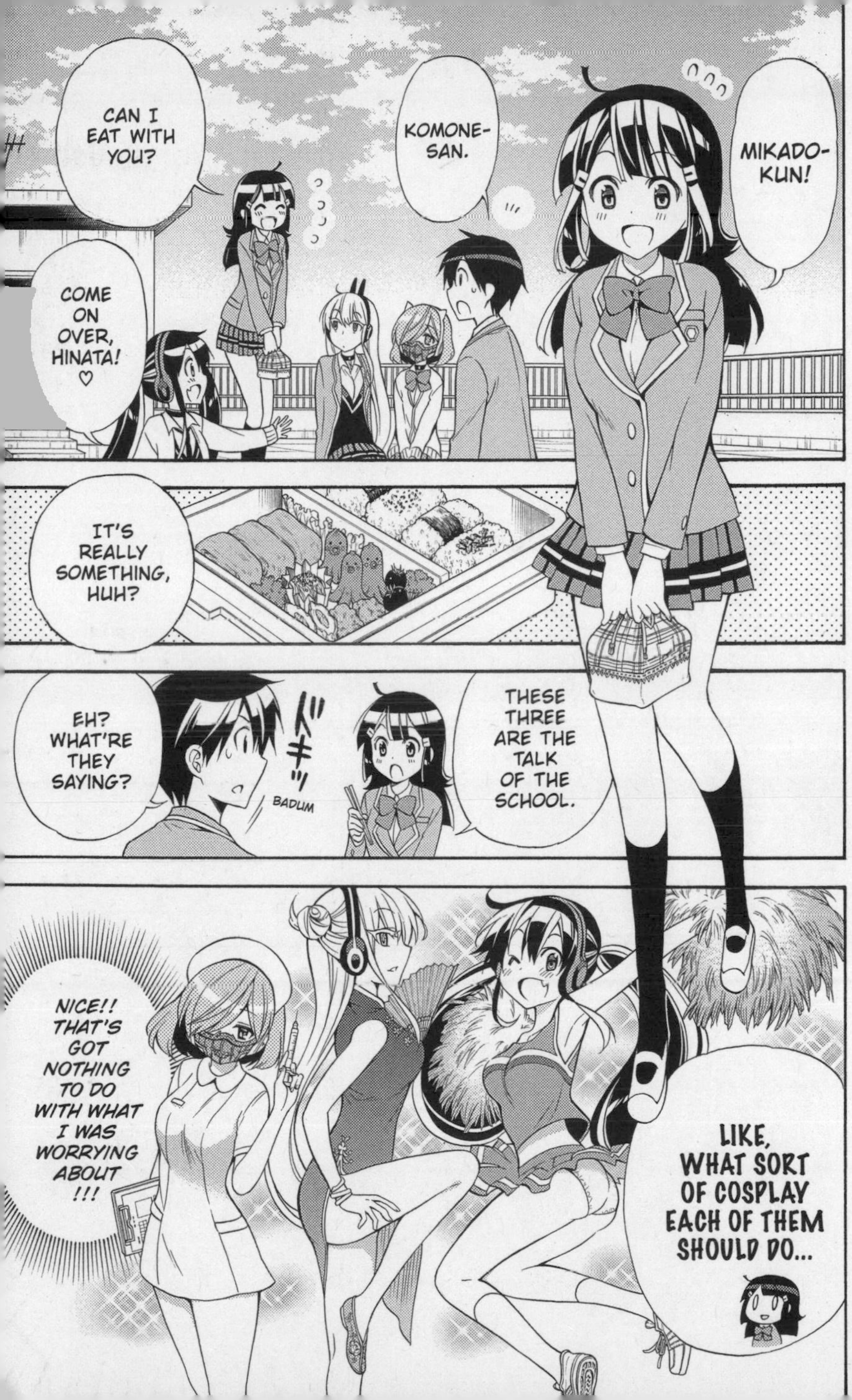
MIKADO-KUN!
KOMONE-SAN.
CAN I EAT WITH YOU?
COME ON OVER, HINATA! ♡
IT'S REALLY SOMETHING, HUH?
THESE THREE ARE THE TALK OF THE SCHOOL.
ドキッ
BADUM
EH? WHAT'RE THEY SAYING?
LIKE, WHAT SORT OF COSPLAY EACH OF THEM SHOULD DO...
NICE!! THAT'S GOT NOTHING TO DO WITH WHAT I WAS WORRYING ABOUT!!!

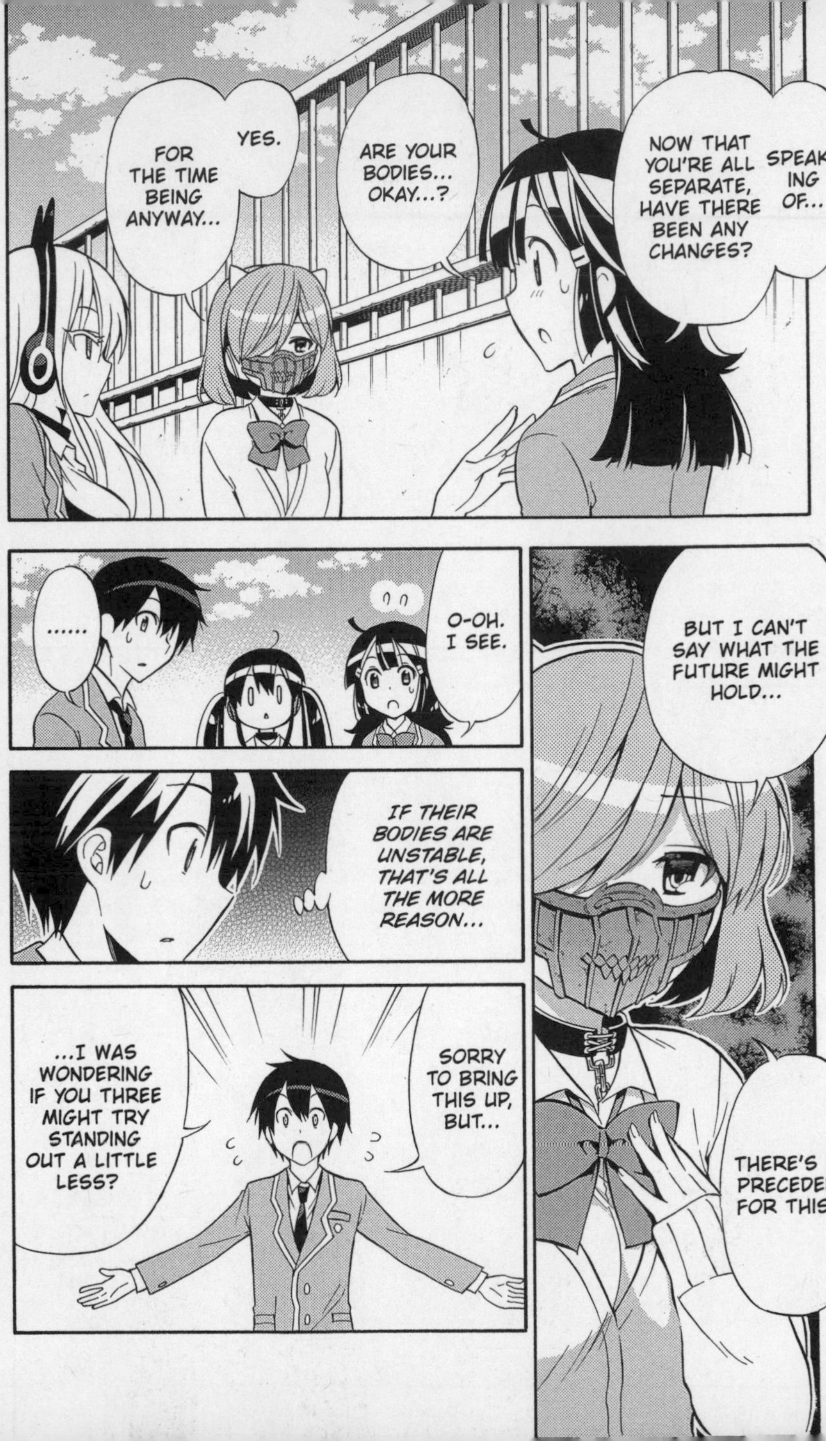
SPEAKING OF...
NOW THAT YOU'RE ALL SEPARATE, HAVE THERE BEEN ANY CHANGES?
ARE YOUR BODIES... OKAY...?
YES.
FOR THE TIME BEING ANYWAY...
BUT I CAN'T SAY WHAT THE FUTURE MIGHT HOLD...
THERE'S NO PRECEDENT FOR THIS...
O-OH. I SEE.
......
IF THEIR BODIES ARE UNSTABLE, THAT'S ALL THE MORE REASON...
SORRY TO BRING THIS UP, BUT...
...I WAS WONDERING IF YOU THREE MIGHT TRY STANDING OUT A LITTLE LESS?

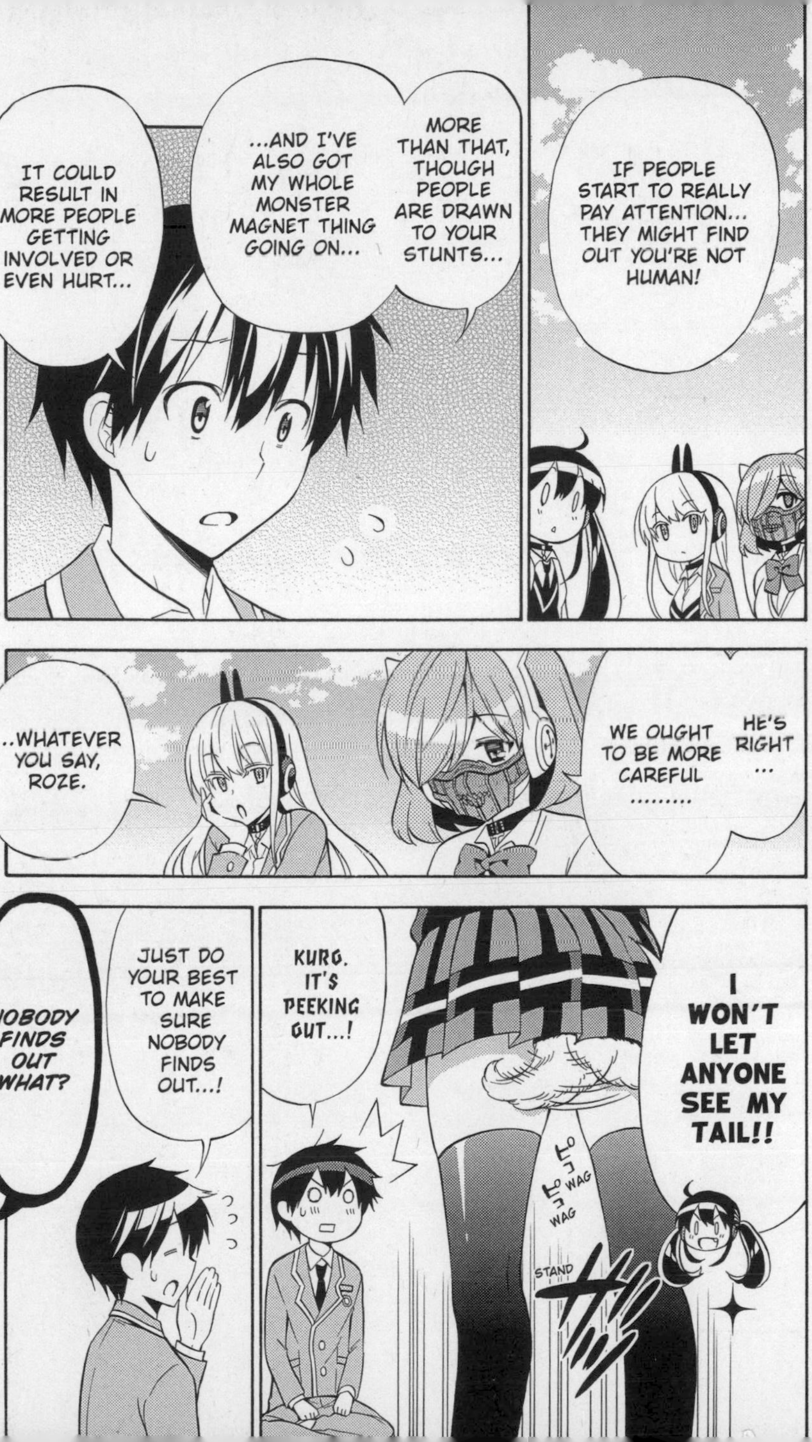
IF PEOPLE START TO REALLY PAY ATTENTION... THEY MIGHT FIND OUT YOU'RE NOT HUMAN!
MORE THAN THAT, THOUGH PEOPLE ARE DRAWN TO YOUR STUNTS...
...AND I'VE ALSO GOT MY WHOLE MONSTER MAGNET THING GOING ON...
IT COULD RESULT IN MORE PEOPLE GETTING INVOLVED OR EVEN HURT...
HE'S RIGHT ...
WE OUGHT TO BE MORE CAREFUL ....
...WHATEVER YOU SAY, ROZE.
I WON'T LET ANYONE SEE MY TAIL!!
WAG WAG
STAND
KURO. IT'S PEEKING OUT...!
JUST DO YOUR BEST TO MAKE SURE NOBODY FINDS OUT...!
NOBODY FINDS OUT WHAT?

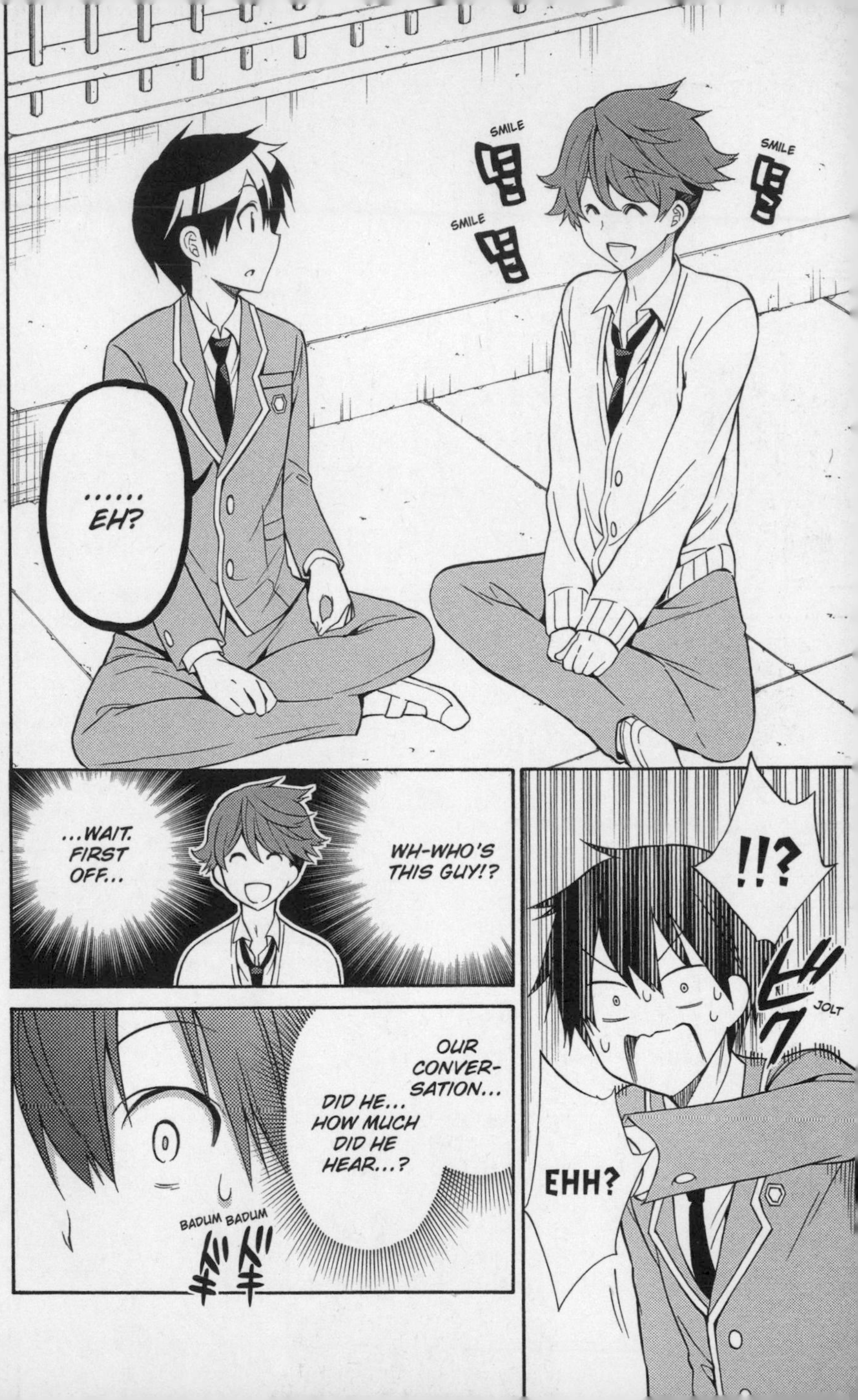
SMILE
SMILE
SMILE
...... EH?
!!?
JOLT
EHH?
WH-WHO'S THIS GUY!?
...WAIT. FIRST OFF...
OUR CONVER-SATION...
DID HE... HOW MUCH DID HE HEAR...?
BADUM BADUM

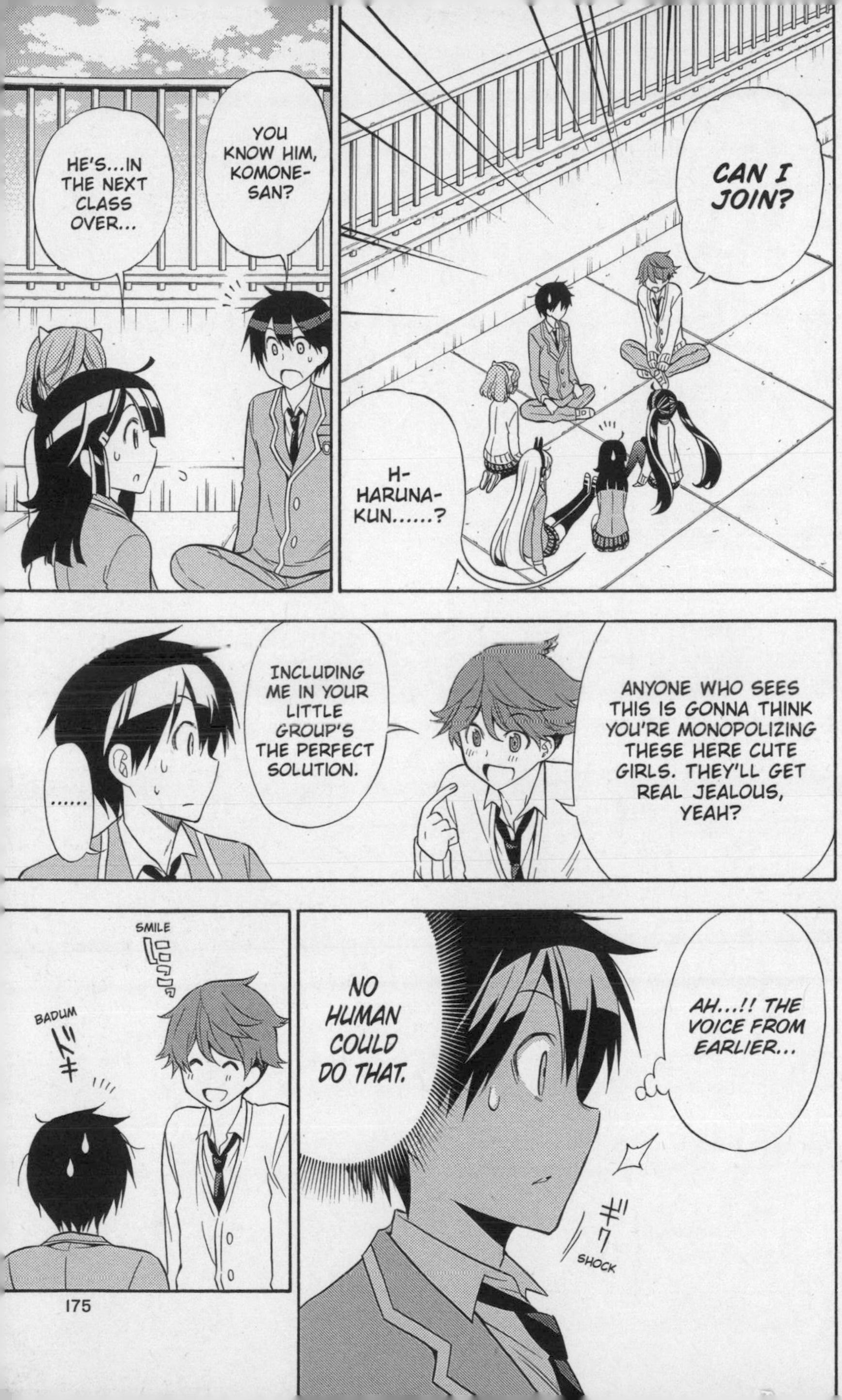
CAN I JOIN?
H-HARUNA-KUN......?
YOU KNOW HIM, KOMONE-SAN?
HE'S...IN THE NEXT CLASS OVER...
ANYONE WHO SEES THIS IS GONNA THINK YOU'RE MONOPOLIZING THESE HERE CUTE GIRLS. THEY'LL GET REAL JEALOUS, YEAH?
INCLUDING ME IN YOUR LITTLE GROUP'S THE PERFECT SOLUTION.
......
AH...!! THE VOICE FROM EARLIER...
NO HUMAN COULD DO THAT.
SHOCK
SMILE
BADUM

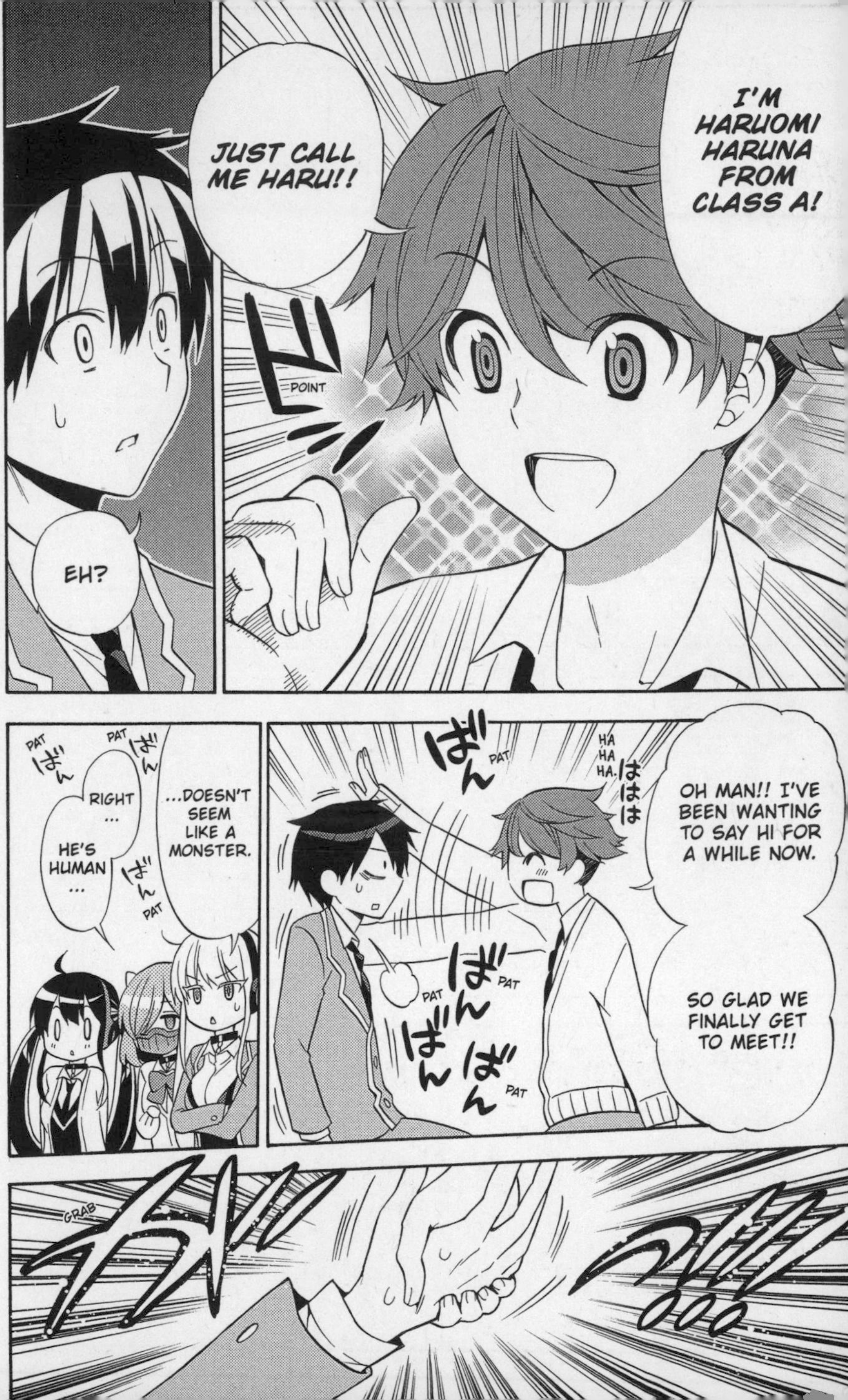
I'M HARUOMI HARUNA FROM CLASS A!
JUST CALL ME HARU!!
POINT
EH?
OH MAN!! I'VE BEEN WANTING TO SAY HI FOR A WHILE NOW.
SO GLAD WE FINALLY GET TO MEET!!
HA HA HA.
ははは
ばん
PAT
ばん
PAT
ばん
PAT
ばん
PAT
ばん
PAT
...DOESN'T SEEM LIKE A MONSTER.
RIGHT ... HE'S HUMAN ...
PAT
ばん
PAT
ばん
ばん
PAT
GRAB

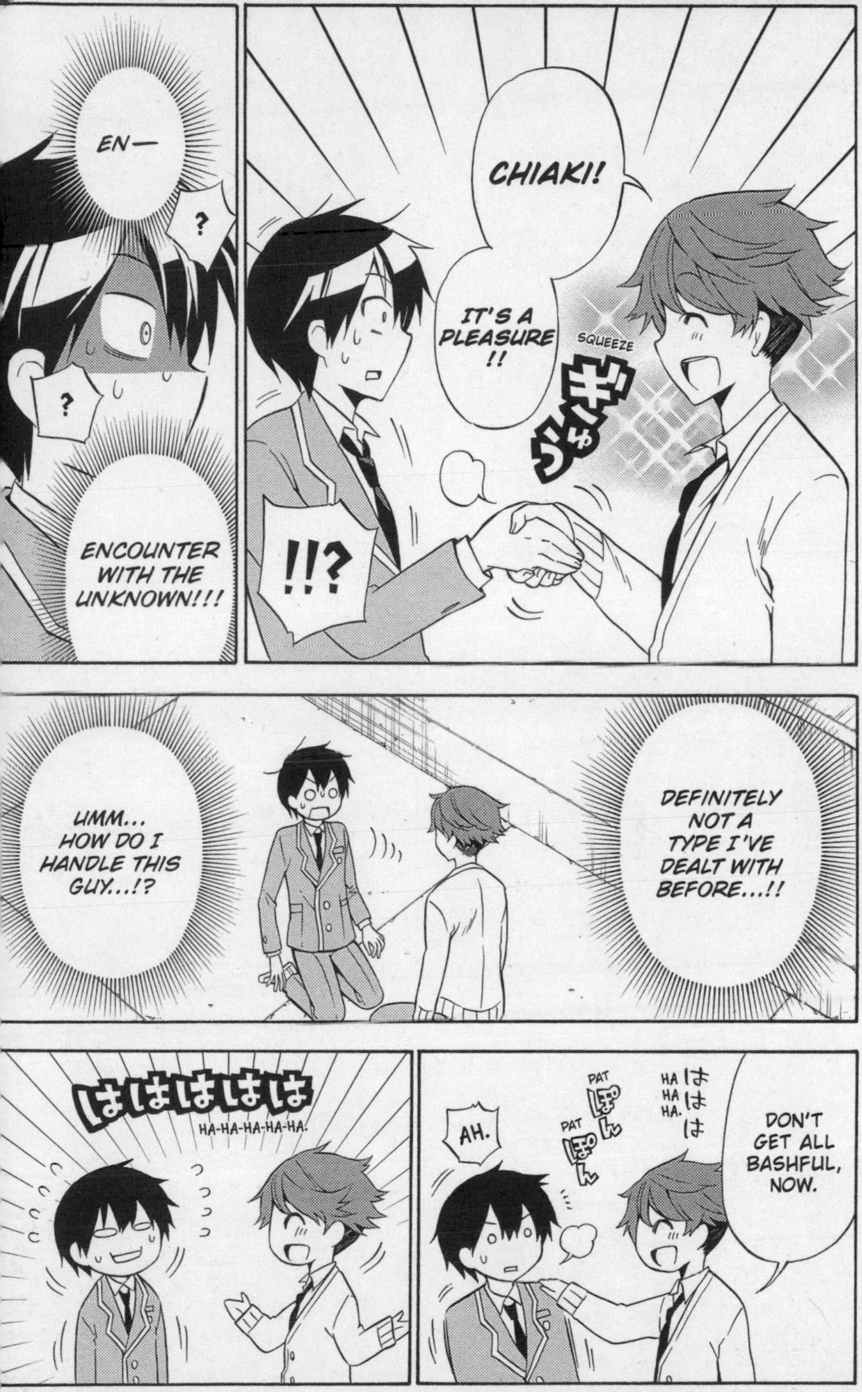
CHIAKI!
IT'S A PLEASURE !!
SQUEEZE
ぎゅう
!!?
EN—
?
?
ENCOUNTER WITH THE UNKNOWN!!!
DEFINITELY NOT A TYPE I'VE DEALT WITH BEFORE...!!
UMM... HOW DO I HANDLE THIS GUY...!?
DON'T GET ALL BASHFUL, NOW.
HA HA HA.
ははは
PAT
ぽん
PAT
ぽん
AH.
はははははは
HA-HA-HA-HA-HA.

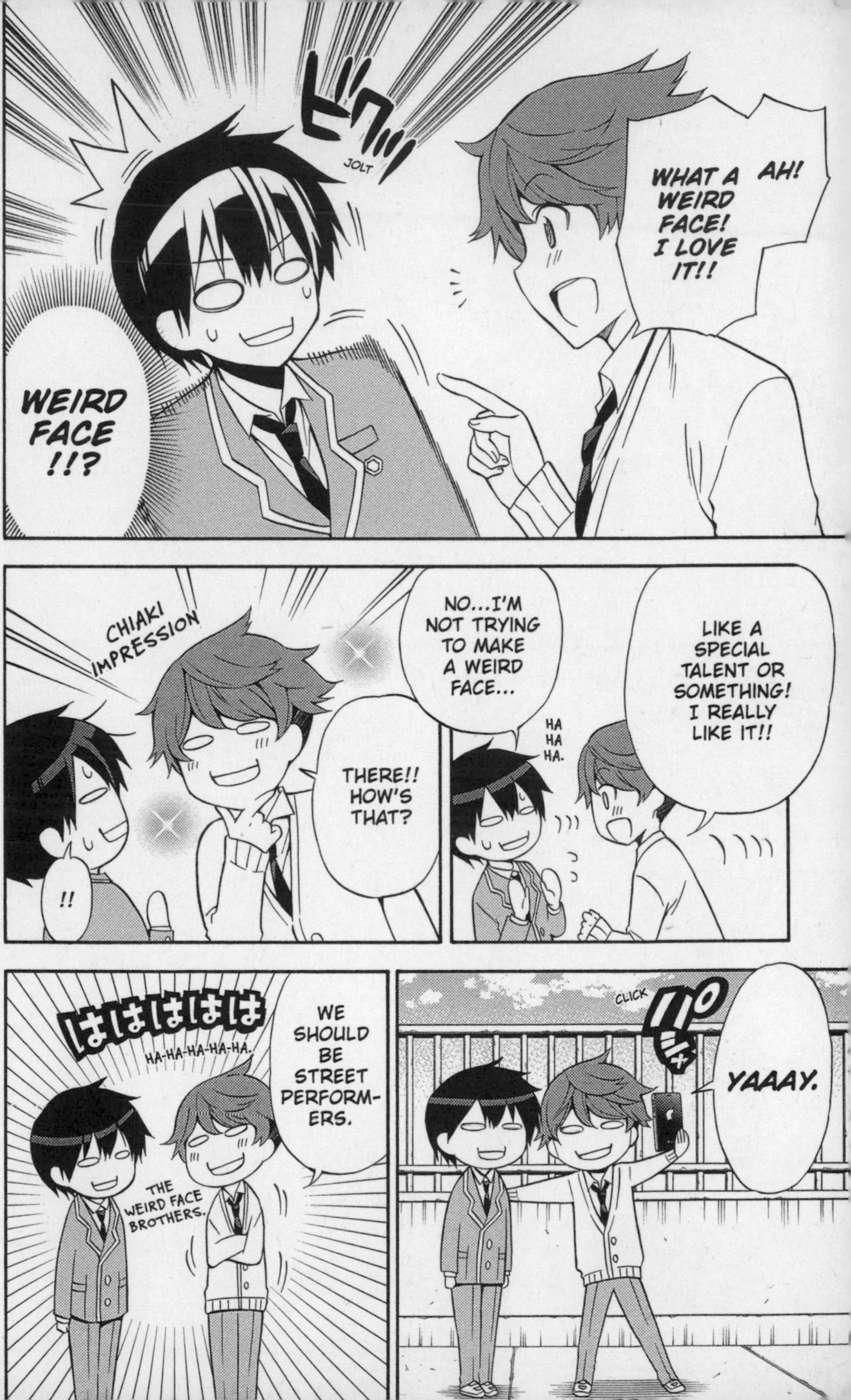
ビクッ
JOLT
AH!
WHAT A WEIRD FACE! I LOVE IT!!
WEIRD FACE!!?
LIKE A SPECIAL TALENT OR SOMETHING! I REALLY LIKE IT!!
NO...I'M NOT TRYING TO MAKE A WEIRD FACE...
HA HA HA.
CHIAKI IMPRESSION
THERE!! HOW'S THAT?
!!
パッ
CLICK
YAAAY.
ははははは
HA-HA-HA-HA-HA.
WE SHOULD BE STREET PERFORM-ERS.
THE WEIRD FACE BROTHERS.

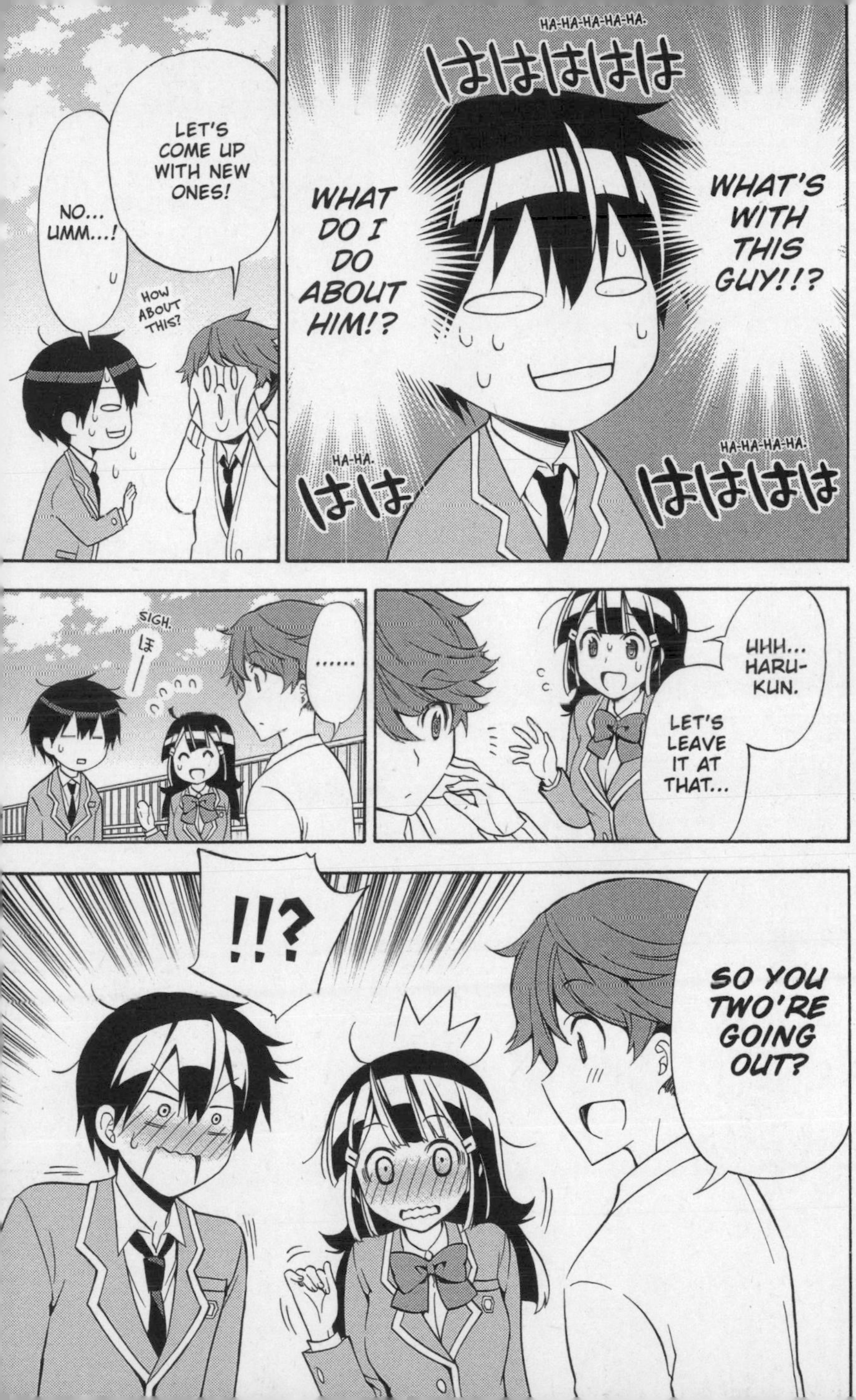
HA-HA-HA-HA-HA.
ははははは
WHAT'S WITH THIS GUY!!?
WHAT DO I DO ABOUT HIM!?
HA-HA-HA-HA.
はははは
HA-HA.
はは
LET'S COME UP WITH NEW ONES!
NO... UMM...!
HOW ABOUT THIS?
UHH... HARU-KUN.
LET'S LEAVE IT AT THAT...
......
SIGH.
ほー
SO YOU TWO'RE GOING OUT?
!!?

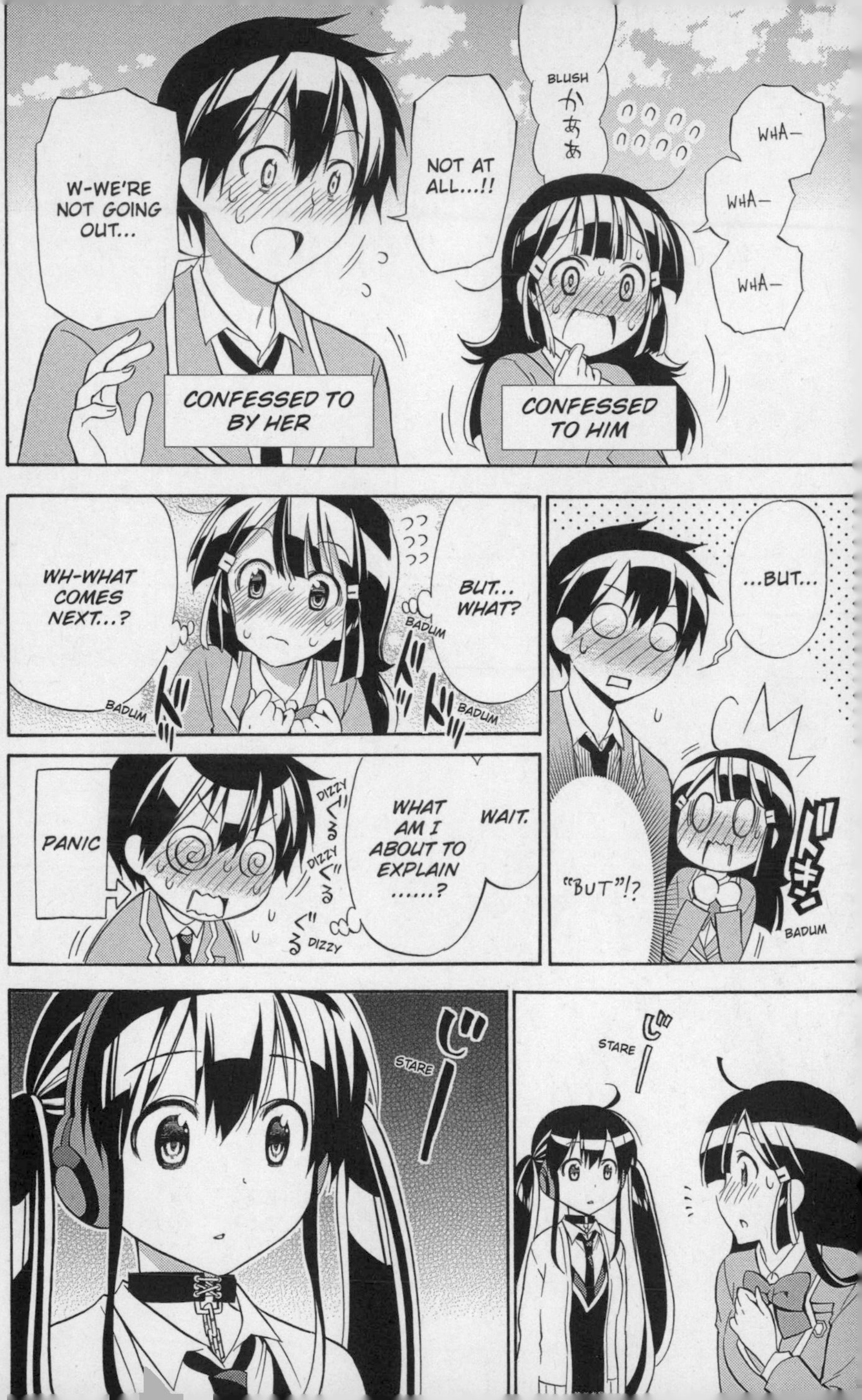
WHA—
WHA—
WHA—
BLUSH
かあぁ
NOT AT ALL...!!
W-WE'RE NOT GOING OUT...
CONFESSED TO HIM
CONFESSED TO BY HER
...BUT...
“BUT”!?
BADUM
BUT... WHAT?
BADUM
BADUM
WH-WHAT COMES NEXT...?
BADUM
WAIT.
WHAT AM I ABOUT TO EXPLAIN ......?
DIZZY
ぐる
DIZZY
ぐる
ぐる
DIZZY
PANIC
STARE
STARE

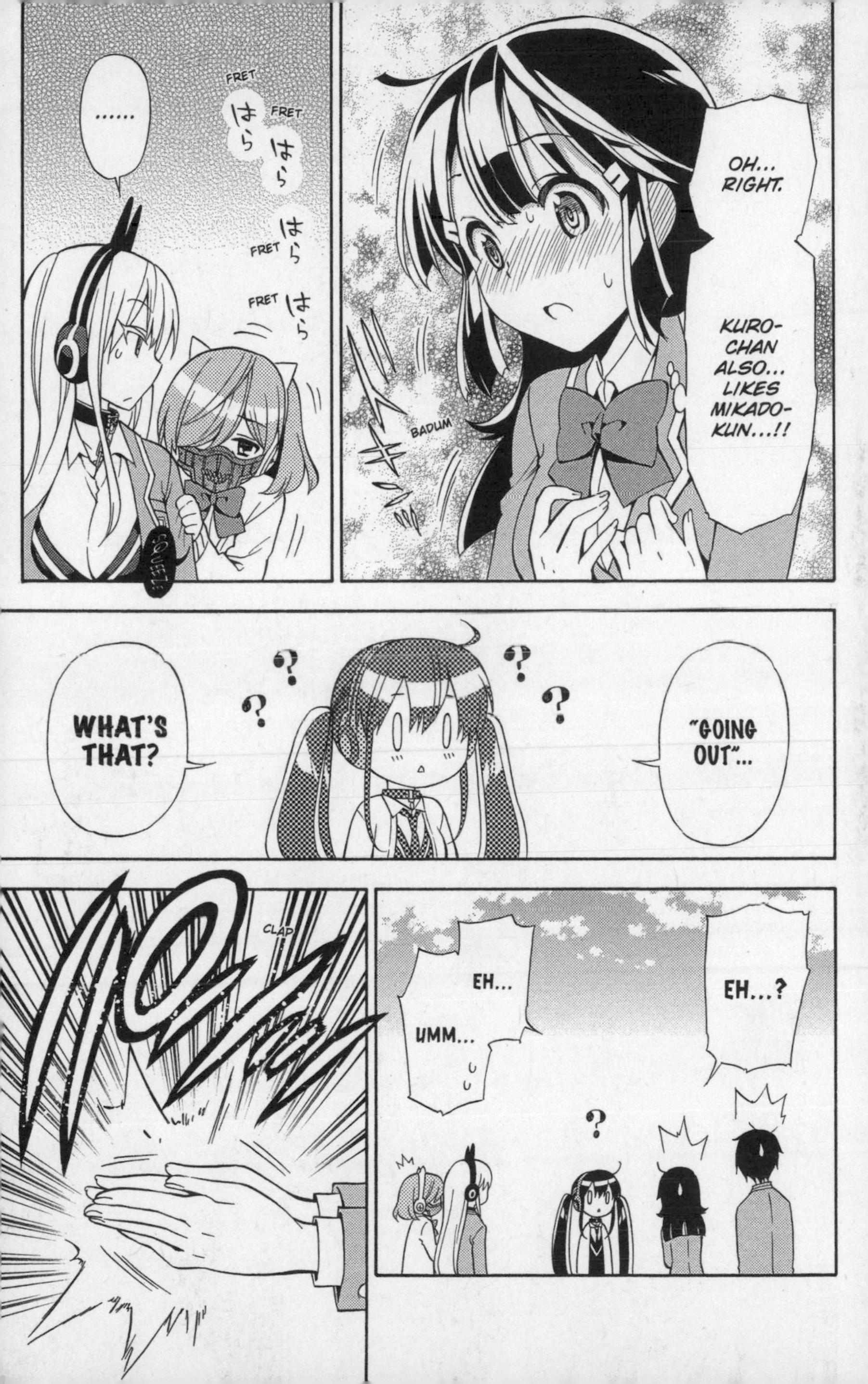
OH... RIGHT.
KURO-CHAN ALSO... LIKES MIKADO-KUN...!!
BADUM
......
FRET はら
FRET はら
FRET はら
FRET はら
SQUEEZE!
"GOING OUT"...
WHAT'S THAT?
EH...?
EH... UMM...
CLAP

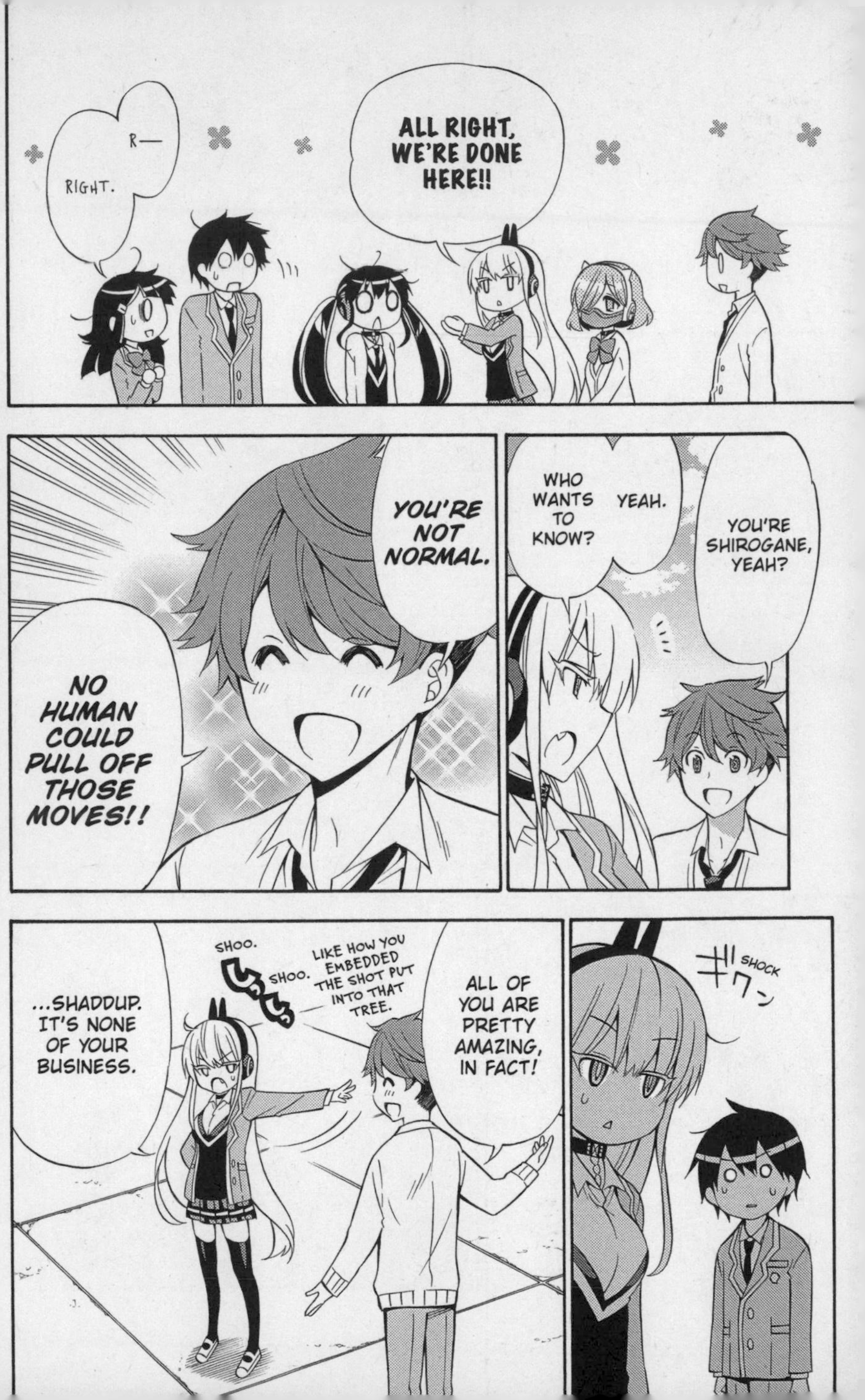
ALL RIGHT, WE'RE DONE HERE!!
R— RIGHT.
YOU'RE SHIROGANE, YEAH?
YEAH.
WHO WANTS TO KNOW?
YOU'RE NOT NORMAL.
NO HUMAN COULD PULL OFF THOSE MOVES!!
SHOCK
ALL OF YOU ARE PRETTY AMAZING, IN FACT!
LIKE HOW YOU EMBEDDED THE SHOT PUT INTO THAT TREE.
SHOO.
SHOO.
...SHADDUP. IT'S NONE OF YOUR BUSINESS.

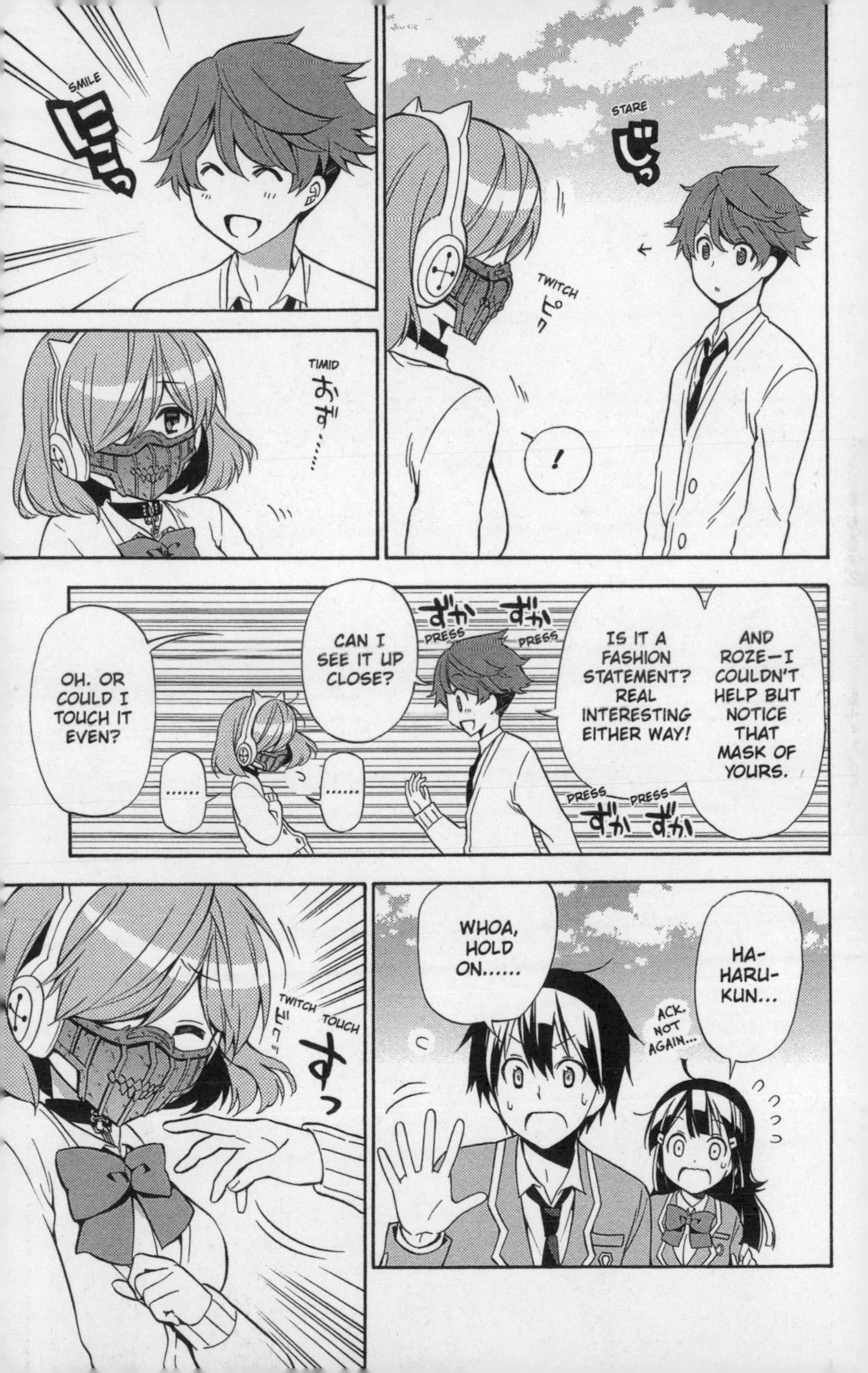
STARE
じっ
TWITCH
ピク
!
SMILE
にこっ
TIMID
おず……
AND ROZE—I COULDN'T HELP BUT NOTICE THAT MASK OF YOURS.
IS IT A FASHION STATEMENT? REAL INTERESTING EITHER WAY!
PRESS ずか PRESS ずか
PRESS ずか PRESS ずか
CAN I SEE IT UP CLOSE?
......
OH. OR COULD I TOUCH IT EVEN?
......
HA-HARU-KUN...
ACK. NOT AGAIN...
WHOA, HOLD ON......
TOUCH
すっ
TWITCH
ビクッ

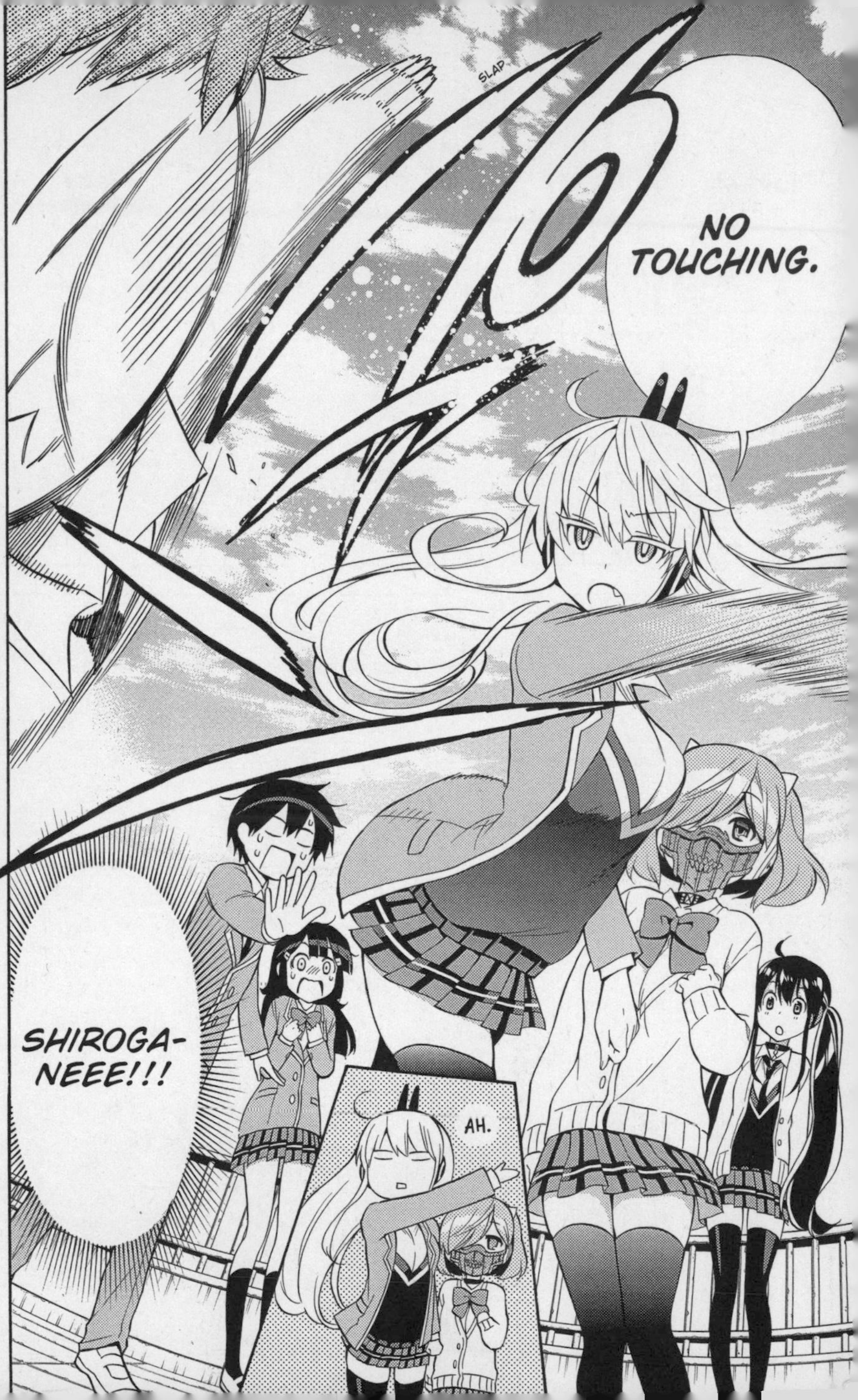
NO TOUCHING.
SLAP
SHIROGA-NEEE!!!
AH.

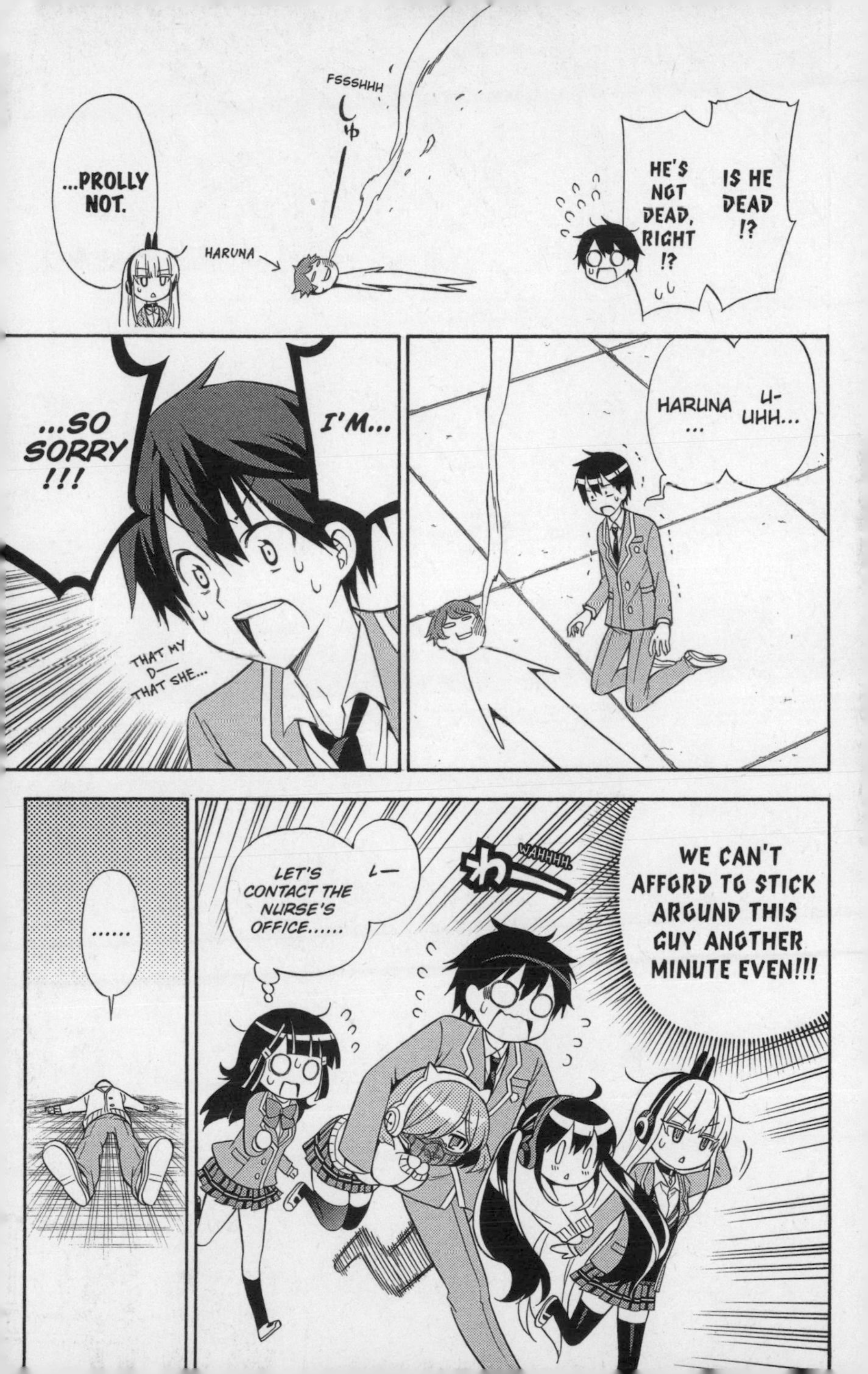
IS HE DEAD!?
HE'S NOT DEAD, RIGHT!?
FSSSHHH
しゅ
HARUNA
...PROLLY NOT.
U-UHH...
HARUNA...
I'M...
...SO SORRY!!!
THAT MY D— THAT SHE...
WE CAN'T AFFORD TO STICK AROUND THIS GUY ANOTHER MINUTE EVEN!!!
WAHHHH
わー
LET'S CONTACT THE NURSE'S OFFICE......
し—
......

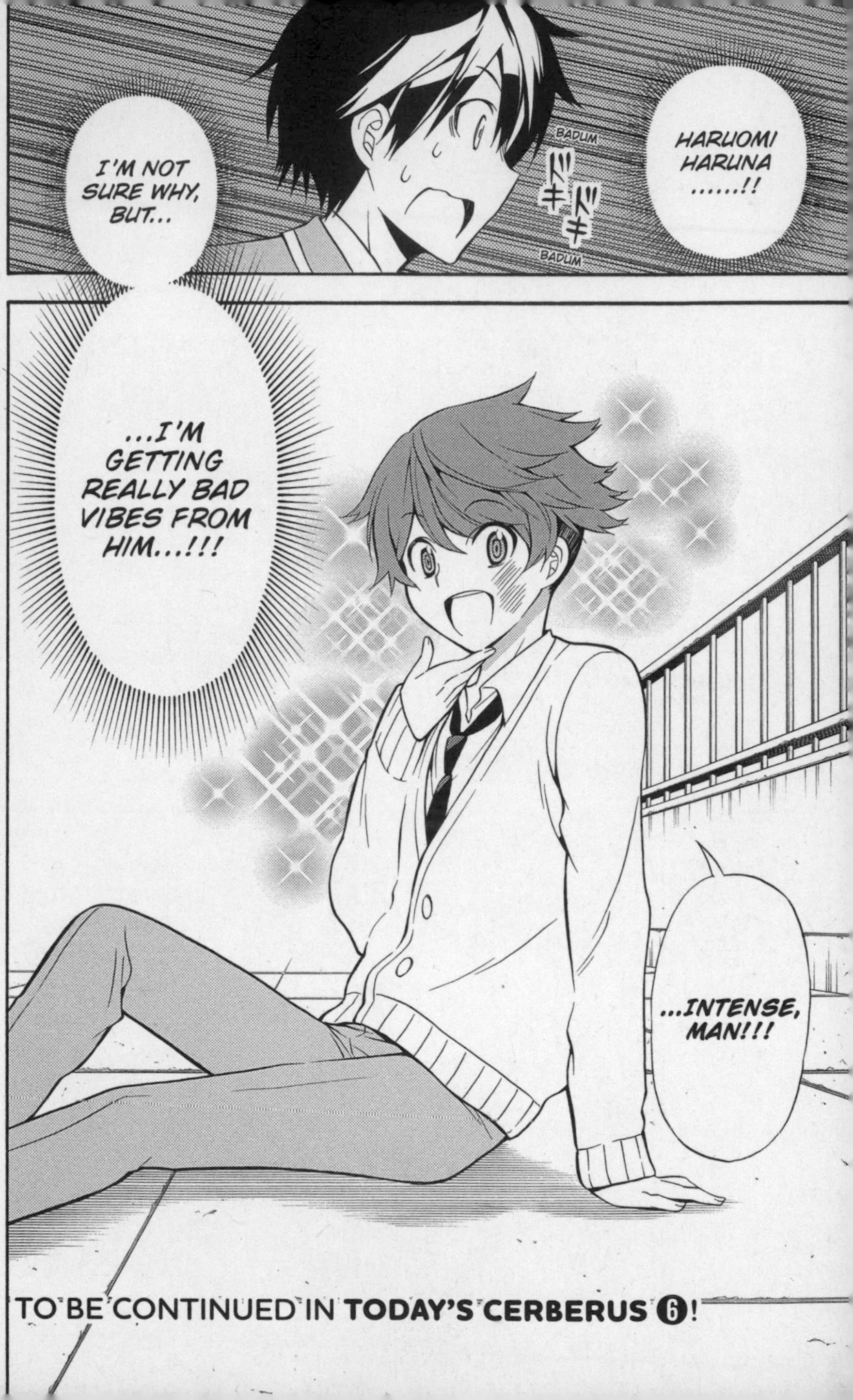
HARUOMI HARUNA......!!
BADUM ドキ ドキ BADUM
I'M NOT SURE WHY, BUT...
...I'M GETTING REALLY BAD VIBES FROM HIM...!!!
...INTENSE, MAN!!!

TO BE CONTINUED IN **TODAY'S CERBERUS 6**!

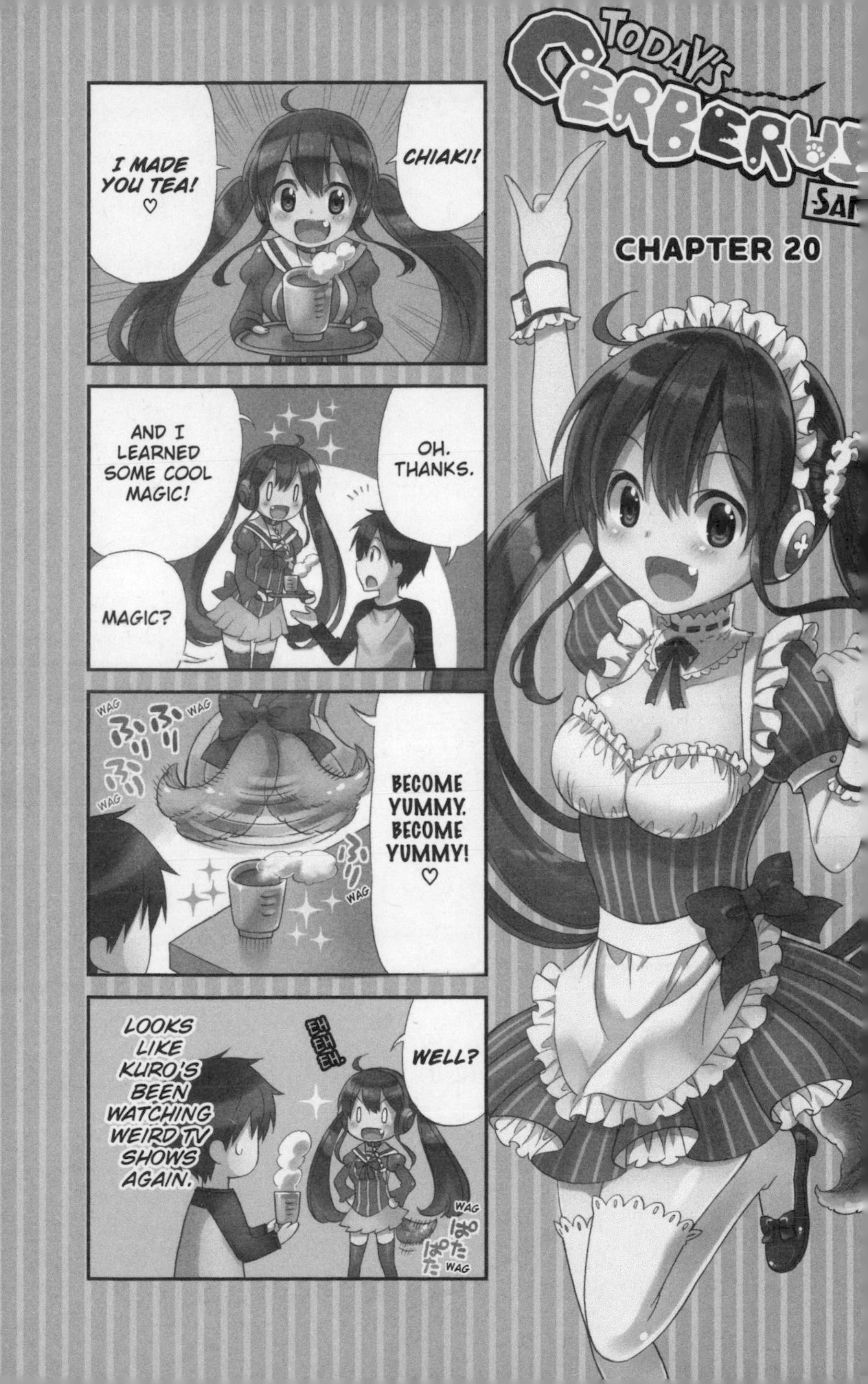
TODAY'S CERBERUS-SAN
CHAPTER 20
CHIAKI!
I MADE YOU TEA! ♡
OH. THANKS.
AND I LEARNED SOME COOL MAGIC!
MAGIC?
BECOME YUMMY. BECOME YUMMY! ♡
ふりふり WAG WAG
ふり WAG
ふり WAG
WELL?
EH EH EH.
LOOKS LIKE KURO'S BEEN WATCHING WEIRD TV SHOWS AGAIN.
ぱたぱた WAG WAG

TODAY'S CERBERUS -SAN

CHAPTER 21

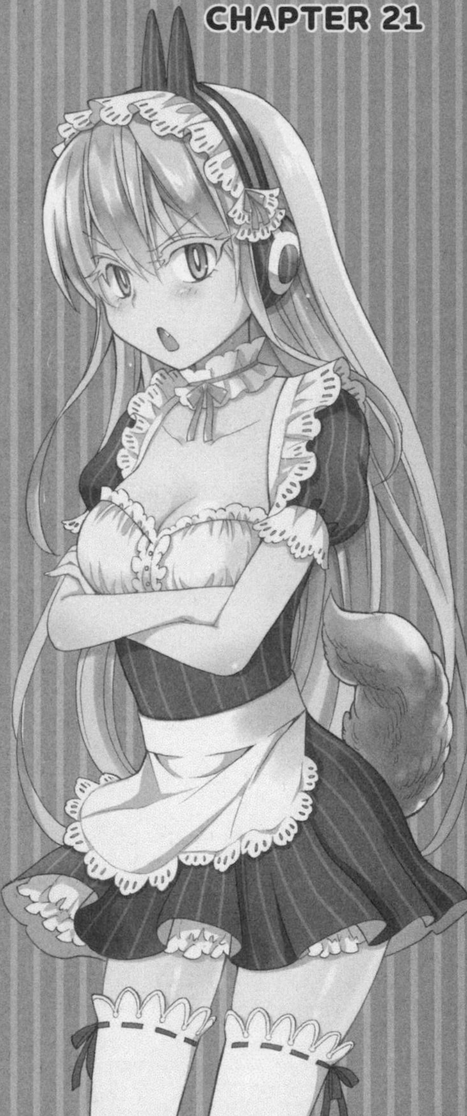

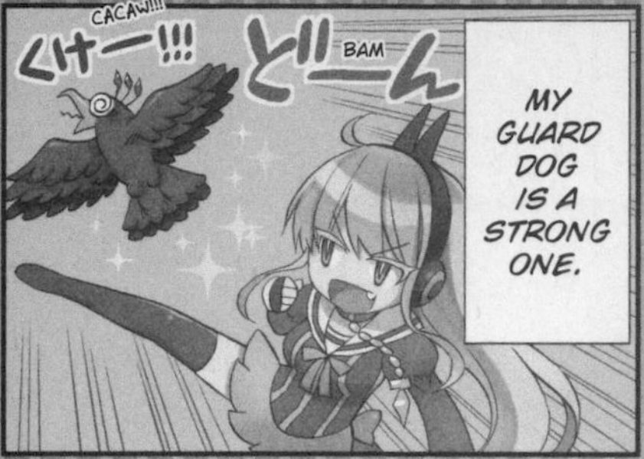
MY GUARD DOG IS A STRONG ONE.
どーん
BAM
くけー!!!
CACAW!!!

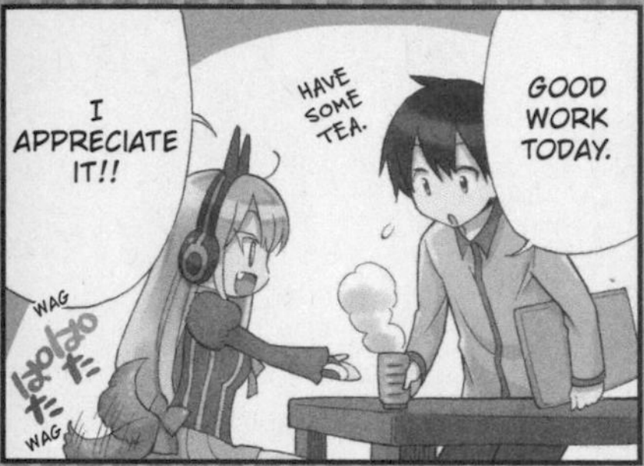
GOOD WORK TODAY.
HAVE SOME TEA.
I APPRECIATE IT!!
ぱたぱた
WAG
WAG

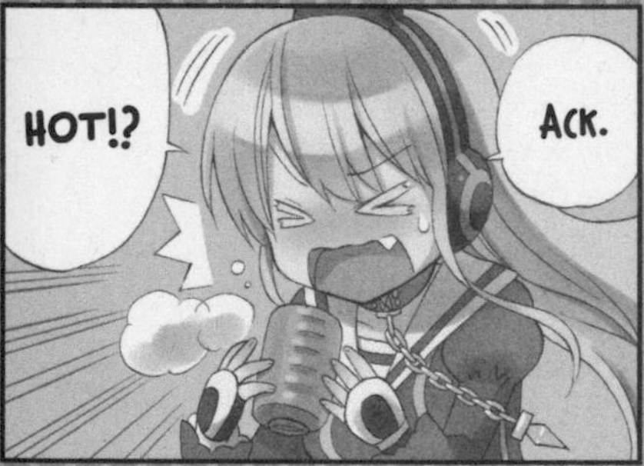
ACK.
HOT!?

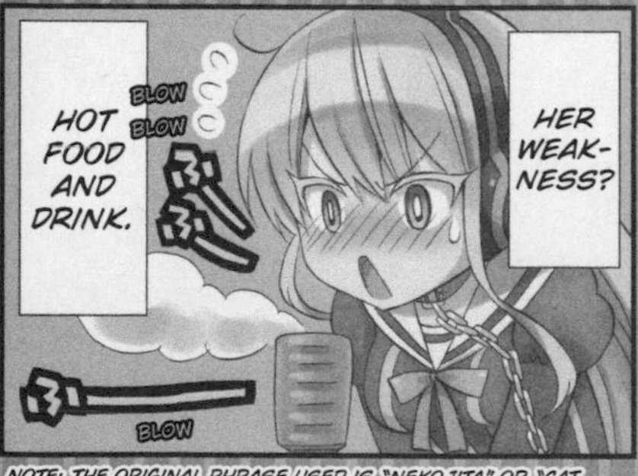
HER WEAK-NESS?
BLOW
BLOW
HOT FOOD AND DRINK.
BLOW

NOTE: THE ORIGINAL PHRASE USED IS "NEKOJITA" OR "CAT TONGUE." IT REFERS TO SOMEONE WHO CAN'T TOLERATE HOT FOODS AND DRINKS, AND ADDS AN EXTRA LAYER OF IRONY WHEN USED TO REFER TO SHIROGANE, A DOG.

TODAY'S CERBERU

CHAPTER 22

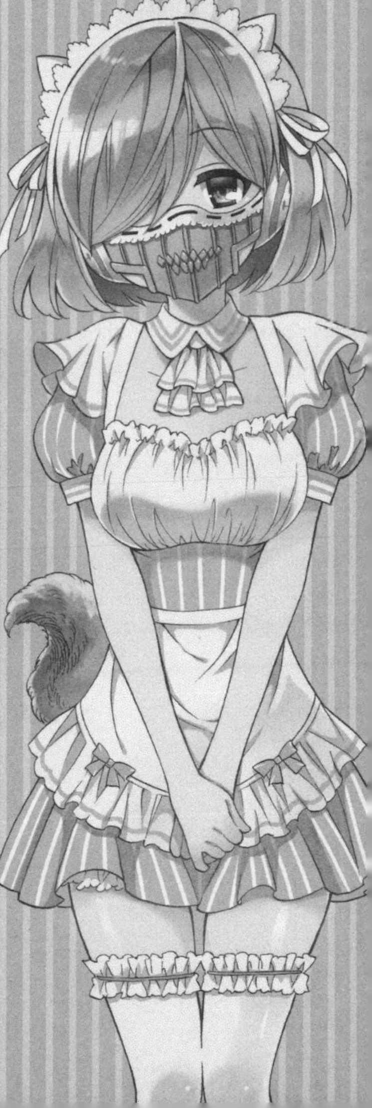

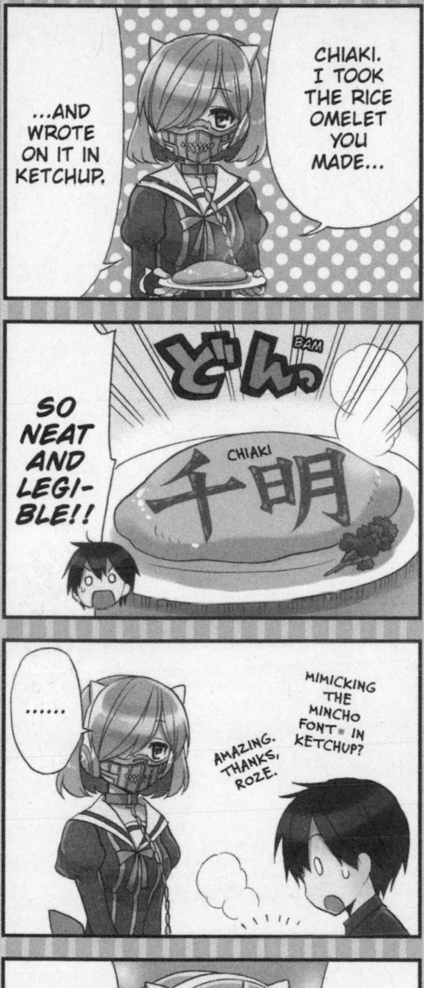

CHIAKI. I TOOK THE RICE OMELET YOU MADE...
...AND WROTE ON IT IN KETCHUP.
どんっ
BAM
CHIAKI
千明
SO NEAT AND LEGIBLE!!
MIMICKING THE MINCHO FONT※ IN KETCHUP?
AMAZING. THANKS, ROZE.
......
I ACTUALLY ...
...WANTED TO DRAW A HEART...

※THE MINCHO FONT IS ONE OF THE MOST POPULAR JAPANESE FONTS FOR PRINTING KANJI CHARACTERS.

TODAY'S CERBERUS -SAN

CHAPTER 23

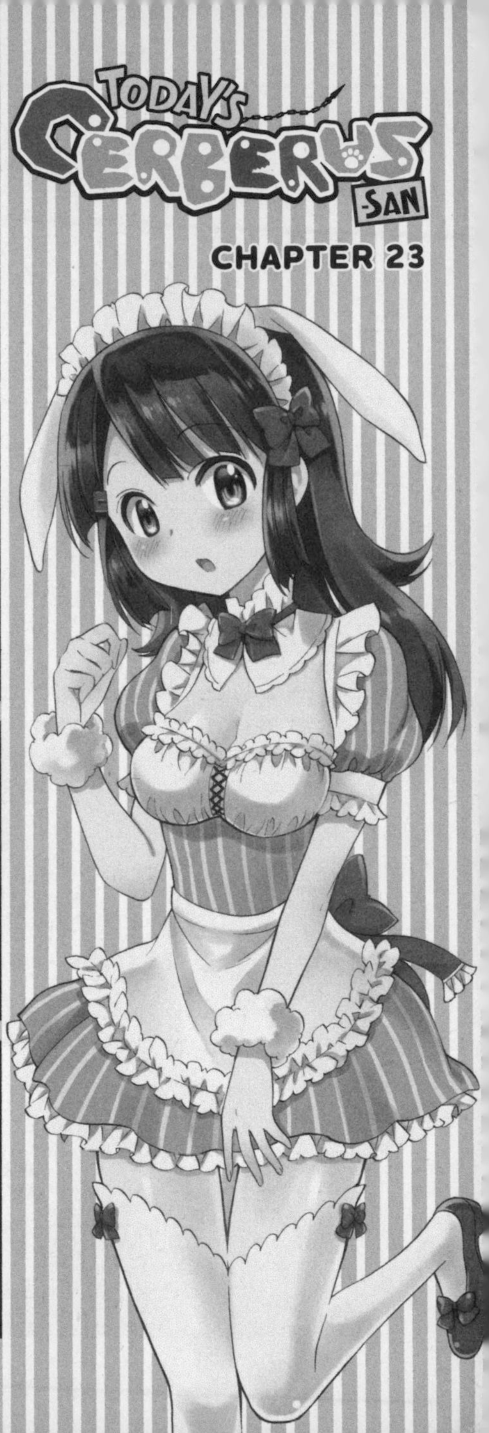

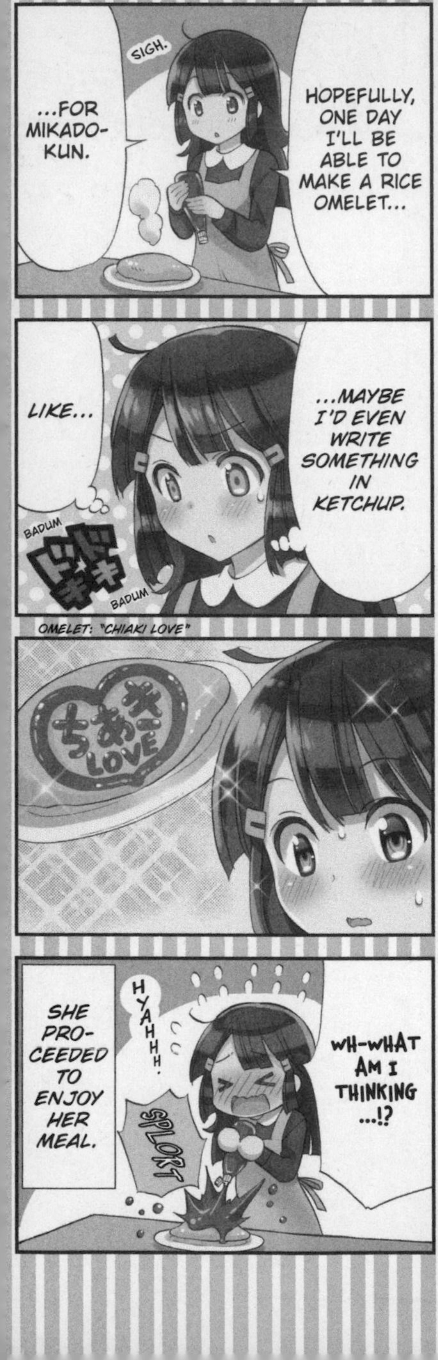
HOPEFULLY, ONE DAY I'LL BE ABLE TO MAKE A RICE OMELET...
SIGH.
...FOR MIKADO-KUN.
...MAYBE I'D EVEN WRITE SOMETHING IN KETCHUP.
LIKE...
BADUM
ドキドキ
BADUM
OMELET: "CHIAKI LOVE"
ちあき LOVE
WH-WHAT AM I THINKING ...!?
HYAHHH!
SPLORT
SHE PRO-CEEDED TO ENJOY HER MEAL.

TODAY'S CERBERUS-SA

CHAPTER 24

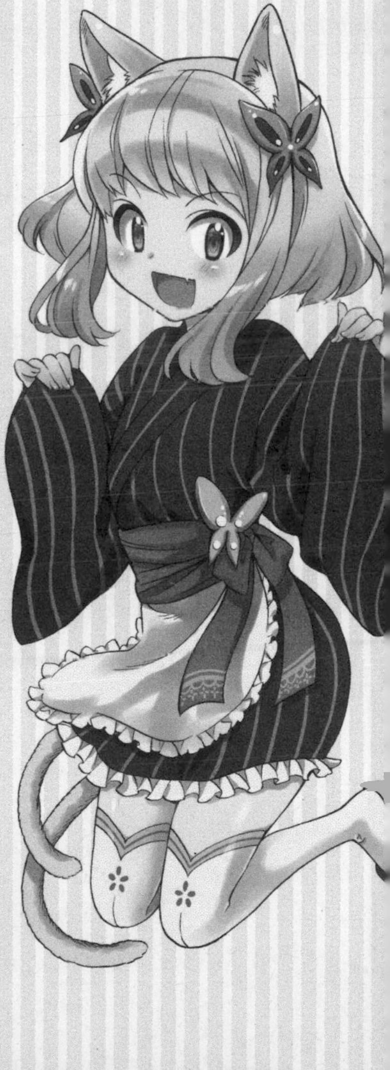

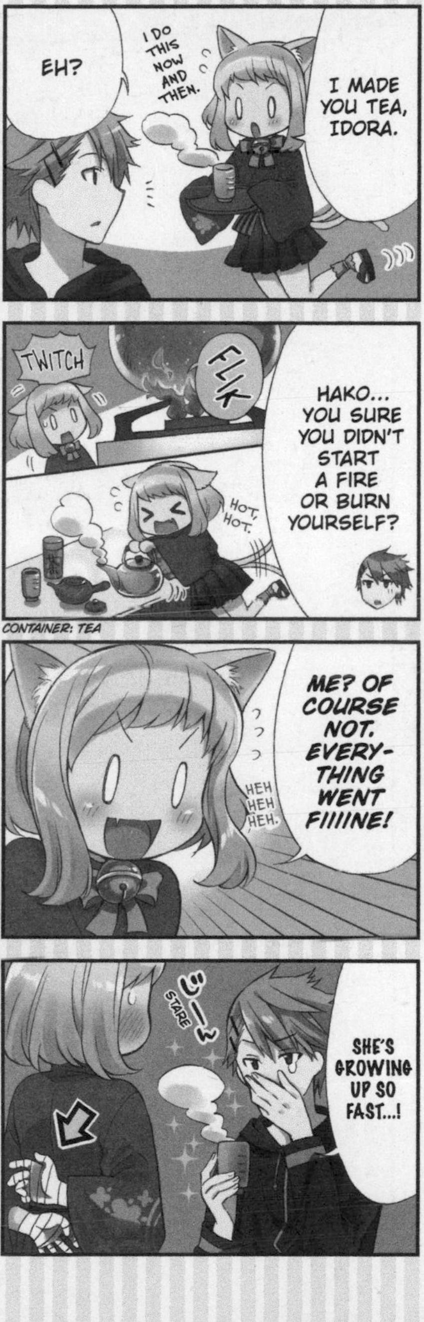

I MADE YOU TEA, IDORA.
I DO THIS NOW AND THEN.
EH?
HAKO... YOU SURE YOU DIDN'T START A FIRE OR BURN YOURSELF?
FLIK
TWITCH
HOT, HOT.
CONTAINER: TEA
ME? OF COURSE NOT. EVERY-THING WENT FIIIINE!
HEH HEH HEH.
SHE'S GROWING UP SO FAST...!
STARE

SEPARATE FOR THE FIRST TIME

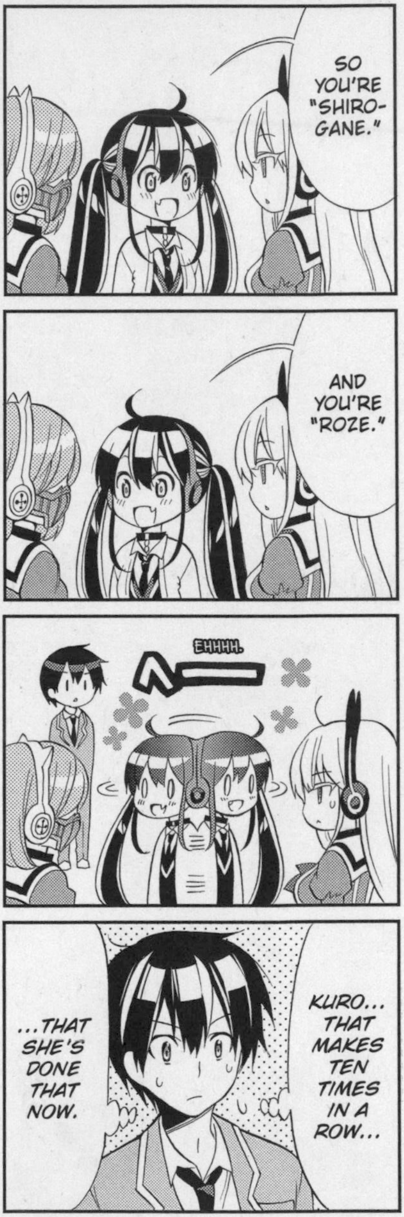
SO YOU'RE "SHIRO-GANE."
AND YOU'RE "ROZE."
EHHHH.
KURO... THAT MAKES TEN TIMES IN A ROW...
...THAT SHE'S DONE THAT NOW.

I WANNA TELL SOMEONE

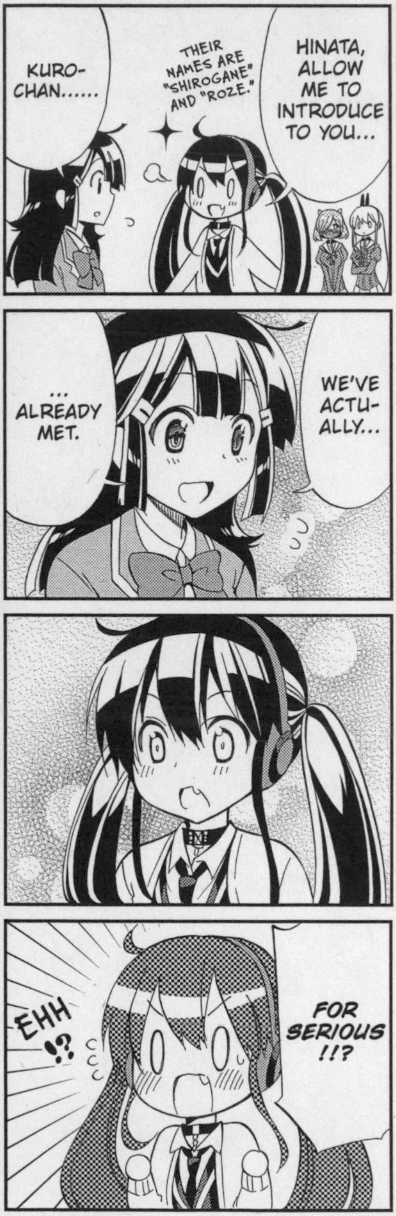
HINATA, ALLOW ME TO INTRODUCE TO YOU...
THEIR NAMES ARE "SHIROGANE" AND "ROZE."
KURO-CHAN......
WE'VE ACTU-ALLY...
...ALREADY MET.
FOR SERIOUS!!?
EHH!?

TRY, TRY AGAIN

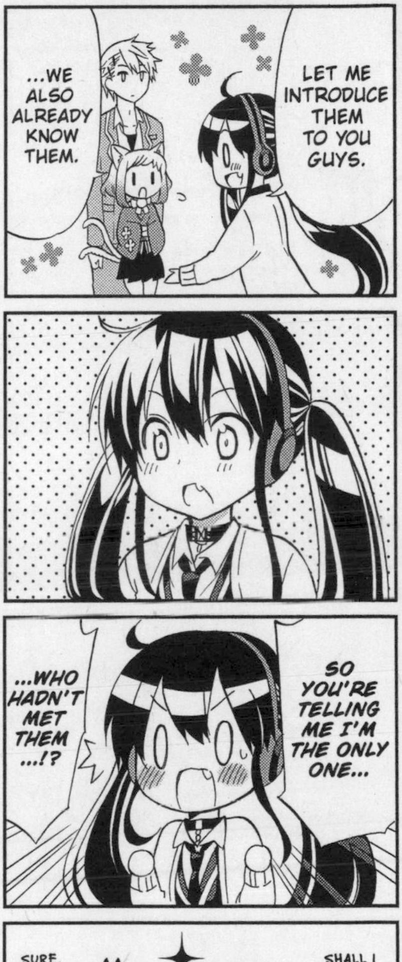
LET ME INTRODUCE THEM TO YOU GUYS.
...WE ALSO ALREADY KNOW THEM.
SO YOU'RE TELLING ME I'M THE ONLY ONE...
...WHO HADN'T MET THEM ...!?
SHALL I EXPLAIN IT TO KURO ONCE MORE?
SURE. GOOD LUCK, ROZE.

I'VE GOTTA TELL SOMEONE

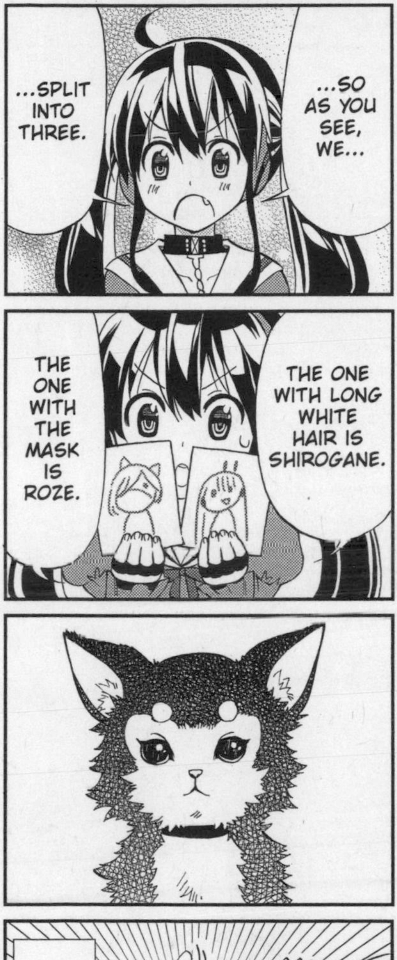
...SO AS YOU SEE, WE...
...SPLIT INTO THREE.
THE ONE WITH LONG WHITE HAIR IS SHIROGANE.
THE ONE WITH THE MASK IS ROZE.
I INFORMED MY MASTER.
SLAP

★STAFF-> MORI, GARAKUTA IMAYAMA, YUU JUNA, YONEDA ★DIGITAL-> WATARI NI FUNE
★COLOR/LAYER SPLIT-> TSUBASA FUKUCHI

TODAY'S CERBERUS ❺

Ato Sakurai

Translation: Caleb Cook • Lettering: Bianca Pistillo

TODAY'S KERBEROS Vol. 5 ©2015 Ato Sakurai/SQUARE ENIX CO., LTD. First published in Japan in 2015 by SQUARE ENIX CO., LTD. English translation rights arranged with SQUARE ENIX CO., LTD. and Yen Press, LLC through Tuttle-Mori Agency, Inc.

English translation ©2015 by SQUARE ENIX CO., LTD.

Yen Press
1290 Avenue of the Americas
New York, NY 10104

Visit us at yenpress.com
facebook.com/yenpress
twitter.com/yenpress
yenpress.tumblr.com
instagram.com/yenpress

First Yen Press Print Edition: September 2017
Originally published as an ebook in October 2015 by Yen Press.

Yen Press is an imprint of Yen Press, LLC.
The Yen Press name and logo are trademarks of Yen Press, LLC.

The publisher is not responsible for websites (or their content) that are not owned by the publisher.

Library of Congress Control Number: 2016946072

ISBN: 978-0-316-43574-1 (paperback)

10 9 8 7 6 5 4 3 2 1

BVG

Printed in the United States of America